EDUCATION AND NATIONAL CONCERNS

EDUCATION AND NATIONAL CONCERNS

Dr. M.H. Syed

Himalaya Publishing House

MUMBAI ❑ DELHI ❑ BANGALORE ❑ NAGPUR ❑ HYDERABAD

First Edition : 2007

Published by : **Mrs. Meena Pandey**
for HIMALAYA PUBLISHING HOUSE,
"Ramdoot", Dr. Bhalerao Marg, Girgaon, Mumbai-400 004.
Phones : 23860170/23863863
Fax : 022-23877178
Email : himpub@vsnl.com
Website : www.himpub.com

Branch Offices

Delhi : "Pooja Apartments", 4-B, Murari Lal Street, Ansari Road, Darya Ganj, New Delhi-110 002
Phones : 23270392, 23278631 Reliance : 3018092 to 96
Fax : 011-23256286
Email : hphdel@vsnl.com

Nagpur : Kundanlal Chandak Industrial Estate, Ghat Road, Nagpur-440 018
Phone : 2721216, Telefax : 0712-2721215

Bangalore : No. 16/I (old 12/1), Ist floor, Next to Hotel Highland, Madhava Nagar, Race Course Road, Bangalore-560 001
Phones : 2281541, 2385461 Fax : 080-2286611

Hyderabad : No. 2-2-1 167/2H, 1st Floor, Near Railway Bridge, Tilak Nagar, Main Road, Hyderabad-500 044
Phone : 26501745, Fax : 040-27560041

Chennai : No. 2, Rama Krishna Street, North Usman Road, T-Nagar, Chennai-600 017
Phone : 28144004, 28144005 Mobile : 09380460419

Pune : No. 11, 3rd Floor, Wing-A, Sahadeo Avenue-II, S.No. 5/9+5/10, Someshwarawada, Baner Road, Pune-411 008
Mobile : 9421053747

Lucknow : C-43, Sector C, Ali Gunj, Lucknow - 226 024
Phone : 0522-4047594

Printed at : New Offset Press, New Delhi-110002

PREFACE

Education is one of the chief concerns of a nation. The higher the ratio of educated citizens, the higher the chances of developing fast. Earlier, the process and the concept of education used to be very complex and cohesive. Various branches of knowledge were to be mastered upon in order to become a successful teacher or a scholar. However, the whole scenario has changed in the present context.

Now, the emphasis is on specialisation. Almost in every walk of life, so many branches and sub-branches of education have evolved and a thorough and comprehensive study of more than one branch would certainly need a prolonged life, which is a thing of the bygone era, now.

Every year, thousands of students are enrolled in colleges and universities. Having attained their targeted academic qualification, most of them seek admission in professional courses in order to get an early job. In a vast country like India, and a mammoth population thereof, it is wellnigh impossible to provide service to everyone.

Of all the job-oriented programmes of study, B.Ed. is a preferred one. It is generally a one-year course, which deals with handling the task of teaching and related matters efficiently. Now, different types of B.Ed courses have emerged, like simple or ordinary B.Ed and specialised B.Ed., etc.

Various universities, deemed universities and colleges affiliated to them offer B.Ed courses. In most cases job is guaranteed, though the exercise, may sometimes be patience-testing. However, sooner or later, B.Ed degree holders are sure of getting job in one or the other institution.

Apart from the traditional methods of teaching and learning, a B.Ed degree can, now, also be achieved either on-line or through correspondence. Basically, it encompasses different theories of education, various approaches of teaching, adopted for training students of different abilities, methods of preparing lesson plans, techniques of holding examination and evaluation, etc.

On the whole, it is a rich and interesting subject on which much more has been written so far. With developing technology, new to newer methods and gadgets keep evolving. Here is a series of books for B.Ed students, as a bold initiative in this direction, which seeks to incorporate the maximum updated information on various aspects of the B.Ed course in a simple language, and with a sense of authenticity and novelty.

This series consists of several books. This particular book is titled: *Fundamentals of Educational Psychology.*

We hope this meticulous work would prove to be a work of worth. It has everything to satisfy and pacify the urge of the teachers, would be teachers, students, academics, intellectuals, scholars and lay-readers alike.

Yet, we solicit and appreciate your comments and suggestions in order to make it all the more useful and authentic, by all means.

—Editor

CONTENT

NON-FORMAL EDUCATION

NEED FOR NON-FORMAL EDUCATION

Article 45 of the Constitution of India lays stress upon providing universal education, but so far, the promise implicit in this article has not been fulfilled. As a result, we find today that the number of uneducated and partly educated, illiterates and partly literate; individuals is on the increase. It is a matter of no little shame for any country if a large number of citizens in it are deprived of the right to education. Therefore, for all those individuals who either could not study at all or were compelled to give up education without completing it, irrespective of their age, sex or class, it is necessary to provide opportunities for education as a part of their working conditions. These opportunities have been given the name of Non-formal Education.

Non-formal Education — a Theory: Education is a lifelong process. In school, child receives education up to a certain age and a certain level, after which he enters society. In keeping with the time, period, environment and individual circumstances, he is compelled to modify the knowledge he has received. This modification occurs through the process of adaptation. In order to live life successfully and skilfully, it is necessary to modify one's experiences. In view of this, we consider non-formal education to be that education which, at all times, in every place, and in every situation, prepares the individual to lead life in a successful way, and which operates both formally and informally. In the opinion of Mehta and Verma, life is changing very quickly because of the rapid growth in knowledge and the high speed of scientific progress, and consequently old assumptions are becoming inoperative. New assumptions are rising on the horizon, and man is constantly becoming conscious of myriad new problems in his life. Not merely this, every child has his own individual problems due to cultural, social and psychological differences, but the organization, syllabus, time period, location, etc., of school education have so much rigidity and formality that it limits the capacity of education to be flexible and dynamic, and to adapt itself to the needs of the individual students. It is evident from this that formal education does prepare the child for life, but it cannot fulfil the need for universal education. Hence, public needs can only be met by providing non-formal education through the medium of other means.

The following ideas have played a significant role in the emergence of the concept of non-formal education:

1. Because of the explosion in knowledge, the knowledge obtained through the stream of formal education remains incomplete, and so the non-formal means of propagation of knowledge can be employed for new knowledge and experiences.
2. The science of educational structure (architecture), is developing rapidly. Because of its hardware and software approach, education has emerged from the classroom and come into the community. Among the effective means of non-formal education are civic life, literacy and cultural institutions; radio, television, pocket books, magazines, libraries, correspondence courses, scientific inventions, films, etc.
3. The responsibility of imparting education is not solely of the school's ; it is the shared duty of all those who know something. Such individuals may well not be a part of the formal stream of education, but their informal functioning as educators is of the highest importance.

From this viewpoint, non-formal education is not the antagonist but the complement of formal education. Non-formal education has its beginning where formal education has its end. It is, in fact, continuing education. For this reason, Mehta and Verma have defined: Non-formal education thus Non-formal education is a system or organization in which the nature of education is determined in accordance with the needs and convenience of the student. It tries to provide educational opportunities for those engaged in some profession, and for those who were, for some reason, deprived of education. It presents such practical foundations of education that education becomes a natural part of life and helps to stimulate society into progressing towards continuous education.

In the modern world, non-formal education is making rapid progress all over the globe. It has come to be believed that the aim of education is to make the individual useful for the fulfilment of personal, national and global needs. Useful individuals make their country useful and their nation strong.

The following suggestions were preferred for acceptance at the 28th All India Indian Adult Education Conference, (1975) held at Jabalpur—"Within the framework of adult education, non-formal education puts forward a new organization. It is neither an alternative for formal education, nor an attempt to displace it. It offers an alternative to those who could not take advantage of formal education or abandoned their education without completing it."

In keeping with its nature, non-formal education attaches the maximum importance to the various forms of a flexible mode of operation and the environment of the individual. It is wrong to conceive of it as the second class or rung of education. Instead, it would be far better to see it as a new form of education. It possesses the capacity to help an individual derive the maximum benefit from formal education.

Thus, non-formal education finds its expression in the following programmes:

1. Education for the 6-14 age group.
2. Education for the 15-25 age group in which functional literacy is inherent. It is suitable for both rural and urban areas.
3. Increase in the skill and productivity of urban workers.
4. Education of women through useful education.
5. Continuous education organized by universities and all classes and institutions.
6. Programme of civic education.

The Government of India has decided to rename the Department of Adult Education as the Department of Non-formal Education, and hence the following changes are visualized:

1. The name of the Board of Adult Education should be changed, it should be reorganized and activated, so that new programmes may be introduced in the sphere of non-formal education.
2. 10 per cent of the educational budget of every state government and the central government should be earmarked for non-formal education.
3. Voluntary organizations should be encouraged to cooperate.
4. The maximum possible number of universities should introduce programmes of continuing education.

For all such programmes, the cooperation of universities, schools, voluntary organizations and other agencies should be solicited.

The UNESCO report on non-formal education, entitled "Learning to be" says that it is necessary to eliminate the artificial obstacles or barriers between the various subjects of education both in formal as well as non-formal education. Recurrent education should be promoted for those who wish to receive it in various form. In other words, this means that an individual should be able to acquire education according to his own needs and conveniences.

Prof. Philip H. Comb and C. Roy have conducted a survey of non-formal education, reported in their work entitled, "New Path of Learning". In the preface to this report, the following concepts have been accepted:

1. Education is a life long process, which cannot be tied to place, time and circumstances.
2. It is necessary for every individual to be aware of the minimum learning skills, who include: (a) creative attitude, (b) creative literacy and organization, (c) scientific attitude, and shackling of the process of nature, (d) earning wealth, civic cooperation and raising the standard of mutual exchange.

In order to make the programme of non-formal learning a success, it is necessary to provide preschool education to prepare children for school, to make arrangements for a desirable and parallel system of non-formal education and to make these arrangements operative with complete dedication.

All these facts emphasize the view that education should continue throughout one's life. Lifelong education is a universal truth which can not be refuted. In the last three or four decades, despite the rapid rate of scientific progress, the rate of social change remained slow. But, in more recent times, scientific development and the spread of education have increased life's necessities manifold., As a result, it has become necessary for every individual to turn to non-formal education if he does not wish to fall behind others in the race of life.

The idea of lifelong education sprouted from India's varna-ashrama system in which there were provisions for the return of 'akshana' (Pitra Dev, teacher and society). In the modern context, it is non-formal education alone which can keep an individual in close contact with knowledge and new skills throughout life.

Formal Education—Features: Formal education possesses the following characteristics:

1. It is limited to the time of learning, not related to the daily routine;
2. Some points of entrance and progress are implicit in it;
3. It is inclined towards the impersonal goals of attainment of knowledge;
4. It is inspired by such motives as employment, appointment, winning of position and prestige, etc.;
5. It is tied to a pre-determined syllabus, comprehension and a definite subject-matter;
6. It is thrust upon the recipient (the student) by the donor (the teacher) without any interaction between the two;
7. It undoubtedly gives rise to characteristics of discipline and obedience;
8. It tends almost exclusively to avoid failure, win success and adopt the approach leading to success;
9. It works within a definite time-space frame, and hence it soon becomes alienated from special changes.
10. It encourages the status quo and discourages mobility;

11. It prepares the individual and society for a particular acquaintance (asmita), which is in fact the need of an immobile and non-developing social and cultural structure.

Non-formal Education: Features

1. It is-lifelong, it is intimately relating to a working life, and it constantly enriches life with novel experiences.
2. It is free from the bondages of admission and progress. It provides opportunities for repeatedly joining the stream or leaving it. It can take place anywhere, at any time.
3. It is a process of understanding, improving and satisfying an individual needs, environment, social objectives and mutual relations.
4. It has its spring of motivation in individual development, self-improvement, and the increase of human potential.
5. It adopts a variety of flexible modes of education which are adapted to the student and his environment.
6. It is a process of mutual sharing and exchange, in which the learner fully participates in the research to obtain analytical results.
7. It shows the path to general or public success, which is both relative and general, and which possesses the virtue of providing general satisfaction by continuous learning by everyone involved in it.
8. It gives birth to free thought, self-improvement and a self-generated and self-satisfying awareness.
9. It accelerates the process of questioning, gives a healthy direction to mobility and aims at progress.
10. It works on the presumption of an unknown future, is always prepared for all possible changes, and hence, not only does it exist in parallel with society, it even influences its changes.
11. It constantly pushes the individual and society towards a continuous dynamic acquittance (asmita)—it keeps both on the path towards continuously moving forward, improving and modifying themselves.

The foregoing description of the differences between formal and non-formal education stresses the single fact that education is meant not only for the illiterate but for all those who constantly want to move forward in the race of life, and adapt themselves continuously to the explosion of knowledge taking place around them.

Non-formal Education—Aims: We have already pointed out that education is a lifelong process. Non-formal education has the following objectives:

1. Understanding the environment and conditions, and arousing awareness of the need to make changes in it.
2. Generating faith in science and technological knowledge and encouraging the individual to adopt their skills.
3. Creating the capacity to learn by working and to increase one's skill.
4. Utilizing acquired experiences in new situations.
5. Performing the role of an agency for bringing the desired changes in society.
6. Generating a desire to participate in and contribute to the general development of the country through the democratic method of working.
7. Developing the tendency to continue for ever one's own learning and teaching others, and generating a suitable atmosphere therefore.

Non-formal Education—Features: It is natural to ask: for whom should non-formal education be made available? What should be its nature? It is, of course, obvious that non-formal education has no relations with formal education. Non-formal education is needed for the individuals who have been cut off from the stream of formal education, irrespective of their age group, caste, class or sex.

For the sake of convenience, these individuals can be divided into two classes: (1) 8-14 years age group, (2) 15-35 years age group.

Students between 8 and 14 Years

There is no dearth of students who abandon school by the time they reach the fifth class, either in order to become economic units for their parents, or because they are the victims of their parent's superstitions or the cruelty of society. In rural areas, such boys and girls become the victims of the evil ambitions of the dominant castes and are thus compelled to live a life of virtual slavery.

Children in this age group fall into two categories: (1) those who have never seen a school, (2) those who have attended school for a short time. But even these latter children soon decline to the level of illiterate children. Dr. Zakir Hussain has opined that if the country has sufficient funds to impart compulsory education for only three years instead of for eight years, he would prefer to provide compulsory education for individuals only of the 11 to 14 age group. The reason for this is that for the 11 to 14 age group, the educational requirements are the same as for the 6 to 14 age group.

For this age group, the syllabus should consist of knowledge related to Hindi, Mathematics, knowledge of the environment, and vocational knowledge. Suitable books should be prepared by skilled writers completely familiar with the conditions and environment of the community. Lessons 'should be concerned with day-to-day experiences. There should also be lessons on human physiology, the science of family, citizenship, etc., to promote the qualities of citizenship. The syllabus should be so structured that, if the child so wishes, he may be able to continue his education through its medium.

Children belonging to this age group should be subject to continuous evaluation. There should be no formal examination. Instead, progress should be based on an evaluation of the progress in the child's performance.

Students between 15 and 35 Years

The second group of students in non-formal education falls in 15 to 35 age group. For educating this group, it is essential to complete non-formalization of time, place and means or tools of education. For them, the purpose is not merely to provide the learner with the tools of reading and writing, but also to bring about an improvement in his efficiency and vocational skills. It will be necessary to provide various forms of education for individuals in this group. This stage has been called Creative Literacy. Learners in this category have fully developed minds and bodies, and hence, economic self-reliance must be a necessary element in their education.

The syllabus for this age group should comprehend the following programmes:

1. Teaching the adults about the means of developing better methods for reducing the labour and maximizing the profit in the profession in which they are, engaged.
2. Giving knowledge and developing the necessary skills of other associated professions.
3. Giving knowledge of health sciences, dietary and nutrition.
4. Improving their knowledge of general social, religious and civic matters.
5. Teaching, reading, writing and arithmetic needed for general use in daily life.
6. Developing an attractive and useful syllabus.

From this viewpoint, the knowledge of language, mathematics and environment should be imparted in such a manner that it provides the learner with many alternatives for slipping into real life.

Non-formal Education—a System: The organization of non-formal education should comprehend the advisory and administrative functions at the centre as well as practical teaching in training centres. In the sixth plan, the major emphasis falls upon non-formal education, a part of the movement for adult education.

Non-formal education should be organized through centres which should be set up whenever they are needed. They should be subject to periodical inspections.

Since the programme is intended to educate the masses, it is necessary to obtain the cooperation of the people. The following factors should be kept in mind with reference to setting up such centres:

1. Thought should be given, in selecting a place for such a centre, to the number of illiterate people, the interest of the local population, and the density of population in the area.
2. Centres of non-formal education may be set up in some school building, panchayat house, the village centre, labour welfare centres, towns, etc., depending upon the convenience of the learners.

3. In selecting instructors of these centres it is necessary to ensure that they do actually possess the ability to direct and implement non-formal educational programmes. They must be possessed of interest, enthusiasm and dedication for the task in hand. They should have organizational talent as well as the skills necessary for educating adults.
4. Instructors of centres must also undergo training. They should be encouraged to teach through discussion rather than lecturing, by reflecting upon problems, and adopting other means of non-formal education.
5. Instructors of centres should be trained at the district level. The district education officer, the senior deputy district education officer, the planning officer, inspector, etc., should join hands to give the right direction to training, inspection and planning.
6. Instructors of centres will make a study of local problems and plan their working according to the local conditions obtaining in their areas.
7. Greater attention must be directed towards the teaching of reading, writing, calculation and knowledge of the environment.
8. People should be encouraged to visit the centre and obtain training after establishing formal contacts with them.
9. Inspectors must also be appointed so that the centres are inspected regularly and at the right time.
10. The centres should also be given the benefit of an administrative system and all necessary assistance.
11. The entire programme should be evaluated regularly.

Non-formal Education and Kothari Commission: The Kothari Commission has defined non-formal education in the context of education. As is the case with innumerable other thinkers, the Kothari Commission also sees education as a lifelong process. It has laid stress upon the following programmes for non-formal education:

Education of Illiterates: It is necessary to put a stop to the rise in illiteracy, as a proportion of the increasing population, if we want to bring about the welfare of the nation. Democracy can succeed only if illiteracy is eradicated hence, it is essential to adopt education based on work experience. For this purpose, it is necessary to make arrangements for universal or full-time schools for the 6 to 11 age group, part-time education for the 11 to 14 age group, either full-time or part-time general as well as vocational education for the 15-30 age group. And, to achieve success in this programme, it will have to be implemented with the cooperation and dedication of all institutions, individuals and agencies as well as leaders. It will be necessary to win the confidence of the illiterate masses and also to make the fullest use of television, radio, films, lecture and all other teaching aids.

Continuous Education: For the development of non-formal education, it will be necessary to evolve education as a continuous process, and for this it must be linked with employment. It will be necessary to impart vocational education which possesses the potential for future development. Such institutions as the Shramik Vidyapith and Gram Vidyapith will have to be set up.

Correspondence Courses: Correspondence courses will have to be introduced for those persons who want to continue their education after having left school. Students enrolled for such courses should get opportunities at regular intervals to meet their teachers in 'contact classes'. Lessons should be broadcast through the medium of radio, television, magazines, etc.

Correspondence Courses should include, apart from the general courses, courses on agriculture, industry and professional training so that national production may be stimulated. A policy of granting recognition to institutions running correspondence courses should be adopted and encouragement should be given to new experiments conducted in this sphere. In addition, facilities should be provided for individuals who wish to appear in university or formal examinations as private or non-institutional examinees.

Libraries: The Kothari Commission has recommended the setting up of libraries all over the country, and the use of school libraries for public benefit. These libraries should make available simple, interesting and useful literature for the reading public.

Contribution of Universities: Universities can make a valuable contribution to the proper development of non-formal education. Each university should have a department of adult education, similar to the

Rajasthan University's department of adult education. Our universities can take on the role of Open Universities, and thereby grant education to those who want to satisfy their desire for knowledge.

In this context our universities should perform the following functions: (1) Social, economic and cultural development. (2) Transmitting to society the advantages of new scientific conclusions. (3) Re-educating workers in various professions. (4) Re-education of teachers. (5) Developing new methods and skills of teaching. (6) Creating awareness of hygiene, cleanliness, population control, etc. (7) Providing training in leadership.

Distance Education

Recomendation regarding technical and vocational education outlines the guidelines in order to bring about improvement in such education.

The Opportunities

1. This Recommendation applies to all forms and aspects of education that are technical and vocational in nature, provided either in educational institutions or under their authority, by public authorities, the private sector or through other forms of organized education, formal or non-formal, aiming to ensure that all members of the community have access to the pathways of lifelong learning.

2. For the purposes of this Recommendation "technical and vocational education" is used as a comprehensive term referring to those aspects of the educational process involving, in addition to general education, the study of technologies and related sciences, and the acquisition of practical skills, attitudes, understanding and knowledge relating to occupations in various sectors of economic and social life. Technical and vocational education is further understood to be:

   (a) an integral part of general education;

   (b) a means of preparing for occupationals and for effective participation in the world of work;

(c) an aspect of lifelong learning and a preparation for responsible citizenship;

(d) an instrument for promoting environmentally sound sustainable development;

(e) a method of facilitating poverty alleviation.

3. Technical and vocational education, being part of the total educational process and being a right as described in Article 26 of the Universal Declaration of Human Rights, is included in the term "education" as defined in the Convention Revised Recommendation concerning and the Recommendation against Discrimination in Education adopted by the General Conference of the United Nations Educational, Scientific and Cultural Organization at its 11th session (1960) and the Convention on Technical and Vocational Education adopted by the General Conference at its 25th session (1989). The provisions of these documents are therefore applicable to it.

4. This Recommendation should be understood as setting forth general principles, goals and guidelines to be applied by each individual country according to its socio-economic needs and available resources in a changing world, with a view also to enhancing the status of technical and vocational education. The application of the provisions and the timing of the implementation will depend upon the specific conditions, and constitutional provisions existing in a given country.

Targets and Motives

5. Given the immense scientific, technological and socio-economic development, either in progress or envisaged, which characterizes the present era, particularly globalization and the revolution in information and communication technology, technical and vocational education should be a vital aspect of the educational process in all countries, and in particular should:

(a) contribute to the achievement of the Societal goals of greater democratization and social, cultural and economic development, while at the same time developing the potential of all individuals, both men and women, for active participation in the establishment and implementation of these goals, regardless of religion, race and age;

(b) lead to an understanding of the scientific and technological aspects of contemporary civilization in such a way that people comprehend their environment and are capable of acting upon it while taking a critical view of the social, political and environmental implications of scientific and technological change;

(c) empower people to contribute to environmentally sound sustainable development through their occupations and other areas of their lives.

6. Given the necessity for new relationships between education, the world of work and the community as a whole, technical and vocational education should exist as part of a system of lifelong learning adapted to the needs of each particular country and to worldwide technological development. This system should be directed to:

(a) abolishing barriers between levels and areas of education, between education and the world of work, and between school and society through:

(i) the appropriate integration of technical/vocational and general education at all levels;

(ii) the creation of open and flexible educational structures;

(iii) the taking into account of individuals' educational needs, the evolution of occupations and jobs recognizing work experience as a part of learning;

(b) improving the quality of life by creating a learning culture that permits individuals to expand their intellectual horizons, to acquire and to constantly improve professional skills and knowledge, and to engage positively in society to utilize the fruits of economic and technological change for the general welfare.

7. Technical and vocational education should begin with a broad base which facilitates horizontal and vertical articulation within the education system and between school and the world of work, thus contributing to the elimination of all forms of discrimination, and should be designed so that it:

(a) is an integral part of everyone's basic general education in the form of initiation to technology, the world of work, and human values and standards for responsible citizenship;

(b) may be freely and positively chosen as the means by which people develop talents, interests and skills leading to an occupation in various sectors or to further education;

(c) allows access to other aspects and areas of education at all levels, including institutions of higher learning, by being grounded in a solid general education and, as a result of the integration mentioned in paragraph 6 (a), containing a general education component through all stages of specialization;

(d) allows transfers from one field to another within technical and vocational education;

(e) is readily available to all and for all appropriate types of specialization, within and outside formal education systems, and in conjunction or in parallel with training in order to permit educational, career and job mobility at the minimum age at which the general basic education is considered to have been acquired, according to the education system in force in each country;.

(f) is available on the above terms and on a basis of equality to women as well as men, and where the learning and working environment is made suitable for the participation of girls and women by removing overt and covert bias and discrimination and seeking, strategies for motivating girls and women to take an interest in vocational and technical education;

(g) is available to people with disabilities and to socially and economically disadvantaged groups such as immigrants, refugees, minorities (including indigenous peoples), demobilized soldiers in post-conflict situations, and underprivileged and marginalized youth in special forms adapted to their needs in order to integrate them more easily into society.

8. In terms of the needs and aspirations of individuals, technical and vocational education should:

(a) permit the harmonious development of personality and character, and foster spiritual and human values, the capacity for understanding, judgement, critical thinking and self-expression;

(b) prepare the individual for lifelong learning by developing the necessary mental tools, technical and entrepreneurial skills and attitudes;

(c) develop capacities for decision-making and the qualities necessary for active and intelligent participation, teamwork and leadership at work and in the community as a whole;

(d) enable an individual to cope with the rapid advances in information and communication technology.

Part of Government

9. Policy should be formulated and technical and vocational education administered in support of the general objectives adopted for the educational process as well as for national and, if possible, the regional social and economic requirements of the present and the future, and an appropriate legislative and financial framework adopted. Policy should be directed to both the structural and the qualitative improvement of technical and vocational education as stipulated in Article 2 of the Convention on Technical and Vocational Education (1989) and further described in the recommendations of the Second International Congress on Technical and Vocational Education (1999):

(a) Although governments carry the primary responsibility for technical and vocational education, in a modern market economy technical and vocational education policy design and delivery should be achieved through a new partnership between government, employers, professional associations, industry, employees and their representatives, the local community and non-governmental organizations (NGOs). This partnership must create a coherent legislative framework to enable the launching of a national strategy for change. Within this strategy the government, apart from actually providing technical and vocational education, can also provide leadership and vision, facilitate, coordinate, establish quality assurance and ensure that technical and vocational education is for all by identifying and addressing community service obligations.

(b) Technical and vocational education is best served by a diversity of public and private providers. The appropriate mix can be found in many ways, with the responsibility of governments being to facilitate choice while ensuring quality.

(c) Government and the private sector should recognize that technical and vocational education is an investment, not a cost, with significant returns, including the well-being of workers, enhanced productivity and international competitiveness. Therefore funding for technical and vocational education should be shared to the maximum extent possible between government, industry, the community and the learner, with government providing appropriate financial incentives. Furthermore, the governments of least developed countries in particular should seek bilateral and multilateral capacity-building cooperation in technical and vocational education.

(d) Within governments, there are often shared and overlapping responsibilities for various elements of technical and vocational education among departments and agencies. It is desirable that governments streamline their own public institutional framework to the maximum extent possible to coordinate the national technical and vocational education effort, create an effective partnership with the private sector, and promote technical and vocational education for the benefit of all stakeholders.

10. Particular attention should be given to planning the development and expansion of technical and vocational education by:

(a) giving high priority to technical and vocational education in national development agendas as well as in plans for educational reform;

(b) evaluating national short-term and long-term needs;

(c) providing appropriate current and future allocations of financial resources;

(d) establishing a national body responsible for coordinating planning in technical and vocational education based on analysis of statistical data and projections to facilitate complementarity between educational policy planning and employment policy.

11. Planning should respond to national and, if possible, regional, economic and social trends, to projected changes in demand for different classes of goods and services, and for different types of skills and knowledge in such a way that technical and vocational education may easily adapt to the evolving scientific, technological and socio-economic changes. This planning should also be coordinated with current and projected training action and the evolution of the world of work in both urban and rural areas.

12. While the education authorities should have primary responsibility, the following groups of relevant stakeholders should be actively associated in polity formulation and in the planning process; corresponding structures, both national and local, taking the form of public agencies or consultative or advisory bodies, should be created to permit this:

(a) public authorities responsible for planning economic and social policy, labour and employment, and for the manufacturing and service sectors;

(b) representatives of non-governmental organizations within each occupation sector from among employer; and workers as well as of the informal economy, small enterprise owners and entrepreneurs;

(c) authorities or bodies responsible for out-of-school education and training;

(d) representatives of those responsible—both in public education and in State-recognized private education—for executing educational policy, including teachers, examining bodies and administrators;

(e) parents', former pupils', students' and youth's organizations;

(f) representatives from the community at large.

13. Policies for the structural improvement of technical and vocational education should be established within the framework of broad

policies designed to implement the principle of lifelong education through the creation of open, flexible and complementary structures for education, training and educational and vocational guidance, considering the provisions of modern information technology in education regardless of whether these activities take place within the system of formal education or outside it. In this respect consideration should he given to the following:

(a) multipurpose secondary education offering diversified curricula linking education to the world of work;

(b) having institutions of higher learning offering flexible admission and programmes ranging from short specialized ones to longer full-time programmes of integrated studies and professional specialization;

(c) establishing a system of equivalencies whereby credit is given for completion of any approved programme and recognition is granted to educational and/or professional qualifications and work experience;

(d) providing articulation and pathways between technical and vocational education and programmes of higher education for the benefit of those learners who may wish to continue their education.

14. Policy should be directed to ensuring high quality so as to exclude discrimination between the different educational streams. In this respect, special efforts should be made to ensure that national technical and vocational education seeks to meet international standards.

15. In order to ensure quality, responsible national authorities should establish criteria and standards, subject to periodic review and evaluation, applying to all aspects of technical and vocational education, including, to the greatest extent possible, non-formal education for:

(a) all forms of recognition of achievement and consequent qualification;

(b) staff qualifications:

(c) ratios of teaching and training staff to learners;

(d) the quality of curricula and teaching materials;

(e) safety precautions for all learning and training environments;

(f) physical facilities, buildings, libraries, workshop layouts, quality and type of equipment.

16. National policy should foster research related to technical and vocational education, with particular emphasis on its potential within lifelong learning, and directed to its improvement and relevance to the prevailing socioeconomic context. This research should be carried out at national and institutional levels, as well as through individual initiative. To this end:

(a) special emphasis should be placed on curriculum development, research concerning teaching and learning methods and materials, and, where the need exists, on technologies and techniques applied to development problems;

(b) financial resources and physical facilities from public or private sources should be made available to institutions of higher education, specialized research institutions and professional organizations for applying the results of this research on an experimental basis in representatively selected institutions for technical and vocational education;

(c) the positive results of research and experimentation should be widely disseminated using all available media, especially information and communication technology;

(d) the effectiveness of technical and vocational education should be evaluated using, among other data, relevant statistics including those concerning part-time enrolment, dropout rates and placement in wage and self-employment;

(e) research efforts to humanize working conditions should be emphasized.

17. Administrative structures should provide for evaluation, supervisory and accreditation services to ensure the rapid application of new research findings and to maintain standards:

(a) evaluation services as a whole should ensure the quality and smooth operation of technical and vocational education by continuous review and action directed to monitoring progress and maintaining standards through constant improvement of staff, facilities, programmes and, most importantly, student achievement;

(b) supervisory services for the staff should encourage improvement in the quality of teaching by providing guidance and advice and recommending continuing education;

(c) all technical and vocational education programmes, including those offered by private bodies, should be subject to approval by the public authorities;

(d) individual institutions should have the autonomy to design their programmes with the involvement of business and industry to suit local needs.

18. Particular attention should be given to the material resources required for technical and vocational education. Priorities should be carefully established with due regard for immediate needs and the probable directions of future expansion in consultation with representatives from the world of work:

(a) institutional planning should be directed to ensuring maximum efficiency and flexibility in use;

(b) the planning, construction and equipping of facilities should be carried out in collaboration with specialists from industry, teachers and educational architects, and with due regard for the purpose of the facilities, prevailing local factors and relevant research;

(c) adequate funds should be allocated for recurrent expenditure for supplies and maintenance and repair of equipment;

(d) institutions should be given greater autonomy in their administration and financial management.

Dimensions of Common Education

19. An initiation to technology and to the world of work should be an essential component of general education. An understanding of the technological nature of modern culture and an appreciation of work requiring practical skills should thereby be acquired.

This initiation should be a major concern in educational reform and democratization. It should be a required element in the curriculum, beginning in primary education and continuing through the early years of secondary education.

20. Opportunities for general technical and vocational initiation should continue to be available to those who wish to avail themselves of it within the education system and outside it ire places of work or the community at large.

21. Technical and vocational initiation in the general education of youth should fulfil the educational requirements of all spheres of interest and ability. It should mainly perform three functions:

    (a) to broaden educational horizons by serving as an introduction to the world of work, and the world of technology and its products through the exploration of materials, tools, techniques, and the process of production, distribution and management as a whole, and to enrich the learning process through practical experience;

    (b) to orient those with the interest and ability in technical and vocational education towards preparation for an occupational field or training outside the formal education system;

    (c) to promote in those who will leave formal education with no specific occupational aims or skills, attitudes and thought processes likely to enhance their aptitudes and potential, to facilitate the choice of an occupation and access to a first job, and to permit them to continue their vocational training and personal development.

22. General technical and vocational studies in schools, having great importance for the orientation and education of youth programmes, should include an appropriate balance between theoretical and practical work. Such programme of studies should be drawn up in collaboration with the professional community and with those responsible for technical and vocational education. These programmes should:

    (a) be based upon a problem-solving and experimental approach, and involve experience in punning method and decision-making;

    (b) introduce the learner to a broad spectrum of technological fields and to productive work situations;

    (c) develop a certain command of valuable practical skills such as tool use, repair and maintenance and safety procedures, and a respect for their value;

(d) develop an appreciation of good design, craftsmanship and quality;

(e) develop the ability to function as a team member and to communicate technical information;

(f) be closely related to the local environment without, however, being limited to it.

23. Technical and vocational initiation programmes in general educational enrichment for youth and adults should be directed to enabling those engaged in working life to:

(a) understand the general implications of technical change, its impact on their professional and private lives, and how to adapt to these changes;

(b) use practical skills for improving the home and community environment, and thus the quality of life and productive leisure-time activities;

(c) inculcate an awareness of the possible impact of technology on the environment, and of the concept of sustainable development.

Vocational Education

24. Given the disparities that may exist between formal education, whether secondary or tertiary, and the employment and career opportunities available, the highest priority should be given to technical and vocational education. Consequently the structure and content of traditional education, whether general or technical and vocational, should be adapted accordingly through:

(a) the diversification of secondary education in the later stages so that it may be pursued in conjunction with employment or training, or may lead to employment or to higher education, thereby offering to all youth educational options corresponding to their needs and abilities;

(b) the development of educational structures and programmes on all levels centred on organized and flexible interchange between educational institutions (including universities), training institutions and the world of work.

25. Technical and vocational education as preparation for an occupational field should provide the foundation for productive and satisfying careers and should:
    (a) lead to the acquisition of broad knowledge and generic skills applicable to a number of occupations within a given field so that the individual is not limited in his/ her choice of occupation and is able to transfer from one field to another during his/her working life;
    (b) at the same time offer both a thorough and specialized preparation for initial employment, including self-employment, and also training within employment;
    (c) provide the background in terms of knowledge, skills and attitudes for continuing education at any point in the individual's working life.
26. Premature and narrow specialization should be avoided:
    (a) in principle, the age of 15 should be considered the lower limit for beginning specialization;
    (b) a period of common studies providing basic knowledge and generic skills should be required for each broad occupational sector before a special branch is chosen.
27. Technical and vocational education programmes should be designed as comprehensive and inclusive systems to accommodate the needs of all learners with special emphasis on motivating girls and women. Their equal access and participation should be ensured by:
    (a) appropriate legislative measures;
    (b) widespread dissemination of information concerning opportunities;
    (c) gender-sensitive guidance and counselling;
    (d) other incentives relevant to the local context.
28. Special provision should be made for out-of-school and unemployed youth and children of socially disadvantaged groups such as minorities, migrant workers, refugees, etc. with little or no primary education, as well as for those not entering education or training programmes after completion of compulsory schooling, in order that they may acquire skills for wage or self-employment.

29. Given the necessity of integrating people who are disadvantaged due to physical and intellectual disabilities into society and its occupations, the same educational opportunities should be available to them as to those without disabilities in order that they may achieve qualification for an occupation to realize their potential and optimize their participation in the work force; special measures or special institutions may be required.

THE MECHANISM

30. Technical and vocational education as preparation for an occupational field should be organized on a national or provincial/ local basis, so as to respond positively to overall social, economic and educational requirements and to the needs of different groups of the population without discrimination.

31. Several organizational patterns of technical and vocational education, including full-time, part-time, open and distance learning options, could exist within each country. The following patterns should be considered:

(a) full-time programmes including general education and practical training, provided in an educational establishment, either comprehensive or specialized;

(b) part-time programmes such as the following, in which general education and theoretical and broad practical aspects of the occupational field are given in an educational establishment, while specialized practical training is acquired during work in the chosen occupation:

(i) the day-release system, providing for workers and apprentices to attend an educational establishment one or two days a week;

(ii) the sandwich system, under which periods in an educational institution alternate with training periods in a factory, farm, business establishment or other undertaking;

(iii) the block-release system, whereby workers are released to attend courses of 10 to 15 weeks per year;

(c) open and distance education programmes provided through:

(i) correspondence;

(ii) special radio and television broadcasting;

(iii) the Internet and other computer-based media.

32. The responsible authorities should encourage part-time education; therefore:

(a) these programmes could be available after completion of minimum compulsory or required schooling, and should continue to be available throughout life;

(b) the qualifications acquired by this means should be equivalent to those acquired by full-time education:

(c) the practical training conducted by employers should be as broad as possible, and should aim to meet international standards.

33. In view of the increasing requirement for qualified middle-level personnel and the increasing numbers completing secondary education or its equivalent, the development of technical and vocational programmes at a tertiary level should be given high priority, by both public and private providers. The following patterns should be considered:

(a) a period of one to two years of guided work experience followed by part-time or full-time programmes of specialization;

(b) part-time and/or evening programmes;

(c) full-time programmes as an extension to those given in specialized secondary or tertiary institutions;

(d) programmes offered through open and distance learning.

34. In view of the high cost of equipment, its usage should be organized to yield optimum benefit. This could be achieved as follows:

(a) centralized or mobile workshops and libraries could be used to serve several educational institutions;

(b) when educational institutions close for the evenings and vacations, their classrooms and workshops should be utilized for continuing education and formal training programmes;

(c) workshops and laboratories should also be used to instal the culture of maintenance and respect for safety standards;

(d) enterprises should be encouraged to make their equipment and facilities available for practical training.

35. Enterprises should be actively involved in the theoretical and practical training of those preparing for occupations in their particular sector, and should interact with educational institutions regarding the organization of such training.

Programmes and Policies

36. All programmes of technical and vocational education as preparation for an occupational field should:

(a) aim at providing scientific knowledge, technical versatility and a cluster of core competencies and generic skills required for rapid adaptation to new ideas and procedures and for steady career development;

(b) be based on analyses and forecasts of occupational requirements by national education authorities, employment authorities, occupational organizations and other stakeholders;

(c) include an appropriate balance between general subjects, science and technology, as well as subjects such as computer literacy, information and communication technology, the environment and studies of both the theoretical and practical aspects of the occupational field;

(d) stress developing a sense of values, ethics and attitudes to prepare the learner for self-reliance and responsible citizenship.

37. In particular, programmes should:

(a) be interdisciplinary in character, as many occupations now require two or more traditional areas of study;

(b) be based on curricula designed around core knowledge, competencies and skills;

(c) include studies of the social and economic aspects of the occupational field as a whole;

(d) include an interdisciplinary perspective to equip students to work in the changing employment environment, and incorporate a multicultural perspective, which may include the study of a foreign language as preparation for international employment;

(e) include the study of at least one foreign language of international use, which, while conducive to a higher cultural level, will give special emphasis to the requirements of communication, the acquisition of a scientific and technical vocabulary, and the need to prepare for international employment and multicultural working environments;

(f) include an introduction to organizational, planning and entrepreneurial skills;

(g) emphasize instruction in safe and environmentally sound procedures relative to the materials and equipment used in a given occupational field, the importance of safe working conditions, and the health aspects relative to the occupation as a whole, including emergency and first-aid training.

38. While based on the above general principles and components, and thus pursuing in all cases broader educational aims, programmes in their practical aspect should be designed taking into account special occupational requirements, especially in "new" professions and those undergoing change, and particularly the use of the new information and communication technology as a tool for enhancing the effectiveness of all vocations, including those considered traditional.

39. Technical and vocational education programmes leading to university qualification, while encouraging research and offering high-level specialization, should be developed with particular attention to:

(a) the inclusion of components directed to developing attitudes whereby those with broad responsibilities in technological fields constantly relate their professional tasks to broader social and ethical goals;

(b) preparing the learner more generally for life and the world of work bearing in mind that technical and vocational education is for economic, personal and social benefit.

40. Programmes of technical and vocational education as preparation for occupations within the agricultural sector should be designed in accordance with the overall social and economic requirements of sustainable development in rural areas.

41. Where lack of resources is a serious constraint, priority should be given to developing programmes for areas experiencing skilled human resource shortages, taking into consideration the projected needs for national economic development and the corresponding labour market growth.

42. Programmes preparing for occupations in small industry, individual farming or the artisan trades, particularly for self-employment, should include entrepreneurship and elementary information and communication technology studies to enable those engaged in such occupations to take responsibility for production, marketing, competent management and the rational organization of the enterprise.

43. Programmes leading to occupations in the business, commercial and service sector, including the tourism and hospitality industries, should consist of:

(a) training in the methods and skills developed as a result of the application of computer-based technology to business and office management, and particularly to the acquisition and processing of information;

(b) training in the organizational and management skills required for the smooth operation of enterprises;

(c) an introduction to marketing and distribution procedures.

44. Special attention should be given to developing programmes for preparing personnel at all levels for the social services system (*e.g.* community and family work, nursing and paramedical occupations, nutrition and food technology, home economics and environmental improvement). Those programmes should:

(a) orientate the special occupational field to raising standards of living in terms of nutrition, clothing, housing, medical services, the quality of family life and that of the environment;

(b) be adapted to the special requirements of local conditions, in particular those of climate and geography, materials available, community organization, and social and cultural patterns.

Open Education

Open or distance education has been in existence for about one hundred years. The different forms of distance education can be identified by their use of technical media and as the basis for the learning materials. By far the great majority of distance education programmes are print based. The teaching basis of the Open University of the United Kingdom, for example, is approximately 80 per cent print based, 10 per cent broadcasting (radio and television) and 10 per cent face-to-face seminars and summer schools.

A real disservice has been done to the field of distance education by overemphasis on terms like 'University of the Air'. Educators, administrators and politicians, not only in developing countries but also in developed countries where finance for education is now being limited, should realize that the vast majority of distance education courses are print-based and will remain so. Exceptions to this in the foreseeable future will come only with population for whom literacy is a problem and perhaps in those regions where there is traditional reticience about correspondence type programmes.

Higher Education

Higher education in the United States of America is an area where an attempt to transfer emphasis to videotape-based or computer-based programmes might be worth considering because of the population's interest in technology and dislike of correspondence study. An interesting variant on printbased programmes are the courses by newspaper developed under the leadership of Martin N. Chamberlain, Dean of University Extension at the University of California, San Diego. The Deutsches Institutfur Fernstudien at Tubingen has recently introduced a similar programme in the Federal Republic of Germany.

Audio-based courses in which the educational content is carried by audio-cassettes or transmitted over radio and to which printed materials are peripheral, if used at all, have been used by distance educators. They are frequently cost-effective, can be used by people with literacy problems and may be a successful method of teaching languages. The University of Waterloo in Ontario is an extensive user of this method.

Distance education can be video-based when the basic educational content of the course is broadcast on television or contained on video-cassettes. Some printed materials containing background, further reading and assessment procedures often are supplementary, to the course. The development of cable television and the possibility of home ownership or rental of VCRs make this an area of interest in some cultures.

Series of programmes for television have already been developed by a number of groupings in America and elsewhere and a series of programmes based on video-cassettes is offered for credit by the independent study division of the University of Minnesota. Such programmes are to be regarded as distance education when they satisfy the characteristics outlined. A variant of both audio and videobased programmes is the educational use of satellites.

Daniel presented an evaluation of the first attempts at satellite based programmes to the 11th World Conference of the L.C.C.E. at new Delhi. Interest has also been aroused by the educational programmes of the Appalachian Area Satellite Project.

A computer can be the medium on which educational programmes that fall within the definition of distance education are based. A number of institutions have developed computer based distance education programmes and the Fall Education Company lists over 300 computer-based courses already developed for the ATO system. They range from Accounting Fundamentals to Zeiss-a model Planetarium. It is known that in America negotiations are in progress for the accreditation of some of these computer-based programmes for college and university credit.

No evaluation of the relative merits of the media described nor of the possibility of developing a multimedia system by combinations of the various components is offered here. Nor can consideration be given to whether it is possible or desirable to combine distance education with on-campus education. That is the work of other studies.

Private, proprietary correspondence schools have made valuable contributions to this field of education since the last century. In recent years standards have been set by affiliation to national accrediting bodies: the National Home Study Council of the U.S.A., the Association of Accredited Correspondence Colleges of the United Kingdom. Some of these institutions are non-profit making and a number receive some government support and they are found throughout the world. Government sponsored schools, colleges and universities have played a role in distance education for the last seventy years.

Many of these institutions are specially structured for distance education: Athabasca University, Edmonton; the Open College of Further Education, Adelaide; the Centre National de Tele-enseignement in France; the Fernuniversitat-Gesam in Hagen. Many other colleges and universities have a department which concentrates on the distance students: the independent study department of the University of Minnesota, Minneapolis; the external studies department of the University of Queensland, Brisbane.

Three forms of didactic structure characterize distance education institutions, especially when considered under the headings: provision for two-way communication and possibility of occasional seminars. Variations of the three models presented here are to be found employed by the different institutional types considered above in their effort to link learning materials to learning. The correspondence schools send learning materials by post to the student, the student studies the materials and posts assignment back to the institution which marks and comments upon them and posts them back to the student.

The correspondence element in distance education is here reduced to a minimum and once the learning materials have been developed and distributed to the students, the emphasis is placed on compulsory fortnightly two-to-three hour consultations. At these, groups of students meet their tutor for evaluation of their home study and for explanation and preparation of the next stage of learning materials. In the third and fourth year of study the frequency of the consultations is greatly diminished.

In a system similar to that of the Open University of the United Kingdom the link between learning materials and learning is promoted by as coherent a structure as possible. The student is supported by a wide range of activities, most of them optional unless the course team has decided otherwise. This tends to strengthen the possibility that learning takes place and that unnecessary dropouts are prevented. From time to time distance education is described as the opposite of face-to-face education. This statement needs to be taken further as there are many forms of what may be considered the 'opposite of face-to-face' education that are not distance education.

Pamphlets, books and teach-yourself manuals fall into this category. The lack of an educational organization is again the major factor which distinguishes these from distance education, together with the impossibility of two-way communication. It is clear that many people learn a great deal from these means, even though they may lack didactical structuring or even an educational goal.

Teaching Kits: In increasing use in face-to-face teachering are kits of various kinds containing samples, games and specimens on which students are invited to work without supervision.

When a lecturer communicates with a student by means of audio-visual aids: slides, film, audio and videotapes, he is teaching indirectly. Depending on the structure of the programme within which they are being used, these forms of indirect teaching can form part either of face-to-face instruction or of a distance education programme. Many people learn a great deal from radio and television and sometimes those media are used in distance education programmes, Kenneth Clarke's *Civilization* or Jacob Bronowski's *The Ascent of Man* were not conceived as part of a distance education programme. Nevertheless they have become part of both on-campus and distance education programmes when offered for credit with accompanying didactically structured assignment, reading and assessment materials.

Programmed learning, which was popular in the 1960s, is a form of indirect teaching which has many similarities to distance education. Both demand extensive preparation of learning materials, careful sequencing and tend towards the individualizing of learning. Computer aided learning is a recent form of indirect education and is used extensively in many conventional teaching programmes. Mention is made here of independent study and private study as two forms of education with similarities to the above. There are many forms of independent study amongst which can be classed study guided by a governess, tutor or counsellor and many contract, independent or external degree programmes in American colleges.

Private study can be seen as neither a form of direct, classroom education nor of indirect off-campus studies. It is widespread and devoid of institutional linkages, though it may be based on materials developed for use within an institution either for traditional classroom students or distance learners. There are certain forms of education which have some similarities to distance education but are not identical with it. Four of the most important are presented here for consideration: extension programmes, University Without Walls, experiential learning, the external degree. Three more general terms: 'non-traditional learning', 'off-campus studies' and 'open learning' are first considered briefly. One cannot define 'non-traditional learning' without first defining 'traditional learning' and that is clearly beyond the bounds of this study. It seems at times that in the United States any educational programme that is not a four-year, residential, university degree programme can be regarded as non-traditional learning, though there are clearly more restricted usages.

"Non-traditional learning' is to be regarded as a vague, generalized term of which distance education is one example. 'Off-campus studies' is another general term for any programme which does not take place on the central university or college campus-distance education is one possibility.

'Open learning' therefore, is a term that is not to be used in an administrative context; rather its context is philosophical to describe, for instance, colleges with 'open' administration policies or a special spirit like Paris VIII at Vincennes, I'Universite Ouverte. Some of these are face-to-face institutions, others teach at a distance. Extension programmes are ways of extending the expertise of a university or college to new population. The terms can imply offering the same programmes as for full-time, daytime students by different means, at different locations or at different times.

An extra-mural department usually has a similar function of extending the expertise of the university to a broader community. Some of these programmes are for credit, others not. The range or extension and extra-mural programmes is very extensive and distance education can be regarded as one grouping of a number of possibilities of providing education outside the normal lecture room. Extension, especially as used in the United States, is a much broader term which can include part-time day or night, conventional lectures on campus.

University without walls implies the design of an individualized programme based on a learning contract for students with clear learning objectives who cannot realize their whole educational aspirations through existing programmes. A University Without Walls programme can include experiential learning credits, ordinary lectures, distance education elements, learning from community sources or job-related activities, all of which can be evaluated towards a college or university degree.

Experiential learning programmes are those which give credit for prior learning which did not take place in a lecture room setting and was not sponsored by an educational institution, but was acquired through work experience including volunteer work, cooperative education or self-study. A degree programme which can be completed in the following manner: a student entering the programme with the minimum entrance qualifications can complete it with less than 25 per cent of the required work taking the form of campus-based classroom instruction.

In the attempt to place some conceptual order around the wide range of study programmes that are associated with non-traditional and distance education, the question of whether or not the external degree should be included within the concept of distance education is the one which poses the most precise definition and research problems. In so far as the external degree serves to describe the programmes whose primary function is to recognize education and attribute to it an appropriate qualification, it does not fall within the concept of distance education as it has been presented in this study.

If, on the other hand, it is used to describe programmes whose function is to provide education for students, then it may be identified with distance education provided that it agrees with the description. One hundred and eighty three college and university degree programmes are classified as external in the American study referred to above.

Distance Teaching

Tele-enseignement 'distance teaching' is an influential term in French because of its use in the titles of the Centre National de Tele-enseignement, (C.N.T.E.), the Centres do Tele-enseignement Universitaire (C.T.U.) and the Tele-universite de Quebec. There are some who would argue that formation of distance 'education at a distance' reflects more closely modern pedagogical theories. The problem with *tele-enseignement* is that many do not realize that the root of 'tele' is the Greek word tele 'from afar', 'from a distance' and does not refer to television. Tele-enseignement appears to be the generally accepted term: The words education a distancia in Spanish and teleducacao in Portuguese seem to be gaining acceptance as terms for 'distance education', side by side with the spread of influence of this type of education in Spanish and Portuguese speaking countries.

In English there are at least six major terms: correspondence study /education, home study, independent study, external studies, distance teaching, distance education. Correspondence study is not a suitable word for what has been described as 'distance education' in this article. It cannot describe radio-based programmes like Ensemble, television-based programmes like The Great Plaine, computer-based programmes in the PLATO series nor the Appalachian Satellite programme.

Communications theory experts tell us that words get tired and if they do then 'correspondence study' is a tired word. It is significant that when the directors of the correspondence schools of the United States of America came together in 1926 to form an association the title chosen was the National Home Study Council and not the National Correspondence Study Council.

Home study is used mainly in the United States of America and is confined to further and technical education. The 1979 listing of approved members of the National Home Study Council contain 94 institutions, most of them proprietary. When the universities of the United States of America which teach at a distance wanted to form an association it is significant that they rejected the title 'Home Study' and chose instead 'Independent Study'. 'Home study' is thus unsuitable and a generic term for the wide range of teaching-learning activities which have been described.

Independent study is the term used in higher education in the U.S.A. The 1979 Guide to independent study through correspondence instruction lists 68 members of the Independent Study Division of the National University Extension Association. Nearly all of these are correspondence sections of extension departments of American universities. In addition to programmes for degree credit, my of the courses are at high school or certificate level.

External studies is the term most widely used in Australia. Its use is confined to that region where it well describes the essence of the 'integrated model' of distance education as found in many Australian institutions: 'external to' but not 'separated from' the faculty staff. It can have little claim to general acceptance because of this limitation and because of confusion with the American external degree. Whether or not the American external degree, especially those associated with Antioch and Nova universities, falls within the concept of distance education has already been discussed. Distance teaching or teaching at a distance has been the term most commonly used by the Open University in the United Kingdom.

Distance teaching is only half the process we are trying to describe: to distance teaching must be added distance learning. The description of distance education as a form of industrialized education will, among other things, be criticized as public opinion is still influenced by anti-technical, or more generally, anti-industrial emotions which emerged in the context of the critique of our modern culture.

'The gospel of humanity cannot be separated from the critique of modern culture,' summarized Litt. In the second part of the nineteenth century cities of culture such as Buskin, Hildebrandt, Nietzsche and Langbehn opposed industrialization, arguing mainly that it mechanizes and factionalizes man. Hans Scheuerl has described the damage done to man by industrialization as set forth by critics of culture.

According to these critics there is a fear that 'original individuality will decline in a mass culture' and will be summarized to mere functional efficiency, that 'the more imitation, the mass production will make the deeper will layers of soul waste away', that stressing external, values will result in the loss of interior values, that the materialistic attitude towards life will alienate man from spiritual contents and their requirements. Altogether, these critics believed that 'the originally wholesome nature' of man is not enriched by the artificiality of civilizatory achievements but 'alienated, endangered and suffocated'. These attacks of the critics of culture have become especially important as their fundamental attitude was mediated by the youth and school reform movements and had strong effects on the theory and practice of education in the first half of our country.

The attitude of several generations of teachers towards technical achievements, the mechanization of instruction, and, therefore, towards distance education as well was influenced by their critique of culture. In spite of this, the return to the critique of culture in order to find out the reasons for the reservations of present-day educationists to distance education seems to be a little inadequate at first glance. First of all, critical discussion of distance education has not yet started on a scientific level. And secondly, we have learnt that the opposition towards other forms of industrialized education, such as programmed learning and cybernetic pedagogy, has been less strong than was expected.

In the meantime, one is often prepared to view industrialization as an irreversible process. Nevertheless, it must still be supposed that the attitude of former critics of culture was handed down by the movement of neohumanistic education and is still potent in the educational world of today, even if it is mainly found below the level of scientific discussion. This may be the reason for the widespread scepticism, lack of interest and even disdain for distance education. As evidence for this are the critics who readily concede that industrialization is, indeed, an irrevocable development, but at the same time consider it dangerous and disastrous.

Judgements of this kind can be heard from modern critics of culture in the conservative camp to the anti-authoritarian and progressive Marxist camp - where they are growing in numbers. Progressive Marxist examples are mainly the attacks on the cultural industry by Theodor W. Adorno, on the consciousness industry by Hans Magnus Enzensberger and Herbert Marcuse's description of the consequences of advanced industrialization on man. There is no doubt that many of the arguments set forth by critics of culture in three different historical periods apply also to industrialized education.

One is, for instance in line with the critics of culture of the second part of the nineteenth century when saying that the original individuality of the teacher and also of the students cannot express itself and is even lost over long periods of the teaching-learning process because of the use of technical media and of fixed goals and procedures of instruction. Teachers and students do not meet as fully developed individuals, but only as reduced and specialized functionaries.

Distance education produces neither funny teaching characters nor notoriously annoying types of students, as is often the case in face-to-face instruction. The systems of distance education are, it is true, 'standardized in order to raise their functionality', and 'production in series', 'mechanization', and 'functionalization' are their important structural traits. Finally, it should be mentioned that the motivation of many distant students derives from a 'materialistic attitude towards life'-that, is, that they strive to improve their conditions of life by obtaining higher qualifications. While this attitude may be a general one in our time, it seems, however, to be typical in a special sense for distant students.

When we consider new arguments - for instance, those of Jochen Kaltschmid, who has proved again in a profound analysis that 'the apparatus, the technicalization, mechanization, division of labour and organization' are all elements of the process of rationalization which shape the existence of man, and that the consequences of this rationalization are that our world is 'dominated by purposes', that we lose our 'inwardness', the 'immediacy of life' and the unity of our psychological faculties then, of course, we have to see that these consequences, indeed, are very likely to be reinforced by industrialized education.

In fact, its rationalized systems of teaching and learning are, as we have seen, structured in such a way that the purposes-the defined teaching goals—are achieved in the best way, the 'inwardness' of the students and the teachers, which is normally preserved by their personal interaction, is more or less lost by the objectivation of teaching behaviour, the splitting up of teaching and learning functions, and by the use of technical media. Also, the 'closeness to life' of instruction is, naturally, reduced a great deal. Teachers and students are no longer involved as whole human beings. And the unity of our psychic faculties is broken up. There are also many current argument about the incompatibility of technical developments and educations which are often emotive and relate to the concept of indus strialized education, as this form of education is—as we have shown-a result of the general process technicalizing of society.

Ludwig Heieck has discussed some of these arguments. According to him, education gives way to the functionalist thinking in terms of expediency in our technical age and abandons man. He says: 'Education derives from history. It is determined by the view that man is a historic being. Technical progress, however, is not historic. Instruction and education, therefore, have not participated in technical progress as they have felt threatened by it'.

The problem cannot be solved in the theoretical framework used so far in other chapters of this book. We have to face the same situation which was characterized by Paul Heimann, when he defended his contention that 'film, radio, and television are the powerful educational institutions of the present'. The objections raised to their educational use in the past also apply to top distance education, especially when it employs such mass media. According to Heimann, these critics were afraid of 'the furtherance of a receptive learning behaviour, an educational and instructional impressionism, the emergence of a dangerous conformism, the immobilization of creative imagination, the artificial increase of optical and acoustical stimuli, the reduction of primary experiences in favour of secondary experiences, the depersonalization, the mechanization of the relation between teacher and taught, and the levelling out of individual instruction'.

Heimann emphasized that these objections must by no means be trivialized, as some of them contain important arguments of educational philosophy. On the other hand, his reflections led to the conclusion that these objections can scarcely be refuted on the level of pure educational thinking. Therefore, he offered arguments dealing with problems of intellectual history and sociology. In this chapter a similar avenue is followed in order to invalidate possible objections of cultural critics to distance education or other forms of industrialized education.

The discussion will have four different starting points. First, the interpretation of a model of the historical development of instruction is to clarify whether distance education really distinguishes itself structurally to such a great extent from traditional education that the teacher and the students are placed in an entirely new existential situation which is not in line with the general historic trend and which must be considered as a development which fundamentally fails to reach the goal of humanity. Secondly, a number of socio-cultural preconditions of distance education and developments in the history of ideas are dealt with, in order to find out whether the objections of the critics of culture remain feasible.

Thirdly, it will be proved by comparing traditional instruction in the classroom with distance education that it integrates into the process of general change of social sub-systems and into the present inevitable development of society, whereby many of the norms defended by the critics of culture appear to be unreal. Fourthly, distance education is interpreted in anthropological terms. It is to be expected that dealing with it in such a way will result in further general arguments for judging the objections of the critics of culture.

If we consider the context of the origin of distance education not in a concrete socio-economic, but in a more general, far-teaching sense, then a new dimension emerges for the understanding of distance education. In order to achieve this it is, however, necessary to describe some structural elements of historical forms of instruction.

Initial Situation

If one relates this initial situation of instruction to our distance education today, a historical model of instruction can be constructed which shows that instruction has fundamentally changed in a development of several thousand years. The dimensions of this change can be determined by the following extreme parameters; the elitist instruction becomes egalitarian, its sacral contents and procedures become profane, the government of the teacher is substituted by the self-government of the student, the intimate group becomes a larger and less intimate group or even an anonymous mass of students, the personal interaction between teacher and students becomes mechanized and automated, and the traditional ties of instruction to a special teacher, a special place and a special time are removed. It is evident that developments have taken place in the dimensions referred to whereby it is not necessary to consider their division into periods or their delays in certain cultural areas.

The entire extent of these changes could be demonstrated on a bipolar scale. Distance education would arrive at the extremes in all cases. However, if one also assesses the present instruction in classrooms it becomes apparent that this form of education has not developed accordingly. A closer examination will show that there is a correlation between the different stages of development and the extent to which principles of industrialization have been applied in each case. Analogously to the historical process of the democratization of political power, which passed through several stages, there was also a process of continued democratizing of teaching and learning and of knowledge. One can even-parallel to the political development-distinguish priestly-aristocratic, bourgeois and democratic forms of teaching and learning and of knowledge.

Whereas in the beginning of the cultural development only small groups handed down their knowledge, which was often kept secret, to the chosen ones, now a phase is reached in which in many countries of the world knowledge is in principle accessible by everyone, whereby traditional ethnic, religious, social and regional boundaries, which still make education privilege to many, can be surmounted-due to the availability of industrialized education. The latest and most convincing steps in this direction have been taken by the Open University in the United Kingdom.

Consequently, in many countries educational politicians consider distance education as a means for equalizing educational opportunities. Such a way of thinking, it is true, overlooks the enormous socio-cultural barriers on the way to education and surely underestimates the real difficulties. Nevertheless, it must be admitted that distance education provides at least necessary technical and organizational preconditions for a universal admission to continued and higher education. An analysis of statistics about distance education reveals that millions of distant students do indeed profit from this industrialized way of education.

Often enough it offers them the only way towards the desired education as all other ways are barred by lack of funds or by other circumstances. Comparison with the conditions under which face-to-face-instruction takes place in the schools of the Federal Republic of Germany as well as in those of other countries can be used to show that we are dealing with school systems organized according to class structures in which access to secondary schools and universities remains restricted, so that people continue to suffer from the inequality of educational opportunities.

The sacral character of instruction can be related to the fact that at the beginning of our cultural development the knowledge and skills which were handed down from one generation to the other were priestly wisdom and ritual ceremonies. Only later were the various scientific disciplines differentiated from the knowledge of the priests. In ancient Babylon the priests were physicians and teachers in one person.

The Indian Veda consisted at first of hymns, prayers, wordings and proverbs which were important in sacrificial ceremonies. Only later varying systems of interpretation and research approaches developed out of them and disciplines like law, logic and dogmatics branched off. The Egyptian priest caste also imparted collections of hymns as part of the holy literature.

The scientific disciplines could emancipate themselves from mythical ideas and ritual reinforcements only later. This applied of course, to the respective instruction as well. In the beginning, however, the forms of instruction corresponded to sacral contents. Everything we still can learn shows us that the priest-teacher was venerated by the students and that the instruction and examinations were permeated by a ceremonial solemnity.

It is obvious that most forms of our present instruction have left those sacral origins far behind them, of course. However, on looking more carefully one can see that the process of secularization has not yet ceased everywhere. As distance education is mainly dependent on indirect interaction and communication it has, so to speak, completed its secularization. The interaction between teacher and student is objectified by rational teaching techniques and the use of technical media to such a degree that even relicts of archaic attitudes are no longer possible. In instructional face-to-face situations, however, one can still find them. In fact, rudiments of an originally sacred teaching-learning behaviour can be identified in the following circumstances:

— teachers—be they in the classroom or lecture hall—see themselves as the source of knowledge;

— the teacher dominates the students verbally in such a way that the intended dialogue between the student which is structurally similar to that of a priest in the pulpit preaching to the faithful;

— the students rise from their seats when the teacher enters or leaves the classroom;

— there are ceremonial greetings and forms of dismissal;

— the teacher-for example, in English public schools and colleges-still wears a gown which recalls a clergyman's vestments;

— the school continues to stick to certain rituals as, for instance, prayers at the beginning of the school day or hymns and other ceremonies during inauguration and graduation;

— school celebrations assume a special significance in the educational process.

These and other aspects of face-to-face instruction have been handed down by tradition. In distance education, however, this tradition is discontinued because of the technological revolution in the methodology of teaching.

The original communicative stance of teachers and students is substituted by a technologically medicated interaction between the two of them. The process of secularization could, therefore, go further than in face-to-face teaching. Under the aspect of hierarchy it can be stated that the structure of all early forms of instruction was characterized by the fact that the teacher assumed the role of the old man, the father, which was connected with wisdom, authority and power. His power derived often from the knowledge of the power bringing formulas and from his knowledge of the tradition. But above all, it was derived from the power of God. Hieros means 'holy'. Accordingly, a hierarchy was originally a 'holy rule'.

The students, who also waited on their teachers, were expected to respect and venerate them. Brunner reports on ancient Egyptian education how the power of the teachers resulted in the punishment of the students. The students were subjected to corporal punishments, were put in the stocks, threatened, admonished, but never praised. In the Middle Ages the status symbol of the teacher was, typically enough, a rod, which he was to hold upright, as may be seen in contemporary pictures. Sometimes, the teacher was supported in his punishing activities by the locates, a school janitor who also carried a rod as a token of his dignity, but-for hierarchical reasons-with the tip facing downwards.

Generally, people were of the opinion that, for instance, in the education of artisans as well as of knights, learning and serving went together. The master-servant relationship which was constituted during the training ceased only when the apprentice was formally released from this relationship after having qualified as a journey man.

The development which started off with the student who was ruled and maltreated in the ways described comes to an end with a student who is able to identify his learning needs and who decides himself which learning goals he wishes to reach and in which way or with the university student who applies the concept of learning by researching. Both approaches orientate themselves to the model of the self-determined and self-governing student. Both of them advocate domination-free learning. There are several reasons why distance education has developed structural approaches for forms of learning which are free from teacher dominance and the influence of the teacher's authority and why, hence, distance education would have its place at the end of this dimension:

— The increased availability and accessibility of distance education enables the learner for the first time to check through the learning material of a number of respective courses and make decisions himself when selecting one of them. The necessary qualification for doing so may still be lacking with most learners as, so far, usually other persons have decided what is to be studied and when and where the studying will take place. It can, however, be acquired with the help of systems of distance education and their counselling services.

— Normally, the teacher is not physically present when the student learns. He effects his learning only indirectly. In the same way as in the political sector the personal power of the king was objectified as soon as his personal exercising of power with the help of written documents which then led to bureaucracy, the personal interaction between teacher and student became objectified by the written word and the use of other media. Thus, a scope of independence and freedom came into being, which, indeed, is used and appreciated by the students.

— The student takes over the control of the time, the frequency and the duration of his learning.

— Very often adults begin to study a course in distance education by their own free decision. In such cases, the relation between the teacher and the student is entirely different from the corresponding relationship in the traditional and institutionalized schools, where the teacher is usually the representative of the power which makes students attend the school and even controls their learning behaviour and school life.

However, the simple fact that a student learns relatively independently does not allow the conclusion that distance education already gives rise to absolutely dominance-free learning.

In particular, if distance education is organized as a part of compulsory general education-as, for instance, in Australia, Canada and the United States, with the military services or in vocational training-repressive effects of those who have the power are not removed, but only distributed in another way and sublimated. Their power cannot be done away with simply by replacing face-to-face instruction by distance education.

In spite of this, it must be stressed that the objectivation of learning processes offers more scope for independent learning than instruction tied to special teachers in special situations.

Above all, it enables the critical cooperation of students when instruction is evaluated even if this happens only in a representative form. When, for instance, selected students are members of the course team their influence upon the intended teaching-learning process can be increased.

Here, dominance-free learning might, indeed, have more scope for its development in distance education than in face-to-face instruction. At the extreme point of this dimension one can place learners who identify their learning goal themselves, select and handle the respective system-of industrialized teaching expertly, and also control the outcomes of their learning themselves.

Obviously, face-to-face instruction is still far from this extreme point, as the learning process is often not only influenced by the teachers' dominance and predilections, as A. and R. Tausch have shown so impressively in their research on the language behaviour of teachers and students, but also by traditional and institutional constraints.

Teaching Behaviour

Criteria of repressive teaching behaviour are corporal punishment of pupils which is still preserved in many primary schools, various forms of disciplinary action at secondary schools, and sending down from universities. In these cases the teaching learning process is still connected to the process of disciplining the students. The double meaning of 'discipline' is, indeed, telling and applicable even today.

The social pattern of instruction was originally modelled after the social interaction in the family. Keay and Brunner agree in that in ancient times instruction began in the family on the basis of the father-son relationship. Obviously, teaching started in the intimacy of a father-son relationship and in the form of private tuition.

Thinking in ideal types, one can assume that there was an initial period in which private tuition dominated; for instance, when a priest introduced his successor into the procedures of secret sacral ceremonies, or when children of aristocratic families were carefully prepared for their future role in society. Our knowledge from history shows us that the subsequent periods must have been characterized by the following communication structures between teachers and students

— group instruction;

— classroom instruction;

— large group instruction;

— instruction of mass audience.

It must be added that each period continued to exist and could even assume new importance in later periods. The changes, however, which came to pass when one period replaced the other must have been considerable, and were, obviously, caused by certain Societal necessities. Brunner, for instance, reported that in ancient Egypt private tuition changed to classroom instruction as early as the beginning of the second millennium-that is, at a time when a rigid administration was established and a technically and ethically well-educated civil service was highly valued.

The ability to rationalize instruction with the help of better organization is obviously a precondition for proceeding from one period to the next one. If one asks how distance education relates to these periods, and especially distance education in the multimedia form which has developed during the last fifteen years and which has already integrated radio and television, the answer can only be that it belongs to the final period. The extreme of mass education has been reached fully. Some projects of this kind provided tuition for groups counted in tens of thousands and even a hundred thousand students.

The traditional instruction in the classroom, however, originated at a very early period. It is, strictly speaking, still closely attached to individual instruction, as classroom instruction is basically often still merely an extended and schematized individual instruction-if one disregards the many efforts to change it into group instruction. Educational theorists, who stressed the individuality of the single pupil, Locke, Rousseau, Herbart, Weniger, Bollnow and Buber may have supported this practice. The traditional teaching and learning behaviours are obviously so stable that they resist the use of technical media and the application of principles of industrialization.

UNIVERSALIZATION OF EDUCATION

Schools and institutions of religion combined proselytizing with literacy, compulsory education later became a duty rather than a right of the child. And yet, getting all children to school is still mistaken for their right to education, although they can be brainwashed, indoctrinated, abused, harmed for life. All rights of the child apply to education and in education. If they do not, human rights will not be achieved through education.

A great deal of attractive rhetoric about integrating human rights education into all education has been generated during the past decade. Teachers are expected to be its conveyers in school, while parents are expected to send their girls to school because it is—in theory—an excellent idea. Bridging the abyss between theory and practice necessitates looking far beyond education to identify all factors which hamper girls' education.

STATUS OF THE FAIR SEX

The girls' right to education is inextricably linked with the rights they can gain through education, but these lie beyond education strategies. A glimpse into detrimental effects of formal schooling on the girls' marital prospects in Uganda and Nepal, demonstrates the need for main streaming all human rights in education strategies. The intrinsic value of education, which is so optimistically assumed in all international strategies, clashes again social norms which confine girls to early marriage, negotiated between their parents and those of the prospective bridegroom.

The price which the girls' parents have to pay to the bridegroom's family, as lamented by a Nepali mother, increases with the girl's formal schooling. It is easy to ignore these real obstacles to the schooling of girls because they are assumed to have been eliminated, that all the rights have already been recognized for all women and girls. Human rights instruments are, as the term 'instrument' indicates, tools which ought to be used to secure equal rights for girls. Trying to promote the girls' right to education without heeding the obstacles to their right to marriage or property diminishes the value of the girls' education for their parents, thus closing off an obvious road towards change.

The advantage which human rights have over the fragmented visions of advances which can be made in isolated areas, such as education, is considerable. The human rights approach forces designers of development strategies for whatever isolated sector to look at all human rights and fundamental freedom. A large number of articles of faith accompanies schooling for girls. Primary education for girls aged from six to eleven is expected to delay marriage, lower fertility, improve the health of the next generation. It is a counter intuitive argument that eleven year old girls, after merely five years of schooling, would not marry and bear children since there usually there is no alternative for them.

Education of girls requires much more than getting girls into schools—it necessitates altering gender roles. The prospects which girls have after schooling influence the attractiveness of schooling for the girls and for their parents. These prospects are determined by the ability of girls and women to exercise all their human rights—from equal political participation and representation, to equal access, to bank loans. It is by focusing on the gender dimensions of education that we learn how much change is needed to transform education into rights-based education. Frank Dall has pointed out how detrimental "the classroom-centred model designed to service a pre-industrial European society" has been. One visible feature of this model are square schools, even if all huts around them are round.

There must be schools whose size and shape fits the environment, but the iron rule of school-building is to make them square. Building schools is usually the first step towards providing education for children, although there is no evidence that the building itself, expensive as it may be, has any effect on children's learning. School uniforms constitute a considerable expense for parents and, again, no association with children's learning has even been established. Taking children away from their family for full-time schooling -especially girls—has often proved impossible but it was only in the 1990s that adjusting the timetable to children's lifestyle started prevailing over the conventional idea of full-time schooling, away from home, with a schedule designed for industrialized countries, and with expectations to match.

Vocational education is twice or even four times more expensive that general education and, when given instead of general education, which parents see as the ladder leading their children to white-collar jobs, tends to become seen as a problem rather than a solution. Many adults recall their school days as exercises in futility, when they were forced to memorize the names of national heroes, the dates of important battles, the exact length of rivers. Ronald Dore caricatured education in 1976 as "ritualistic, tedious, suffused with anxiety and boredom, destructive of curiosity and imagination; in short, anti-educational."

It must be incomprehensible to children why we are forcing them to learn exactly the same things which we neither enjoyed nor found useful ourselves, except for passing exams. Much as the aims and purposes of education are beautifully defined in theory, the practice for most children is drudgery and they alternate from voting with their feet and truanting or going through the ritual of memorizing masses of useless data and hating it. Their right to question and challenge is not theirs, except in theory. Their voice is seldom heard. A boy aged 8 has feared becoming "the smallest unclever" in his family and pursued memorizing things which he found "very boring."

A Bosnian boy aged 13 has agonised over the muddle in his head created by having to memorize all the varied information which the syllabus has inflicted upon him, and has pursued as well. Their own experience is likely to result in their inflicting the same kind of drudgery upon their children. Giving children a voice while they are still at school would make all the difference, as the Convention on the Rights of the Child anticipates. School should be child-friendly, based on the right of the child "to be curious, to ask questions and receive answers, to argue and disagree, to test and make mistakes, to know and not know, to create and be spontaneous, to be recognized and respected."

The enormity of the task embodied in this vision clashes against the reality of schools that may be grappling with the lack of running water and sanitation, with the incompatibility of the school timetable with family and community life, with violence against and among children, with curricula and syllabi that force children to spend their schooling years constantly fearing that they will mix up the masses of information which they are forced to memorize.

From the human rights viewpoint, education is an end in itself rather than merely a means for achieving other ends. Some economists, such as Alain Mingat, define education "as efficient production of human capital and its purpose is then structuring the supply of qualified people over a long period of time to make it more in line with economic demands."

The contrast between the human-rights and human- capital approaches is best illustrated taking children with physical and learning disabilities as example. They may be excluded from school because providing wheelchair access might be deemed too expensive or their learning deemed not to yield a sufficient marginal return on investment. This type of reasoning obviously challenges the very assumption of human rights, namely the equal worth of all human beings.

Is the recognition of the role of "human capital" adequate for understanding the importance of what has been called "human development," to wit the development of the capability of people to do the things they have reason to value and choose? There is a crucial difference here between means and ends. Seeing human qualities in terms of their importance in promoting and sustaining economic growth, significant as it is, tells us nothing about why economic growth is sought in the first place, nor much about the role of enhanced human qualities in making it directly possible for us to lead freer and more fulfilling lives.

Human beings are not only the most important means of social achievement, they are also its profoundest end. Being a fine piece of capital is not the most exalted state that can happen to a human being.

Human capital is commonly defined as the sum of economically relevant attributes (knowledge, skills, competences) held by the working-age population. A human rights response ought to be forged lest the postulate of the International Labour Organization that labour is not a commodity risks falling into oblivion. Furthermore, accepting underlying market value of human capital risks turning upside- down the idea that economy should serve people rather than the other way around.

Theodore Schultz examined in 1962 risks embodied in an imbalance between non-human capital, such as land and physical capital, and human capital, which meant a healthy and educated population at the time. Schultz advocated investing in people so as to raise their capabilities. The literature on human capital has evolved in the past decades from the relationship between education and income, focusing on the economic value of schooling and/or the rate of return on schooling, especially private, to then affirm the productive utility of human knowledge.

This is only one out of many purposes of education. Such reductionism precludes defining education in terms of the full development of human personality, frustrating the very foundations for human rights education which require sharing knowledge rather than trading it and cooperating rather than competing. The human-capital approach moulds education solely towards economically relevant knowledge, skills and competences to the detriment of human rights values.

Education should prepare learners for parenthood and political participation, it should enhance social cohesion and tolerance and more than anything, it should teach the young that all human beings—themselves included—have rights. A productivist view of education depletes it of much of this purpose and substance. The human-capital approach has, however, revealed the importance of public investment in education as well as disparate prospects for attaining knowledge-based economies.

The current international priority for basic education has led to a halt in financial support for post-basic education. This fares ill against findings that the foundation necessary to enable individuals ‘to build up their human capital' is upper-secondary education. Moreover, without secondary and university education, what education will teachers have so as to be able to teach children?

We have not enabled all children and young people to go to school and discussing the right to education thus requires exposing and opposing the abyss between the normative and empirical worlds. Children, more than adults, should but often do not have the right to education. Recognizing and guaranteeing their right to education thus remains priority. Once in school, children can be subjected to indoctrination as well as beaten into submission hence merely getting them into schools secures only one part of their right to education.

International human rights law has therefore from the very outset guaranteed fundamental freedom in education. Mere respect of such freedom, without guaranteed access to education for all children and young people, leaves the poor condemned to illiteracy or schooling of such poor quality that it cannot meet even the most generous definition of education.

The right to education straddles the division of human rights into civil and political, on one hand, and economic, social and cultural, on the other hand, thereby affirming the conceptual universality of human rights. Both the right to education and rights in education thus ought to be recognized and protected. Moreover, many human rights can only be accessed through education, particularly rights associated with employment and social security. Without education, people are impeded from access to employment. Lower educational accomplishment routinely prejudices their career advancement. Lower salaries negatively affect their old-age security.

Denial of the right to education triggers exclusion from the labour market and marginalization into the informal sector, which is accompanied by the exclusion from social security schemes because of the prior exclusion from the labour market. Redressing the existing imbalance in life chances without the full recognition of the right to education is then impossible. Moreover, illiterate people are routinely precluded from political representation.

In many countries, literacy in general or in a particular language is prerequisite for becoming a candidate in elections. As recently as

1985, illiterate people were precluded from having a right to vote in Brazil. There is thus a large number of human rights problems which cannot be solved unless the right to education is addressed as the key to unlock other human rights.

Education operates as multiplier, enhancing the enjoyment of all individual rights and freedom where the right to education is effectively guaranteed, while depriving people of the enjoyment of many rights and freedom where the right to education is denied or violated.

The right to education is easiest to analyse by focusing on the corresponding governmental obligations on two levels:

— on the level of individual states as is customary in human rights, and

— on the level of global and regional intergovernmental structures within which governments act collectively.

While individual states are held primarily responsible for ensuring that human rights are effectively safeguarded, global economic and fiscal policies can constrain both the ability and the willingness of individual governments to guarantee the right to education.

The identification and elimination of obstacles—especially financial—to the realization of the right to education is the key to progress. There is, nevertheless, no commitment to the right to education by international financial institutions such as the World Bank and the International Monetary Fund, nor the international donor community as a whole. The main reason are corollary duties and responsibilities.

The collective voice of governments has been supportive of education but less so of the human right to education, indicating that there is a difference between the two. This difference is epitomized in the post-war history. An international commitment to universal primary education for all children in the world was made once per decade. None materialized. Each betrayed pledge was followed by a similar pledge, which was also betrayed. The difference which human rights bring can be expressed in one single word—violation.

The mobilizing power of calling a betrayed pledge a human rights violation is immense. Moreover, legal enforcement of human rights obligations makes violations expensive. Resort to legal enforcement requires pre-existing individual and collective commitment to the right to education. The turn of the millennium has been marked by attempts to forge consensus within the international community on diagnosing problems faced by the whole world and devising solutions for them. High hopes have been focused on these global summits, hopes that a global vision of our common future will emerge and that commitments will be made to translate it into reality.

The established practice has been convening a follow-up global conference for each issue—women, environment, social development, or children—where one was held in the 1990s. The one on education was held ten years after the Jomtien Conference in 1990 had instilled a great deal of optimism by forging a set of global commitments.

The Fourth Global Meeting of the International Consultative Forum on Education for All took place in Dakar on 26-28 April 2000. This meeting has been referred to as Jomtien+10 in popular parlance as it was based, as the title of the final document indicates, on the acknowledgment that commitments made at Jomtien in 1990 had not been met.

The 1990 commitment had been to achieve universal primary education by the year 2000 but the target year was postponed to 2015. Whether we will do better in the first decade of the new millennium than in the last decade of the previous one is an open question. Answers tend towards pessimism unless corrective action is urgently undertaken.

The 1990 Jomtien Conference was convened against the diminishing coverage of primary education in the 1980s, especially in Africa, where the proportion of primary-school age population in school declined by 10 per cent. Further retrogression was feared and could only be halted through parallel measures at the global level and in individual countries.

The Jomtien Conference was a historic event intended to enhance priority for basic education through a global mobilization around time-bound targets. The language of the final document adopted by the Jomtien Conference merged human needs and market forces, moved education from governmental to social responsibility, made no reference to the international legal requirement that primary education be free of-charge, introduced the term 'basic education' which confused conceptual and statistical categories.

The language elaborated at Jomtien was different from the language of international human rights law. Those who saw Jomtien as a donor-driven process were proved right because donors' support for education did increase in the immediate follow-up to the Jomtien Conference.

Schemes for Women

As a corollary, many developing countries started elaborating education-for-all strategies through assessments of basic learning needs (in the Jomtien jargon) and estimates of the associated resource requirements. The gap between the needs and the funds did not diminish much although the Jomtien meeting noted that "the downward trend of falling enrolments that we witnessed during the 1980s has been reversed." Reversing the retrogression of the 1980s necessitates profound domestic and international changes: Too few have taken place as yet and retrogression, was only halted, perhaps temporarily.

While individual governments were traditionally deemed capable of complying with their human rights obligations if they exhibited the necessary political will, the tumultuous 1980s showed that the political will of many individual governments of poor countries was no longer sufficient to halt and reverse previous retrogression.

A great deal of global mobilization, within and outside the United Nations, was necessary to 'adjust adjustment,' to challenge and change the fiscal austerity which had badly affected primary education, making the right to education an un-affordable luxury in open contradiction to the international human rights law.

Human rights obligations demand that the maximum of available resources be allocated to human rights, thus explicitly targeting fiscal austerity. This line of reasoning would have been immensely helpful in drafting education strategies at Jomtien and, ten years later at Dakar, but was absent from both.

From the human rights perspective, no significant improvement was achieved in the year 2000. The status of the right to education in these global education strategies was obviously controversial because the formulations that were ultimately agreed upon in Dakar replicated 'the language of Jomtien.'

Suggestions to adopt the language of international human rights law, with its definitions of rights and obligation, violations and remedies, were apparently not heeded. References to human rights and to some treaties in which these are defined were more numerous than they had been in 1990, but the corresponding obligations were not mentioned.

The process of negotiating the final text adopted at Dakar had started in 1999 from a 30-page draft to end with a 5-page text in April 2000. Difficulties in reaching an agreement on collective commitments which the Dakar Conference was to finalize thus must have been considerable. The consequences of defining education as a human right are corollary duties and responsibilities, entailing changes in policies and practices of the respective agencies. Rights entail corresponding obligations as well as remedies for violations.

There were few financial commitments to carry out whatever transpires to have been agreed in Dakar; the $300 million was apparently spent to review the situation and reach an agreement that ultimately could not be reached—what to do after the conference has ended to reverse the ill fate of education, especially in the allocation of public funding. A sideshow was a heated debate as to whether education was or was not a human right.

On the positive side, the advocates of selling and purchasing education lost the battle as references to the right to education were included in the final document. On the negative side, the advocates of buying and selling education won the war because there has been no financial commitment needed by the millions of poor children to get education as a matter of right.

The Dakar Conference has not done much to eliminate barriers in the way of the right to education. These are easy to articulate and this is done here by presenting a series of misconceptions, starting from the key obstacle which is routinely singled out for hindering the right to education—poverty. Similarly to the reluctance exhibited by the key actors at Jomtien and Dakar, barriers that need to be overcome on the road to the right to education can be traced to the price which recognizing the right to education entails.

In the case of international agencies such as the World Bank or the International Monetary Fund, their policies have to be adjusted to making free primary education available and accessible to all children. This is costly for them because it often interferes with debt servicing by the respective governments, while they are owed much of this debt.

In the case of individual governments, budgetary allocations have to be adjusted to the requirements of international human rights law, education law has to be altered to recognize children as the subject of the right to education, curricula and text-books have to be altered to accommodate all human rights for all, methods of instruction hindering human rights have to be eliminated. In the case of parents, accepting that their children are not their property but people with rights necessitates challenging the worldwide heritage of denying that children have any rights.

The way to the right to education is long and uphill. It is necessarily a relay-race because obstacles are many and diverse. First and foremost, economists and statisticians are needed to facilitate creating rights-based economic and fiscal policies and the associated statistics.

A range of professions and academic disciplines are necessarily involved in moulding education so that it can contribute to poverty eradication. It is, however, the principal task of the human rights community to dismantle misconceptions about linkages between poverty and human rights and these are addressed first.

At the beginning of the new millennium, the new vocabulary of donors' policies in education includes human rights and poverty eradication. Neither of the two is new but the linkage between them is novel. Clearly and powerfully articulated human rights-both in education and in poverty eradication-are necessary in order to prevent the current focus on poverty from lowering the goals of international development cooperation.

The changes in donors' policies have come at a time of constantly decreasing aid hence this fear. The shift from development to poverty eradication may lower the goal of helping individuals, communities and countries to develop by merely halting impoverishment. The shift from education to basic education focused donors' funding to the lowest rung in the education pyramid, sometimes also diminishing the age-range of beneficiaries from the previous 6-15 to 6-11.

Investment in education for all children was historically assigned to the state because it yields economic returns with much delay and, moreover, only in combination with other assets. The history of compulsory education did not revolve around economic arguments alone but these carried considerable weight. The need for a large pool of literate people was a driving force behind compulsory education during early industrialization as was the need to keep children out of the labour market thus enabling adult workers to negotiate and uphold fair wages. The economic rationale behind compulsory education also included ensuring that people can support themselves after leaving school lest they become a financial burden on public authorities.

Nevertheless, today education rarely attains the priority in budgetary allocation which international human rights law requires, and where it does, allocations tend to favour higher at the expense of primary education. South Korea is a favourite example of the sound economic rationale for investing first in primary and then secondary education, with two-thirds of public funding having been allocated to primary education in 1960-1975, followed by allocating one-third of the total to secondary education in 1975-1990.

The importance attached to secondary education differs from the current global emphasis on primary education as the passageway out of poverty. The example of South Korea is important because disappointments with education which has been ill-suited to income generation have been many. Recently they have been evidenced in Eastern Europe, where the generally high levels of education have not proved to have been a sound economic investment.

It is indicative that only one in seven young people in Central Europe has rated education as essential for getting ahead in life. With scarce natural resources, Korea has relied heavily on human resources to develop its economy. Education being a major source for trained manpower, educational policies have changed in accordance with the types of human resources demanded by a changed economy.

In the 1950s, when low-level skilled workers were needed in manual industries, efforts were geared to undertake a massive scale literacy campaign to produce a manual workforce. In the 1960s, skilled workers were in great demand for light industries, and the focus was shifted to expand vocational education at the secondary school level. As the importance of heavy industries grew in the 1970s, technicians who could deal with complex modern manufacturing processes were in demand. The government responded by expanding junior technical colleges. The number of junior colleges nearly doubled in this period.

Fiscal Elements

In the 1980s, economic competitiveness based on high level technology and information industries became fierce and this challenge urged the Korean government to strengthen research and education in basic science and technology. Though there have been some mismatches, it is generally agreed that secondary school enrolment and investment in education have a positive and crucial relationship with economic growth in Korea.

Expansion of secondary enrolment and public investment in secondary education were very important in offsetting diminishing returns to investment in physical capital, and thus made significant contribution to achieving sustained per capita income growth. It is often pointed out that the positive effect from public investment in secondary education was made possible because Korea had a universal elementary education and had, as well, comparable rates of investment in physical capital along with export-oriented growth strategies. In other words, Korea expanded and universalized elementary education followed by secondary education, and only after achieving this, shifted its emphasis to the expansion of higher education.

The economic rationale for education in South Korea what Korea did right in the 1970s was that it spent four-fifths of its education budget on basic education, while countries with similar level of economic development focused on higher education. One significant effect of this improvement in basic education was that due to increased number of women with a basic education, the number of school age children remained stable.

Thus a growing amount of resources could be devoted to a stable number of children, allowing for improvements in the quality of education. In contrast, other countries which neglected the importance of basic education observed a growing number of school age children, and had to direct their educational resources to build more schools, with less resources left to improve the quality of education. Amongst the other ingredients of the relatively successful story of Korea's educational development, a right choice of policies, and an undisrupted implementation of these policies are deemed to have been crucial.

Disillusionment with education which is producing armies of unemployed graduates is well known throughout the world and demonstrates the necessity of adapting education to the children's future, to their prospects for supporting themselves. When this is not done, the parental choice not to send their children to school easily falls into the pattern described for Burkina Faso:

People who do not send their kids to school cannot solely be discarded as 'ignorant' but might have made a rational choice. Firstly, education is conducted in French, the official language, which is not spoken by most people. When children come to school, they first have to learn French before they may be able to access other subjects. Secondly, unemployment is common among the youth with years in school.

The economic incentive to send children to school is thus less convincing today. A main problem is that many children who go to school do not return to farm work any longer. To send children to school might constitute a double loss: first they cannot participate in farming and herding and thus contribute to subsistence, and, second, they might be able to get a job after school but would be unwilling to accept farming again.

A contribution to poverty alleviation of thus-designed schooling is unlikely because of the abyss between educational systems (as these have historically developed) and poverty reduction strategies (which have started in earnest at the turn of the millennium as a condition for debt relief). Educational systems were routinely designed to enable children to progress to post-primary education and ultimately acquire jobs, for which—as in Burkina Faso—French was essential as was migration to cities where post-primary education, and later the jobs, were. The most likely employer was the government. Redesign of formal schooling so as to enable young people to create their livelihood in rural areas, and to make it attractive for them to do so, remains a challenge yet to be met.

Education alone cannot even start addressing key problems. Poverty-alleviation strategies anticipate meeting this challenge and, to do so effectively, they would need to analyse the process of impoverishment (and enrichment) so as to discern the chain of causality. This is seldom done and poverty remains a notion that is not deemed to be man-made, which it almost always is.

The statement that poverty is a human rights violation sounds good because people can intuitively sense that poverty and human rights clash against each other. Everybody can feel that something is wrong when children cannot go to school because they are too poor, and nobody is today publicly advocating that primary-school children should be working as was done in earlier times.

Going to school in comparison to working is idleness, and the longer boys continue in this easy sort of life, the more unfit they will be when grown up for downright labour.

The change in the past two centuries has been profound; although children are often forced to work, nobody is openly demanding that they should do so. On the level of rhetoric, there is agreement that children should be at school until they reach the minimum age for employment, usually set at the age of 15. There is no underlying commitment to make this happen, however. Poverty is routinely cited as the major cause of child labour.

Conventional wisdom relates the lack of access to education to poverty and sees the solution in throwing money at, the problem. A recipe of pouring money into countries where too many children are precluded from going to school might -paradoxically—do no good. Suffice it to mention that only 60 per cent of educational budgets in Benin, Burkina Faso and Mali were spent in the late 1990s 16 although the need for additional funding was—and is-constantly emphasized.

Increasing an educational budget of a central government does not automatically translate into funding to teachers, schools, text-books, and everything else that children need. Most children are not in national capitals hence their schooling necessitates a functioning country-wide educational system.

Problems are inversely related to the proximity to the national capital—the more distant, the less likely they are to be addressed. The willingness and ability of governments to raise funds and use them to educate children varies a great deal; neither should be presumed to exist already. Child labour constitutes a huge obstacle for children's education because it is mostly poverty-driven as children have to contribute to the survival of their families. Our fragmented manner of addressing these issues leads to singling out poverty in some regions and territories while not in others.

Myopic images of peace-making, as they were put into practice in Kosovo, have revolved around ethnicity and religion, autonomy and statehood, but not about education for the young and the price which children and young people have to pay when the survival of their families is jeopardized.

Unsurprizingly, "adolescents out of school and work request intensive courses for computer and foreign language skills so that they become qualified to work for international organizations" and these adolescents have pinpointed the core problem:" if parents had jobs, adolescents would have to work less."

To attain meaning, statements positing that poverty is a human rights violation would have to be followed up by identifying the actor (more likely, actors) who are perpetuating, or even increasing poverty. This is not the case and poverty becomes like the weather—everybody is complaining about it but deeming it to be beyond anybody's control. All donors are today committed to the eradication of poverty but so they were in the 1970s and there is not much to be shown as successful eradication of poverty. Something did happen, however. Poor school children seeing donors and their employees driving in their shiny four-wheel jeeps have learned one important lesson.

The then Norwegian minister of development cooperation has found that children have a very good idea how not to be poor after schooling:

> In a classroom in Tanzania, the pupils were asked what they wanted to be when they grew up. Everybody answered: aid worker.

The flip-side of the statement that poverty is a human rights violation implicitly equates the antipode of poverty (which must be wealth) with the realization of human rights. Children whose parents purchase for them the best education that money can buy are then assumed to have their right to education recognized and realized. If the parents are at same time paying tax for an education that should but does not exist, they will not think so. The children are paying the price of corruption twice: firstly, they have been deprived of education, and, secondly, they will have to pay back the loans which successive military governments had taken and spent.

The placement of corruption on the agenda of international financial agencies and the donor community promises a change, but making this change happen will require a great deal of courage and determination. The postulate of international human rights law whereby governments should use the available resources to their utmost to secure all human rights for all serves as ready-made guidance.

International cooperation is defined as the principal means for facilitating the realization of the right to education but its prospects are hampered by a vicious circle. The volume of aid is at its lowest in history. The constantly diminishing aid flows include assertions that much aid is misappropriated or misused. Alongside corruption, nuclear weapons are a frequent target of critique. Amartya Sen, Nobel laureate in 1998 for restoring an ethical dimension to vital economic problems, has been asked about India's resources and priorities. He has suggested that the government should prioritize education, health care and land reform. Asked where India would find the money, Sen replied:

> "If one has any sense of priority, to say that India does not have the money is absolute, utter, unmitigated nonsense."

From the recipient's perspective, the glaring discrepancy between vast aid needs and minuscule aid flows does not give donors moral credibility to demand accountability. In its extreme, such attitude becomes give-us- the-money-and-go away. Children who cannot go to school because the dialogue between donors and recipients has worked itself into a blind alley have no voice.

Getting the children, their parents and teachers involved in securing that funds for education reach their destination is not a particularly difficult task. It would rupture the vicious circle of enrichment of intermediaries and impoverishment of beneficiaries which aid often sustains.

Rights-based development is a syntagm that has spread within international development cooperation at the turn of the millennium. The term indicates that development should be founded upon human rights. Previously, the rights of actors funding and carrying out development interventions were asserted and protected but not necessarily the rights of beneficiaries.

These beneficiaries were treated as objects of development interventions (developees) with developers retaining all the rights. It is against this heritage that the term rights-based development has been coined. In the words of Claire Short, Britain's Secretary of State for International Development, there are three particular changes that ought to be made so as to make development aid rights-based:

— if we want to work for human rights we must be willing to take risks and reach out where we can, rather than sit smugly at home and feel good about hectoring governments that oppress their people;

— this new approach also has implications for the way we work. In our White Paper, the Government commits itself to a rights-based approach to development. This means making people the central purpose of development. Not by speaking or acting on their behalf, but by allowing them to speak for themselves—to articulate their own interests and needs;

— strategies for development should not be a secret deal between governments—done behind closed doors.

The heritage of changing vocabularies in international development cooperation entails a risk that human rights language may be appropriated without its contents. There are no self-activating safeguards against abuses of the term 'rights' or 'rights-based.' As these terms have been divorced from their grounding in international human rights law, there is a risk that 'rights' will become a weasel-word into which almost any contents can be fitted. The process whereby this is done is well known and entails exercise in power. It would thus benefit from the application of human rights simply because human rights are safeguards against abuse of power.

Partnership has become a keyword in international development cooperation, also at the turn of the millennium. Partnership between indebted governments and their creditors assumes a relationship of equals. Where one side desperately needs a cheque while another holds the cheque book, it takes a great deal of creativity to define such a relationship as one of equals. The language of partnership assumes relationships which would have made human rights work redundant from the outset. The term 'partnership' disguises inequalities and hampers identifying, exposing and opposing abuses of power. Those who wield power may abuse it hence human rights safeguards are necessary, always and everywhere.

Human rights NGOs have been established to expose and oppose human rights violations, and this role neither will nor can be taken over by governments, individually or collectively. Moreover, human rights work cannot always be carried out in partnership with governments. There is an adage shared amongst human rights NGOs whereby one cannot work in human rights and be popular with governments. Human rights work necessitates identification of those who wield power so as to be able to prevent or remedy its abuse.

Despite this new language of rights-based education and partnership, the practice of selling and purchasing education is gaining ground, embodying a risk that education will be moved from international human rights law to international trade law. Contemporary changes can be illustrated by an increasing resort to the term 'rights' to denote shareholders' or creditors' rights 28 rather than in the sense attributed to this term in international human rights law.

In education, UNESCO has thus defined the danger of depleting the rights-language of its original meaning:

> In so far as the 'right to lifelong learning' is understood to include a 'right' to continuing education, it would seem in practice to amount to little more than the 'right' of any citizen to participate, at his or her own expense, in the market for goods and services generally, with more or less encouragement from public funds depending on the situation in individual countries.

This process of transforming the rights-language so as to make it fit the prevalent ideological commitment to the free market is accompanied by broadening and deepening inequalities in access to education. Donors' concentration on basic education has made universities, particularly in Africa, starved of funding. The profits of exporting education services to people who have no access to them in their own countries dwarfs aid for basic education. Moreover, information and communication technology is referred to as a global phenomenon, although only 5 per cent of people in the world have access to it.

A new term—digital divide—has been coined to depict this new abyss. Public investment in education has led to the completion of upper-secondary education by more than half of the working-age population in the OECD countries. The OECD has moved to almost all-encompassing enrolment at the secondary level, while for most developing countries not even data on enrolment are available.

Children aged 5-15 constitute 13 per cent of the population in OECD but 30 per cent in developing countries. UNESCO has perceptively observed that adults in the OECD countries are running out of children to educate and attention has thus switched to prolonging their own education ('right to life long learning'), which fits the aging population.

In developing countries, meagre funds have to be stretched to educate a large proportion of children. As a consequence, virtually all children will complete 11 years of compulsory education in the OECD, while in developing countries all-encompassing primary education has yet to be attained; providing 11 years of education to all remains a distant dream. The abyss between knowledge-based and education-deficit regions is not likely to be narrowed spontaneously but rather to increase. International trade in education services is emerging as a principal means for increasing this abyss.

The globalization of professional and academic qualifications has been based on "a relatively uniform culture, set of business practices and language" and has re-actualized the phenomenon of brain drain. The linkage between aid for education and trade in education services is evidenced in donors' allocations for students from developing countries, which makes such funding into both aid and export revenue. Diminished aid for higher education in developing countries leads to increased numbers of students going to study abroad.

A further link is diminished public funding for higher education in the donor countries themselves, which pressurizes educational institutions to seek ways to overcome financial shortfall, including through exporting their services. This circulus inextricabilis has attracted attention but too little is known about it as yet.

Data ought to be compiled and collated from a maze of public and private institutions, with a further difficulty inherent in the protection of commercial confidentiality of such data. More importantly, the underlying conceptual change treats education as a commodity to be sold and purchased and necessitates reaffirmation of education as a right. Another conceptual change has been brought about by sanctions, which are imposed against a particular state but, because the state is a legal rather than real-life concept, they harm the country.

Sanctions against Iraq have been particularly long and comprehensive, and their effects on education harsh. There have been pronouncements of human rights bodies on this issue, with the Committee on Economic, Social and Cultural Rights lamenting that humanitarian exemptions do not encompass access to primary education, and the Commission on Human Rights reaffirming that food and medicine should not be used as tools for political coercion, but not mentioning education. Deprivation of education can be encompassed by sanctions which would then, according to Marc Bossuyt's study for the Sub-Commission on the Promotion and Protection of Human Rights, constitute a violation of the right to education.

Children are a popular object for fund-raising because they elicit a sense of guilt when deprived of food, water, schooling, or clothing. Statistics on children deprived of access to school are used a great deal, even if they show two sides of the coin. On the one hand, such data reflect this sense of guilt towards children who we have failed as adults.

On the other hand, these data show that we really do not know how many children we have failed, not even to the closest ten million. The full scope of investment necessary to make schools really rather than nominally available is hidden because the most frequent internationally used indicator—enrolment—does not capture either out-of-school children or the real-life schools.

A UNESCO/UNICEF pilot survey of primary schools in the least developed countries has revealed that electricity or piped water is an exception rather than a rule, while many children finish primary school without ever seeing a single text-book in their mother tongue. This reality is often hidden behind the existing education statistics—nominally available schools are counted in, children registered at the beginning of school year are counted as if they attended school the whole time, teachers are presumed to be teaching although their salaries may not have been paid for months or even years.

Quantifications have become a hallmark of every international strategy; education is no exception. A desperate search for the exact number of children precluded from schooling yields precise, if varying data from 100 to 150 million. The purport of such exercises is to demonstrate precision, to delineate the scope of the problem and assess the effort needed to solve it. No matter how much they vary, the numbers of out-of-school children are numbing and tend to elicit apathy or frustration rather than decisive action. Moreover, poor starving children tend to be portrayed not as subjects of rights but objects of charity.

The effects of their marginalization spring to global attention when they strive to make their way to rich countries or get involved in wars which are seen as senseless from these rich countries. The tendency to romanticize poverty interferes with common sense.

Rather than seeing poverty as brutalizing and dehumanizing, with the instinct for survival pressurizing people towards selling their children or their own organs to survive, poor people tend to be portrayed as waiting for a solution to their problems while patiently starving to death. A widespread approach has then emerged prioritizing the counting of poor people so that measures could be devised to somehow alleviate their poverty. Education has become part of the package which routinely follows from this approach.

A commonsensical approach holds true that education could be the first step on the ladder out of poverty, but unless additional steps are in place, education on its own cannot do much, if anything. Teaching landless peasants the alphabet does not lead to their land ownership or to productive use of that alphabet unless they can create some way of earning their livelihood. The full range of issues to be built into education strategies often turns out to be too complicated or costly, and sights are then lowered to getting children to school. A drawback is that nobody knows how many children are out of school, where they are, who they are, how old they may be, why they are not in school, which language they understand. A hunt for figures follows, with varying outcomes.

Counting the children makes obtaining the figures costly in time and resources because it requires fieldwork. Mathematical modelling comes to rescue by facilitating the creation of data which exhibit the desired precision at low cost. Would it really make a difference if we knew that precisely 107,982, 346 children lack access to any education whatsoever? It is unlikely that we could ever get the figures right because quite a few children would die while being counted because they regularly lack not only education but also food, shelter and safe water. Those children who are encompassed by enrolment statistics, and thus counted as having access to education, do not necessarily have their right to education recognized. The way from access to school to education that is compatible with human rights is long and progress is impeded by another set of conceptual obstacles.

The assumption that education is inherently good is as prevalent as it is unfounded on reality. Images of education not being good-and-desired are rare. One has been unearthed by Victoria Britain in Angola: "When a soba (chief) explains that people do not want to send their children to school because they see that those who go become politicians or businessmen and are thieves and liars, you know you have got a really fundamental need for a change."

Because negative images of education are rare, the assumption that it is inherently good is widespread and seldom, if ever, challenged. Discussions about Education Statistics is governed by the rule of correlation: it is the least available for those countries where education is also the least available and the need for data is thus greatest.

The consequence is resort to technological short-cuts. Mathematical models are applied to invent the size of the population of Angola or Afghanistan. Nobody can fault it because nobody knows how many people there may be in these two and many other countries.

Statistics on school enrolment are created by estimating the numbers of children in each age bracket, pupil-teacher ratios are construed by associating the statistically created numbers education tend to focus on how to provide it and how to increase the provision. Any subject which is taught can be abused. Anti-human-rights messages can be found in mathematics as these examples show:

— In Hitler's Germany, a mathematics text-book nudged learners to calculate financial savings that would ensue from eliminating mentally ill people: "The construction of a lunatic asylum costs 6 million DM. How many houses at 15,000 DM each could have been built for that amount."

— One maths book, printed in the US during the Afghan war for use amongst Afghani refugees, offered the following mathematical problem: "If you have two dead Communists, and kill three more, how many dead Communists do you have?"

— A school text-book in Tanzania in the 1970s included the following mathematical problem: "A freedom fighter fires a bullet into an enemy group consisting of 12 soldiers and 3 civilians all equally exposed to the bullet. Assuming one person is hit by the bullet, find the probability that the person is (a) a soldier, (b) a civilian.

The widely shared belief that getting all children into school is always a solution, never a problem persists, however. Parents whose children have been beaten in school so badly that they ended up in emergency ward to be treated for injuries know better. Abuses of education became institutionalized through re-education camps, where political dissidents were (still are) brainwashed into regurgitating the dogma espoused by the powers that be. Throughout history, education has been particularly effective in the militarization of boys. Participation in warfare has been part of traditional initiation rituals, through which boys become men.

Glorification of war continues through history text-books which are dotted with wars and war heroes, through the promotion of violent sports, and limitless commercialization of computerized war games. Education for war has, unfortunately, a much longer tradition and commercial attractiveness than education for peace. An image that education is good and one just needs to secure additional funds to provide more of it could never be endorsed by the indigenous peoples in Latin America, who have experienced education as oppression.

Those who dared to rupture the denial of education and ventured to school were severely punished. Women who remain openly indigenous while schooling children have three layers of prejudice to overcome. A judgment about the contribution which education made to the genocide in Rwanda by creating and reinforcing mutual Hutu-Tutsi prejudices is pending.

The UN Special Rapporteur on Rwanda at the time has noted how successive governments conditioned the population to the acceptance of ethnic discrimination and moulded education to fit this aim: The schools took it upon themselves to develop actual theories of ethnic differences, based on a number of allegedly scientific data which were essentially morphological and historiographical. In the first case; the two main groups can be differentiated by appearance, as the Tutsi are 'long' whereas the Hutu are 'short'; the Tutsi are handsome, genuine 'black-skinned Europeans' while the Hutu are 'ugly', genuine 'Negroes'.

The fact that the Hutu occupied the country before the Tutsi makes them indigenous, whereas the Tutsi, as descendants of Europeans, are invaders. These purportedly scientific data inevitably created a psychosis of fear and mistrust which gradually became a veritable culture of mutual fear and led to another theory, that of pre-emptive self-defence based on the 'kill or be killed principle'. This theory was a major factor in the 1994 genocide.

Using human rights safeguards to constrain the power inherent in writing history books, from which the coming generations are going to learn their own history, is often needed but lacking. The issue is deemed to be 'technical' regardless of its often being a veritable political minefield. Regarding the discrimination that still affects the indigenous woman, in her traditional skirt, the Vice-President of the Republic, Victor Hugo Cardenas, made the following statement in a press interview: "Cardenas recognizes that progress is slow, though tangible, and does not deny that indigenous communities still suffer from Dubravko Lovrenovic, a professor of history at the University of Sarajevo, has recalled a voice which euphorically told him by phone on the eve of the war: "It is now our turn to write history."

Writing history to describe to both Tutsi and Hutu children what happened in Rwanda, how and why, will inevitably be as difficult as it is important. The emergence of truth commissions has played a pioneering role in quite a few countries by rewriting recent history, often negotiating a history that can be accepted by the victims and their victimizers, by the oppressed and their oppressors.

More than fifty years after the end of the Second World War, the pre-war history is being rewritten throughout Europe. Moreover, the role of education in conflict-generation is seldom portrayed in history text-books. They tend to remain confined to consequences, especially violence, while keeping silent about the myriad of factors which generated and facilitated the underlying conflicts.

The initial enthusiasm for mass education at independence soon gave way to the institutionalization of inequality. Mass enrolment at the .beginning of primary school did not lead to mass persistence throughout primary and secondary education to continue at the university and education was slanted towards the interests of the narrow elite whose children actually made it all the way up to the university. Frustrated expectations of early school leavers—especially boys have been shown to lead to criminality, violence, and warfare. Their abandonment by the system of education to their own fate was accompanied by the paucity of lawful methods for securing livelihood and the attraction of pursuing unlawful ones with impunity.

The abundance of bad models to imitate and the absence of good ones made the choice of many adolescents a foregone conclusion. The neglect of adolescents, highlighted in Sierra Leone, has been an unintended consequence of the priority for primary education in global education strategies as of the 1990s and will hamper efforts at peace-making unless it is reversed. An important obstacle to universalizing the right to education is a view that education is not indispensable for human survival nor required for subsistence, that families can function with children labouring rather than learning.

Oppressed Lot

The absence of education for victims of armed conflicts and disasters dooms them to remain recipients of assistance while preventing them from becoming self-sustaining. Water, sanitation, medical services, shelter, clothing and food constitute the 'survival package' which is offered through humanitarian relief. Including education in this package is a development of the 1990s, but overcoming the previous 'ideology of survivalism' has yet to become institutionalized. Arguably, the most negative aspect of Sierra Leone's elitist system of education has to do with a complete failure to cater for those who do not make, it within the system.

School dropouts are simply not provided for in any serious or meaningful way. Thus, those who do not survive and rise to the top of this narrow and competitive system simply become the 'forgotten aspirants' in a very elitist educational process. In situations where only a tiny minority can get a complete and reasonable quality education, the price of ignorance weighs more heavily on those who have some schooling than those who never had access to school.

The role of education in spawning warfare Sierra Leone aspirants', which is turn could serve as a time-bomb waiting to explode. It is not surprizing therefore to find 'forgotten aspirants' playing a role as combatants on both sides of the rebel war in Sierra Leone. Because of the demonstrated impact of education in promoting social mobility in newly independent Sierra Leone, wrong signals have been sent to the subsequent generations.

This has given rise to unrealistic expectations about what can be achieved by virtue of mere school attendance and certification. At independence in 1961, the drive for indigenization meant that nationals with little more than secondary level qualifications were catapulted to top positions. Later, the new and expanding population of university graduates were guaranteed high-level jobs regardless of specialization.

Most secondary school graduates could also be certain of reasonable jobs within the public sector. When economic growth and job creation began to lag behind output of universities and schools, reality dictated that educational qualifications *per se* could no longer be a guarantee of any job, much less top level jobs. Unfortunately, expectations continued to fly in the face of this new reality. The belief that schooling leads to good jobs could not be questioned. Hence a strong sense of delusion persisted amongst learners that society owes them something once they have gone through the education system.

Designing rights-based education necessitates eliminating barriers which keep human rights separated from education. It is not only parents and children but also teachers who have rights. The status of teachers can be forgotten in education strategies and it often is. It is much too easy to define teachers as a production factor in the manufacturing of human capital and forget that they are people with rights.

Probing into the teachers' fate can reveal that neither their labour rights nor their trade union freedom are recognized and that their salaries are much too low to enable them to teach as they have to combine three or four full-time jobs to be able to feed their families. Although it is possible to imagine schooling taking place without schools but not without teachers, the attention to schools and text-books in international education strategies is immense while they are relatively silent about teachers.

The advantage of teaching being labour-intensive is that employment of large numbers of people is possible—necessary—to educate the millions of children and young people in the world. Since teachers are locally trained, hired and paid, the additional benefit is that there is no need for foreign exchange, different from schools or schoolbooks that may be provided through loans which ought to be repaid. It seems, however, that instead of being seen as an actor indispensable for schooling, teachers may be perceived as an enemy of their own vocation.

One reason for viewing teachers as a burden rather than asset is the proportion of education budgets allocated to teachers' salaries. In a country where school-age children represent one third of the population, a ratio of one teacher per every fifty children makes teachers 0.6 per cent of the population. As there is little besides teachers in the schooling process in many poor countries, teachers salaries necessarily form the bulk of the education budget. The consecutive crises through which education has passed in the recent decades triggered a constant search for cutting down education budgets. Because teachers' salaries constitute the bulk of education budgets, they were the obvious first target for budgetary cuts and an ideological rationalization has followed. The protection of human rights of teachers sometimes slips into oblivion if teachers are defined as an education-production-factor rather than being treated as people.

The applicable international human rights standards are many because the problems teachers encounter are complex and multi-layered. They range from the application of the internationally prohibited grounds of discrimination to teachers' recruitment and deployment, to the protection of their professional and academic freedom, or to the role of teachers in human rights education. Problems in enforcement have ranged from the teachers' status as civil and/or public servants leading to the denial of their trade union freedom, or a definition of teaching as an essential service leading to the denial of their right to strike.

The expectations upon teachers to integrate human rights education throughout the curriculum, against the background of denials of their own rights, demonstrate why human rights are indivisible. Acknowledging that all human rights ought to be recognized and protected clashes, however, not only against human-capital approaches but also against the trust in democracy as a substitute for human rights.

Without human rights correctives, resource allocation in education looks pretty much the same worldwide. Most money goes to universities, whose learners are the most expensive to school, the fewest in number, and the most likely to pertain to the country's elite.

The lack of political voice of primary-school children, especially in rural areas, makes the allocation of funds for education a foregone conclusion. University students are present in national capitals, politically articulate, and regularly come from the wealthiest segment of the population.

The language of rights effectively favours university students and fits into the paradigm depicted by Massimo Cacciari through his homo democraticus, who has all the rights but no corresponding duties, is unwilling to accept any limitations upon his freedom, including freedom of spending to satisfy all his desires, easily setting aside the needs of the next generation because they do not have a political voice.

Low budgetary allocations are typical for categories that lacks a political voice hence human rights law strives to alter this pattern by remedying the lack of political voice through bestowing legal rights. Primary school children cannot form a political party, get elected to parliament and secure budgetary allocations for themselves.

International human rights law requires progressive realization of the right to education where primary education ought to be made free of charge, and this should gradually extend to post-primary and, ultimately, university education. This approach is known as progressive realization and is exactly the opposite to results of political processes taking place in the absence of human rights correctives.

Retrogressive realization of the right to education then provides those at the very top of the education pyramid with most funding while ultimately precluding those at the bottom—the youngest—from even getting started. The proportion of children in the northern part of the world is small and their parents can secure funding for education by combining their political voice with paying tax. In Africa, children constitute the majority of the population but obtain a vote after becoming adults and joining the minority who has the right to vote.

Few of their parents pay tax, many because they earn too little, and their vote seldom affects budgetary allocations, often because there is too little to distribute after foreign debt has been serviced. Children's right to education thus goes beyond national and regional borders, it is universal and addresses governments collectively. It also highlights what an abyss there is between democracy and human rights, which have erroneously become treated as they were one and the same.

The absence of an enforceable claim upon governments to allocate a specific amount to education highlights the need to focus on the procedure whereby allocations are decided upon. Human rights are seldom costed because human rights standards do not determine how much should be spent on specific items, but define substantive and procedural human rights standards; the latter encompass the process of decision making. Exercise of political rights thus becomes the necessary instrument for attaining economic and social rights, imposing upon those who exercise them a duty towards others.

University students are politically vocal, primary school age children are not, and the latter can easily be neglected in the allocation of resources. The proverbial preference for university students in budgetary allocations within education (in the extreme exceeding up to one thousand times the allocation for primary education) vividly illustrates the necessity for introducing the human rights rationale throughout the process of resource allocation, from global to local.

As adults we should (but never do) acknowledge that we routinely abuse our power over children. International human rights law affirms the parental choice for education of their children, but requires states to constrain it where this choice jeopardizes the best interests of the child. This postulate has yet to be translated into practice. A visiting Martian would have a great deal of difficulty understanding what the humanity, as species, is really trying to do.

In one country we are expelling girls from school because they are wearing a headscarf, in another we are precluding them from access to school because they are not wearing a headscarf. Nobody would be able to persuade such a visiting Martian that we really care about our children's education or about their rights.

Assuming that advancing human rights is easy clashes against conflicting rights, as is often the case with parents and children. In a rare case where a child, sixteen years old, has been accorded the right to challenge parental disagreements about the choice of school for her, justice Dalcq in Bruxelles has acknowledged that the best interest of the child should prevail. The case involved a girl whose divorced parents disagreed as to which school she should attend. The girl had ultimately refused to attend the school chosen by the mother (who exercised parental rights) and ended up attending no school, to then legally challenge the mother's attempt to force her to attend the school which her mother had chosen.

The child's choice of school was judicially vindicated so as to prevent further jeopardy of the child's right to education. An implicit agenda of schooling may be to keep children conformist and deferential, forcing them to kneel when addressing adults, training them to recite the, official dogma without allowing them to ask questions, getting them to accept physical punishment for faults which children often cannot even understand.

A text-book for Christian religious education used in East Africa highlights obedience as the explicit purpose of education: "At school we have to obey people who are not our parents and this is real preparation for life." An excerpt from a text-book on children's accounts of their childhood, used by fifteen year old Ugandans in the 1970s, describes the fearful, uncomprehending obedience which was instilled through schooling.

Children were trained from their earliest years to be respectful, obedient and mannerly, these being the standards by which adults became acceptable in society. All parents, and fathers in particular were very stern with their children who in any way departed from such standards. Furthermore the punishment for children who misbehaved, however harsh, had to be accepted without question or complaint. Thus the children, respectfully submissive, learned to fear their fathers as harsh and severe. Strong feelings of dislike though dutifully suppressed were very frequently mixed with this fear.

Inculcating obedience easily leads to children's following orders without questioning them, especially when punishment accompanies failure to do so. Corporal punishment socializes children into accepting violence, and the combination of obedience and violence easily makes them ideal child soldiers. The curriculum is often design to accommodate what the closely involved adults, principally parents and teachers, are comfortable with rather than what children need and nominally have a right to get.

There are few explicit assertions of children's right to learn about sexuality in school, a rare example was included in the Children's Charter, which was adopted on 1 June 1992 by the Children's Summit of South Africa. It posited that all children had the right to adequate education on issues such as sexuality. This was a courageous and immensely ambitious statement, at odds with the adults' proverbial intransigence regarding children's access to sex education. The 10-year United Nations Girls' Education Initiative, launched at the Dakar Education for All Forum in April 2000, requires a great deal of human rights input in responding to the Secretary General's challenge to empower girls to protect themselves against HIV/AIDS.

Prevented from going to school, girls are denied information about how to protect themselves against the virus. Without the benefit of an education, they risk being forced into early sexual relations, and thereby becoming infected. Thus, they pay many times over the deadly price of not going to school.

There is no need to point out how controversial human sexuality, an inevitable part of HIV/AIDS-education, has been, and how much effort is needed to design and put into practice educational modules acceptable to all relevant actors. Progress is evident from the attention paid to children's right to obtain knowledge necessary for their self-protection, which has replaced the silence of the past decades.

Education law has traditionally treated children as objects of education, specifying the rights of parents, teachers and the state. The affirmation of the rights of the child has not yet been accomplished in most countries. There is a welcome move in this direction, which prioritizes the best interests of the child as a step towards child's rights. The Supreme Court of Canada has affirmed that restraint should be exercise by adults, particularly parents, in order to mould education towards the best interests of the child.

For a child who is young or unable to communicate his or her needs or wishes, equality rights are being exercised on his or her behalf, usually by the child's parents. Moreover, the requirements for respecting these rights in this setting are decided by adults who have authority over this child.

For this reason, the decision-making body must further ensure that its determination of the appropriate accommodation for an exceptional child be from a subjective child-centred perspective, one which attempts to make equality meaningful from the child's point of view as opposed to that of the adults in his or her life. As a means of achieving this aim, it must also determine that the form of accommodation chosen is in the child's best interest.

The Supreme Court of Colombia has taken this rationale one step further, holding that school children should have the possibility to express their personality. It was examining a case involving a boy, who had been wearing an earing in class, whereupon the teacher commented that this earing suggested that the boy was a homosexual. The Court faulted the teacher's inappropriate behaviour and insisted that relations between pupils and teachers should be altered.

The subjects of the educational process are not divided into passive recipients of knowledge and active depositories of wisdom. The constitutional principle which guarantees the free development of personality and the right to participate in the educational community have transformed the learners into active subjects who participate in education through their rights and duties....

The relation of pupil-teacher is not based upon the authority which the teacher can exercise as the ultimate depository of wisdom or through his hierarchically superior position, but rather upon reciprocal respect of the subjects of the educational process with the same possibility for free expression, under the sole condition of not jeopardizing the rights of others or the just order.

The most far-reaching interpretations of the rights of the child have focused on children with disabilities. These overruled the previous exclusionary approach, whereby children had to fit into the existing schools and, if they could not remain out-or-school or be segregated into special schools. Children relying on wheelchairs for their mobility could not access schools which were built without access for wheelchairs.

Children unable to conform to criteria of linguistic proficiency or successfulness in testing were segregated into special schools. A veritable conceptual revolution has been created by turning around such premises, whereby the school had an implicit right to turn away the child because the child did not fit. Affirming the best interests of each child, and gradually equal rights of each child, has reversed the premises for decision-making—it is the school which has to adapt to the child, not the other way around. The German Federal Constitutional Court has affirmed the need to design specific solutions through explicitly balancing all pertinent human rights dimensions.

The current state of pedagogical research does not indicate that a general exclusion of disabled children from integrated general schools can be constitutionally justified.

Education should be integrated, providing special support for disabled pupils if required, so far as the organizational, personal and practical circumstances allow this. This reservation is included as an expression of the need for the State to consider all the needs including the financial and organizational factors, of the community in carrying out its duties.

Globally, under all categories, the children most frequently excluded are girls. Gender continues to be the major causal factor in children being left out, and pushed out, of school. The denial of a girl's right to education remains a pernicious and persistent characteristic of many societies on a purposive basis, for reasons of culture and family choice.

Beliefs that the formal education of girls is inappropriate or unnecessary, and failures to make schools safe, secure and empowering places for girls, continue to create systemic gender bias in who goes to school and successfully completes a basic education. Girls are excluded by cultures insisting on early marriage and preparing for that role by young years focused on domestic chores, caring for siblings and protecting virtue. They are excluded when, due to pregnancy, they are forced to dropout of school and rarely given support by either home or school to return.

The figures are well known but none the less dramatic: approximately two-thirds of the 130 million primary-school-age children not in school are girls. In Africa, almost 26 million girls are out of school.

In Afghanistan, under the Taliban, net primary attendance is only 36 per cent for boys, but a tragic 11 per cent for girls; while 47 per cent men are literate, only 15 per cent of women are. In the Lao People's Democratic Republic, of the 64 per cent of adults who are literate, only 35 per cent are girls and women. In Yemen, girls' participation is only about 31 per cent, some 42 points behind that of boys. They are the especially vulnerable. Children limited in realizing their full potential for learning by being denied access to a good quality education are also children who are physically, intellectually or emotionally vulnerable.

This includes children who have been put at risk by the inadequate pre- and post-natal care available to their mothers, by their own nutritional deficit or by an early home environment that failed to nurture or stimulate them. The 120,000 children who survived iodine deficiency disorder in 1990 and are now afflicted with cretinism; the 250,00() who survived vitamin A deficiency and are now blind; and the thousands who are manned annually by landmines, are all children whose right to learn and be educated to their full potential has been put at risk.

Children are also systematically excluded in many cases on the basis of what the society and school define as disability. Like much else about exclusion, beliefs and actions around disability cause a great deal of suffering, but few clear answers.

Of an assumed 10 per cent of children in a population with some form of disability, it is estimated that as few as 3 per cent of those in developing countries have access to rehabilitation services. Globally, it is the tragedy of these children that along with the special efforts they themselves have to make in order to participate, they have to deal with education systems which define them out by failing to apply a framework which creates environments better suited to all learners.

Children are excluded where no provision is made to support them when physical, emotional or intellectual difficulties interfere with their learning. It is estimated that only 1 per cent of such children are in school. In more-industrialized countries, where they do often have access to school, the participation of these children may still be marginal.

The poor pedagogical training of teachers can limit both the effective management of the particular learning needs of these children and their integration into the social relationships of the class. Elsewhere, these problems are exacerbated by an overall lack of resources, child-accessible facilities and expertise.

Most insidiously, perhaps, these children are excluded by being rendered statistically invisible: not included among the potential total school-going population and, therefore, not missed when they do not turn up.

In near-crisis proportions for some countries and new since Jomtien, the answer to the question of who is being excluded is children affected by HIV/AIDS. Clearly traumatic for children in terms of their health, HIV/AIDS is also having tragic impacts on their right to be protected by and participate in their society, and on their ability to protect and manage themselves. One of the enduring traumas for affected children is that the discrimination associated with HIV/AIDS can put certain of their rights (of access to care and learning) at jeopardy of others (their right to confidentiality).

Children are also being negatively affected when their parents and other family members are infected and die. AIDS has created over 8.2

million orphans between the critical school ages of 6 and 12), a figure that is expected to reach 40 million by 2010 (UNFPA, 1998, p. 18).

HIV/AIDS is thus creating children who are suddenly responsible not only for their own protection and care, but also that of younger siblings and other infected relatives, and with few human or financial resources to bring to bear in doing so. With an HIV/AIDS affected family typically comes a downward spiral of exclusions: economic problems, leading to inability to pay school fees and dropping out; food insecurity and difficulties with other basic needs; sometimes loss of land and possessions to relatives, and a move into the street where vulnerabilities increase exponentially.

Children's ability to access services, and the quality of those services, are most certainly being affected. This includes limiting their ability to go to, and stay in, school and the ability of schools to ensure that the teachers will be there when the children do come. In Zambia, 680 teachers were reported to have died of AIDS-related illnesses in 1996, 624 the following year and 200 in the first few months of 1998, 'figures which translate into more than 2.1 per cent of trained teachers or almost two per day'.

Monitoring the progress and impact of the epidemic on different groups of children at risk and on their learning is fundamental to ensuring appropriate action on their behalf. As education systems fail, however, any mitigating influences for children in terms of the nurturing, knowledge, skills and protection that might come from education are being even further reduced.

They are minorities and indigenous. Children excluded from education are frequently the children of ethnic minorities and indigenous groups. These two types of community are often distinguished in terms of the intensity, persistence and scope of their exclusion from mainstream societies. Common to them in terms of their children's education, however, is the serious risk that many are facing from schools which fail both to treat children equitably as learners and to respect their cultures as valid systems of knowledge and values.

For both indigenous communities and long-standing ethnic minorities, the fact of exclusion is real, and it is serious. In 1994, 70 per cent of Peru's Quechua-speaking people over 5 years of age had not been to school; in Guatemala, 80 per cent of the rural indigenous population was illiterate. In China's Qinghai Province, an area of nomadic herders, attendance at the secondary level has dropped more than 66 per cent over the last decade, largely as a result of rising school costs and fewer jobs, making these costs less tenable. These are not rare instances.

The questions for education concern the nature and impact of this isolation on quality of life, and how the situation should be addressed to ensure effective learning and equity. The questions go beyond issues of poverty and marginalization. They include how the rights of these children and communities will be preserved, and their best interests ensured, when their very history, culture and language serve both to exclude them and to put them at risk of never being able to achieve 'inclusion'.

In most cases there is no reasonable possibility of these communities remaining outside the mainstream. Without the dignity of any choice, however, education systems are excluding these families and their children by leaving them to handle the balancing of socio-cultural integration, assimilation and disintegration as best they can.

Many of these children will not go to school; most who do go, will not stay. The Karimojong of Uganda provide a cogent example. A semi-nomadic people in a 'highly fragile and precarious ecological environment', the formal primary school:

> ... has failed to provide... children with the necessary knowledge, attitudes and skills relevant to their roles and livelihood... which neither equips them to become productive members of their society nor prepares them to take up meaningful life outside it undermines their values, traditional knowledge and skills, cultural traits and form of education which are crucial to survival. The curriculum is generally irrelevant does not stress preparation for self-reliance, (a) positive image of pastoralism for the emergence of traditional and modern pastoral cultures which would enhance the economic contribution of pastoralism to the national economy.... The formal primary-school education continues to threaten social ethics... and has rigid instructional methodology. On top of all this, it is also

expensive and requires full-time attendance unsuited to a nomadic culture.

Indigenous and ethnic-minority children are continuing to be excluded because partnerships and negotiations between the community and externally oriented schools are not sufficiently effective or open. Creativity and flexibility in curriculum choices, appropriate balancing around language of instruction and use of traditional versus child-oriented teaching styles, are not common.

While a community such as the Karimojong is able to bring considerable strengths to any serious effort seeking its participation, it is rarely invited to do so. The tragedy of these communities and their children is that so many interventions assume that they have nothing on which to build, nothing to contribute to the analysis of problems or to the development of alternatives. The tragedy of education systems in dealing with these communities is that so few provide the professional competency, motivation and material resources necessary to allow such participation.

Cutting across all categories of excluded children is the situation of those who are, in fact, no longer really children. Except for those who get into trouble of some kind, capacity, knowledge and lifestyle issues of concern to young people in that period of transition called adolescence (usually between 11 and 18 years) have not tended to be specifically addressed in much of the EFA discussion.

The situation is changing as young people of this age are increasingly recognized as being particularly vulnerable and at risk. Maternal mortality and morbidity are higher for girls under 20; violence, delinquency and substance abuse are on the rise in this age group; 6510 of the reported cases of HIV/AIDS in Thailand are here. Most child-soldiers, labouring children and those who are sexually exploited are here.

In many African countries, over 50 per cent of the population is under the age of 18, but youth is 'an excluded category in terms of policies, services and participation'. Adolescents are becoming a larger proportion of prison and detention centres population, and are often those same ones who have not completed school and, while inside, remain without access to regular or good quality education programmes.

Adolescence is a period of life with a special need for supportive caring relationships, to feel respected and appreciated, to have a sense of belonging and membership in families and communities which can help young people to develop the 'inner strengths' and resilience for effectively managing themselves and acting on their environments. Unfortunately, although these are still children for whose learning families, schools and the wider community are responsible, they are the ones very often denied support.

Teachers and parents frequently do not recognize the nature of the changes they are going through, treating their confusion and testing behaviours as undisciplined, aberrant and hostile. Schools that supply little beyond custodial management and rote teaching methods are ill-prepared to provide supportive, flexible learning environments for youth struggling with the demands of an adult world. They are excluding and opening up these children to risk by failing to provide them with protection from, and opportunities to acquire skills and knowledge about, the dilemmas and threats of HIV/AIDS, drug use, early pregnancies, exploitative relationships; or how to meet the challenges of an unknown future.

As a result, these young people are becoming increasingly disaffected and discouraged, angry and sometimes hopeless. In all societies, more are coming to see themselves as not only without a sense of security and personal worth now, but as potentially without a better future. In Western countries, violence in schools and among street gangs is growing along with dropping out of school, home and community. Homelessness is becoming a permanent condition of their lives rather than a passing teenage phase.

In developing countries, whole communities of youth are living in and with marginality as their life condition. Some of UNESCO's efforts to give these people a voice are producing not only a platform for them, but a window for the adult world on how serious the situation is becoming. 'But really young guy, you won't go to school. Of course not, you're too poor; your father and your mother, they have no time; they are too busy serving for more. Days come and go until sudden death. Your life is as hard as stone; don't forget you're raw to the bone'.

Existing Position

In situations of poverty. The vast majority of children excluded from their right to education are those living in conditions of absolute poverty. Poverty is the most persistent and inexorable of all exclusionary factors. Because of this, it is also the least dramatic and the least likely to mobilize action. The fact that whole communities of children and parents are not participating in education is a reality often unseen except in annexes of international reports. Exclusion by neglect becomes an intergenerational, effectively natural, condition for families who come to assume irregular, inadequate and dysfunctional schooling and for societies which ignore them.

Absolute poverty is also universal. In both developed and developing countries, in both rural and urban areas, it exists. On a national level, it is reflected in governments not having the resources or the willingness to meet their social development obligations, including provision of functional education systems with competent teachers and enough schools.

On a more human level, it is an all-inclusive condition of families not being able to meet their basic needs of survival, health and development. Poverty affects every dimension of a family's life and the lives of its children. In particular, it diminishes their individual and collective sense of control over immediate and long-term options, making education a less compelling value. Poverty at this level is about having few real choices and limited flexibility. From a national socio-political perspective, absolute poverty among the population is sometimes a happen stance. More typically, it is a matter of persistently failed public policy, corruption and civil or environmental trauma.

Children are excluded by poverty in countries where policies of national and local governments create and exacerbate it by cutting social expenditures in response to structural adjustment programmes, subsidizing an urban middle class, building up the armed forces or large-scale infrastructures, or sustaining corruption. All of these deny large numbers of children adequate schools, trained teachers and good curricula. They are excluded in countries or provinces where policies, by action or default, distribute resources, power and access to information inequitably and sometimes not at all. They are excluded in families and communities without the qualities of health, income security or sense of a 'future benefit' that might incline them to send their children to school—even to pay the fees, were good schools available.

Absolute poverty exists in countries where it should not exist. A growing body of US-based research on children having problems in school or dropping out points to chronic poverty, often confounded by race, as the common factor. Families in both rural and urban poverty tend to have more children with special needs; they certainly have fewer resources to address those needs, or the psychological margin, social support and self-confidence to collaborate in affirmative action with schools. Research on the state of urban education in developed countries indicates that poverty significantly reduces the likelihood of communities 'bucking' the trends of low attendance and achievement, patchy standards and dropouts.

In Canada, with 20 per cent to 25 per cent of children considered to be living in poverty, the effects on their education are clear: poor performance, chronic stress and adjustment problems, conflicts at home and school, feelings of rage and despair and, especially among Native American communities, teenage suicide.

In situations of traumatic change. Children already made vulnerable to exclusion by living in poverty are pushed even further into crisis by being in situations of severe economic decline and traumatic changes in socio-economic governance systems. In times of such stress, already-fragile education systems push marginal children out with special harshness, usually without clear or committed strategies for protecting the gains they have made or for bringing them back. Some of the countries in South-East Asia have served as an important object lesson in recent years in how quickly this can happen. In Indonesia, entire cohorts risk being lost as children are forced to dropout of the system and do not come back. Even where some are financially able to return, and want to, schools are likely to have trouble accommodating them where classes will be full and many children over-age for their level. It is a condition becoming critically worse as the social dislocations of ethnic conflict begin to take hold.

The countries of the Commonwealth of Independent States present another version of a near-systemic exclusion of children created through abrupt economic reversal and political change. In this case, the dramatic recasting of the socio-economic paradigm of these countries has changed equally fundamentally the nature of the education system and families' relationship to it. Children are being excluded as the costs and benefits of participation lose their previous equilibrium.

In a situation of 'major educational melt-down', more than 32,000 Russian pre-schools have closed, contributing to a decline of close to 20 per cent of children in kindergarten (UNICEF, 1999a, p. 1). Fees for schooling have risen significantly. State support for teachers' salaries and training, for curriculum materials, for school meals and medical care, for subsidized clothing and other incentives have all fallen or been eliminated. Most at risk, of course, are the already vulnerable: children from the poorest, chiefly rural, families, ethnic minorities, children with disabilities. A new and very large generation of excluded children and adults is being created as stratification in access is denying 'equal education to the poorest and most marginalized children'.

In situations of structural adjustment and debt. Excluded children are also to be found where international agencies and national governments have insisted on the strict application of structural adjustment or debt repayment regimes. They are excluded further where these interventions are applied without sufficient consideration of their implications for vulnerable groups, and are not monitored for their impact on these groups. Impacts have certainly been felt, especially in Africa. Painting a quite graphic description of broad-brush, systemic, exclusion from the perspective of Senegal, for example:

> Many families were plunged into relative or absolute poverty and children of poor families paid the heaviest price:... between 2,000 and 3,000 children live in the streets. Around 100,000 children beg in the streets. Worse than that, the number of child beggars increases from year to year. In 1997 there were 6,300 children begging in the streets of Dakar, compared to 1,000 in 1991... more than 60 per cent of these children are between 7 and 12... 33 per cent suffer from malnutrition in rural areas, and 22.4 per cent in urban areas. If these children fall sick they have no access to either curative or preventative medicine.

Reconfirming the 'close, and incontrovertible, relationship between poverty, health and education', the crisis has had an impact on survival strategies of Senegalese families. According to a World Bank report, 70 per cent of the income of poor families is spent on food, while only 2 per cent is dedicated to education. The state budget for education is considered insufficient in view of population growth and educational demand, and even those children who go to school find themselves in crowded classrooms in which quality teaching is impossible.

On the Street: Children living with poverty and other conditions putting them at risk are increasingly to be found as children on the street: as beggars, scrap pickers, street sellers, prostitutes, petty thieves. This categorization is complicated by the fact that these children are not a single 'type', the label being based on where donors and society find them rather than who they are or what they are doing. While many do live on the street, alone and with other children, many others live at home.

The street is the place where they earn income and find their social networks. Most are in some risk of servitude to adults who use them in their prostitution, drug and other criminal activities, and many find themselves involved with the law as a result of direct and indirect criminal activity. Many leave the street to go to worse situations, into indentured labour and into prisons. Few are in any kind of educational programme. As with working children generally, the specific conditions under which these children come to the street, and stay there, are still not well understood. Data as to numbers, causes and conditions are limited.

There are assumed, however, to be over 100 million worldwide, chiefly young boys. It is clear, however, that while their conditions vary, they all include exclusion at other levels—lack of health care, security from violence or sexual exploitation, or sporadic access to educational opportunities.

Some choose to be on the street; the majority, however, are there because they have few other choices. They are the victims of dislocation caused by conflict or economic crisis or of parental abuse and/or abandonment. They are victims of family poverty, forced out to fend for themselves or to augment the family income. Schools also contribute to sending children into the street where, instead of serving to 'offset and even compensate for society's and parental failings, by providing a propitious environment for human growth have themselves become scenes of violence.

In Institutions: Excluded children are also found in institutions. Placing children with disabilities, in trouble with the law, or without adequate family and community support away from society's sight happens in most countries, to varying degrees and for varying reasons. Though justified in terms of serving the child's 'best interest', the underlying rationale is often one of making the management of that child, by society or the sector, easier. In not all cases, of course, do such children fall within the parameters of exclusion as used in this chapter.

Professionally managed, child-friendly and rights-based institutions, with strong links to the community, can provide precisely the kind of support at-risk or abused child needs to establish a sound intellectual and psychosocial footing, from which he or she can then move forward.

But these conditions are not the norm. Brazil is but one country where children and adolescents from the streets make up a significant proportion of the population of detention centres, children with no access to resources or to school. In Eastern Europe, the practice of institutionalizing children considered to be 'uneducatable' persists, based either on a perception that the influences of disability cannot be mitigated, or on a disinclination to try. Institutionalization is also based on inflexibility in the face of cultural or linguistic differences, especially of groups considered to be ethnically inferior. And it is based on an unwillingness to invest limited resources in children not seen as able to 'pay back' society's investment through their eventual financial independence. All of these are reasons for policy and practice decisions to put them aside.

In countries that have come through war or economic crisis, children are in institutions as a result of a breakdown in the ability of communities and social-support agencies to provide more light-handed support. In Cambodia, for example, serious shortfalls continue in the human and fiscal resources of its social welfare sector which, when coupled with the many still-unstable communities, results in children continuing to be put into 'orphanages'. These offer little more than basic custodial care.

Not all such children are orphans; many are abandoned because of poverty or family breakdown; because they have disabilities of some kind; or because their parents are lost. Regardless of cause, few are adequately supported in these institutions. They are rarely helped to realize their full psychosocial or intellectual development. Only recently have efforts been made to facilitate linkages to the formal schools and wider community.

In War and Conflict: With increasingly horrific damage, excluded children are in situations of war, or the persistent communal conflicts and dislocations which are the precursors and aftermath of war.

Over the past decade, in addition to the estimated 2 million children in armed conflict, several times that number have been injured and permanently disabled, exploited as soldiers, starved and exposed to extreme brutality. Millions snore have been displaced, internally and into other countries.

For all these children, the entire fabric of their societies has been torn to pieces-homes, schools, health systems and religious institutions. And these social traumas have not tended to be short-term, one-off instances, but to drag on for long periods with no clear beginning or end, creating in yet another way, a cycle of serious and endemic exclusion and endless struggles for survival. Long after fighting ends, many children continue to feel its repercussions, forced on to the street or into factories as communities, governments and even their families focus on priorities other than children and education. They are further excluded where the focus of education reconstruction is on replicating previous elitist structures, or bringing in a foreign, often donor-preferred, system without considering the implications for social dislocation.

The significance of this for children and adolescents can be tragic. Facing the same trauma as adults, they often do so without the capacities they need to act in their own best interest and without the support of families, communities or opportunities for learning.

Children who suffer most from exploitation and abuse, as child soldiers or girls forced into prostitution, are likely to be those already at risk or in trouble from exclusion. Conflicts tend to grow from conditions of social disintegration, and many of these children were previously found in communities where systems failed and forced them away from support services, including school.

Even where schools exist, children may not be able to enrol because they lack proper documentation, are not considered residents of the area or are unable to pay school fees. Feelings of exclusion, and the struggle for survival and protection, may lead children to join parties to the conflict or to become street children. In the course of the ten-year Liberian civil war, the number of teachers is estimated to have dropped from 12,000 to 4,000-5,000; approximately 10,000 to 15,000 child soldiers acquired little education and no marketable skills; and 20,000 to 30,000 primary-school-age children have not attended regularly in the last seven years.

Vulnerable and excluded children are found where their government's military and civil action against domestic minorities or other perceived threats blatantly make them the weapons as well as the victims of war. Burning school, intimidating and murdering teachers and destroying books are all weapons of choice in policies to deny children both the immediate opportunity to learn and undermining any potential they might have for recapturing a life of normal development and effective participation later on. International sanctions imposed against hostile countries can also exacerbate exclusion when they are applied 'too bluntly' and where they are inadequately monitored to ensure that the impact does not fall on children.

A most critical message for education from Machel concerns the durability and scope of conflicts, and their permanent impact on the exclusion of large numbers of children. Persistent instability, unpredictability and randomness of even low-grade violence 'which never begins or ends' produces a generalized vulnerability years of lost schooling and vocational skills will take equivalent years to replace and their absence imposes a greater vulnerability on the ability of societies to recover after war.

The interdependencies of exclusion will guarantee that this 'greater vulnerability will fall most heavily on those least able to cope, already-marginal families even more hard-pressed to find financial and psychological resources for ensuring the health and emotional well-being of children, and less likely to have a future-looking faith which might make ingesting in education a sensible use of resources. Systems have fewer opportunities to provide them and those they have are 'of lower quality'. Funds are short; the supply of materials slow and erratic;

fear and disruption making it difficult to create an atmosphere conducive to learning.

In Refugee Settlements and Displaced: Immediately consequent to children being excluded through war, they are being excluded in their millions in refugee camps and as the internally displaced. For many such children, this nether world is a more-or-less permanent condition. Lao and Palestinian refugees, for example, have seen several generations born in camps; Afghan refugees have been in the Islamic Republic of Iran for some twenty years. As with other social-support structures, the education available to these children and their families is precarious.

Host governments rarely allow open access to the regular school system; even when able to attend, refugee children often face exclusions of discrimination, social harassment and failed communication (cultural and/or linguistic). Motivation within refugee communities to educate their own children may be high, but their capacity to manage coherent and consistent programmes is typically not. In the Afghan case, in the few refugee schools which are run, classes in all of them are very small, overcrowded and under-equipped. Implying ongoing exclusion, they are also not formally recognized and no certification is given.

They are working. Among the most obvious causes and consequences of exclusion is the fact that children who are not in school are not sitting idle. They are at home, generating income or filling in for working parents; they are in the field, in factories, and on the street. Definitions of work vary by type, level of hazard or exploitation and the amount of time involved, making detailed figures on working children difficult to calculate with certainty. Broadly, the number of children in the developing countries estimated to be working, full- or part time, is 250 million.

Asia, reflecting conditions chiefly in South Asia, continues to have highest absolute numbers of working children. As of 19.97, 120 million children between ages 5 and 14 were 'fully at work', and there are many more for whom work is a secondary activity.

In Cambodia, 1996 statistics indicated 16 per cent working children between ages 5 and 17, most of these in fisheries and agriculture and the rest in domestic service, scavenging and small factories or sweatshops. In some East Asian and Pacific countries, one in three households depend on their children's labour; and 2 per cent to 16 per cent of the region's gross national product is earned through a sex industry in which, for some Mekong countries, 33 per cent of those involved are under 16.

Statistics from elsewhere are no better. In the most seriously affected provinces of Brazil, over 700,000 children aged 10 to 14 are working and not attending primary school; over 2 million work and attend part time.

Another 2 million or so of 15- to 17- year-olds are similarly distributed. In addition, close to 600,000 5- to 9-year olds are 'in the work market', and while below official school starting age, are seriously risking both their future life and their eventual success in school by undermining their health and establishing patterns of family income earning which are hard to break.

Poverty statistics on working and street children relate closely to their exclusion from education. In 1993 in New Delhi, 63 per cent of working children were illiterate; 17 per cent completed primary school and 61 per cent of the girls had never been to school. In Yangon, 39 per cent had no schooling and 54 per cent had dropped out by second grade. 64 per cent of Cambodian street children are estimated not to attend school, most are girls; estimates for minority children in remote areas are worse.

Histories of working children with respect to exclusion from education are all too similar: rural areas with no or incomplete access to primary schools; low-income families, single parents with limited educational background; marginal urban areas with few, over-crowded schools; communities and schools with high levels of crime and violence; school failure, repetition and abuse. Two critical issues for all these children are choice and consequences. Research suggests that many want to work—to support families, have the freedom to make their own life-decisions, avoid ineffective and unfriendly schools. The fact is also that many do not.

Interviews with eighty-four Cambodian street children found that the majority aspired to go to school because they wanted to read like other people and get a job. Where children do choose to work, many of these choices are pyrrhic; the consequences serious and long term. Their jobs may give them immediate and necessary income, but little of the knowledge or skills to enable them to move to better, more flexible, stable or financially secure employment. Much of the work is informal, providing a life of limited alternatives and increasing dependency on the vagaries of uncertain economies, unscrupulous adults, political expediency and fleeting charity. It also creates a great deal of personal risk, subjecting girls especially to sexual abuse.

Working children of seasonal migrant families are probably less at risk than those who work on their own, protected for the most part within the framework of a coherent community structure. They are, however, vulnerable to exclusion on a wide range of social dimensions, including education, given families' often high levels of poverty, the unhealthy working conditions and the instability of an enforced transient lifestyle. In Mexico, over 3.5 million people are estimated to be in seasonal agricultural work, with numbers increasing 'as one of the few alternatives to survival' given the endemic poverty, lack of productive infrastructure and deteriorating natural resources of their communities. Approximately 900,000 of these are children, 50 per cent under 14. Their contribution to family income is critical, estimated at over 30 per cent, but at a cost: 40 per cent illiterate; 21.5 per cent never in school.

Globally, the number of children in this situation is again difficult to assess. The living conditions and size of such 'floating communities' are often not well monitored by governments; nor is their children's absence from school. The dilemma is in how to provide appropriate educational opportunities and facilitate learning when the children's work is so intimately woven into their lives. It is clear that there are risks to both the children and their families in forcing them into educational arrangements in ways that undercut the stability they have managed to create. But without an education, their future is unlikely to be less vulnerable than their present.

The Growth

On the plus side, progress has been made: the decade since Jomtien has laid a solid groundwork for action against the exclusion of children, in terms both of education as a defined sector, and of learning as a cross-cutting process necessary to all aspects of survival and development.

The World Conference on Education for All (WCEFA) was a watershed, a critical juncture in global thinking about the legitimate place of learning and education as core to all human and social development. Jomtien established an unarguable link between poverty and exclusion, for the individual and the society; exposed the failure of most nations to provide adequate basic education for all their citizens; and confirmed the inevitability of future exclusion for those children and their families who are denied access to such education. Critically, it set a new 'expanded vision' for education and declared national and global responsibilities for taking action.

The Convention on the Rights of the Child (CRC) provided the critical overarching framework for EFA in making the education of all children their right. It committed a global imperative of action to ensure all children an effective education, not simply to a seat in school and not simply for those who turn up. Governments, civil societies and donors are now compelled to give highest priority to an explicit and intensive focus on the chronically excluded: under the CRC umbrella, all children are owed an education which meets their basic learning needs and enables them to live an individual life in society in the spirit of peace, dignity, tolerance, freedom, equality and solidarity. Responsibility for providing this quality of education for all rests with everyone in world society, at global, national and—by extension—local levels. Ultimately, of course, much of the onus for children's learning and education falls on families and schools.

The Salamanca Statement and Framework for Action on Special Needs Education further refined and focused the message of EFA, committing the international community to addressing the large-scale and typically systemic exclusion of those children with special learning needs. This continues to be a problem in all countries to some degree, both by education systems omitting to identify, count or support children's special learning needs, and by their committing actively against them, declaring children who are 'different' as incapable of learning or participating. For children in either context, Salamanca was important in placing more explicitly on the global EFA agenda the imperative of recognizing, valuing and managing their learning; and doing so in ways that ensure their full participation in education, the successful realization of their learning goals and, ultimately, their independence as adults able to sustain themselves as parents, workers and citizens.

Salamanca was also the key to reinforcing and extending the EFA principle of an expanded vision of education, one in which 'ordinary schools should accommodate all children, regardless of their physical, intellectual, emotional, social, linguistic or other conditions'. 'Inclusive' schools give particular attention to enabling the learning of each child, serving to integrate all and not to segregate any. They serve to bring all children into mainstream education. Salamanca recognized that 'regular schools with this inclusive orientation are the most effective means of combating discriminatory attitudes, creating welcoming communities, building an inclusive society and achieving education for all'.

Less a formal international commitment than a global re-declaration of the central place of learning and education for all, the Delors Commission served further to underscore the role of education as a basic element of individual and Societal development and peaceful coexistence. In confirming the capacity to learn as the 'treasure' everyone has within them, the task of education is to ensure all children and adults the right to lifelong learning along four core dimensions or pillars: learning to know, learning to do, learning to be and learning to live together. Some have added a fifth: learning to transform oneself and the world around one.

In both general and specific terms, all these initiatives placed education at the centre of action in support of the children who are most excluded, as both a tool for their development and a place for their protection. Regional meetings in Stockholm, Oslo, Cairo, Amsterdam. Beijing and other international actions have, through the remainder of the past decade, made substantive contributions to the EFA framework. Their discussions and commitments have taken a harder look at the realities of the especially vulnerable and forgotten child and, within this framework, the special protection and development rights of girls and women.

The World Summit for Social Development (WSSD), Copenhagen, March 1995, was especially important in looking specifically across all groups and sectors to consider the interactive nature of socio-economic exclusion and development. In consequence, it stressed the need for integrative strategies and collaborative actions by domestic institutions, NGOs and international agencies to deal with them.

Suffering to some degree by not having a clear constituency to keep its 'Action Framework' on the table, the WSSD nevertheless presented a significant opportunity to push the critical role of learning as the enabling dimension of all organizational and social change aimed at social integration:

> "... the capacity of people to live together with full respect for the dignity of each individual, the common good, pluralism and diversity, non-violence and solidarity as well as their ability to participate in social, cultural, economic and political life.... It requires the protection of the weak, as well as the right to differ, to create and to innovate."

The WSSD thus made critical distinctions between inclusion and conformity and between diversity and exclusion, distinctions and implied directives central to realizing effective and equitable education. It went further, urging specific actions to mobilize funding of the 'Agenda for Development' to which the summit participants had committed themselves: reduced military spending; enhanced transparency and accountability at all levels; better focusing on basic human needs; recognition and support to alternative financing mechanisms; open exchange of technology, knowledge and skills; application of the 7 per cent Official Development Assistance/ODA commitment, debt relief, and action on the 20/20 initiative.

All these factors, if coupled with concerted action to address the professional quality of teachers and curricula, would clearly have gone far to ending education exclusion. The UN Development Assistance Framework (UNDAF), though not yet as far advanced as it needs to be in mobilizing and ensuring effective collaborative and consistent action on children's exclusion, is clearly the way to go. Multilateral agencies, NGOs and bilaterals each have their own areas of comparative advantage, mandates and partners. Each, however, shares a common constituency of people who are excluded, marginalized and living in poverty, and to whom it owes action that is relevant, sustainable and of high quality.

On the other side, more is to be done. Progress in following up all of these global agreements is far from wholly positive. While enrolments and school spaces have increased, these have not been matched by gains in ensuring that pupils persist in their schooling and emerge from primary school with the knowledge and skills they need expected benefits are being undermined by significant levels of dropout' in both developing and developed countries.

The Jomtien target of 80 per cent completion for primary school is still a very distant goal in sub-Saharan Africa, South Asia and much of Latin America. The 80 per cent figure is no longer, of course, tenable under the CRC. In presenting this number as sufficient, Jomtien may have suggested that 'the rest' could legitimately be left to fail or not to count at all—in effect, serving to legitimize exclusion.

In focusing on UPE as an expressed goal, and defining that within the specific context of schooling, Jomtien ironically may also have served to undermine the probability of its own key concept of the 'expanded vision' taking root. Education for all has become minimized in too many countries and too many agencies as school for all. The expanded vision of basic education is inclusive of, but clearly greater than, formal schools and traditional classroom methods. Though the WCEFA strongly endorsed the place of alternative educational arrangements within the vision, the UPE-cum-schooling emphasis appears to have left them relegated to a second-class, choice-limiting status. The CRC is significant in changing the paradigm. Eight out of ten children completing primary school is no longer the issue; two out of ten not completing is.

The EFA Declaration was important in establishing the core of what effective education and learning systems should be, the 'what' of basic education. Jomtien and the succeeding decade have been less clearly successful, however, in making explicit, and putting into effect, the 'how' of mobilizing subsequent action; of stimulating demand and improving supply. The Mid-Decade Meeting of the International Consultative Forum on Education for All provided a useful, albeit justifiably modest, stocktaking of the progress made in the first five years. It, too, was unfortunately vague in analyzing the 'how' of why the Framework was not being fully implemented. Where and what the implementation gaps were, and how to fill them—especially with respect to such fundamental issues as the training of teachers and mobilizing of sustained political action—remained largely unknown.

Nor has the decade finished strongly in terms of tracking the progress of EFA targets. While anecdotal evidence suggests that many innovations are showing good effects, there is little systematic assessment of them. Many of the advances reported are based either on broad averages, or narrowly focused pilot efforts, both of which have drawbacks in terms of informing wider practice.

Monitoring and tracking systems remain universally weak, not well able to determine the real quality and impact of many of the interventions on, or the deeper reasons for, continuing exclusion. Rare also are the comprehensive case studies and implementation analyses that might present the kind of integrated social development picture urged by the WSSD. Instances of serious and interactive exclusion remain without good explanations as to how to disentangle them.

Highlighted throughout the Johannesburg Sub-Saharan Africa Conference, for example, were the multiple needs of creating stronger capacities for analysis, of undertaking research, and of using results to inform policy and practice. Data throughout the continent are considered to be weak in quality, narrow in scope and limited in quantity. In particular, too little is known of patterns and trends on such key issues as participation and achievement, especially concerning the children who are at risk and excluded—girls, children with disabilities, minority groups. Analysis is often poorly carried out, not considered sufficiently reliable, and not presented with sufficient assurance, to mobilize, guide or evaluate change.

School and community-based action research is rare. Teachers, parents and students have little input to assessments made within the education sector as it affects them. What is happening in the classroom, what teachers and students are actually doing, is rarely observed let alone analyzed.

While a wide range of innovations and pilot programmes are being tried through the region and may well be relevant to the excluded—on community and out reach schools, multi grade classrooms, double-shifting, use of quasi-professional resource teachers—few are being systematically assessed to determine whether or how they are making a difference, to which children, and under what conditions. Lack of analysis makes it difficult to take corrective action on the unsuccessful ideas; to strengthen and extend those that are effective; or to share lessons.

The types of study currently being promoted by the UNESCO/ UNICEF Monitoring Learning Achievement/MLA project and by regionally-based projects such as the Southern African Consortium for Monitoring Educational Quality, are steps in the right direction. They will focus particularly on the more qualitative factors impeding access and successful participation of especially vulnerable children, and on the relevance of what they are learning. These assessments also need to be persistent and participatory. The use of 'pilot' projects as the mechanism for focusing and managing action for the excluded also merits closer attention. Pilots are often undertaken because difficult for people to agree on the pace of change; they let small groups of mobilized people do it on their own.

Unfortunately, the logic of pilots often fails in application, leaving them 'outside the mainstream, threatening people in the rest of the and causing resentment. Eventually, most of these programmes collapse, not from lack of value, but from lack of support'. Where they involve marginal communities, those with few resources and little room for experimenting, they are often too demanding to be sustained. Real control over planning, design and implementation of most pilots rests with interveners rather than with the schools and communities involved; and efforts to develop local capacity are often too limited to shift the ownership. Sustaining the results of innovation requires serious, long-term attention to the change process, to organizational learning and to participation. These are the necessary conditions of 'full scale' implementation, which many EFA pilots have tended not to give.

Ministries of education need to assert their strong commitment to the excluded in this area. Although the educational innovations targeted to various excluded groups are often managed and executed by NGOs, it is essential that the Ministries are involved from the initial [stage] by, for example, assigning officials to work with the innovations or by directing some resources; and later adopting the innovation for dissemination. Separate projects which are not well incorporated in the framework of the national education system tend to be short-lived.

There are recurrent themes and common threads, principles of action which appear to characterize moves towards more effective and sustainable action, not simply against exclusion, but in support of inclusion.

These themes are not new. Broad participation and synergy, within a holistic framework and using enabling processes to ensure local relevance. These are the concepts and principles underlying all the international commitments noted above. What must be new for the next decade is that action is taken to actually implement them—by states, civil societies and the international community.

Great Participation

Perhaps the two most significant advances of the decade since Jomtien in reaching excluded children, indeed all children, have been (a) the increasing realization that education, like learning, is a necessarily holistic and integrated system, and (b) the persistent movement towards greater participation of communities, families and children in matters concerning learning, education and schools.

Coincident with both of these has been a more sensitive appreciation of teachers and school as critical actors; a distinct trend toward focusing the reform efforts at a level nearer to the 'action': the school itself.

None of these developments is revolutionary. All, however, are fundamental and mutually reinforcing in reaching the excluded. They recognize that no education policy will be sustainable by attempting to mandate attitudinal or behavioural change from the centre, or in one narrow aspect of the system. They acknowledge that genuine implementation of change in classrooms, families and communities that are socio-culturally and economically marginalized and at risk requires equity, transparent accountability and joint responsibility.

The Family: Participation in the context of excluded children most particularly concerns their families. The concept of the family as a place of security and support for children and as a partner of the school has been slowly emerging over the past decade as efforts are made to find better ways to address the rights and needs of all children to education. Facilitating that emergence should be happening more quickly.

The CRC in particular recognizes families and parents as the first line of intervention in, and support for, children's emotional, psychosocial and intellectual learning. The capacity, or incapacity, of families to act on behalf of the survival, protection and development of their children is especially critical in the early years, and not much less so as children become adolescents and begin to confront the confusion of uncertain and conflicting choices and demands. Families are the key in keeping children out of exploitative working conditions and in school; the opposite is equally true.

Again recognizing exclusion as a cycle, the education level of the family is the 'single best predictor of how long children will stay in school and how well they will perform'. It is much more difficult for illiterate parents and those who have been harmed by schools to see the value of education for their children, or to help them to participate even when they do. Programmes promoting parent literacy, therefore, are also likely to have positive effects on children's learning. Mobilization campaigns to get girls into school are most successful when they take place in collaboration with the family—and with community leaders, civic groups and NGOs—the bodies that are often in closest touch with the values and needs of families and so most able to influence their decisions. The particular importance of the family during times of stress is clear. Conflict, forced migration and economic crisis are periods when family stability and consistency are the child's best link to learning, adaptation and sense of identity, and when the loss of family can be especially devastating. The effectiveness of action such as that by the World Bank and the Asian Development Bank in working with Indonesian families to put in place scholarships for the children most at risk will be critical in this regard.

One area in which gains have been made in this respect is the greater attention being given to early childhood care and development interventions. Most successful where set within the context of their families, ECCD programmes recognize that only with whole-hearted parental participation can such programmes succeed.

They are critical in countries such as the Lao People's Democratic Republic where, especially among indigenous families, primary-school attendance is very low. The village based early childhood education project is concerned with children's early learning within the framework of support both for their own developing capacities, as well as the capacities of their care givers, especially mothers. The project strengthens family knowledge and practice in basic nutrition, hygiene and health and child development, including infant stimulation and ways to increase language ability. It links with women in development/WID and basic-education interventions so that there is support for increased income generation, village planning and schooling; and with the media and early childhood education sub-project to produce educational radio broadcasts, videos and print material on good parenting, nutrition and child development practices.

For seriously at-risk children, and those unlikely to have access to reasonably effective schools, ECCD interventions may be the only quality learning support that they will have. It is, therefore, especially critical that the interventions should be of high quality: learning and learner-oriented, interactive and participatory, culturally sensitive and responsive, holistic and engaged with all family members and the community agencies with which they also interact.

Programmes which are able to engage with marginalized families, to work with them in the context of the constraints and strengths of their own setting, and which bring them together to support one another, are the most effective. They impose less risk to vulnerable families, allowing them to find their own 'best way' in developing strategies of childcare and learning that they are able to sustain in collaboration with neighbouring families and local support agencies.

A main difficulty with efforts to engage such families in changing their relationship with the school is, of course, their own negative history with education—if they have had one at all. Parents who have themselves been excluded from school are less likely to have the knowledge, skills or psychological 'margin' for risk-taking which would make them feel naturally comfortable in their children's school. One example of an attempt to overcome this distance is the school-based education project in Peru. Working through activates aimed at developing a shared vision, breaking down dysfunctional perceptions and creating a partnership among parents, students and teachers, the underlying strategy of the programme has been to start a dialogue on the child as a priority for parents and for teachers in terms of their shared responsibility in the child's education. Parents and teachers work together to formulate solutions and alternatives which could help create the 'ideal' school. At the same time, teachers develop 'converzations' with students, on the assumption that they, too, are in a position to have opinions about the quality and content of their learning and have the capacity to contribute.

The task is an evolutionary and open-ended one, attempting to create a culture of inclusion where both community and school are able to bring together their expectations and priorities, evaluate options for 'translating them into reality' and developing frameworks of action they can then work to apply. Interventions such as this are critical to building on and strengthening the learning within families in ways that will help them engage with the school. It is important that schools themselves reach out to support families, especially the vulnerable ones, in doing better, to encourage them to be involved throughout their children's schooling.

The results of a large-scale study of poor inner-city schools in the United States, for example, showed clearly that effective schools were those that were able to help parents to change the ways in which they connected to the school and promoted their children's learning as they moved through the system. Beginning when children were very young, these schools helped parents to help their children in 'building the skills' they needed to do well in school.

They 'coached' parents in how to talk to teachers, helped them to monitor their children's progress and support them with their schoolwork. Effective schools helped parents to learn 'how the system works' so they could be better advocates for their children, to make decisions, about how to make the school better, and to make sure that their children were learning what they needed to know.

The Community: It is important to recognize families *per se*, their unique role in creating and raising children and the need to take them into one-to-one partnership. But most excluded families and their children live in the context of a community. Less a geographical construct than a sociological one, communities are important here as the primary reference group for families and their children (especially older ones).

Particularly in traditional societies and cultures, communities can play a major role in defining a family's available resources and support structures, its social obligations, and its core values, attitudes and expectations. The community in this sense is especially critical in addressing exclusion. No attempt to create equitable and inclusive education programmes for children and families will succeed independently of their surrounding community.

Using this broad definition of community, the learning and education of excluded children can be enhanced where families and local groups come together to support them in formal and non-formal programmes, with and without government support. Excluded children can also be supported through 'communities of interest', networks formed among them as individuals who share a common bond of vulnerability. These are child labourers or street children who form family type bonds; or support groups formed by adolescents affected by HIV/AIDS. Mutual support and exchange associations of these kinds can constitute significant forms of psychosocial 'margin'. They provide a sense of belonging, a nurturing role and guidance; often they also provide very pertinent and effective venues for learning information and skills. They can provide critical focal or entry points for education interveners, as interlocutors able to interpret between an NGO or school out reach initiative and children unable to communicate effectively or from a position of equal participation what they want and need to learn.

Communities, whether geographical or interest-based, can also play a critical role in finding and engaging 'missing' children. Informal associations of child carpet-workers in India, for example, have proved to be much better able to locate other children and convince them that it is safe to get involved in learning programmes than are officials from the ILO International Programme for the Elimination of Child Labour or from the government.

Somewhat more systematic, Lok Jumbish in Rajasthan is another example of community-based mapping of the excluded, where and as they are. Working with community members interested in educational improvement, it creates an 'inspirational group' which then undertakes to depict every household in the village visually on a simple map indicating the schooling status of every household member aged 5-14'.

Serving as an 'occasion for interacting with the community', block-based interviews help to show where special help is needed and what priorities families see as barriers to their children attending school. Leaders of the village and the local community draw up a set of proposals based on the mapping data, where new schools and NFE centres are needed and where present ones need fixing.

The methodology is intended to be empowering as well as informative, allowing even non-literate families to be involved in the analysis. The follow-up is also community-based and is critical in fostering 'continuous evaluation'. Attendance of children is locally monitored and neighbourhood blocks are free to determine and revise appropriate issues and strategies (creating residential study camps for girls, for example).

The Myanmar All Children in School (ACIS) project is concerned with fairly broad systemic reform to reduce the severe national-level exclusion. In order to achieve this it focuses on an integration of three levels: the community, engaging people in enrolment surveys and school mapping, local data management and PTA training; teachers, providing decentralized training for multi-grade and learner-centred teaching, in-class supervisory support and materials development; and school structures, through promotion of school clusters and improved monitoring and evaluation.

Significant for the potential sustainability of increased student participation, ACIS appears to be having a positive impact on the relationship between community and school: local teachers hired through community donations; a 'growing willingness' of teachers to talk with parents about their children's progress; and community- based identification and enrolment of previously 'invisible' children such as migrant workers.

The Kolondieba District community schools project in Mali aims at addressing deep-seated, poverty-based exclusion. It is a particularly cogent example of the dilemmas facing communities and their children as they try to act on the very mixed 'causes and consequences' of that exclusion. Poverty is clearly the over aching issue for the communities, which have very few resources and minimal national support. Families live at subsistence level, speak the local language with a limited capacity in French, and have little access to the few and distant government schools.

At the project's start in 1992, only 1210 of the 207 villages in the district were reached by the formal system and there was little to indicate that the situation would change. Community schools appear to be succeeding, however, as a way to shift the paradigm—from one of children trying and failing to accommodate within the formal system, to one of the community ensuring a school designed to suit them.

Based on explicit commitments by the community to ensure enrolment, regular attendance and girls' participation, and to pay salaries of locally hired teachers and monitor their work, the project has created learning environments to which children apparently want to come and in which they are, on the whole, succeeding. Teaching is in the local language, of subjects selected by the community as important to their children's current lives. Literacy, mathematics and French are also taught, as a base for children who eventually choose to move into the formal system.

The success of the schools appears to lie specifically in these efforts to localize content, process and ownership; but so, too, lie their core dilemmas. Teachers can be hired locally because they are minimally trained, and paid locally because they are paid very little. Curriculum can be relevant because it is developed locally, but it has little reference to the national system. All these characteristics are consistent with the fundamentals of creating inclusive learning, but not necessarily with inclusion beyond the community.

Critical questions must then be asked of all such community-based programmes. Whether the approaches are sustainable, and whether they should be; whether they risk confining excluded children to further exclusion in 'pockets of learning', positive but inevitably isolating. Children are learning in their community schools; in the Mali case, they are even laying a basis of French-language competency and there appears to be interest at the national level for extending the approach. Nevertheless, these communities and their supporters need continually to explore the children's long-term 'best interest': if the structures and methodologies of the education can be adapted and sustained; whether eventually the students must move out of the community to move up in the education system, and whether that system can somehow come into the community without undermining the latter's coherence and culture.

Programme of Action

One example of a community-based programme which has gone a considerable way towards answering some of these questions has done so because it has developed an integrative programme for excluded children and their families. Based in a slum area of Jaipur (India), the Bodh Shiksha Samiti is a good example—in the extent to which it has become part of the very fabric of the community, in the long time scale it has allowed itself, and in its forging of a genuine two-way link to the formal system.

The effective owners of the Bodh schools are the migrant and landless labourers, disadvantaged castes and traditional artisans who live in the community. With no previous access to schools sufficiently affordable, flexible or 'welcoming' for them, the community agreed in the late 1980s to engage with a small group of social activists to create a school as a form of 'collective endeavour' for their children's education.

Seven schools have been built by the community over the past decade. A 'sense of ownership' and a bridge between school and community have also been built. The Bodh has ensured children's inclusion by becoming part of the community itself.

It has been a process through which people in 'an organized framework pool their ideas, concerns, aspirations and resources, and develop a dynamic networking of communication among students, parents, teachers and Bodh organizers'.

Together, they have worked through many of the core issues of exclusion: dealt with the absenteeism of working children and appropriate forms of discipline; negotiated teaching methodologies, balancing the benefits of active versus rote learning; selected curriculum topics appropriate to the life of the community; created relevant and affordable teaching materials; and jointly assessed children's ongoing progress. Confronting many of the barriers to the inclusion of socially marginalized children, the Bodh programme is holistic. It includes all aspects of community education, from preschool through to adult literacy. Mothers and older children are trained as part-time resource teachers, creating another tie between school and community.

At the same time, emphasis is put on the continuous training of the full-time teachers in methodologies stressing participatory learning.

The entire primary curriculum is divided into three broad ability groups, among which children can easily move as appropriate to their competencies rather than being fixed by age.

Curriculum topics are flexible, but ensure coverage of basic issues, such as hygiene and nutrition, which are immediately useful to children and their families. A core of community—agreed generic-skills training (language and mathematics, analysis and reasoning) and attitude development (independence, cooperation, motivation for learning) aims at building children's capacities for future learning.

All this is intended to give the act of learning, and the process of education, a more valued place in the community, encouraging parents and children to pursue further study in the formal system.

In preparation for this end, text-books and written examinations are eventually introduced and, important in realizing that 'seamlessness' which is the key to inclusive education, an 'adoption programme' has recently started to work with and train teachers from the formal system in the main principles and teaching approaches of the Bodh programme. The aim is systematically to integrate aspects of the two educational approaches.

Within Schools: Reaching excluded children and encouraging their participation requires making education, and especially schools, easily accessible, physically and emotionally welcoming and oriented to each child's learning capacities and needs.

This may seem a self-evident point, but both the international community and national education systems have taken a long time in coming to it. In the broadest sense, it means paying much greater attention to conceiving and organizing schools holistically.

More specifically, it means assessing schools, and acting to improve them, on the same lines as they have been using to keep out the most vulnerable children:

— quality of the environment, to create safe and girl-friendly physical facilities, policies and practices of non-violence and mutual respect;

— modes of delivery, to explore use of school clusters, multi grade teaching, double-shifting and distance technologies;

— methods of facilitating learning, to use interactive small group arrangements, peer and child-to-child tutoring, teacher-generated curriculum;
— role of the teachers, to encourage teacher-teacher support groups, peer counselling, in-service monitoring;
— partnerships with families, to develop school linkages, school-based ECCD, parent literacy and work-related programmes, PTA and school councils.

Such actions imply major shifts in thinking, in perspectives, in relationships and in ways of working. They require that those designing the innovations, and especially those delivering them, be open and ready for change, for taking risks and for reflective experimentation. This extent of support for learning is, unfortunately, not often provided in education reform efforts, especially when the targeted community is of low status or politically invisible.

However, while application of change may not have gone very far since Jomtien, and the traditional top-down, information-transfer model of schooling remains the norm, serious efforts continue to be made to cast doubt on the efficacy of that traditional model and to create a new one. The nomenclature for identifying these more holistic approaches varies among agencies and organizations. However, while problematic for the outsider trying to sort through the terminological stew, common threads are visible across most of them.

The latest education policy framework of the UK Department for International Development (DFID), for example, speaks of a whole school development approach, 'designed to bring together and integrate the many inputs and processes which constitute the learning environment and the learning experience of children'. The approach includes inter alia a focus on school-based planning, on motivating and supporting teachers, on creating safe and secure school environments, on partnerships with families and community agencies, and on setting and monitoring reachable learning goals.

The wholesome education school programme in Bhutan, supported by SC-US, has a similar point of departure. Set within the broader context of an education reform effort with community-based change as its base, it includes aspects of community development education, participatory rural appraisal/PRA and skill-development for out-of-school youth, and children's clubs. The programme's goal of increased inclusiveness is reflected in its integrative schools-based management and teacher-focused orientation. Considering 'the needs and rights of the whole child, bridges health and education', encouraging schools to 'come up with their own plans' and helping them develop 'a self-assessment tool help sensitize teachers to the concept, and show them that there are things they can do and concrete steps can take'.

One of the potentially most influential initiatives in this regard is the concept of the child-friendly school (CFS). Perhaps most energetically promoted by UNICEF, the concept is becoming increasingly reflected in similar approaches of agencies such as the World Health Organization, Save the Children and Radda Barnen, bilateral donors and a number of national governments. In essence, the CFS framework aims at creating education systems and school settings that are inclusive, effective, equitable and secure for all children.

The child-friendly school seeks to engage children and their parents in all aspects of the learning event; to be more welcoming of the diversity of children, and to keep them longer in the educational environment. It seeks to be more nurturing, academically professional and programmatically flexible. The underlying premise of the CFS is that all children must be provided positive learning opportunities, and that all must be expected to succeed no matter what their background and whether in or outside the formal school setting.

The child-friendly concept thus widens the framework. It assumes that learning, and society's commitment to supporting it encompass children from birth through adolescence, whatever capacities they bring and whatever their learning needs.

It assumes the need for partnerships with families and communities in developing facilities and programmes which are physically safe, foster a sense of security, well-being and self-confidence, and help children to respect themselves and others. It aims, at promoting responsible and collaborative citizenship through abuse-free schools, codes of conduct, anti-bullying policies and training in peer mediation for 'peaceful playgrounds'.

For teachers as well as children, it includes norms against all forms of harassment, no-tolerance policies against violence, and development of positive disciplinary alternatives to corporal punishment which are clear, consistent and provide support to teachers in their fair application. By engaging with families, the CFS seeks to become a place where children and adults can have converzations about issues of immediate concern to them and about the values, attitudes and behaviours underlying them.

While certainly applicable to all children, then, the flexibility and responsiveness inherent in the concept are especially important for reaching the excluded in the 'especially difficult circumstances' where children, adolescents and families are particularly at risk. They are important when normative social controls are breaking down-due to the rapid and unmanaged social change of communal conflict, urban stress or rural dislocation; and when families are not able to support their children because they are themselves fighting fragmentation or alienation.

Two programmes currently under way in Thailand reflect different approaches and emphasis to the child-friendly concept and give a sense of its scope.

Working under the auspices of the Office of National Primary Education, the Children's Integrated Learning and Development (CHILD) initiative in the north-east (with input from UNICEF) and the Child-Friendly Schools (CFS) programme in the north (supported by SC-US) are both intended as fairly holistic interventions.

Each involves several layers of activity, various strategies for engaging with schools and their communities and different types of content. Both deal with a range of schools and children, confronting problems of exclusion to varying degrees. Situated in the poorest region of the country, child takes a broad-brush approach to the child-friendliness concept, aiming to create a 'constructive context' in which children's learning is enhanced through the school, in collaboration with the community and in a holistic way. It begins with a 'futures search', to mobilize teachers, parents and students in thinking and talking about children's protection and development rights and agreeing to take action.

The first most concrete action, offered as an enabling incentive, is on the micro level, introducing for the school's consideration a relatively simple computer-based management information system/ MIS technology. Including computer and training, the technology helps teachers to organize and track data related to students' academic and health status. The innovation at this level is not dramatic.

It is easily accessible to teachers of even the most resource-poor schools and is, for the most part, manageable in its first stages by the expertise available. It moves previously scattered pieces of hand-noted data on each child into more visible patterns, 'whole pictures' of a student's developmental progress. In this, the key strength of the intervention is that it allows teachers to do more easily and effectively what they already do.

At the same time, the project allows for growth. Teachers and schools are becoming increasingly more interested and expert in analytical manipulation and in thinking and talking together about students in more holistic -and integrative ways. Some are looking for ways to add new and more locally important data to the MIS 'on drug use, absenteeism, nutrition—and are working with students and parents on ways to address problems revealed by their analyses.

The Child-Friendly Schools project operates on the other side of the country, in a region characterized by relative wealth, the persistent social inequities and social trauma of marginalized hill-tribe communities, high rates of drug abuse and child prostitution and epidemic levels of HIV/AIDS.

The project is framed explicitly within the core themes of survival, protection and development, equity and participation. It begins with a relatively intensive Self-Assessment Process asking parents, teachers and students to define their ideal of a child-friendly school, and to contrast that with what they perceive to be the current situation. It then pursues a broadly focused intervention strategy based on a negotiation of the perceived gaps and creation of an agreed 'school charter'. Specific activities aim at strengthening home-community-school links, promoting the safe and secure psychosocial development of children, and introducing the notion of participatory active learning into classroom practice.

The logic of the child-friendly and teacher-engaged school appears to be proving intuitively sound in both regions, irrespective of social, economic and cultural differences. In large part, the positive response is a function of the holistic and non-restrictive nature of the concept, which allows each of the projects to be framed and implemented with considerable flexibility and adaptation. Each has been able to base the precise entry point, focus and evolution of its interventions on its respective schools, teachers and students as coherent organizational 'systems'.

More problematic here, and in 'piloting' initiatives generally, are the physical and psychological distance of the programmes from each other and from the national education policy centre, making communication and joint action difficult. From the perspective of articulating, managing and sustaining a nationally coherent and integrated 'child-friendly reform programme', it is obviously more difficult to promote change in a situation where each reform application and trajectory is different in approach and emphasis.

It is more complicated to create and organize training materials and action, to plan inputs, or to track outcomes jointly. If the impact is to be sufficiently national in support and scope, it is especially important for projects like these to create and maintain transparent and regular communication, horizontally between the work in the field and vertically with the policy centre. Underlying principles of action must be openly and regularly discussed and implementation must be monitored and outcomes assessed in cooperation with the communities expected to be benefiting.

Though with limited attention to teaching and learning quality and academic performance, the overlapping health promoting and healthy school initiatives of the World Health Organization are conceptually consistent with that of the child friendly school. They also are concerned with a holistic conception of children, with their lives both inside and outside the school and with building linkages between the school, family and community. Their main emphasis, however, is on mental and social health as the underpinnings of children learning to make sound choices (on factors such as nutrition, sexual behaviour, interpersonal relationships) and to protect themselves from high-risk behaviours, violence and abuse (to make better judgements, for example, and assess the veracity of advertised information).

They aim to foster healthy school environments, deliver appropriate health messages and interventions through the auspices of the school and its curriculum, and promote healthy lifestyle behaviours. They also project a more activist role for the school in providing input to health-promoting and violence reducing public policy; reorienting community health and referral services to ensure effective diagnostic and remedial support for vulnerable children; and mobilizing community participation around child health and protection issues.

A third variation on this same theme is that of inclusive education, introduced at Salamanca. Intended to capture the ideals of CRC and EFA commitments through schools which are welcoming of all children, irrespective of capacities, UNESCO in particular is promoting this terminology as a direct counterpoint to education which excludes. Inclusive education aims to be 'transformative'.

It includes advocacy (creating public platforms for people with disabilities), capacity development (training teachers, decision-makers, community leaders) and management strengthening activities (guidance for school staff, curriculum developers, supervisory systems).

As with child-friendly and health-promoting schools, much of the focus of 'inclusive schools' has been on networking and professional development to spread the idea in principle and ground it in practice.

It is concerned with identifying all forms of exclusion and barriers to learning within national policies, cultures, educational institutions and communities. It has implications for redirecting resources, inter-sectoral collaboration, teacher training, curriculum development, local capacity building and community involvement.

It is about developing an education within communities which is relevant to local needs and maximizes the use of community resources to overcome problems. It requires everyone involved in supporting learning at whatever level in identifying and responding to priorities for development as they exist locally. It emphasizes the roles of communities and centres of learning in creating and sustaining each other.

All these programme approaches are, or should be, attempts to create learner-friendly schools; schools with teachers and managers who are able to recognize and build on the differences children bring to school, in gender, age, background and capacities. Simultaneously, they should be schools that actively seek out and remove the barriers to learning which might exist within their own arrangements and resources, barriers which prevent accommodating the mix of children who do come and which serve to keep others out.

As a typology, it is critical that these are schools in which ECCD programmes are given high priority, tailored to the specific learner characteristics of the young child and the active inclusion of their primary care givers. They must be schools that also give consideration to the particular learning styles and priorities of adolescents, as children in transition, to provide opportunities for genuine participation and to help them make linkages between the knowledge and skills of the school and those of the world outside.

They must be schools that help students at risk to test the parameters of their values, knowledge and capacities to act by inviting input from, and collaboration with, other youth-oriented institutions and services of the community.

The recent efforts to implement a stronger life-skills orientation in and across programmes, to strengthen students' abilities to translate knowledge, attitudes and values into action' are especially critical for students in marginal communities who may have no chance other than school for guided exploration.

They are important, too, for specific at-risk children and adolescents—for child workers, young soldiers, teenage parents, those who are HIV/AIDS affected—who may be able to engage only in non-formal education settings. Again, the priority must be on forging links, on developing a porous education system, one allowing children and young people to move back and forth as their changing situations warrant.

An example of an effort to move in the direction of greater synergy among various education development initiatives is beginning in the Lao People's Democratic Republic, a country with few resources, little bureaucratic capacity and almost no civil society participation. Most of its children are indigenous and most remain vulnerable, excluded from even minimal learning opportunities.

Educational interventions, however, are beginning to happen in a number of sub-sectors. The overarching framework of all the donor interventions is important in their attempt to be explicitly integrative. One of the more important structural components of these activities is the cluster school, intended to serve as a way to increase the participation of parents in the schooling of their children, to improve access to good teaching and learning materials, to increase learning achievement and decrease wastage rates especially among remote and indigenous areas.

The cluster, an arrangement of some half-dozen schools linked administratively, serves to promote common use of materials and interaction among teachers and principals, including extended opportunities for joint training and more regular supervision. Parents are also encouraged to use the facilities of the cluster, and to contribute to its governance.

The administrative clustering of schools and implementation of joint activities is no doubt a necessary condition of sustainable synergy; it provides the skeleton. Equally important in this case, however, are the apparent commitments to ensuring that all other educational interventions also reinforce one another in content, process and community focus; and that all are based within an essentially learning-for-implementation paradigm. Thus, clusters are located in the same communities as village-based early childhood programmes, creating and facilitating parent-teacher student associations to deal with issues of access and retention, especially for indigenous children.

Resource centres are built to train teachers from the clusters in materials production and localizing curriculum. These, in turn, complement efforts of the National Teacher Training Programme to upgrade untrained and unqualified indigenous teachers in the use of child-centred methods, increase their knowledge of the new curriculum, and help them work in multi-grade classrooms which comprise the majority of schools in ethnic areas. None of this is very dramatic in the telling; it is also labour-intensive and slow in such a vertically managed and centrally controlled country. Nevertheless, it is an approach suited to institutionalizing an inclusive system.

With out-of-school learners. Holistic education recognizes the fact and critical importance of learning beyond the school. The Jomtien

Conference opened wider the door unlocked a decade or so earlier by the Faure Report to the legitimacy of non-formal education. In its potential for flexibility of out reach and interactive teaching methodologies, out-of-school learning is not only legitimate, it is necessary if all children and young people are to have access to a comprehensive and truly seamless education. Community, non-formal, literacy and adult education are all terms which, in principle at least, operationalize the EFA 'expanded vision" of all people being able to address their basic learning needs at any and all points in their lives. 'For basic education to be equitable', and for it to be useful and inclusive, 'all children, youth and adults must be given the opportunity to achieve and maintain an acceptable level of learning'. NFE is intended to do this.

Building on considerable experience from the previous half-century, the decade following Jomtien has seen an increasingly positive recognition accorded to the right and value of this kind of learning. It is often seen as the basis of marginalized and fragmented communities becoming 'empowered'. Much of this progress has been realized under the ambit of specific communities of people at risk (women, people affected by HIV/AIDS, subsistence farmers, street children) or of sectors with a strong out reach agenda (primary health care, water and sanitation, management of the environment).

Although evaluations as always tend to be somewhat anecdotal, many of these programmes appear to have been fairly effective in mobilizing change at the grassroots level, at least for the short-term benefit of those involved. Much of the change has involved children's learning, directly and indirectly through early childhood development programmes and functional literacy or job training for youth. Unfortunately, there appears to have been relatively little community-based education aimed specifically at designing NFE programmes for the long term. Nor has there been much attempt to strengthen linkages between families and the formal school; PTAs and other such mechanisms often remain little more than channels for eliciting school fees and local services.

One potentially significant impact of the increased status being accorded to non-formal education with particular relevance for excluded children, however, are programmes allowing them to come back—

either to formal schools or more informally organized learning activities. Children who for whatever reason have been kept, or put, out of school are being given more opportunities to find appropriate 'learning spaces' when and as they are ready, irrespective of age or school history. Such second-chance education is especially positive where it combines curriculum elements of the formal system with more non-formal delivery arrangements: another movement towards the critical criterion of seamlessness.

The Mauritius basic education for adolescents (BEFA) programme on the island of Rodrigues addresses a situation of primary completion rates at less than 50/0, with few children who dropout having the knowledge or skills either to manage their lives or to find productive work.

The BEFA programme provides a mix of life and livelihood-skills modules, delivered through a variety of venues, often facilitated by secondary school students. Participants are, in part, drawn to the programme by mobilization and out reach activities; in part also because the community and their families are active supporters of it. Unfortunately, while there is some cooperation with the formal school in BEFA management, there is less indication that the strengths of BEFA (learner-centredness, participatory approach, links with the community, peer-peer delivery) are being adopted by the formal side.

Uganda's Complementary Opportunities for Primary Education (COPE) project is in a much stronger educational environment and, while also concerned with presenting formerly excluded children with 'an alternative educational strategy', it has been able to do so with greater expectation of sustainable results.

Significantly, COPE takes cognizance 'of the fact that many of these children have stayed out of school through conscious family decisions based on the logic of their circumstances. Living in poverty, families have considered their children's ability to work as outweighing the vague potential of an education system seen as low quality. COPE is important in being a strongly community-based initiative. The community's choice of teaching times, school year and instructors gives it the power to provide an acceptable alternative to the formal system.

The project is important, too, in attempting to de-link age from grade, involving children age 8 to 14 in multi-age groupings and learner-centred methods. Classes are small enough to allow some use of participatory methods, individualized attention and continuous feedback to students on their progress. Significantly, it also emphasizes strengthening the capacity of locally recruited teacher-instructors through community-based in-service training.

COPE is understood to be a temporary solution to the problem of excluded children, one that will no longer be needed once the formal system is able to provide quality, affordable and accessible opportunities for all children. This may be an overly short-sighted perspective in situations of probably fairly chronic poverty.

Even once the formal system is better established, it seems likely that significant numbers of children and youth will continue not to enrol or to dropout early. This suggests that permanent action against exclusion requires programmes such as COPE to serve in an equally permanent role, extending the parameters of what constitutes 'legitimate' education. Non formal education, functional literacy and training programmes have long provided a recapturing role of a kind, but rarely in ways that allow learners to draw on, or integrate with, the resources and contents of formal education and more rarely do they do so in ways that may bring change in the system.

Primary and Secondary Education

Primary Education

The concept of 'primary education' as a distinct area of development was fully established five years before the next report of the Consultative Committee appeared. Certainly the Board did everything it could to keep the concept alive, and after its publication in 1928 *The New Prospect in Education, L.E.As* drew up schemes for the full provision of 'post primary' education for children of 11+ along with the lines indicated in the Hasow Report. There is a tendency to look upon it as little more than a historical curiosity; certainly beside the Plowden Report of 1967 it appears a very slim and modest volume, indeed, and although it took two years to produce its gross cost was minute compared with the cost of Plowden.

After a fairly lengthy introduction on general principles, the report provided a historical sketch of the development of the idea of primary education from the beginning of the nineteenth century. It went on to describe the physical and mental development of children between the ages of seven and eleven; and it is interesting to note that, just as Plowden leans quite heavily upon Piagetian thought, the 1931 report used and quoted Padget's *Le Language et la Pensee chez l'Enfant,* published in France in 1923 and translated into English in 1926.

The report then went on to consider the age limits for the upper stage of elementary education, which it felt should be fixed at the age of eleven; that is, the transfer from the primary to the secondary school should take place between the ages of eleven and twelve. It went on to discuss in some detail the arguments against separate 'infant' and 'junior' schools, but finally recommended that, in those areas where it was possible, there should be separate schools for children below the age of seven, and that in all primary schools there ought to be a well-defined line of education between the younger and older children.

The report made it clear that the primary school should not be regarded merely as a 'preparatory department for the subsequent stage': primary school course were to be planned and conditioned by the specific needs of the child at that particular phase in his development, both physical and mental.

The internal organization of primary schools was next discussed, including such problems as the size of classes and co-education at the upper stage of primary education. The report adduced evidence from a variety of sources to establish that classes in junior schools should be kept small, preferably about thirty five, and it further made the point that it would be impossible to put into operation many of its suggestions if large classes were retained in primary schools. The size of primary classes was indeed one of the most urgent problems facing education administrators. Concerning co-education the conclusion was that there was no valid objection on general or sociological grounds, provided due regard was paid to the differing needs of girls and boys in games and physical activities generally.

Problems of mental and educational retardation were considered in detail, and the chief causes, detection, diagnosis and treatment dealt with. Retarded children required special attention between the ages of seven and eleven, and it was recommended that special classes should be organized for this purpose and that they should be small.

The traditional curriculum of the public elementary school was next analyzed, and the general principles on which the upper stages of primary education should be based were elicited. The report considered the complexity of 'modern industrial civilization' and the bearing this has upon the work of the primary school. It emphasized the uselessness, as well as the innate danger, of seeking to inculcate what AX Whitehead has termed "inert ideas'; and it deplored and deprecated the fact that, whilst a great deal of teaching was good in the abstract, too little of it directly assisted children to enlarge and vivify their instinctive hold on the condition of life by enriching, illuminating and giving point to their growing experience.

In its further consideration of curriculum detail the report emphasized the desirability of devising new methods on approaching its various branches, and in particular dealt with the project method and 'centres of interest' as set against the traditional practice of treating the curriculum in terms of 'subjects'. It warned, however, against the dangers of such methods when used without due consideration or caution-music and drama were often merely 'dragged in' in order to fulfil what were regarded as the claims of a principle.

The staffing of primary schools and the training of teachers were next considered, and it was argued that teachers with general qualification rather than specialists were best suited for work in primary schools.

A brief survey was made of school premises, equipment, school and class libraries, visual and auditory aids to teaching, school visits and playing fields. There followed a discussion of examinations in primary schools and it was recommended that, in classifying pupils leaving the infant school, of consultation between the teachers concerned. Any classification should be merely provisional, and should be subject to frequent revision.

Secondary Education

The council felt that as the provision of various types of secondary education was extended in the way proposed in the report on The Education of the Adolescent, the need for selecting by competition those children who would pass on to grammar and selective modern schools would diminish.

It was convinced, however, that some sort of qualifying test or examination would always be required for the purpose of classifying pupils, and argued for the use of written papers in English and arithmetic as a basic test of capacity and attainment of children at the age of eleven, together with carefully devised group intelligence tests. Throughout the report of The Primary School there was a lively sense of the needs of the children themselves. It considered that what any wise and good parent might desire for his own children was precisely what the nation as a whole must desire for all children.

The primary school was on the way to becoming what it should be, namely, the common school of the whole population, so excellent and so generally esteemed that all parents will desire their children to attend it. In 1933 the Hadow Report on the Infant and Nursery school was published and, like its predecessor, it emphasized the need to build new schools for young children more on an open-air plan. It also made it clear that the best place for very young children was in the home; but if this were not possible there was a great deal to be derived from attending nursery schools.

There is a recognition of the child as a total being who has specific and differing needs within the realms of character and intellect, and additionally the need to be initiated into the world of work and life itself in such a way as to be able to cope practically as well as intellectually. Eaglesham may be right when he comments that whilst there is to be preparation for life there is to be no vocational education.

The children are to be trained in habits of careful observation and clear reasoning so that they may gain some intelligent acquaintance with some of the facts and laws of nature and this is hardly 'followership'! The school must further arouse in its pupils a lively interest in man's ideals, achievements, literature and history; it must give them 'some power over language as an instrument of thought and expression'—surely more keeping with education for leadership! All sound education should make pupils and students aware of the limitations of their knowledge and encourage a due sense of humility within the realms of learning-whether they are leaders or followers.

The code consequently adds that, while the school should make pupils conscious of their limitations it should provide thoughtful study as it will enable them to increase that knowledge' when their school career is over, and by their own efforts. This, indeed, is still one of the prime purpose of education—to demonstrate to pupils how to acquire knowledge and learning for themselves. The influence in practice of the 'sloud' movement is to be seen in other elements of the introduction which suggests that the school should encourage the natural activities of the child's hand and eye 'by suitable forms of practical work and manual instruction'; and the general, though gradual, movement towards hygiene and health is suggested by the training of pupils in physical exercises, organized games and the simple laws of health.

It is true that the code saw the possibility of discovering 'individual children who show promise of exceptional capacity', and that such children should be qualified to pass at the appropriate age into the secondary schools and there be enabled to derive the maximum benefit from the education offered them. Whilst this was a recognition that some children rather than others were fitted for further education it is worthy of note that there was a clause in parenthesis which had the sort of contention which many educators have put forward in more recent years against the streaming of children in primary schools for the 11+ examination, and the gearing of the whole of the primary curriculum for the benefit of the academic few to develop their special gifts. The introduction was not an exhortation to industry, respect and reverence in quite the same sense as that implied in pervious codes and reports.

There was little or no suggestion of 'fellowship' subservience in the terminology of the code. It was implied that there was a great responsibility on the part of the teachers to lay the foundations of conduct; and by their influence, example and personal sense of discipline, which should pervade the school, to inculcate in the children 'habits of industry, self control, and courageous preference in the face of difficulties' training suited, surely, to the middle and upper classed as well as the working classes. Reverence was to be taught, not for the nobility bur for what was noble; and children were to be ready for self-sacrifice and to strive to the uttermost for purity and truth. The respect which was to be fostered was not that for 'their betters', but for others, 'which must be the foundation of unselfishness and the basis of all good manner's. The corporate life of the school was the basis for the development of the instinct for fair play and sense of loyalty to one another-the very 'germ of a wider sense of honour in later life'.

Some of the introduction, for good or ill, reads almost like a public school code. The introduction concludes that school, parents and home should all unite in an effort to enable the children to reach their fullest development as individuals, and also to become useful and upright citizens in their community. Whether Morant was interested in forwarding elementary education or not, there was a certain liberalizing and humanizing purpose expressed in this introduction. And this was supported by the Blue Book issued by the Board of Education in 1905, which was a handbook of suggestions for teachers involved in the work of public elementary schools.

Uniformity of practice throughout such schools was not desirable, but rather that each teacher should think for himself and work out his own methods according to the school's conditions and requirements. Above all the teacher should know and sympathize with the children he was teaching. The entire process of education was viewed as a partnership for the acquisition of knowledge.

Facts were not to be dealt with in isolation but in relation to the total experience of the child 'each lesson must be a renewal and an increase of that connected store of experience which becomes knowledge' The Blue Book was in line with the introduction to the code in that it insisted that the latter should fully realize his duty to use his innate powers to the best advantage.

Life must be presented as something at once pleasant and serious, and in consequence the work being pursued in the schools was in a real sense a preparation for life. Moreover, the teacher's influence in all this was a very vital one, however short the period of influence might be. The First Education Act of 1918 enforced compulsory attendance at school up to the age of fourteen years, and it also underlined the need for a complete reorganization of what today is more specifically referred to as primary education, that is, the education of young children below the age of eleven years.

Officialdom had learned a lot from the less orthodox and more progressive movements already mentioned, but despite all this, many of the school buildings were inadequate and unhygienic. And despite the general desire expressed to make the primary school curriculum free from the pressures of selective examinations at the upper end of the school, in practice their classes were geared largely to preparation for secondary school work at the subject level and to some sort of 'scholarship' examination at 11+.

The White Paper on Education Reconstruction which appeared in 1943, suggested in particular that children of 11+ should not be classified on the basis of a competitive test, but rather upon the assessment of their aptitudes based largely upon school records and intelligence tests. It felt that competitive examinations at the age of eleven were wrong in principle, not only because of the strain to which children were subjected but also because the future schooling and careers of children were largely decided at this one point in time. An age when children's minds were nimble and receptive, when their imagination and curiosity were strong and fertile, they were subjected to a cramping and stultifying curriculum in which considerable emphasis was placed upon 'ways and means or creating the examiners.

The White Paper also stated that there should be separate schools for infants and juniors; and, whilst attendance was not compulsory before the age of five, L.E.A.s must make adequate provision for either nursery schools or, where these were considered expedient, nursery classes in infant schools.

The Butler Education Act of 1944 gave the primary school statutory authority in this country, and it defined primary education in Section 8 as full time education suitable to the requirements of junior pupils'. The Act forced a clear break between primary and post-primary education between primary and secondary education. We are not here secondary education, the developing tripartite system, put ever increasing pressures upon primary schools to act as forcing grounds for grammar schools.

The aims, so clearly expressed in the Hadow Report on The Primary School, were very soon forgotten in the cut-throat competition for grammar school places, and the more enlightened development of primary school methods was somewhat delayed. There was a very real sense in which the firm, separate, statutory establishment of primary and post-primary educational institutions postponed the liberation of primary school methods and the Central Advisory Council for Education was probably not being over-pessimistic when it stated in 1947 that "the gap between a reasonable provision of primary schools and the existing provision was formidable" 'half a century's unremitting efforts will be required before we can hope to have good primary schools for all'. A lot, of course, depends on the connotation of the word 'good' in this context: the verdict of the Plowden Report, twenty years later, was quite simply expressed in these words, 'the primary schools are giving good value for the inadequate amount of money spent on them'. But it made it quite clear that the financial inadequacies has seen severe educational repercussions, as we shall presently see.

In August 1963 the Central Advisory Council for Education was asked by Sir Edward Boyle, then Minister of Education, 'to consider primary education in all its aspects, and the transition to secondary education'. Their report was concluded in October 1966 when it was presented to Anthony Crosland, Secretary of State for Education and Science, and it was published in January 1967. Volume I presented the report, and Volume II the statistics derived from a national survey of 20,00, schools.

The total cost of the report was slightly over 120,000. Part one formed an introduction to the whole investigation and referred in particular to the close association between the home background and academic achievement.

The importance to individual of his family and social background was emphasized, and among question raised in general terms was that of whether 'finding out' had really proved to be better than 'being told' and stressed the enormously wide variability in physical and intellectual maturity amongst children of the same age, particularly during adolescence, and the tendency for children to mature physically earlier than formerly.

It went on to discuss the interaction of heredity and environment, the stages of child development as outlined by Jean Piaget, and the measurement of IQ. It found a correlation between children's IQs and parental occupations-the children of professional parents have an average IQ of 115, emphasized that the child was a total personality, and that its emotional, social and intellectual aspects were closely intertwined.

Some of the implications of this section include the fact that individual variations between children of the same age are so great that any class, however apparently homogeneous, must always be treated as a body of children needing individual and different attention. Until a child is ready to take a particular step forward, it is useless to try and teach him to take it. Since any child grows up intellectually, emotionally, and physically at different rates, his teachers need to know and take account of his 'developmental age' in all three respects.

The child's physique, personality and capacity to learn will develop as a result of continuous interaction between his genetic inheritance and his environment. Whilst the genetic factors are not as yet under our control, the environmental factors largely are Part Two of the report, therefore, suggested the need of a very personal approach to the pupil in the primary school, with a special study of each child's 'readiness' for any particular form of learning or operation; and, at the same time, the provision of a sound, healthy, amenable sort of environment in order to present the best learning situations and conditions.

A minimum programme was suggested for the participation of parents in the education of children a welcome to the school, meetings with teachers, open days, information for parents via brochures about the organization of the school, and reports for parents. There should be a concerted effort that the primary school should be used as fully as possible, out of ordinary school hours, as a sort of community centre. Community schools should be developed in all areas, but particularly in educational priority areas, where there was need for constant communication between parents and teachers if the schools' aims were to be completely understood.

The report emphasized the need for colleges of education to have stronger and more efficient links with such schools and to develop courses to meet the needs of immigrant children in particular.

The Suggestions

There was a very strong suggestion that the training of teachers generally should take more account of those social factors which affect school performance, and also of the structure and functions of the school services. It recommended the initiation of experimental schemes in the joint training of teachers and social workers, and already there are colleges of education which are devising courses for social and youth wing work as well as general welfare work. The report made it very clear indeed that the primary school has a social role in the community, as well as an immediate and individual adductive role.

There should be three years in the infant school and children should not be transferred until the age of 8 years; this would permit both children and teachers to work steadily and without anxiety. The age for admission to a secondary school was suggested as 12+, since this would give a four-year course in the junior or middle school, with a median age range from 8 years 6 months to 12 years 6 months. It should be noted here that the definition of primary education provided by Section 8 of the 1944 Education Act was amended by Section 3 of the 1948 Education Act.

Primary education was there defined as 'full time education for children below 10 years 6 months and children above that age but below 12 years who it is expedient to educate with them'; whilst the 1964 Education Act allowed proposals to be submitted to the Secretary of State for the establishment of new schools with age limits below 10 years 6 months and above 12 years The report emphasized the need for the fullest possible documentation of each pupil before transfer to the secondary school, and it detailed the type of contents that a folder on each child should contain.

The ill effects upon primary education of selection for secondary schools were lessening, and the council recommended that authorities still employing selection procedures should no longer rely on an externally imposed battery of attainment and intelligence tests. Part five dealt with the children in the schools, with curriculum and internal organization. Among a large variety of aims and purposes mooted, and dangers to be avoided, the following aims of primary education were accepted in somewhat general terms, with the provision that generalities have limited value and can quickly become little more than platitudes; it was agreed that a pragmatic approach to the purposes of education was more likely to be fruitful'.

(a) Adaptability-to fit children for the society into which they will grow up, and to train them to be capable of adjusting to their changing environment.

(b) The all-round development of the individual child.

(c) The acquisition of the basic skills necessary in contemporary society.

(d) The religious and moral development of the child.

(e) Physical health, intellectual development, emotional and moral health, aesthetic awareness, a valid perspective, practical and social skills, and personal fulfilment.

(f) Values and attitudes must be mediated to the children. The school is not merely a teaching shop but a living community in which pupils learn primarily to live as children and not as future adults.

The work of Piaget was emphasized as a sound developmental approach to children's learning, and the importance of children's 'cultural' play was made clear. The report went on to consider certain particular aspects of the curriculum, and throughout there was an enlightened approach to both content and method, and a balanced attitude towards heuristic principles.

The council has no doubt that 'children's questions about sex ought to be answered plainly and truthfully whenever they are asked'. It gave validity to the modern, both relaxed and friendly, approach within the primary schools as a much better preparation for life in contemporary society than the old authoritative one.

Whilst accepting "discipline", the council were clear that this connoted neither heavy punishment nor soft and flabby relationships; discipline, it felt, was impaired by such elements as disorder, untidiness and slackness. It could flourish only in an ethos of order and purposefulness, in which boredom had been eliminated. There must be, in all this, a healthy combination of individual, group, and class work and learning. Due consideration was also given to the education of both handicapped and gifted children. The role of the teacher was discussed, and it was argued that teachers must enlarge their endeavours and enlist to a greater extent parents' interest in their children's education. It was extremely important to diagnose the child's needs and potentialities and there would be increasing demands on the knowledge of the teacher, whether literary, scientific or mathematical.

Teachers said the Report 'cannot escape the knowledge that children will catch values and attitudes far more from what teachers do than what they say Unless they are courteous, they cannot expect courtesy from children: when teachers are eager to learn and turn readily to observation and to books, their pupils are likely to do the same'. The report, in effect, asked not only for more teachers but also for better quality ones, It went on to discuss teachers' aides, or trained ancillaries, who might give substantial help to teachers inside and outside the classroom, and who would have equal status with nursery assistants and have comparable training.

The council considered that colleges of education, in general, were too remote from the problems of the school; it recommended a full inquiry into the system of training of teachers, and suggested that there should be more joint appointments to college and school staffs. Further, a network of residential teachers' courses should be developed.

(i) The Department of Education and Science should consider taking steps which would require all independent schools to state on their prospectuses whether the schools were recognized or registered and what this implies. The Department of Education and Science should reconsider the terms "recognized" and "registered" and try to devise more informative ones.

(ii) The Secretary of State's powers to serve Notices of Complaint on independent schools should be based on more stringent criteria. The construction of "objectionable" should be widened to include any conditions, physical or educational, in which children's welfare was not thought to be adequately safeguarded.

(iii) All head teachers of independent schools should be qualified teachers. After a data to be specified, only qualified teachers should be appointed as heads in new schools, or when there is a change of head teacher.

(iv) In-service courses should wherever possible allow some places for teachers from independent schools. The independent schools themselves should take through their professional organizations to "increase the facilities for in-service training for teachers in independent schools."

The primary schools were giving good value for the inadequate amount of money spent on them, and went on to state that teachers were too few in number and too unevenly distributed to do the job adequately.

The first priority was the establishment of education priority areas; the recruitment of teachers' aides would be an essential and immediate source of help to the schools everywhere, the essential improvement of bad primary school buildings must be undertaken as soon as possible wherever they existed; and nursery education must be extended through increased accommodation and staff. Planning should begin on changes in the national dates of entry, and also on the ages of transfer between the different stages of primary education.

The Plowden Report represents one of the most thorough investigations into any area of education ever produced. Perhaps not least of its achievements was its virtual unanimity, which is reflection on the goodwill and singleness of purpose of its twenty-five members over a period of three years of intensive work and study. Out of every 100 women who enter our colleges of education, only 47 will be in the schools after three years of teaching; and after six years of service only 30 will remain. Perhaps the most sanguine way to look at the figures is simply to argue that 70 women out of every 100 so trained have, at least, qualified in a profession to which they may later return, but in any case they have found one way of obtaining higher education, with often minimum of entry qualifications; and as mothers, in the majority of cases, they will have a better understanding of educational problems.

Basic Syllabus

The problems that arose for those charged with managing the curriculum at the school level can be analyzed in three discrete categories: curriculum time allocation, teacher expertise, and resources in primary schools. The first reason for unmanageability is the apparently simple matter of time allocation how much time is needed for each subject and for the whole curriculum. The problem has been commonly represented as the result of the statutory orders and the pint pot of the teaching week. If you are sitting on a national committee inventing or revising the statutory curriculum, it must appear merely a mechanical matter. Reduce the content until the whole curriculum matches, or is slightly less than, the time available.

The second reason concerns the task demands on class teachers attempting to deliver the whole curriculum-most obviously the range and level of subject knowledge required, the pedagogical skills necessary, including differentiation, the sheer detail and number of Statements of Attainment, and techniques necessary for reliable assessment. These have now been seen as unrealistic demands to make upon normal classroom teachers by all save the dismal succession of Ministers of State parading before us to assert that primary teaching, especially at Key Stage 1, is not a particularly demanding job, needing for its successful performance neither graduate knowledge nor long training.

The third reason concerns resources. Primary schools are staffed less favourably than secondary schools, even when the comparison is based on only Key Stage 3, yet the range and demand of their educational activities, and therefore their staffing needs, are almost identical. When Kelly ran a computer model of Stockport's curriculum led staffing, she found that it led to staffing needs that were more-or-less identical across the five to sixteen age range.

The first difficulty faced by teachers was simple; there was too much curriculum for the time available. One reason commonly given for this was that the statutory curriculum had been invented by means of committees of subject enthusiasts who were unable to consider how their subject had to fit into the whole curriculum.

There was some truth in at least the first two of these sentences, but the extent of policy error was substantially greater than Graham and Tytler allow. First, at an early stage Ministers had worked on a broad view that the Education Reform Act would create a curricular framework in which the national prescription should cover substantially less than the whole curriculum.

This was because Religious Education and other important curricular areas such as health education and moral development were conceived of as lying beyond national prescription. The consultative document suggested that in schools where there was 'good practice' the National Curriculum subjects would occupy 70-80 per cent of curriculum time.

Three implications arose for curriculum management from the notional time allocations in this table. The most important is that they represented an error that was to have disastrous effects as the curriculum was implemented. The notional time for English and Mathematics combined, was dramatically lower than was conventionally provided by primary teachers, according to every study that had examined time allocations in the post-war period.

A summary covering much of the relevant research in the last fifteen years showed that 50 per cent of time was typically given to English and Mathematics, excluding their application to other subjects. Empirically, the phenomenon of 50 per cent of time on these two subjects-what we might call the 'basic instinct' in the primary curriculum-is firmly established. Indeed, a study by Meyer et al., which is an examination of official elementary and primary curricula worldwide across this century until the late 1980s, argues that the phenomenon has been a global constant-irrespective of region, political economy or state of development.

The second point refers to the time available for the whole curriculum. It relates to 'evaporated time', a term coined in a professional development programme and used by Campbell and Neill to indicate time technically available for teaching but used for non-cognitive purposes such as supervising children changing for PE, moving them from one location in the school to another, lining up and clearing away.

It is important because it is assumed to be available for teaching, but the studies referred to above that took account of this time by excluding it from teaching time, showed that something between 22 per cent of teaching time evaporates in this way, the amount depending upon the age of the pupils and the physical layout and size of the school and the methodology of time analysis. In general, younger pupils and those in open-plan settings experience more evaporated time.

It occurs in small units of time in any one day, but in Campbell and Neill's research, based on time logs of over 3000 days from over 300 primary teachers, the average evaporated time per week was calculated at nearly two hours per week, equivalent to nearly 10 per cent of the teaching time available and equal to the notional time allocated for at least one of the non-basic subjects, in the National Curriculum.

Long hours spent on repetitive computation exercises do not necessarily mean challenging learning for bright pupils any more than do long hours spent by low-attaining pupils on tasks too difficult for them. Nonetheless, the conclusion from the research findings on time showed no general problem in primary classrooms about the adequacy of time being spent on teaching and learning the two basic subjects. Evidence after the introduction of the National Curriculum suggested that little had changed, with Campbell and Neill showing 51 per cent and 49 per cent of time devoted to the basics. The reasons for this state of affairs are three well-known ones.

First, as Ashton's research showed, drawing on a national sample of 1500 primary teachers in the early 1970s, the highest curricular priority was given to the basic skills of Reading, Oracy, Mathematics and Writing. Art. PE, Music, Sex Education, Science and Technology and a second language were given low priority. A follow-up study by Ashton with a less representative sample at the end of the 1970s, showed, if anything, higher priority placed on Mathematics and formal language competence.

Thus, commitment to the basics has always been at a premium in the professional culture. Second, parents and governors place highest curricular priority on the basics also, as Thomas's investigation of London schools showed, and the Government has required greater teacher accountability to parents and governors. Third, there has been a long tradition, stretching way back before 1988, of formal testing focused on Reading Comprehension and Mathematics, a tradition reinforced by National Curriculum assessment arrangements, though it is now slightly broadened by the inclusion of Science in the core. Such testing washes back into curriculum priorities.

The basic instinct is sustained and reinforced by the workplace culture in primary schools. Thus, it becomes startlingly clear that the National Curriculum in primary schools, introduced by a series of Secretaries of State who had constantly banged on about the need to get back to basics and to raise standards of literacy and numeracy, put in place policy guidance designed to reduce the time typically spent by primary teachers on the basics, and especially on English, where the astonishing reduction of about one-third of existing time was proposed.

With respect to time allocations, the policy guidance outstripped the practice in the schools for liberality and breadth. It offered a fundamentally different concept and ideology of curriculum balance. The guidance given to the working group devising the English curriculum was such as to encourage infant teachers to reduce the time they typically spent teaching children to read and write from about seven hours to little over four hours a week. No wonder there was widespread stress at Key Stage 1 with infant teachers accurately reporting that, against their own professional judgment, they were having to reduce the time on hearing children read in order to fit in everything else.

As if to confirm this interpretation of the general policy, the National Curriculum Council issued guidance on planning the Key Stage 2 curriculum in which three presumably recommended case studies of school planning were provided: two of them (year 6 and 5 classes) suggested that the basics should be planned to occupy 41 per cent and 37.5 per cent of curriculum time respectively.

The Year 5 class plan was developed into a yearly programme in which Mathematics and English occupy 316 out of the 846 hours available, some 37 per cent of curriculum time in their terms. Schools are urged by the NCC to review the exercise, including reviewing whether the time allocations are appropriate.

In this context, it is interesting, but confusing, to see that in the summer Update from the NCC, the curriculum planning in a Coventry primary school was celebrated; it initially used a plan which involved only 40 per cent of time on basics, but after training, it changed to 50 per cent.

There was thus built into the curriculum at national level a four-pronged problem for every primary school: too much planned prescription overall; too much content in the statutory orders for each subject: not enough flexibility to allow for evaporated time; a pretence or assumption that there would be more time available for the non-basics than there was in actuality.

The task demands placed on class teachers by the National Curriculum have been analyzed by Thomas, who shows that in the slimmed down curriculum, teachers at Key Stage 2 had to be familiar with about 500 statements of attainment, detailed and confusingly presented programmes of study, poorly defined cross-curricular themes and religious education.

In addition they would have to possess subjects knowledge in the ten subjects up to about Level 6, or to be able to differentiate the planning, teaching and assessment across at least 4 levels or the curriculum in each subject. To achieve all this they would need to be the curricular school equivalent of Albert Einstein. Marie Curie and Lanford Christie rolled into one. The evidence about subject expertise sometimes takes a narrow view of the concept.

There are serious deficiencies in individual primary teachers' understandings, especially but not exclusively in the science and technology areas. Graduate students training for primary teaching provide no greater reasons for being sanguine, if those studied by Bennett and Carre are typical. They brought with them to their PGCE courses misunderstandings of everyday phenomena, such as the energy in a sledge moving down a hill, the explanations for night and day, and basic arithmetic competencies such as expressing $18 as a percentage of $120.

Bennett and Carre's research used tests in Mathematics, English and Science based on National Curriculum levels 4, 5 and 6, and Assessment of Performance Unit (APU) tests. In some of these latter, the top 20 per cent of primary pupils scored higher than the average of the PGCE students.

Technically, of course, the curriculum demands are placed on the whole school rather than the individual teacher, but in practice for the medium term further, most teachers will remain responsible for teaching most of the curriculum for the pupils in their class. Given the research findings, Alexander, Rose and Woodhead's assertion that 'Teachers must possess the subject knowledge which the statutory orders require' sounds like a plea of desperation.

The Management

A major management issue therefore becomes how the specialist expertise in the whole staff group can be deployed to extend the work of class teachers, with the overarching purpose that, as Richards argued, such deployment should 'support not undermine' the class teacher's role. The previous two problems for manageability apply to all schools irrespective of location, size or other factors. Resource issues affect schools differentially. depending upon funding formulae, school size or pupil characteristics. There is however one key resource issue—the level of surfing. The disadvantage for primary schools of historic staffing allocations has been acknowledged for almost a decade, although the difficulty of translating the acknowledgment into staffing resources has been enormous, particularly since the acknowledgment occurred in a period of public expenditure restraint.

If primary schools are to develop more specialist approaches to the curriculum, if class size should rarely exceed 30, and if teachers are to have some time free of class teaching in the school day; if, in short, the schools are to be enabled to implement the National Curriculum without stress and overload remaining a chronic feature of teachers' work, some improvement in the resourcing of schools is required. Acknowledgment is no longer enough. The funding formula at local level and the approval of schemes of devolved management at national level will need to be based on realistic assessment of the work activities now required of teachers in modern primary schools. Without the development of such national or local policies there will remain constraints on the extent to which the curriculum reform policy can succeed.

For the management of primary schools, the Dearing review's interim report appeared to hold out seductive promises to make the curriculum manageable by slimming it down. In terms of the analysis provided so far, however, it was limited to the issue of time allocations, and the evaluation of Dearing start form this recognition; the review had nothing to say about subject expertise or resourcing perhaps more fundamental problems than time allocation. Even the restricted problem-solving of the final report is a sleight of hand in respect of the 'curricular arithmetic' of time allocations, according to Alexander and Campbell.

Dearing's approach was to allocate 20 per cent of curriculum time for discretionary use by the school and to free two weeks of the school from any curricular prescription, and then to offer guidance on time allocation for the remaining time, viz for 80 per cent of thirty-six weeks. In discussing his own arithmetic, Dearing acknowledged that it was difficult to apply it to primary schools: 'Specific time will have to be set aside for work in English, but the full 30 per cent (KS1) and 25 per cent (KS2) does not have to be found in addition to time given to other subjects.' Perhaps too defensively Dearing added, "This is not sleight of hand; it is a statement of fact based on the realities of teaching expressed by teachers'. His own arithmetic was presented in a table in para, 4.20. With the bracketed figures referring to cross-curricular application, and therefore not counted in the total. Added percentages based on the total annual hours of 612 and 675 for which national prescription was envisaged, and these percentages appeared to reflect the historic practices of teachers, at least at KS1, with about 50 per cent given over to the basics.

There was however an assumed reduction in the proportion given to English at KS2. Alexander and Campbell however provide an alternative arithmetic, based on the overall time, not just the 80 per cent. Their arithmetic is given. Expressed this way, Dearing appears to have rendered almost a quarter of the school curriculum year discretionary, and therefore to have solved the manageability problem. However, as Alexander and Campbell show, there are five reasons why this has not really happened. First, the percentages for English and Mathematics are dramatically lower then previous or current practice, and time will have to be taken from the allegedly discretionary time to restore the basic instinct of 50 per cent time on them. Second, there is no educational or research-based justification for Dearing's assertion that as primary children become older they need less time on English.

The DES Primary Staffing Survey found 27 per cent allocated to English in the junior stage, and while it is obvious that the nature of English at KS1 is different from that at KS2 it is not clear why it should take less time. Nor has it done so in practice. Third, time on science has been reduced from what was previously proposed as necessary and the 10-15 per cent of time that was actually needed for the science curriculum. Fourth, national testing remains focused on the core subjects, pressing in on school management to ensure that teachers give priority to them in time allocation.

Alexander and Campbell calculated that all discretionary time would have to go to the core. Fifth, the time remaining for the other subjects will be inadequate, especially for those that are time consuming, such as PE, Music, Art and Technology. Sixth, without good reason, excessive time has been set aside for RE. As a consequence, the only way the curriculum will become manageable is if it is recognized for what it is, underneath the Dearing rhetoric a return to the elementary curriculum of the basic and RE updated with some Science and Information Technology. But manageability will have been gained at the expense of breadth and balance.

Management implications of the argument is based on two assumptions about the relationship between a national quango and individual schools. National quangos are not good at details, and have little competence in respect of the curriculum organization of individual schools. For example, within the space of nine months the National Curriculum Council and the School Curriculum and Assessment Authority could not even agree on the simple technical matter of how many hours per year should be considered as available for instruction.

Second, as Thomas pointed out, the National Curriculum was established by reference to the best practice in each subject. To the Test' or even good at everything is not common in individual human beings or their institutions so that there was and is a certainty that virtually and schools would, to some degree, fail to meet the statutory requirements. He added that 'Schools in other countries commonly fail to meet the requirements of their national curricula'. If these two assumption are confirmed, the first lessons for school management are that it is in the individual school, not a national agency, that will create a curriculum that can be made to work for the school concerned; and that concern to cover the whole curriculum will have to be tempered by consideration of quality and standards in pupils learning. This latter goal might be more readily arrived at by the school establishing its curricular priorities than by attempting to deliver every statutory prescription equally well.

It was, after all, the quango charged with the inspection of schools that first made clear that coverage had been achieved only at the cost of depth in pupil learning. To restore confidence in their own professional judgment, it may first be necessary for teachers to lose faith in the ability of the national agencies to manage the curriculum implementation process sensibly. Dependency on external forces is as counter productive for the whole school staff as it is for the head and is likely to reduce rather than increase empowerment and accountability. On this basis six possible ways forward may be identified, though each will be contested by some teachers because of the value assumptions it contains.

First, in respect of time allocation, there is the possibility that much more of the teaching of English and Mathematics than currently might be planned, delivered and assessed through their application to other subjects. This is a position advocated for at least fifteen years by HMI, but has been found problematic in practice.

The problem is not helped by the framing of the curriculum in single subjects, nor by the tendency for mathematics and English schemes to be subject-specific. It is a good example of how a staff would have to have confidence as HMI had, that standards in the basics would improve by their being applied to other subjects. Unfortunately, it may be easier for staff in schools where pupils already have high achievement to develop such confidence than for staff where pupils appear to need substantial amounts of time on basic skills. Second, schools might consider the use of homework as part of their overall policy, especially perhaps at KS2. If there is shortage of time for English, part of the solution might be to cease to consider the pupils' curriculum time as synonymous with the timetabled school day.

Successful experience at KS1 with parental partnerships provides exemplars for developing similar approaches at KS2. Some opposition might be raised by those who would see such a systematic approach to homework as increasing the disadvantages of pupils who live in unsupportive families or physical conditions unconducive to doing homework. School based provision for facilities for doing homework, while a contradiction in terms, might go some way to mitigating the difficulties, though at a cost in staff supervision time.

Curriculum Problem

A third solution to the problem of curriculum time might be to extend the school day, week or year. This is clearly sensible for those schools who currently spend less than the minimum expected weekly hours on instruction. It will be opposed on grounds of workload and of inappropriateness in rural areas where pupils have to travel long distances. It might also be surmised that while the current assessment and testing policy remains in place, any extra time would be devoted to the core and thus not release time for the non-core, which is the problem. A solution to teachers' lack of confidence and competence in subject expertise could be remedied by a greatly expanded In-service training programme along lines similar to the DES twenty-day courses. This is obviously true, assuming that the courses are effective, and that their effects are long-lived, an assumption that Bennett and Summer's review of research questions in part.

However, the problem for primary schools is that extensions of in-service training programmes are also extensions of the times when teachers have to be away from school and their class, so that a substantial programme of In-service Training in the school day may have disadvantages for pupil learning where schools do not have access to good quality supply cover.

A second possibility lies in suggestions that schools should deploy their staff in ways that enable their subject expertise to be exploited more effectively to the benefit of the school as a whole, whether as specialists, semi-specialists or as coordinators. Again, within limits, this might offer gains to some schools, especially those with staffing allocations that permit some flexibility of deployment. For most schools, however there is almost no flexibility, and, as school size reduces, the range of subjects in which there is staff expertise also reduces.

A third possibility is that more use should be made of class texts in which the teachers can have confidence that the intellectual content is reliable, freeing them to concentrate more upon planning for how pupils may learn more effectively from the texts. There may be some reluctance in the profession to the purchase of texts for whole classes, since it is seen as at odds with concepts of good practice which stress learning from first hand experience, building on pupils' interests, and practical investigation. While recognizing that purchasing class texts will not solve all problems, perhaps influenced by past images of whole classes sitting reading class text-books at the same pace, each pupil being asked to read aloud with the rest of the class following. The way texts are used with primary classes is obviously an important matter, but the adoption of good quality class texts would be the quickest way of helping class teachers cope with both the cognitive demands of the whole curriculum and the time demands of preparing all learning materials for their pupils.

There is something puritanical in a professional culture which implies that the virtuous teacher is the one who prepares every worksheet herself. One of the few ways that a national quango could make itself useful to teachers would be to issue 'kitemarks' to texts to indicate that the statutory orders were accurately and adequately covered by them and that there were useful assessment activities integrated into them.

This is, politically speaking, quite different from requiring that schools use one particular prescribed text.

Little use can be added about the formulate by which, external, resources are allocated to schools, beyond what has been argued earlier. On the internal allocation of the resources when allocated, one further point needs to be raised. In most primary schools lack of time, especially lack of time in the school day, has been a major obstacle to effective delivery of the curriculum. Yet Campbell and Neill showed that teachers spent about eighteen hours a week teaching, and between five and six hours a week on low level routines, such as mounting displays, supervision, moving pupils round the school, registration, and collecting dinner money, etc. Where teacher had more time with a non-teaching assistant, they tended to spend more, not less time on such routines, probably because of the 'collaborative cultures' operating in them.

Yet there is something unsettling about the picture of teachers naming lack of time as the main obstacle to achieving the cognitive objectives of the curriculum while spending so much time on non-cognitive routines. Given that teacher time is the most valuable and most expensive resource available to a school, it is worth the management of the school exploring the advantages of re-thinking the use of time of all adults on the staff of the school, to see whether the non-teaching assistants' time might be used imaginatively to free up teachers' time. Professional groups validate their professional claim by reference to 'expert' knowledge, supposedly hard-won and rigorously tested, but few people are naive enough to believe that in a job as complex as teaching such formal training provides the sole resource for subsequent professional thought and action.

Experience plays a substantial part. 'On the job', teachers develop skills and insights through constant interaction with children; they come to recognize patterns, commonalities and recurrences in behaviours, situations and problems and thereby develop habits of diagnosis and response whose practical effectiveness they can confidently demonstrate. Similarly, to an extent perhaps not sufficiently recognized, teachers draw on their pre-training experience; for, uniquely among professionals, they are engaged in a process with which they have already been involved, continuously and unremittingly, since the age of five or earlier.

Their teacher training course is but a brief part of this total, cumulative educational experience and the latter, as much as the specifics of the one to four year training course, shapes the view of the educational process and its purposes within which they operate as teachers. It is a commonplace that many young teachers teach as they were taught in school rather than as they were urged to teach in college. Significantly too, teachers themselves display ambivalent attitudes towards initial training.

In the context of debate and negotiation about salary and status the teacher is a 'trained professional' in possession of expertise denied to all but those who submit themselves to the rigours of Certificate, B.Ed, or PGCE. But in everyday discourse, good teachers are 'born, not made' and that same expert knowledge may be dismissed as 'irrelevant' theory.

The truth is that it is empirically impossible to isolate initial training from earlier, contemporaneous or subsequent experience for the purposes of demonstrating its precise impact on the way a teacher performs in the classroom. It seems sensible to assume that it does have an impact, but to avoid the extremes of the grandiose strategic claim prepared for negotiation with Burnham on the one hand, and the dismissiveness of teacher folklore and Staffroom conventional wisdom on the other.

Instead, two hypotheses can be supported. One is that by incorporating in its emphasis on certain sorts of knowledge and skill particular views of the teaching role, the nature and needs of young children, the initial training course tends to facilitate some lines of subsequent professional development and to discourage others. Second, initial training influences subsequent development as much by what it omits or does badly as by what it treats positively; or, to use for the sake of convenience some mild jargaon, a course may 'de-skill' as well as 'skill'.

This latter point is particularly opposite in the present context, given that we have seen how primary ideology may relate to professional insecurity The ideology, it will be recalled, is most strongly focused and most forcibly expressed in relation to those aspects of primary teaching where empirical study shows the greatest weakness.

Therefore it is not firm evidence of behavioural causality—element *X* in initial training produces action *Y* in the classroom—so much as a succession of positive and negative correspondences between training and subsequent practice which are sufficiently pervasive and exact as to leave little doubt about a causal relationship of some sort, albeit diluted by the power of experience, circumstance and contingency, and mediated through each individual's unique combination of personality, intellect and worldview.

To provide a framework for the analysis which follows it is necessary at this point to give a brief resume of the overall structures and contexts of courses. There are two main routes into primary teaching, the four year B.Ed and the one year PGCE. The former is a post 'A' level undergraduate course and the latter, self-evidently, is taken by graduates in subjects which could equally well lead to other careers.

Deferred student choice and flexibility were major aspirations; this was the era of the 'container revolution', of courses which students put together from a wide selection of units and modules, and which often meant that professional study and work in schools were deferred until the second or even the third of four years. By the late 1970s, deferred choice, consecutive training and modularity were running into the logistical problems attendant upon contraction, for such courses had to be large to be viable. There were other criticisms chiefly revolving round the continued lack of sufficient professional emphasis, the perceived divorce of theory and practice and the split between subject and professional study.

A large number of institutions had transferred from university to CNAA validation and alternative notions of 'degree worthiness' had begun to be explored. Mark III B.Eds lasted the full four years, were usually honours only, and included serious attempts to put professional concerns at the centre of the course and at last to break down the barrier between subject and professional study. But by that time, during the early 1980s, there were countervailing pressures.

Population Education

The population explosion is the most potent cause of the crisis which the world is facing. This explosion has come about through a natural and automatic process, but it has been implicit in its very far-reaching consequences. The increase in material resources and every individual's right to live have created an upheaval in the world of education.

When we forget the international arena, and think of this problem in the context of India, we find the situation even more pitiable and disheartening. In every five year period, the addition to our population is more than the existing population of England, and if this situation continues, there can be no reason to doubt that problem of foodgrains will assume truly alarming proportions.

Education of Masses

The notion of remaining constantly aware of the increase in population and its future consequences arose in 1960. Efforts were then made to define and clarify the concept to relate it to education. Stressing the importance of this, Philip M. Hauser remarked that "It is about time for twentieth century school curricula to comprehend and understand twentieth century demographic findings in the context of their 20th century implications."

In India, it was Prof. Sloan Wayland of Columbia University, who gave concrete shape to the notion of population education. According to him, irrespective of the nomenclature, we are concerned with the fact that the public policy on family planning, nation and family, the desirability of family planning, etc., should be comprehended under the counselling system in formal education. At the same time, studies should be conducted into the economic and social development of education, size of the family, and the dynamism of the qualities of a nuclear family. Hence, it is necessary to develop a special method of education at the school level under the linguistic provisions in a particular society.

Burleson has conceived of population education as population awareness. In his view, the increase in population brings about an increase in the already increasing expenditure on education. Education can modify the problem by arousing a population awareness among teachers and students. Population education is the awareness of knowledge relating to population. It has two objectives(1) Educationists and others concerned with them should understand the importance of population, the disadvantages of its nature. (2) Teachers and students should understand the nature of their own tendencies.

Mass Education—Aims: Population education is essential for the reconstruction or restructuring of our modern, rapidly changing society. The NCERT has set up a special wing entitled Population Education. It has set out the following objectives of population education:

1. Orientation of the school teachers towards preparing training units on which students will obtain information about the increasing population and the problems created by it and also take interest in finding solution to the problem.
2. Conducting experiments in extra-curricular courses in selected schools, and implementing similar experiments on a larger scale if successful.
3. Preparation of suitable teaching material for population education in schools.
4. Making provisions for research and study concerning population education in schools and making the programme more effective.
5. Evaluating the productiveness of students covered by the programme and developing the necessary skills.

It is evident from these objectives that in the programme of population education, it is necessary to keep in mind the ecological complex. According to Duncan, Ecological complexes are built up out of changes in the environment, changes in the structure of population measures for fighting the problem of population and the mutuality of factors, and an account of these complexes amounts to population education.

In the same way, Chauls has expressed the following opinion on population education. He says that population education should comprehend the culture of the students, the population situation of their society, their own views about the existing situation, their logical, reasoned and organized ideas on the situation of the population and its effects.

The UNESCO workshop defined population education in the following terms "Population education is our educational programme which provides for a study of the population situation in family, community, nation and world with the purpose of developing in the students rational and responsible attitudes and behaviour towards coping with the situation."

Mass Education—A Need: It is only natural to ask why we should have population education. The answer is very obvious. Today, population is increasing at such an alarming rate that material resources have completely failed to keep pace with it. There is a complete imbalance between material resources (food, clothing, housing and the size of the population. The existing situation naturally encourages exploitation and misery, thus leading to increasing social injustice.

In order to face and overcome these conditions, educationists and demographers have come to feel that the problem must be given the form of a revolution in ideas. This implies that the problem of population must be given the form of a revolution in ideas. This implies that the problem of population must be integrated with education.

In India, the task of educating people about the problems of population is being done by the governmental agency, NCERT, and the informal agencies-Family Planning Association, All India Federation of Education Association, etc. These programmes are directed at: (1) schools, colleges and other educational institutions, (2) those who have left school or have not received any education, (3) those imparting training to teachers, teachers themselves and those who impart education through training, counselling and guidance.

Indian Mass Education

In India, the concept of progress means industrialization, exploitation of resources, improvement in the standards of living through material progress, and acceptance of education as the medium of the foregoing. Population is the focal point of the fulfilment of these objectives. The cooperation of all possible agencies is essential for understanding the problems likely to arise in the future and for promoting this programme of population education.

Programme for Mass Education: The Family Planning Association of India has prepared the following for population education:

Growth of Logic

1. Family and the individual focal points of population education at these levels, determination of scope and syllabus.
2. Nation
3. The World

The following elements will be comprehended under these objectives:

Population, Factors and Results: (Rates of birth, death, life and increase).

Human, Situation and Environment: (Population, reduction in consumption and production).

Social, Economic and Development Aspects: Production, national production, health, education, housing employment.

Family Life and the Individual Aspect: (Family and social institutions, education for family life, sex education, position of women).

Fundamental Values and Qualities of Life: Objectives of society, techniques, a consumer's society, utilization of resources.

These programmes will be implemented through studies, discourses, regional schemes and research.

Group: an Outline

1. The objectives outlined above will be achieved with the help of the ministries of education and health and other ministries, administrators; educationists, principals and teachers.
2. Arrangements will be made for discourses, contact with the people, publication, guidance cells, training syllabi, etc.

Plans Ahead

(Syllabi, extra-curricular activities, etc., in village/city).

1. This programme will be implemented through the medium of schools, colleges, social education classes, adult education classes and classes for the employed.
2. For this purpose, arrangements for reading class units, context books, hand-books, audiovisual material, information centres and library facilities will be made.

Active Research and Study (Village/City)

1. Studies into marriages in villages and cities, sex, family life, population problem, awareness of the population problem and the attitudes towards it.
2. A survey of guardians of school-going children for an understanding of begetting of children, sex, family life, population awareness and study of problem.
3. A study of the knowledge of teachers with a view to introducing population awareness, marriage, family life, sex relations, begetting of progeny, etc., into the syllabus.
4. A study of the leaders of education in the contexts outlined above.
5. Active research into teaching methods and techniques, pertaining to sex, family planning, population education, problems, etc.

For all these programmes, close contacts will be established with educational research institutions, teachers' training institutions, social welfare institutions and voluntary agencies so as to impart speed to the programme.

At present, the Population Education Department has taken the following steps under the Fore mentioned programme:

(a) preparation of context books, hand-books and publications,

(b) preparation of teaching material,

(c) publication of a monthly magazine,

(d) establishment of libraries and information centres,

(e) issue of teaching materials to schools at low prices, and

(f) preparation of kits for population education.

At present, all of us are being swept onwards by the inexorable flow of an ever-increasing population, but we must try to escape from this flood and also forestall it for the sake of our own existence. Today, the crowds in universities are growing larger, colleges lack even an inch of spare space. Our population annually increases by 13 millions, which is equal to the entire population of Australia. In the next twenty-five years, our population will double itself. In order to solve the problem of the future, we should adopt the following programmes:

1. Departments of education should make arrangements for in-service training, research and programme implementation.
2. Various departments of universities should conduct research and prepare desirable literature.
3. Departments of science should conduct factual experiments into the evil consequences of rise in population.
4. Various programmes of population education should be implemented through seminars, discourses, exhibitions, etc.
5. This programme should be made a part of education at every level.
6. The United Nations Fund for Population Studies has been set up at Bombay with the cooperation of the World Health Organization and the United Nations for the purpose of combating the problem of education at the international level.

It is hoped that through the implementation of this programme, the increasing population will be brought under check, and our future generation will be freed from the spectre of a gigantic problem.

METHODS OF TEACHING

In this unit, you will get acquainted with different method of teaching, including traditional and modern methods such as Lecture Method, Project Method, Seminar Method, Discussion Method and Demonstration Method. An attempt has been made in this unit, to discuss the need for using different methods, the characteristics and uses of these methods along with their limitations. Lastly, integration of different methods of teaching has been discussed in the unit.

AIMS AND TARGETS

On completion of the unit, you can:

(i) Know the necessity for using various methods in teaching

(ii) Get the meaning of various methods

(iii) Acquaint yourself with the nature and characteristics of the selected methods of teaching

(iv) Identify the types and advantages and requisites for these methods of teaching

(v) State the limitations of these methods

(vi) See whether integration is possible between the methods.

VARIOUS TECHNIQUES

According to the *Challenge of Education* (1985) the teaching practices in our universities and colleges of education continue to be the same as in forties, and methodologies in the teaching-learning process should lay emphasis on learning and developing analytical, critical and conceptual abilities rather than on memorization and reproduction. The National Policy on Education (NPE, 1986, p. 14) has aptly enunciated that higher education provides people with an opportunity to reflect on the critical, social, economic, cultural, moral and spiritual issues facing humanity. Developing such reflective, critical and analytical power should be the chief general objective of higher education that contributes to national development through disseminating of specialized knowledge and spirit. This will actually ensure the effectiveness of higher education.

Higher education is to realize its objectives through suitable methods and techniques. These are mostly reflected in the curriculation and syllabus which are transacted through various teaching-learning activities. The Report of Secondary Education Commission (1965, p. 85) has aptly observed, "But every teacher and educationist of experience knows that even the best curriculum and the most perfect syllabus remain dead unless quickened into the life by the right methods of teaching and the right kind of teachers."

A method is not merely a device adopted for communicating certain items of information to students. It links the teacher and his pupil into an organic relationship with the constant mutual interaction. It motivates and reacts not only in the mind of the students, but also on their entire personality, their work and judgement, their intellectual and emotional equipment, their attitude and values. Good methods which are psychologically and socially sound may raize the whole quality of their life and bad methods may debase it. Good methods of teaching should aim at realizing all the objectives, cognitive, cognitive and affective, besides the various specific objectives.

Teachers need be "Skilled Artists." An American Teacher Lowman (1987, Preface) has cogently stated, "Excellent teaching captivates and stimulates students imagination with exciting ideas and rational discourses. Students satisfaction as well as motivation are stressed important criteria for successful teaching." Thus successful teaching and student satisfaction are strongly correlated and teaching and learning are not thought of as cold and technological, but warm, exciting and personal. Rather college teaching should be personal and an incisive enterprise involving human beings and their personalities.

It should not be compared to mechanical cause and effect relationship. Modern electronic media and materials like radio, television, films and computers have revolutionized the methods of teaching by making them innovative, interesting and successful. By imaginative use of audiovisual aids, the methodology becomes more effective and efficient. Moreover, multimedia package and multi-disciplinary approaches can make the teaching-learning process more productive, cost effective and time-effective.

There should be adequate scope for students' participation, interaction and activities. Wise and experienced teachers know how to balance the individualized and group methods. Good methods must enable students to acquire the qualities of leadership, initiative, cooperation, discipline, etc., and should develop problem-solving ability, capacity of personal achievement and independent work, besides team/group activities.

Many a Method

Methods of teaching vary according to the size of learners groups. For instance, lecture or seminar method is followed effectively in a big class of 40 to 50 or above and role-playing or brainstorming techniques can be adopted with profit in a small group of 15-20. There are some age old methods like lecture, discussion etc., which are followed invariably in most of the classrooms, particularly at the stage of higher education.

In a class there is scope for interaction, collective perception, emotional cohesiveness, shared aims, and so on which contribute to the effectiveness of group teaching in more than one way. But learning according to individual capacity is possible only in individual teaching like programmed learning, or assignment or tutorials. But group discussion, simulation exercises, buzz group techniques, etc., are efficiently adopted in small groups. Activity Method, Heuristic Method, Project Method etc., can promote practical skills and abilities. Hence, variety and multiplicity of methods should be encouraged in classroom practices.

Through Lectures: Lecture method is generally followed in the colleges and Departments of Universities. It is the most commonly and traditionally used method through ages at the higher education stage.

It is mostly a teacher-centred and expository method involving one way communication and transmitting good quantum of knowledge or subject matter to a large number of individuals. Lecture is also found to be a feasible method of teaching in higher classes to the students who are motivated and required to achieve the desired learning objectives. The advantages and limitations of this method may be discussed here for providing necessary insight and guidance to teachers.

The Features

The lecture method has the following characteristics which have to be capitalized for better outcomes.

(i) *Imparting Good Amount of Content Knowledge*: Since the lecture method is mostly one way communication process and meant for adult learners, a big quantum of content knowledge can be transmitted and many teaching points can be covered through this. Thus economy of time and energy is ensured in this method.

(ii) *Providing Better Opportunity for Clarification of Concepts*: While teaching through the lecture method, a teacher knows the background and reception of the students from the attention and interests shown by them. He can assume and ascertain to what extent they have been able to appreciate and understand. Accordingly, he can clarify the difficult points or repeat the point not got by students properly. Thus he can carry the class with him getting proper feedback.

(iii) *Vitalizing Dry and Dead Ideas*: Spoken words are more effective than printed ones. In a lecture a teacher not only speaks but also changes tone, gestures, postures and facial expressions. He can thus use various devices for bringing in life, blood, colour, vivacity and vividness to the dead, dry and dreary material.

(iv) *Making Presentation more Psychological than Logical*: A lecture can present the subject matter according to psychological and educational principles and not merely logically as is done in writing textual material. It, therefore, becomes emotionally appealing and psychologically sound.

(v) *Ensuring Flexibility and Adaptability*: The lecture method can ensure adequate flexibility according to the needs, ability, interests and previous knowledge of the pupils. A lecture is not just a straight jacket readymade method or material. It can be adjusted or adapted, suiting to the requirements and capability of students for whom it is intended.

Limitations: The lecture method has the following limitations which should be taken into account for improving the same.

(i) *Lack of Feedback:* Since the lecture method is a one-way communication. The lecturer proceeds to deliver a speech without getting or without caring to get the reaction from the audience. This delimits the effectiveness of a lecture.

(ii) *Want of Active Participation of Audience:* Learning is an active process. But in the lecture method, students become passive audience without getting any scope for interaction and participation. This does not provide adequate environment for learning.

(iii) *Developing Dry Monotony:* Since the lecture method does not wait for interaction or discussion with the students, it develops deadening monopoly in the class. But very invigorating speeches make the class interested and involved in the process.

(iv) *Substituting the Teacher Only:* Lectures are generally presented as various chapters of a text-book. Heavy dose of content knowledge is imparted without giving scope for creating interest and curiosity among the students.

Uses of Lecture Method: As discussed earlier, the lecture method is generally used in the higher classes where students are of higher age-group, adequately knowledgeable and properly motivated to listen to lectures attentively and benefit from the knowledge packed exposition of teachers who are mostly subject experts. However, in order to make lectures effective, some supporting and supplementary inputs are given by good teachers. These kinds of lectures are discussed as follows:

Although there are several limitations to a lecture, it has been accepted as a popular method of teaching particularly at the stage of higher education. It has proved its effectiveness for transmitting a good quantum of knowledge at a time and for covering a vast area of subject matter. With a view to overcoming the drawback, however, lectures occasionally are modified and enriched or supported with different features and materials which help in enhancing the learning experiences of students. These modified forms of lectures are, for example, lecture-cum-demonstration, illustrated lecture, lecture cum buzz sessions and lecture cum discussion. These are discussed below:

Lecture-cum-Demonstration: A lecture is sometimes supported and enriched by demonstration which provides scope for students to observe and understand certain object or system in action and operation. Demonstration enables them to learn skills and get concepts clarified.

The lecture explains the various parts of the material and different steps of an operation showing the actual objects of relevant audio-visual aids. Such lecture-cum-demonstration method is found quite useful for teaching science, language and different skill subjects involving practical activities.

Illustrated Lecture: Various types of illustrations may be used by a lecturer in course of his presentation. These illustrations may be projected ones like slides, film strips, transparencies etc., and non-projected ones like models, charts, maps, pictures, diagrams and even blackboard writing. A lecturer carefully selects or prepares various AV aids to show and explain different concepts, ideas and objects in the classroom. The illustrations must be related to the topics and properly sequenced and planned so that these can be used in right time and at the right place. Otherwise instead of helping, these may hamper the acquisition of learning experiences.

Lecture cum Buzz Session: A topic is presented in a lecture at first and about ten to fifteen minutes before it is concluded, the entire class is divided into some groups of five to ten students for discussing and finding solutions to certain problems involved to give practical suggestions for improving the existing condition. Such discussions in small groups are called buzz sessions which may last for a few minutes, generally for five minutes. Then the group leaders present their views or findings in the class and the lecturer tries to moderate and conclude their observations.

Lecture cum Discussion: Since a lecture is a one-way communication, attempt is made to discuss some salient points with students in order to involve them and elicit their reactions. Such discussions may be held intermittently or at any stage of the lecture according to the need and convenience.

In this process questions are asked by the teacher or the students and the method of interaction, the lecture, is able to clarify some important points through discussions and lecture is modified after getting feedback from the students. Thus, the rigid structure of one-way communication is broken and the subject matter is made meaningful through introduction of adequate freedom flexibility and feedback.

How to Make Lecture Effective?: With a view to making the lecture method more effective, the teachers should consider the following guidelines meant for necessary activities at three distinctive phases *i.e.,* (i) Preparation (ii) Presentation and (iii) Evaluation.

Preparation

a. The first step in the process is to define the objectives in clear and specific terms. The lecturer should be aware of the purposes for which he is going to teach.

b. The lecturer should be clear about nature of the audience or the students, their background, needs, interests, and so on. This will help him to plan his lesson accordingly.

c. He should know the duration of the period during which his lecture will be delivered. This will enable him to decide the quantum of content to be covered during that period.

d. The lecturer should prepare sufficient subject matter or teaching points for dealing with the students. It is better to collect more material than is usually required for teaching a class in a particular period, so that he may not run short of content before the lapse of time.

e. It is advisable to develop a synopsis of the lecture giving the important teaching points at various steps along with a list of reference materials. This will save the teacher from pointless digressions and save students from undue distractions. Thus, it can save time and energy of the teacher and the taught.

f. The lesson of the lecture should be planned in a sequential manner which will facilitate logical presentation of facts starting from known to unknown and from concrete to abstract.

g. Relevant audio-visual aids can be thought of while planning and adequate preparation for their use in right time and place be made earlier to presentation.

Presentation

a. The lecture should create curiosity and motivation among students from the very beginning and should continue the same throughout the class. That is the introduction should be interesting as well as motivating, and similar atmosphere may be sustained in the class.

b. Various techniques of creating interest and motivation should be utilized according to the proficiency of the teacher. Some of these examples are narrating illustrative stories, anecdotes, contemporary incidents, newspaper items of relevance, visual presentations, highlight of the previous lecture etc.

c. There must be variation in the style of presentation like voice modulation, change in speed of delivery, pausing for emphasis or emotion and combining auditory with visual presentation. A well modulated voice and combination of various techniques are desirable.

d. Unnecessary movements, gestures or postures which are named as mannerism should be avoided as far as possible during the lecture. Some teachers, for example, move up and down in front of the class or unnecessarily make some gestures or use some words more frequently.

e. Blackboard writing as an art needs special skills. Important points—names, year and drawings should find place on the blackboard during presentation. A lecturer should however not show his back to the class longer than is necessary. The use of overhead projector at present has reduced this difficulty.

f. The lecturer should distribute his attention throughout the classroom That is, he should look at various places and individuals in the class, not at any place or anybody particularly. He should also convey thanks for encouragement and reinforce responses by a smile or similar non-verbal techniques.

g. Too many facts and figures should be avoided in the lecture which lead to boredom or drudgery. The lecturer should know that there is explosion of knowledge of course, but the sources of knowledge also are so many, starting from converzation among friends and peers to radio and television programmes.

Assessment of Lectures

a. The lecturer should always try to get feedback to his lecture, so that he can improve upon the methods and techniques followed in the same.

b. He can get readymade feedback from the interest evinced and attention paid to his presentation by the students or audience. The faces in front of him can reflect the same like living mirrors.

c. Besides such informal methods of evaluation, the teacher can develop a proforma or a small questionnaire for formal evaluation by collecting views or reaction of the students on the lecture delivered in the class.

d. The sole objective of this evaluation is not to test the students but to ascertain the effectiveness of the lecture and to improve the learning experiences of students. The proforma and questionnaire should contain specific items and rating scales indicating the degree of response.

e. Such evaluation can be done in the beginning or in the middle to know students' entry behaviour or status of their knowledge on the topic. But it is usually done at the end of a lecture to assess its effectiveness and locate the level of understanding and difficult concepts or ideas of students.

f. A colleague can be requested to assess the effectiveness of a lecture with the help of a checklist or proforma. The teacher can also use a self-evaluation proforma or checklist to ascertain such effectiveness of his own lecture.

g. Like in micro-teaching, recording of a lecture can be done with the help of a tape recorder or video recorder so that it can be played back and the lecture can be evaluated on the desired aspects or points.

By Projects: The Project method is a dynamic and democratic approach to teaching, particularly suitable to the stage of higher education.

This method centres round a project which is a practical unit of activity having educational implications and aims at achieving not only knowledge, but also understanding, application and skills. It involves investigation, documentation and solution of problems. This is a student-centred method and planned by the student with the help of the teacher and conducted in a natural and real life situation.

Meaning and Characteristics: An educational project is defined by Stevenson as "a problematic act carried to completion in its natural setting." According to Kilpatrick "A project is a whole-hearted purposeful activity proceeding in a social environment." It has been defined by Good (1973) as "a significant practical unit of activity having educational value and aimed at one or more definite goals of understanding, involves investigation and solution of problems" and is carried to completion by pupils and teachers in a natural real life, manner.

The characteristics of the project method are as follows:

a. The project method aims at teaching the students to get the best out of life and to prepare them for life. It is not meant merely for the future living, but also as a part of the present living.
b. This method is an attempt to utilize experiences as the truest and best lesson which cannot be forgotten.
c. It brings out the best of the potentiality in the student and provides opportunities for self-expression.
d. This method enables the learners to translate theories into practices. It not only solves problems, but also the activity is actually carried to completion.
e. In this method the activity chosen becomes the core and all learning experiences become incidental. The curriculum is reset and all barriers of subject matter are broken in organization of the project.
f. This method provides opportunities of working out purposeful projects of any character according to learners taste and interest *viz.*, presenting a play or producing a class magazine. It may increase technical knowledge or motor skills.
g. Although a project is undertaken with all sincerity and seriousness, a relaxed atmosphere prevails through this method. In spite of hard work, a project gives more satisfaction to the learners.

h. In the project method, the workshop techniques are followed through which learners acquire more learning experiences according to the principle of "learning through doing."

i. A project is usually organized in a life-like situation which provides actual and meaningful experiences to the student like "that of an apprentice learning his trade" as remarked by Dewey.

j. The project method naturally implies group activity which means: cooperation, fellow feeling, sense of responsibility, mutual sharing and respect for others.

Use of the Project Method

a. The method follows the psychological principles of learning. For example, the law of readiness, the law of exercise and the law of effect are very well taken care of in organizing a project and providing learning experiences through it.

b. It gives ample freedom to the learners which is so valuable for self-direction, self-learning and self-satisfaction. In absence of external direction and imposition, the learners plan, implement, experiment, explore and learn according to their interest and ability.

c. It enables pupils to derive social values like cooperativeness, sharing responsibility, dignity of labour, respect for the individual etc., which are possible usually in a project work.

d. It provides training in citizenship which is very essential for success of democracy. Since the students select their project, plan the same, distribute responsibility among themselves and organize with understanding and cooperative spirit, they are practically trained in citizenship.

e. It is generally a problem solving activity in which pupils are made active, responsive, involved, motivated and responsible. Students try to sort out a particular problem in a cooperative manner. They get practical experience as well as insight into the solution of a problem.

f. This method gives a sense of reality as a consequence of its practical and social implications. In this method school activity is related to social needs and situations which make students' learning experiences more realistic and relevant to their life.

g. It gives a feeling of satisfaction of completing the whole task by sharing a part of it. A project is divided into various tasks and series of activities are distributed among the students according to their interest and ability. But as the project is completed, the individual students feel the satisfaction of fulfilling their objective and completing the whole activity.

h. It is economical and efficient as learners are made interested and motivated in learning through participation and sharing in the project work. In an atmosphere of spontaneity and freedom, they learn more within the short time. Further, whatever is learnt by them is retained.

i. It gives dignity of labour in particular and dignity of the individual, in general as the students are required to work personally in completing their assignments of various kinds small or big, manual or mental. That is why, this method is more democratic and dynamic than any other method.

j. This method is particularly successful and effective in teaching of science, geography, language, art and craft in which students are required to do some practical work.

Limitations of the Method

a. In the project method, systematic learning may not take place. Actual learning is apt to be incidental and accidental as teaching is not possible in an organized manner and many things are left to the interest and initiatives of students.

b. Progress of instruction may not be up to the mark or as per schedule, as the students are likely to waste more time in planning and organizing activities. That is why, the course cannot be covered in time and students may experience difficulty in the formal examinations.

c. In this method, communication plays a minor role. Emphasis is laid on activities. In this age of knowledge and information explosion, unless adequate facts and figures are given in the shortest possible time, students will face problems in competition and evaluation.

d. This method is time consuming and cost-intensive as the project for proper organization must call for more materials, more accommodation and more facilities. All students are not adequately motivated and involved and teachers cannot control their progress and activities.

e. This method may not be suitable to the bright students who need speedy progress and efficient acquisition of knowledge and skills. That is why, they may lose interest and feel bored with the unsystematic and time consuming process.

f. This method is likely to leave gaps in the pupils' knowledge as learning does not follow a logical and systematic arrangement. The teachers are required to keep note of these gaps and fill up the same in time.

g. This method needs more correlation of topics and objectives in order to make learning effective. But such correlation is not always possible, particularly in academic subjects.

h. This method should be followed occasionally and as sparingly as possible since progress cannot be made adequately as per schedule.

i. In this method the teachers' role is quite significant and proper guidance as well as directions are to be provided by him. For this resourcefulness, training and experience of teachers are essential. Otherwise, the teaching-learning process is apt to be haphazard and superfluous.

Through Seminars: The English author Francis Bacon rightly said long ago, "Reading make the full man, writing the exact man and conference the ready man." That is the skills of reading, writing and speaking are essential for development of the personality. These skills are well combined and well developed through the Seminar Method.

The term "Seminar" generally refers to a structured group discussion that may precede or follow a formal lecture. It may be either in the form of an essay or a paper presentation. It may be done by experts or academicians at a seminar or conference organized by an institution or an association or by individual students in a class or group of peers as a part of the source of work. In any case, the audience critically examine the paper and discuss the content or findings of the paper.

They make queries -for clarification or elucidation on any point and the writer of the paper is required to clarify these queries with further facts and figures. The special nature and the professional setting distinguish the seminar from group discussion. The seminar method is very suitable for higher education or professional discussion when the level of attainment of the group is relatively high and the nature of discussion is expected to be analytical and technical.

Characteristics of the Seminar Method

i. The seminar method is stimulating and motivating.

ii. It is an effective mode of testing the students' understanding and knowledge in the subject or the topic.

iii. It evaluates their skills in arranging, formulating and presenting facts in a systematic manner.

iv. It develops the sense of responsibility and cooperation as well as the powers of self-reliance and self-confidence.

v. It is an advanced means of socialization and instruction involving students' participation, preparation and interaction.

vi. It breaks the monotony of traditional teaching and promotes academic excellence.

vii. It stimulates and tests the students power of comprehension and understanding.

viii. Seminar is mostly subject oriented and deals in depth a particular topic and issue at hand.

ix. The presenter or the teacher is tested in his skill of arranging ideas in a sequence and sustained manner.

x. Seminar promotes the power of delving deep into the matter and deriving principal from the context.

xi. Questioning power is developed through participation in this process of intellectual model.

xii. Seminar develops self-reliance, self-confidence, sense of cooperation and responsibility.

xiii. It is an advanced technique of socialization and serves the very useful purpose of creating interest in intellectual pursuits.

Uses of the Seminar: The teacher concerned of the college or department should take initiative and acquaint the students with the objectives of the seminar. In case of a professional organization or association the head or chairman gives an idea about the purpose of the seminar and a backdrop of relevant activities or progress made so far. The students and participants should be made aware of the potentialities of the seminar and motivate them to actively participate in the same.

The student or scholar who is required to present his paper has to prepare himself in all respects. He has to search and research the relevant material and develop the paper which needs proper sequencing of facts and figures and effective reporting. The teacher may give guidance in locating literature or references and preparing the paper in an objective as well as scientific manner. He may suggest the audio-visual aids to be used for presenting the paper effectively.

A seminar can be held for two-three hours, and about 30-45 minutes may be devoted to presentation of the paper. Participants should also be encouraged to seek clarification or elucidation on various aspects of the paper. Thus discussion may take one or two hours giving adequate time for interaction according to the degree of interest shown by the students or participants. Necessary facilities should be provided for the use of various projected and non-projected materials.

Like other intellectual and academic activities, seminars may be evaluated formally or informally. The presenters of papers should be able to get adequate feedback for improving their paper and removing the defects or deficiencies therein. An observation schedule can be developed for getting formal feedback and objective assessment of the paper and participation of the students or audience. The data collected may be analyzed and interpreted for further discussion or guidance of the presenters and teachers concerned with the programme.

STYLE OF DISCUSSION

It is said that "two heads are better than one." When a number of heads combine to solve a problem, results become wonderful. Discussion Method makes use of these tests particularly in teaching

Social Sciences. An issue or a problem in which there is a difference of opinion, becomes a fit topic for discussion method of teaching.

In this method ideas are initiated, expressed and exchanged, and the factual basis is traced out. The participants are engaged in interaction, interpretation and interpolation of facts. A kind of "Competitive Cooperation" takes place. Agreement is the declared purpose of such discussion. If it fails to achieve an agreement at all, there is value in discussion for clarifying the concepts and widening the horizons of knowledge and understanding the issue in question.

Characteristics: Discussion as a method of teaching may have the following purpose.

a. Laying plans for new work.

b. Presenting facts and figures from various angles.

c. Sharing and exchanging information and data.

d. Respecting various points of view.

e. Clarifying ideas and concepts.

f. Inspiring interest.

g. Taking decisions in the matter.

h. Evaluating the progress from time to time.

According to some characteristics, discussion takes different forms *viz.*, classroom discussion, debate, symposium, panel discussion and round table discussion. In the classroom discussion the teacher initiates presentation of a topic or issue giving the background and then elicits points of view and ideas from the students. In the debate usually a group of students argue in favour of, and another group against the issue or topic in question. In the symposium, different specialists or speakers make presentations dealing with the topic from different perspectives. Such presentations may be written. A panel discussion raises issues, provides facts and stimulates interests in a selected topic. A panel of experts or speakers interact with each other on various aspects. In a round table conference, similarly, arguments are made from two opposing groups to seek solution to a current problem.

Some other characteristics are as follows:

i. This method can be used both for junior and senior age-groups.
ii. This method enables students to learn together, make suggestions, provide facts, share responsibility and comprehend the topic.
iii. It clarifies the issue and sharpens curiosity to know further.
iv. It crystallizes the thoughts and concepts relating to the topic.
v. It helps students in discovering what is not known already.
vi. It is an intellectual teamwork for working out the details and seeking solution to the problem.
vii. It helps the teacher to identify the potentiality and talent of students for promotion.

Uses: Discussion method, in order to be effective, has to pass through the following stages.

Planning: Considerable planning is necessary for holding successful discussion. Discussion for producing the desired results follows a well-directed procedure which can be divided into three stages, such as preparation, discussion and evaluation.

Preparation: The teacher should at first introduce the topic and may read out the method purposefully and critically. Points need to be arranged in a sequence logically. The points may be written on the blackboard for re-reference of the students. The problem to be discussed should be a burning problem.

Discussion: The teacher should see that discussion is conducted in a disciplined manner. Face to face talk should be arranged. Adequate data and information has to be presented, and viewpoints exchanged by the students freely and frankly. It must be ensured that everybody takes part in the discussion. Queries may be made and comments made for clarifying the concepts and sorting out solutions to the problem faced.

The teacher should see that discussion is made in a relaxed and cooperative manner. He has to discourage heated exchanges and wild comments. He ought to ensure that proper support is created for cooperative and unbiased discussion.

Evaluation: Discussion aims at achieving certain specific results. It is to be evaluated whether these results have been secured through discussion, whether knowledge has been increased, prejudices have been removed and interest increased in the burning issue.

Limitations

i. Discussion Method is time-taking and often taxing.

ii. It requires active participation of all which is not so easy.

iii. The teacher should be more alert, careful and skilful for making discussion logical and systematic.

iv. Students coming from various backgrounds and having various levels of interest cannot contribute to discussion adequately.

v. This method can be followed sparingly as the entire Course of Study cannot be covered through this method only.

By Way of Demonstration: Demonstration Method lays emphasis on demonstrating experiments for teaching a particular topic, usually in science. The teacher performs all kinds of experiments in the classroom or science laboratory and explains the use of apparatus, chemicals and operations. This method, although mostly teacher-centred, encourages students' participation in conducting experiments.

Many unfamiliar things become familiar and many abstract things become concrete, when students see with their own eyes and handle some of the apparatus and chemicals themselves. Since students are motivated to see new experiments, they observe attentively and learn everything critically.

Demonstration method proved to be one of the best methods in explaining new concepts and anecdotes. But the demonstrations are to be well-planned and rehearsed by the teacher. Otherwise, if all experiments fail in the classroom, it will have a very bad effect on the students. Once all experiments are well conducted, demonstration becomes successful and teaching becomes effective for achieving the objectives.

Characteristics: There are several characteristics of the Demonstration Method which may be taken as criteria for ensuring success in teaching. These are as follows:

i. Demonstration Method makes use of several experiments involving a series of operations.

ii. These experiments need to be well-planned and rehearsed well in advance.

iii. Success of experiments encourages and their failure discourages students in learning.

iv. Students need encouragement to participate and involve themselves in conducting experiments.

v. The teacher and students should be clear of the institutional objectives in lessons delivered.

vi. The teacher must have adequate confidence and preparedness for demonstrations.

vii. Students have to observe the operations with attention and know all apparatus with interest.

viii. He should involve students as much as possible and seek their cooperation in performing experiments.

ix. Questioning should form an important part of demonstration in order to get feedback from students about their understanding and assimilation.

x. Difficult or new concepts need to be explained to them in simple and clear-cut language and style.

xi. Important points and terms are to be mentioned on the chalkboard which is to the back of the teacher and in front of students.

xii. The apparatus for demonstration should be arranged earlier in a sequence.

xiii. The experiments need to be visible to the entire class and for the purpose, the demonstration table should be higher than students' desks/tables.

xiv. Demonstration should fit in the timetable and according to the season/occasion.

xv. Students' interest should be maintained throughout demonstration.

xvi. The teacher should see that students write in their notebook what is written on the chalkboard and found in the experiments.

Uses

i. Demonstration Method is found to be economical in time and money.

ii. It is psychologically based as the pupils are shown all apparatus and operations conducted in their presence.

iii. Students' participation is encouraged and their involvement ensures effectiveness.

iv. Abstract things are made concrete by teachers and observed by students.

v. The teaching-learning process becomes very efficient and meaningful through experiments.

Limitation

i. Students often do not get chance to perform the experiments themselves in the classroom.

ii. "Learning by Doing" maxim becomes ineffective in Demonstration Method.

iii. Unless the teacher rehearses the experiments and plans them in sequence, there may be delay and failure in conducting demonstration bringing about adverse effects on students. With adequate planning and rehearsals, however, these limitations can be overcome.

TECHNIQUES OF TEACHING

It is to be borne in mind that not a single method should be adopted in teaching. The method has to be selected according to the nature of the topic. But very often, one or two or more methods are to be followed for making teaching effective and efficient.

For example, unless the lecture method is used for initiating teaching, for giving the background knowledge and explaining certain content, demonstration or experiments cannot be effective or understood properly by students. Hence lecture cum demonstration method is usually adopted in teaching science subjects. Similarly, discussion method is also followed along with lecture method.

Project method is to succeed the lecture method which is used by the teacher to introduce the problem, lay down guidelines, forming groups and giving some ideas about the project earlier. In the seminar method also, the teacher may be required to initiate and conclude the discussion and deliberation of the points relating to the project.

Unless the scattered points are properly summed up and inferences are drawn, the entire exercise may fall flat on the students. Therefore, methods have to be properly integrated for making the teaching-learning process successful and meaningful.

In this unit, the need and importance of methods of teaching and their uses are discussed. Different objectives and criteria for good methods have been spelt out for developing an insight and purposes of these methods. You have been told about the necessity for using various methods in different contexts. The characteristics, uses and limitations of Lecture Method, Project Method, Seminar Method, Discussion Method and Demonstration Method have been discussed and you have been made familiar with the merits and demerits of these methods.

Now, you can select any method found, suitable for transmitting the knowledge, skills, attitudes and interests in teaching a particular topic. Sometimes you may find an integration of one method with another benefiting the students more than in any one method. In order to maximize learning experiences, you can either utilize any one suitable method or an integration of different methods may be utilized.

VALUE EDUCATION

An important feature of value-education is the ability of the educator and the educatiors skill to discriminate between right and wrong. What may be nectar for one may be poison for another. We may be clearing forests to build human habitats, which is a laudable objective, but in the process we may be depriving animals of their natural shelter and food and humanity of many environmental benefits.

In many Indian communities, a wedlock between a girl and a boy may not be permissible unless the two are removed from each other by a gap of some generations; whereas among some, marriage between cousins may be auspicious. A debate on the subject can go ad infinitum without coming to any precise conclusion; but as pointed out earlier every community has its own written as well as unwritten behavioural norms which it expects its members to observe.

PART AND PARCEL OF SYLLABUS

In order to decide if the educational institutions should play some part in the dissemination of these accepted norms, the following statement was included in the questionnaire for students:

> "Value-education *i.e.*, education regarding discrimination between what is right or wrong, should be impacted in schools and colleges." (S-1)

The reaction of the five categories of students, constituting the total student-population of 267 was as follows:

S.No.	Category Agreeing	Number Undecided	Number Disagreed	Number persons who expressed no opinion
(1)	Total no. of student respondents (267)	254 (95.2)	6 (2.2)	61 (2.2)
(2)	School students (Male) (70)	68 (97.2)	1 (1.4)	1 (1.4)
(3)	School Students (Female)	84 (97.6)	1 (1.2)	(86) (1.2)
(4)	College Students (M)* (34)	27 (79.6)	4 (11.8)	3 (8.8)
(5)	African College students (M)* studying in the Delhi Colleges. (7)	7 (100)	3 —	4
(6)	Indian College students (F)* (70)	68 (97.2)	— —	11 (1.4)

*(i) Abbreviations M and F stand for Male and Female respectively throughout this work.

*(ii) The following norms has been adopted in this study for categorization of scores:

Below 26% Poor 50%Average 51-74% Above Average

26-49% Below Average Above 74% High

It is thus observed that every category of students expressed high degree of agreement for making a provision of value education in the educational institutions. Speaking in comparative terms, more of college students (males) expressed their disagreement with the statement or were undecided in this regard.

Therefore, if one were to work for a programme of moral or value-education in our educational institutions, one is likely to come across a receptive rather than an indifferent audience, provided the programme is given due importance in the curricula and the teacher imparting value-education is capable of doing justice to the job.

The following news-item appearing in one of the national dailies in India shows that there is a worldwide demand for imparting moral education to the students.

"The (U.K.) Government is to direct its latest attack on violence, disorder and crime at children as young as seven". In a Cabinet meeting it was felt that 'the roots of criminality' must be tackled early and that "moral dimension will be added to the new national curriculm".

Sometime earlier to it in the economic summit in Toronto (Canada), Mrs. Thatcher, the British Prime Minister had raised her concern on the behavioural problems of the young people. She said that although western nations had gone a long way to bring about a technological change, they had to do much in terms of training people to have respect for the law.

The Government (of U.K.) had proposed preparing experimental lessons for the youth with this objective in view. For example, in such lessons the school going youth may be told about a young man who drinks, steals a car, becomes a hit-and-run driver and ultimately one day lands in the custody of the police.

The lesson may depict the consequence (jail etc.) to be faced by the delinquent youth, misery of the family whose members had been hit by this criminal and also the misery of the criminal's own family because of his unlawful act. For this purpose parents, teachers and media have to unite. Teachers cannot provide lessons which are the responsibility of the parents.

Resembling the above statement (S-1) in the questionnaire for students, there was a statement (G-13) in the questionnaire for the general public. The statement was as follows:

Moral education *i.e.*, education regarding what is right or wrong should be imparted.

(a) In schools

(b) In colleges

(c) Through mass media such as radio, TV, newspapers etc. (G-13)

Role of Mass Media

Number of persons who agreed, disagreed with the above, three parts of the statement or were undecided in this regard was as follows:

S.No.	Category	No. Agreeing	No. Undecided	No. Disagreeing	No. of persons who expressed no opinion
(a) In schools	Total no. of respondents (881)	717 (81.6)	136 (15.5)	16 (1.8)	10 (1.1)
(b) In colleges	Total no. of respondents (881)	510 (57.9)	315 (35.8)	43 (4.9)	13 (1.4)
(c) Through mass media	-do-	655 (74.4)	194 (22)	16 (18)	16 (1.8)

The above statistics show that the elements of disagreement and indecision are comparatively higher in the case of part (b) of the statement.

Also the largest number of the respondents appeared to be of the opinion that moral education should be imparted in schools.

Parts (a), (b) and (c) of the statement were further analyzed with reference to age, educational qualifications and income of the respondents. Some of the results obtained were as follows:

The analysis in the case of the statement 13(a) indicates that in comparison to the remaining age-groups of the respondents, those between 18-25 years of age expressed lesser degree of agreement (of 71.2 per cent) with this statement. The remaining 28.8 per cent of the respondents in this group were undecided.

Analysis of the reactions of the respondents on the basis of their educational qualifications revealed that quite a large number of respondents in every group, sub-group seemed to be undecided on the issue whether moral education programme should be introduced at the college stage. The reasons for this must be as follows:

(a) Higher education is a stage of specialization in one or the other discipline, therefore general education in morals was not supported by any sub-group as was done in the case of the school stage.

(b) The college students are mature enough to decide for themselves as to what is right and what is wrong.

Analysis with Reference to Ages of the Respondents

S. No.	*Category of Respondents*	*No. Agreeing*	*No. Undecided*	*No. Disagreeing*	*No. of Persons who expressed no opinion*
1.	Below 18 years (11)	9 (81.9)	2 (18.2)	—	—
2.	18-25 years (52)	37 (71.2)	15 (28.8)	— —	— —
3.	25-40 years (234)	191 (81.6)	38 (16.2)	2 (0.9)	3 (1.3)
4.	Above 40 years (574)	474 (82.6)	79 (13.8)	14 (2.4)	7 (1.2)
5.	Those who did not indicate their ages (10)	8 (80)	2 (20)	—	—

Analysis with Reference to Educational Qualifications of the Respondents

S.No.	Category of Respondents	Number Agreeing	Number Undecided	Number Disagreeing	Number of persons who expressed no opinion
(1)	Below High school	6	7	2	—
	(15)	(40)	(46.7)	(13.3)	—
(2)	High school or equivalent	66	50	5	2
	(123)	(53.7)	(40.6)	(4.1)	(1.6)
(3)	B.A. or equivalent	157	96	13	1
	(267)	(58.8)	(35.9)	(4.9)	(0.4)
(4)	M.A. or above or equivalent	274	157	23	10
	(464)	(59.0)	(33.8)	(5)	(2.2)
(5)	Those who did not indicate their educational qualifications	7	5	—	—
	(12)	(58.3)	(41.7)	—	

Analysis with Reference to Monthly Income of the Respondents

S.No.	Category of Respondents	Number Agreeing	Number Undecided	Number Disagreeing	Number of persons who expressed no opinion
(1)	Below Rs. 1000	16	11	-	1
	(28)	(57.1)	(39.3)	-	(3.6)
(2)	Rs.1000-1999	68	27	1	2
	(98)	(69.4)	(27.5)	(1)	(2)
(3)	Rs. 2000-3999	246	75	10	3
	(334)	(73.6)	(22.5)	(3)	(0.9)
(4)	Rs. 4000 or above	318	74	5	10
	(407)	(78.1)	(18.2)	(1.2)	(2.5)
(5)	Those who did not	7	7	—	—
	indicate their income	7	7		
	(14)	(50)	(50)	—	—

It would be interesting here to study the attitude of male and female college teachers to the same statement *i.e.* 13(b).

S.No.	Category of college teachers	Number Agreeing	Number Undecided	Number Disagreed	Number of persons who did not express any opinion
1.	Female	25	11	2	1
	(39)	(64,1)	(28.2)	(5.1)	(2.6)
2.	Male	37	10	1	2
	(50)	(74)	(20)	(2)	(4)

The degree of support expressed in case of statement that moral education should be imparted in colleges is considerably more both by female and male college-teachers than the overall support given by the general group. College students themselves (of both sexes) also expressed considerable support to the idea of providing moral education in our educational institutions while reacting to statement S-1.

In the case of statement 13(c), maximum agreement was expressed by the income-group having a monthly income of Rs. 4000 and above. Starting with this, as we come to the sub-groups with lower monthly incomes, the degree of agreement to this statement successively decreases. May be that the people with higher incomes have a better appreciation of the role of mass-media on account of their greater exposure to these media.

Propagation through Conduct: It would be desirable to briefly mention here some basic factors which influence our thought and behaviour pattern.

Samskaras or Natural Tendencies: Every person is born with certain propensities, likes and dislikes, potentialities-inherited or otherwise. The ancient thinkers of India called them samskaras or impressions accumulated by an individual spirit in its previous births. All this is called individual's inherent nature which differs from person to person. The nature of an individual plays an important role in determining his or her behaviour.

Education and Environment: It may be difficult to say if an individual's nature or his nurture plays a greater role in shaping the individual's conduct; but it goes without saying that nurture in the form of education and environmental influences have a significant impact in shaping the character of a person.

Free Will: Every individual is endowed with a 'free-will'. By exercising his free-will an individual becomes the architect of his own destiny.

Every individual, when he enters this world, brings with him a set of samskaras—impressions, tendencies, and attitudes. As he goes through his life, by the process of education and interaction with various situations in the social milieu, he acquires new samskaras and his old samaskaras get modified.

With the judicious application of one's free-will, every individual raises the behavioural edifice of one's life and becomes the architect of his own future.

The Background

History of education reveals that in ancient times, say up to the 6th century A.D., many countries laid considerable emphasis on character-training of the young children. In India, religion emphasized ethical conduct, art, literature, jurisprudence, etc. In Rome, cultivating respect for traditions, austerity and frugality was an important function of education.

Character-training was a salient feature of the Mauryan education. Chinese regarded moulding of character a prime concern of education. Zoroastrians, in ancient Persia, attached considerable importance to training the young in practices of good thoughts, good words and good actions. Byzantine system of education went even to the extent of mostly confining itself to religious instruction to students and encouraging among them ascetic practices and thus developing in them an attitude of indifference towards secular subjects.

Athens, the cultural centre of ancient Greece, was known for the stress it laid on moral training of the youth and cultivating good conduct and grace in them. Sparta in Greece, besides training the youth (from the age of seven) in physical culture, taught them the art of lying and theft etc., as these were some of the values with the Spartans. Spartan morality, however, demanded that this kind of

Machiavallianism was to be practised only while dealing with the foreigners.

During the medieval India, when there was Islamic rule in the country, maktabs, *i.e.* institutions of early education taught the students to say their daily prayers as indicated in the Holy Quran. In the institutions of higher learning *i.e.* madrasas, Hadit was taught. A number of denominational schools in India still teach students religious practices of their respective faiths. Bible discourse is still compulsory in the schools of England. In Russia after the great Revolution character was attempted to be moulded through the teachings of communism:

Role of Schools and Colleges

Educational institutions constitute the biggest organized sector for imparting various kinds of training, including moral training, to the growing youths. As regards the stage at which moral education programme should begin in the educational institutions, Meriel Downey says:

> "It (moral development) is an area to which no pupil owes 'cold', since moral learning, the development of values and attitudes begins at birth and is fed from many sources. For this reason, it is not something that can be delayed, like, say, the learning of Latin, until we feel that pupils have readied an appropriate stage of mental development to cope with the demands which it will make upon their intellectual abilities".

A number of people are of the view that moral education, in the school system, should begin from the pre-primary stage so that students develop proper samskaras and attitudes from the early years of their lives.

Maintaining Records

It would be relevant to study the views of various commissions and committees on the subject of moral education

Pre-independence Period

(i) The Education Commission of 1882 had recommended that, based upon the fundamental principles of natural religion, an attempt be made to prepare a text-book on moral education. This book should be taught in all Government and non-Government colleges. The principal or one of the professors in each Government and aided colleges should deliver a series of lectures to all the classes on the duties of a man and a citizen.

The Government, however, rejected the proposal by its Resolution No.10/309 of October 2, 1884.

(ii) Thereafter a significant recommendation in this regard was made in the Memorandum of the Post-War Educational Development (1944). The recommendation runs as follows:

"Religion in the widest sense, should inspire all education and that a curriculum devoid of an ethical basis will prove barren in the end".

(iii) The Religious Education Committee of the Central Advisory Board of Education (CABE) recommended in 1945, "Spiritual and moral teachings common to all religions should be an integral part of the curriculum and provision/facilities for instructions therein should be the responsibility of the State."

Post-independence Period

(i) The 42nd Constitutional Amendment of 1976, inserted as Article 51A in Part IVA of the Indian Constitution lays down ten Fundamental Duties (or values) for each citizen. This amendment was inspired by the idea of arresting the falling moral standards in the country and that of ensuring higher level of moral conduct from the citizens.

(ii) The University Education Commission (1948-49) recommended that: "unless morality is taken in a larger sense, it is not enough. If we exclude spiritual training in our institutions we would be untrue to our whole historical development".

(iii) The Secondary Education Commission (1952-53) asserted that 'religious and moral instruction played an important role in the growth of individual's character.

(iv) Sri Prakasa Committee on Religious and Moral Instruction (1959) held the view that:

"Many ills that our world of education and our society as a whole is suffering from, resulting in widespread disturbance and dislocation of life, are mainly due to gradual disappearance of the hold of basic principles of religion on the hearts of the people—The only cure, it seems to us, is in deliberate inculcation of moral and spiritual values from the earliest years of our lives."

(v) The subject was also dealt with by the Indian Education Commission (1964-66), which recommended that:

"Conscious and organized attempts be made for imparting education in social, moral and spiritual values with the help, wherever possible, of ethical teachings of great religions".

(vi) Challenge of Education (1985), published by the Union Ministry of Education, summed up the position in this regard as follows:

"Thoughtful people in all walks of life are greatly disturbed by a progressive erosion of values and the resultant pollution of public life. The fact that this crisis of values is as pervasive in schools, colleges and universities, amongst teachers as well as students as in other walks of life, is seen as a highly dangerous development. It is, therefore, being urged that the process of education should be reoriented and young people should be made to realize that exploitation, insecurity and violence cannot be contained nor can an organized society be sustained without adhering to and enforcing some norms of social, political and economic behaviour. Learning from past experience, it is expected that a coherent and an operationally viable value-system would be inculcated through educational process, based upon rational and scientific and moral approach to life".

(vii) The Document on Approach to the Seventh Five Year Plan (1985-90) published in July 1984, states, " Value-orientation in education should constitute a special thrust in the Seventh Plan, teacher-education in particular-being reoriented for this purpose".

Various Methods

(1) At the boyhood stage, individual's physical propensities have a full play; during manhood and old-age intellectual and spiritual

values start dominating the corporeal values. Therefore, while imparting moral education, educators must keep this fact in view and no attempt be made to burden the students with intellectual exercises in moral education during early years of their lives.

(2) Value-perspective may be two-dimensional or three dimensional. A two-dimensional view is caring for oneself as well as fourth other because both need each other and any transgression of values may harm both sides. USA and USSR had been very unfriendly till the eighties of this century; but both have respected each other's sovereignty because either of these countries could destroy the other with the pile of destructive weapons it possessed. This kind of need and reciprocity-based value-system would be followed by many people. When the value system is ideal-based as well, it becomes a three-dimensional value system. The three dimensional value-system can be followed over a long period of time by a few persons only.

(3) The Education Commission (1964-66) suggested that social, moral and spiritual values should be imparted both through indirect and direct methods. The Commission remarked, "We attach great importance to the role of indirect influence in building up good character. The school atmosphere, the personality and behaviour of the teachers, the facilities provided in the school, will have a large say in developing a sense of values. We would like to emphasize that the consciousness of values must permeate the whole curriculm and programme of activities in the school. It is not only the teachers incharge of moral instruction who are responsible for building character. Every teacher, whatever be the subject he teaches, must necessarily accept this responsibility.—The school assembly, the curricular and co-curricular activities, the celebration of religious festivals of all religions, work-experience, team games and sports,, subject clubs, social service programmes—all these can help in inculcating the values of cooperation and mutual regard, honesty and integrity, discipline and social responsibility. These values have a special significance in Indian society today, when young men and women are passing through a crisis of character,"

In regard to direct moral instruction, agreeing with the recommendations of the Sri Prakasa Committee, the Commission stated that " one or two periods a week should be set aside in the school timetable for instruction in moral and spiritual values".

At the early school-stages, moral instruction can be imparted through parables or stones which have an appeal to the emotions of the children. At the secondary stage, there can be discussions between the teacher and the taught on the values to be imparted, thus resorting to an intellectual approach to the subject. According to V.K.R.V. Rao, one time Union Education Minister, "Ethics should be taught only through parables, stories, religion, and sayings of great people and their lives. Right from the start, children should be taught about the founders of great religions of India. Films should be shown to them depicting temples, mosques, gurudwaras etc."

(4) In ancient times, some states imparted moral education through edicts or some other forms of permanent writings. For example, the Romans expected the children to learn by heart the Twelve Tables of laws. The Japanese employed the imperial edicts for this purpose. One example of the edict is given below:

"Our imperial ancestors have founded our Empire on a basis broad and everlasting and have deeply and firmly implanted virtue; our subjects, ever united in loyalty and filial piety, have from generation to generation illustrated the beauty thereof. This is the glory and the fundamental character of our Empire, and herein also lies the source of our education. Ye, our subjects, be filial to your parents, affectionate to your brothers and sisters; as husbands and wives be harmonious; as friends true; bear yourselves in modesty and moderation; extend your benevolence to all; pursue learning and cultivate arts, and thereby develop intellectual faculties and perfect moral powers; furthermore, advance public good and promote common interests; always respect the Constitution and observe the laws; should emergency arise, offer yourselves courageously to the state; and thus guard and maintain the prosperity of our imperial throne. So shall ye not only be our good and faithful subjects, but render illustrious the best traditions of your forefathers."

(5) In the teaching of moral practices, both theory and practice are of equal significance, because cognition, feelings and action are

interdependent. The quality and depth of information and its sources-all play an important role in influencing our attitudes. Without a proper conceptual background, all action may be reduced to a blind ritual only. However, translation of information into proper action is of great importance, because simple parroting of Ten Commandments cannot make a Moses of an individual. Emphasizing the superiority of example over precept, N.K. Dutt says:

"Albert Camus once experimented with inculcation of moral values through teaching. He encouraged students to write an essay on 'Truthfulness'. The best essay was written by the biggest liar of the class. He further said that if the purpose of education is merely to impart information and skills, then thanks to the present day teaching technology, perhaps an idiot can teach another idiot calculus."

The same remarks apply to speech-making also. A person may play a big hoax on the people by play of words and thus claim to be a big preacher of values whereas his own actions may be just the opposite of what he might say:

N.K. Dutt adds that according to Mao-Tse-Tung, "The thoughts of intellectuals are like arrows in a quiver which scratch the back but never fly".

(6) Value orientation is a continuous process. As man evolves intellectually and otherwise, his expectations also get modified. This is true in regard to values also. Society's expectations rise in respect of moral values also, therefore imparting of value-education and adjustment to values should be a continuous process.

Apart from the educational institutions mass media, *i.e.* media which has the potential to transmit messages to the masses at large, can play a far-reaching role in any scheme of imparting value education-formal, nonformal or informal. Some of these media are privately owned and independent of the government whereas others are directly under the government machinery. Although some government departments bring out various kinds of journals, etc., but by and large press and publications in India are free of government control.

Some of the mass media under the Union Government are television, radio, Department of Field Publicity, Publication Division, Department of Advertising and Visual Publicity and Song and Drama Division. Though there is a Films Division under the Union Ministry of Information and Broadcasting, it produces documentaries only. Feature-films production is totally in the private sector and this medium is very powerful in influencing the attitudes of the people.

One may, of course, argue that in India mass-media has not been the mass media in the real sense—some of the reasons for this being as follows:

> According to 1981 census, India had nearly 140 million families and only 25 million radios and one million TV sets. If TV sets are possessed by the same 25 million who own the radio sets, the reach of these two media is only to 17.9 per cent population and if the TV sets are considered to have been owned by some who own the radio sets and some who do not own the radio set, even then the reach of these two media is to a maximum population of 18.6 per cent of the country's population. The total circulation of newspapers and journals in India is around ten million which comes to less than 1.5 for every hundred people. As nearly half the population in the country is still illiterate, the newspapers and journals have a limited impact on the education of the masses. One may agree that the mass media are not able to reach the vast masses of India inhabiting the length and breadth of the country, yet they have, admittedly a great potential of wielding a considerable influence on human minds, therefore these media can be gainfully employed in the moral education programme.

It is, thus, observed that there is a general consensus that moral education should be imparted in our educational institutions as well as through the mass-media. Various commissions and committees on education have been stressing the need for social, moral and spiritual education programme being introduced in our educational institutions. Any programme of value-education must take into account the age and other factors of the target population. The programme, in order to be useful, should lay equal emphasis on precept and practice.

The character of the teacher or any other person imparting moral education is of greater significance than his precepts as actions always speak louder than the words and the totality of the educator's personality is far more important than his utterances, howsoever loud and pious these might be. Mass media, which have a deep and powerful influence on human minds, should also devise a well-planned programme in respect of moral education and thus contribute to resolving the present crisis of character in the society.

Religious Values

The *Concise Oxford Dictionary* defines religion as a "particular system of faith and worship—human recognition of superhuman controlling power and especially of a personal God or Gods entitled to obedience and worship". The main components of any religion are theology, rituals and code of conduct.

It is believed that in India, the conception of Supreme Being, the first cause of the universe *i.e.*, the Brahma, had a great impact on the moral code of the Aryans. Starting from the worship of various elements of nature such as the sky, the earth and various forces of nature, there was a trend towards finding unity in them. Polytheism was correlated to monotheism just as forces of nature namely, heat, light, electricity to one single thing 'energy'. This Single Cause of the universe, was impersonal, absolute, passionless and beyond consciousness, just like energy in this material world, is the primal cause of the universe. This chain of thought led our ancestors to one of the greatest philosophical conceptions—that the whole world was one.

The concept of religion is bound to vary from person to person and from society to society. For example, in Hinduism, the equivalent of religion is 'dharma', which is far more a comprehensive word than the word religion. The word 'dharma' is from the root 'dhra', which means something which holds the society and this universe together.

As such, 'dhama' lays greater stress on one's goals, functions, obligations and duties. It is, difficult to say which conception of religion (which) the respondents had in mind when reacting to the following statement:

It would be appropriate to impart moral education,

(a) Without reference to religious teachings;

or

(b) With reference to teachings in various religions.(G-2)

Positive Role of Religion: Thus more than 50 per cent of the respondents favoured moral education with reference to religious teachings. There could be several reasons for it, some of which may be as follows:

(i) Religion plays a positive role in the moral uplift of man. It may, at times, be the fear of gods which may be the motive factor for individual's right conduct. William Newton Clarke considered the role of religion in imparting moral education as that of a school master. He wrote in his book *The Christian Doctrine of God*.

"Doubtless the ethical life of the world has suffered much from religion, but it owes to religion immeasurably more than it has suffered from it. Faulty enough indeed the influence has been, but the ethical life of the world has on the whole been greatly reinforced and purified by its religions."

(ii) All religions are creations of superb minds. Religious writings are replete with episodes which have great moral lessons far man. It would be lack of wisdom on the part of man not to benefit from the wealth of experience stored in the religious books.

(iii) We, in India, are not trying to create an irreligious society. What we have accepted is a variously religious society, and not a society which has nothing to do with religion. Therefore, religion cannot be rejected merely on the ground that we are a secular state.

The Other Side: Those who are opposed to assigning any role to religion in the sphere of moral education may have some of the following arguments in mind.

(i) According to Article 28 (1) of the Constitution of India,

"No religious instruction shall be provided in any educational institution wholly maintained out of State Fund."

This, of course, does not apply to the educational institutions run by private trusts. In regard to such institutions, Article 28(3) of the Constitution lays down the following policy.

"No person attending any educational institution recognized by the State or receiving aid out of State funds shall be required to take part in any religious instruction that maybe imparted in such institutions or to attend any religious worship that may be conducted in such institutions or in any premises attached thereto unless such person or, if such a person is a minor, his guardian has given his consent thereto."

(ii) Religion is identified by some people more as theology, a set of rituals, fear of God and greed for heaven rather than a code of, conduct evolved over a period of years. Such people see no link between religion and morality. In his work 'Christianity and Hinduism', Bishop Caldwell writes:

"We meet with a moral Hindu who has broken altogether away from religion and, what is still more common, still more extraordinary, we meet with a devout Hindu who lives a flagrantly immoral life. In the latter case no person sees any inconsistency between immorality and devoutnes."

'The Karma Theory' which is one of the fundamental principles of Hinduism proclaims the importance of virtuous acts. The following legend in a Hindu sacred-book brings out very aptly the higher place of a kind act than the performance of rituals. A rich man, once, performed the ritual of offering 1000 mangoes to the sacred Ganges. One of these mangoes was picked up by a poor beggar to satisfy his hunger. The same night, the rich man, in his dream saw the goddess Ganges who told him that she had accepted the offering of the mango only! The 'devout Hindus' of Caldwell experience are therefore, not truly religious.

(iii) People project their moral conceptions in the shape of gods; but once created these divinities react on the conscience of their creators. Examples are not wanting where divinities created by the priest class and other powerful sections in the society have had an adverse influence on the morals of the society. It is in the name of some divinities that injustices are perpetrated on the weaker sections of the society.

(iv) To many people, religion has meant forcible proselytization at the point of bayonet or economic and social exploitation of others. Religions have led to feuds among the co-religionists as well as between people of different faiths.

(v) Communists as well as many other people have no faith in any religion. Religions like Buddhism make no reference to God. If moral teachings are to be based on religion, it would amount to imparting no moral education to persons who do not believe in religion.

(vi) Some of these people hold that moral education should be based on rational thinking only. In ancient Greece, where there was no priestly class, the country had no theocratic morality. Aristotle discussed only scientific foundations of morality. In ancient Rome, morality was based on patriotism and not religion.

(vii) The great Hindu codifier of values, Manu, makes no reference to rituals and supernatural things in his definition of dharma.

Those who hold that moral education should be imparted independent of religion argue that if some day a person rejects his religion (and this can happen with the growth of materialistic values), he would reject morality also. It would, in a way, amount to throwing the baby along with the bath tub.

(viii) Today, many societies are pluralistic and have a markedly different value-system arising from their respective religions. Therefore, there is an inherent difficulty in linking morality with religion.

Critics and scholars have also pointed towards several disintegrating factors in various religions. For example, Judaism, Christianity and Islam, which have a common catchment area, believe in an exclusive God. Their God brooks no rival, whereas according to Hinduism, all Gods are manifestation of the same Brahma; only the sages have described Him differently.

The Judaic God commands his worshippers that when they enter the land of their enemies, they will "destroy their altars, and break their images, and cut down their groves, and burn their graven images with fire". (Bible, Deut 7.5). Iconoclasm, temple razing has been preached and practized by Islam to a similar degree. It is told that Walid was sent by the prophet to destroy the idol of al-Uzza at Nakhle worshipped by the tribal people there. Wherever the followers of Christianity went, they destroyed gods and religious places of the 'nonbelievers'. When America was discovered, the Benedictine monks who came in the train of Columbus boasted of having destroyed single-handed 170,000 images in Haiti alone. Juan de Zummarage, the first Bishop of Mexico, writing as early as 1531 claimed that he destroyed 500 temples and 20,000 idols of the heathens.

In our own country, in Goa, Jesuit fathers destroyed many Hindu temples. The Hindus, at one time, had to pay 'Jazia, only because they were Hindus and not Muslims. A law laid down that infidels could not build their temples. The Laxmi Narain Temple in New Delhi is reported to have come up in the country after a lapse of about 700 years. Various religions, thus, appear to have been reduced to mere denominations only.

Verticals for Thoughts

In case educational institutions adopt an attitude of indifference to religion, it would mean leaving the interpretation of religion to the reactionaries and half-educated people only and jeopardizing the process of social evolution.

The works of the religiously inclined saints and sufi poets and philosophers like Namdev, Tukaram, Kabir, Kurral, Jaisi, S. Radhakrishnan and others in different languages express moral truths in epigramatic phrases. All such works have had a great moralizing influence on the society and it would be a mistake not to make use of them for their literary and moral value.

Every religion lays down some code of conduct for its followers and contains in its books numerous legends to inspire its faithfuls to observe certain norms of behaviour. It would be useful to make use of this heritage, for imparting ethical education to students.

Each religion preaches spiritual fulfilment, withdrawing from the lower pulls to higher recesses of mind, prayer, meditation, inculcation of virtues like compassion, contentment, good actions, self-surrender, service of mankind and all that can elevate man and the society.

Whatever be the source of the material employed for moral education, all discussions on the value-system should be on rational basis only and not wrapped in meaningless myths and superstitions. For example, it would be an incorrect approach to say, 'Respect women because it is written in *Manusmriti.*

yatra nariastu poojante, ramante tatra devata,

yatraiatastu na poojante, sarvaatatraphala kriya.

'Homes where women are worshipped become the abode of gods but where women are not given respect, all the actions of the people there end up in failure'.

Instead, students should be told with examples that whenever and wherever women have been given an opportunity in education, services or other spheres,, their contribution has been no less than that of men. On this account as well as on account of the sacrifice which women make as mothers, they are worthy of great respect.

It would be wrong to attribute some of the existing social ills solely to religion. Foreign aggressions, alien rule, present day consumerism and absence of developmental work over long periods are vital factors responsible for moral decay of the society.

Factors in Faith

To the statement that—"Students should be given an intelligent understanding of the codes of conduct of various religions", (G-9), the respondents reacted as follows:

S. No.	Category of Respondents	Number Agreeing	Number Undecided	Number Disagreed	Number of persons who expressed no opinion
1.	Total population (881)	798 (90.6)	39 (4.4)	44 (5)	—
2.	Age-Group 18-25 years (52)	43 (82.7)	4 (7.7)	5 (9.6)	—
3.	Above 40 years (574)	532 (92.7)	20 (3.5)	22 (3.8)	—
4.	High School (123)	115 (3.5)	1 (0.8)	7 (5.7)	—
5.	MA or above (464)	414 (89.2)	27 (5.8)	23 (5)	—
6.	With income from Rs. 1000-1999 p.m. (98)	88 (89.8)	6 (6.1)	4 (4.1)	—
7.	With income of Rs. 4000 p.m. (407)	369 (90.7)	16 (3.9)	22 (5.4)	—

All the categories of respondents listed above lent a high degree of support to the statement. Religion has played a central role and is still playing an important role in the life of the Indian people. All our works of ancient art, literature, dance, music, etc., are intimately interwoven with religious myths and thought. Sciences such as astronomy and geometry, etc., were cultivated in India initially for religious purposes only.

Therefore, it may not be possible to eliminate religion from our lives without the grave risk of cutting ourselves from our roots. According to a news-report, a record number of 19.92 lakhs pilgrims visited the holy shrine of Vaishno Devi during 1988, exceeding-the previous year's mark, by 1.35 lakhs. These pilgrims came from all over India. Even a number of politicians who swear by secularism visit the holy shrines located all over India.

The visit by these leaders may be politically motivated, but they indicate the 'direction of the wind' in our country. Due to great appeal which religion has for the Indian masses, religion was used as an effective weapon during the freedom struggle of the country. V. Subramaniam writes:

> "Annie Besant's use of the *Bhagvadgita* and theosophy appealed to the urban high-caste Hindu—while Tilak widened the base of appeal through using the Ganesh Puja as an instrument of politico-cultural revivalism quite apart from his Karmayogic (activist) reinterpretation of the Bhagvadgita. Bengali radicalism drew inspiration from the Mother Goddess right from its early days—and Gandhiji's efforts to appeal to the widest public included the slogan of Ram Rajya and the singing of Ram Dhun. In short, the nationalist movement though never exclusively Hindu nor theocratic, nevertheless used Hindu religion cultural symbols and slogans as the most practical instruments of mobilization of the Indians-in spite of strong criticism both from the Right and Left, from Liberals such as Sapru or Kunzru and Leftists such as Jawaharlal Nehru, the from Socialists and the Communists."

The motif 'Yoga is efficiency in action' '(Yoga Karmasu Kaushlam) adopted by the National Academy of Administration and the National Productivity Council is from the holy Bhagvadgita. Of course, the choice of the motif would have been on account of its appropriateness and eloquence and not religious considerations but this is all the more reason that the students should be given an intelligent understanding of various religions and the useful messages contained in the religious text.

"The Indians," remarks Sir Harcourt Butler, "are as essentially religious as the Europeans are essentially secular. Religion is still the beginning and the end, the alpha and omega of Indian Life". This belief finds expression in a bitter satire of the Urdu poet Akbar, of which the gist is " The East is spiritual, the West is material. Mansur (the Sufi Pantheist who was executed in Baghdad in A.D. 922 for blasphemy) declared, 'I am God.' Darwin announced " I am the son of an ape".

Strength of Religion

As regards the role of the religious institutions, the questionnaire for the students carried the following statement:

"Religious institutions such as temples, mosques, churches should play greater role in propagating moral values in the society". (S-11)

Religious Organizations

(a) College students agree with the statement to a greater degree than do the school students.

(b) Male students are more in favour of the idea that the religious institutions should play a greater role in propagating moral values than the female students.

(c) In each case the degree of agreement with the statement is less than 75 per cent.

More than 25 per cent of the respondents were undecided on this issue or were opposed to the idea of religious institutions taking up the work of the propagation of moral values, possibly due to the fact that the respondents were skeptical about the ability of the religious institutions to achieve results. Some of the following steps could be considered for equipping the religious institutions for working effectively in the sphere of value-education.

(i) It should be ensured that the temple-priests or other similar personnel involved in the work take a progressive and not an obscurantist's view of religion. For this purpose, a system would have to be evolved on a national basis for entry to priesthood. Individuals wishing to become priests should go through an adequate course of training and education. In the USSR, prior to glasnost and perestroika, notwithstanding that communism is antagonistic to religion, the priests; before they could take up priesthood, have had to go through a course of adequate training and education in religious and other allied texts. If government can successfully intervene with the administration of the Vaishno Devi temple in J and K State, there is no reason why a similar system cannot be introduced or at least experimented in India.

(ii) The education programme of the priests must drill the trainees in the concept of oneness of the Supreme Being and certain degree of the comparative study of various religions. *Ahura Mazda* in Zoroastrianism, Allah in Islam, Heavenly Father in Christianity, Iswara in Hinduism, and Sunyata in Buddhism are only different names given by different people in different geographical and linguistic regions for the same cosmic, creative, infinite and eternal energy. The leaders of religious institutions should be trained to remain free from bigotry.

(iii) The people in religious institutions, like all other people, should bear in mind that as a society evolves intellectually, spiritually and socially, its value-system undergoes a metamorphosis. In case religious institutions refuse to accept this logic, they would lose their credibility. A couple of examples of a progressive and a rational approach in this regard are given here.

Example-I: Among the Muslims it was held for a long time that the *Zakat* or the *Wakf*, *i.e.*, the money collected for charity purposes, is to be spent, among other things, for religious education only as distinct from secular education.

In recent years, rational Muslims have justified the utilization of Zakat for secular education. According to these progressive thinkers, the Holy Prophet Muhammad had sent a number of people to India and China to receive education. Evidently these people had not gone to these countries to receive Quranic education. Therefore, it is perfectly in accordance with the Islamic thought to utilize Wakf for imparting secular education.

Example-II: Islamic tenets, on theocratic basis, divide the world into two sections-Dar-al-Islam and Dar-al-Harb' It was said that no taxes be levied by Muslim countries for imports from the former category of countries whereas taxes maybe levied in the case of the second category. The rationalist Muslims have, in recent years, changed this view in this manner. They say that Islam upholds the essentiality of survival. As money is necessary for survival, therefore taxes maybe levied in the case of all categories including the first category.

Example-III: According to Islam, Muslims are not allowed to charge interest from anyone, even from banks. The modern thinking among some Muslims is that banks invest money-deposits of the individuals in various projects and business deals and earn profits. As sharing of profits is not specifically banned by Islam, the depositors can accept these profits.

The issue is still a debatable one as Muslims of the conventional types view that trade has an element of profit and loss and risk. As bank deposits do not have this element, bank interest cannot be equated to trade profits. They argue that this is a circuitous way of accepting the bank-interest by changing its nomenclature; but then if religious leaders refuse to accept these changes, the changing society would just ignore them and their sermons as well.

Preaching Values

There was the following statement in the questionnaire relating to mass-media. "Indu and Joginder Singh were discussing radio and T.V. coverage of such programmes which are religious in character. Indu justified such coverage whereas Joginder Singh felt that such coverage violated the principle of secularism. Who, in your opinion, was correct?

(a) Preventing the mass-media from doing such a coverage would, to some extent, mean working for a closed society. The endeavour, on the contrary, should be to depict all religions, cultures as well as sub-cultures rather than drawing a curtain on them. India's mission to evolve a society with composite culture and not one which is indifferent to all cultures.

(b) Any belief or custom which becomes a part of the mainstream of life no longer remains exclusively religious. It becomes a part of the social life of the community and deserves to be depicted by the mass-media. The immense popularity of the *Ramayana* and the *Mahabharata* T.V. serials from the Doordarshan network amply establishes the justification of projecting such programmes through the mass-media.

(c) Secularism has two forms. There is the 'absolute secularism' which is practised in the communist world where religion has no place in the planned affairs of the country. There the religion is a totally private affair.

The Indian view of secularism is, however, different. In India, all religions can flourish. The government does not give preferential treatment to any particular religion. Therefore, if a balanced coverage of important programmes of all religions is undertaken by mass-media, it would lead to better understanding of all cultures by different communities inhabiting the country.

Those opposed to the use of mass-media for religious programmes primarily may be of the opinion that the Preamble of the Indian Constitution declares India a secular state, therefore the government should not dabble with religion. They may be interpreting secularism as communist societies do this. Some persons in this category also have a feeling that the government massmedia occasionally, give a preferential treatment to the programmes of one religion vis-a-vis programmes of other religions.

Difficult as it may be to totally ward off such an imbalance or an error of judgement in the selection of programmes for the mass media, its incidence can be reduced by drawing up a clear and a well-thought out policy. The question is—which is more hazardous in a multi-cultural society—to deprive the people of the chance of having an intelligent understanding of the cultures and religions of other communities and interaction with them, or taking a calculated risk of the consequences which would flow if there is some error in the choice of programmes for dissemination through massmedia. Perhaps, the latter course may be a better choice.

It may be argued that humankind had started observing some kind of moral code earlier than it evolved any kind of religion. Merial Downey and Av Kelley held that:

> "..... morality has to be seen independent of religion. If there is a connection it is not that morality is dependent on religious beliefs, it is much more likely that man's religious beliefs are a result of his moral awareness". As Kant said, "Belief in God is grounded in moral consciousness rather than moral law on belief in God."

The question, however, is not if the moral code preceded the evolution of religion or it was vice versa; but whether in the present context moral education should be undertaken with or without reference to religion. In this context two things are to be kept in view:

(a) Have we evolved adequate secular literature for imparting moral education?

(b) If religion is divorced from theology and belief in supernaturalism, is there any harm if its moral code, and fables, stories and other relevant material are used for imparting moral education?

In this connection one cannot overlook that only 532 per cent of the respondents supported the application of religion for moral education, whereas 43.3 per cent supported that moral education should be imparted without reference to religious teachings. However, it is not known what was the picture of religion that the respondents had in mind while reacting to this statement. If the picture of religion before them was that of bigoted priests, performance of unmeaningful rituals, sermonizing doctrines, one would agree that religious teachings should be kept aloof from moral education; but if religion means harmony of the individual with all forms of life and matter in the cosmos, religion provides a sound basis for moral education.

In view of the above, it would be desirable, as corroborated by about 90 per cent of each category of respondents (in G-9) to give students an intelligent and a rational understanding of the code of conduct of various religions, so that students are not deprived of the wealth of experience stored in these books.

If our dilapidated value-system is to be restructured and saved from decaying further, it is essential that religious establishments should also play their full role in this regard. For this purpose, it would be necessary to have an educated priesthood which has a comprehensive view of various religions and can see the elements of unity behind all religions. The mass media should also take a balanced and a rational view while projecting customs, traditions and programmes, etc., connected with various religions and intended to impart information to the viewers on different aspects of the national and cultural life and for inculcation of moral values among them.

Social Values

Life with 'values' is all meaningful. Whereas life in the absence of 'values' is of no use and is not good at all. A person who gives importance to values is good, is considered good by others and is also held in high esteem in the social group he belongs to.

Every good person values time. Such a person is very mindful of time. He/she gives importance to it by giving the significance to every moment-minute or second. He/she is always keen to make the most of his/her time. Thus, whatever has its importance and worth may be called value. Truth, Honesty, Beauty, Goodness etc. are values, whereas a lie, dishonesty, badness, ugliness are disvalues. "The choice before present humanity is either total annihilation or coexistence through ethical and spiritual values"—Bertrand Russel.

According to N.T. Ram, "A value is what is desired or what is sought. Values may be operationally conceived as those guiding principles of life which are conducive to one's physical and mental health as well as to social welfare and adjustment and which are in tune with one's culture."

Manual work is important for every human being. In Indian culture. there is due emphasis on this value. Guru Nanak Dev advocated the value of 'Kirat Karna'. In this regard, Mahatma Gandhi said, "Those who do not work with hands soon lose the music of their life." In our system of education the dignity of labour is held in high esteem.

Education Commission (1964-66) recommended work experience for the youth for the inculcation of dignity of labour.

Various Theories

(a) According to Clyde Kluckhohn, "Value is a conception, explicit or implicit, distinctive of an individual or characteristic of group, of the desirable which influences the selection from available-means and ends of action."

(b) R.K. Mukherjee says, "Values are socially approved drives and goals that are internalized through the process of conditioning, learning or socialization and that becomes subjective preferences, standards and aspirations."

(c) Allport observes, "The term value means the relative prominence of the subject's interest or the dominant interest in personality."

(d) D.H. Parker puts forth the views:" Values belong wholly to the inner world of mind. The satisfaction of desire is the real value, the thing that serves is only an instrument. A value is always an experience, never a thing or an object."

(e) R.B. Perry says in his general theory of values, "Any objective whatever it be, acquires values when any interest, whatever it be, is taken in it, just as anything what so ever becomes a target when any one who so ever aims at it."

(f) In this regard Edgar Brightman remarks, "In the most elementary sense, value means whatever is actually liked, prized, esteemed, desired, approved or enjoyed at any tune. It is the actual experience of enjoying a desired object, or activity."

(g) According to John Dewey, "The term Value' has two quite different meanings. On the one hand, it denotes the attitude of prizing a thing, finding it worthwhile, for its own sake or intrinsically. So value in this sense is to appreciate, but to value also means a distinctly intellectual act, an operation of comparing and judging to evaluate."

(h) Dr. Prem Kripal says, "Values may be defined as:

(i) what we believe (professed values);

(ii) what we practise (operational values); and

(iii) what we learn from experience in order to adopt and renew traditions received from the past (traditional values)". He further remarks, "Values should be operational and also relevant and dynamic. Values should not be crystalized and frozen to the point of rigidity, stopping further growth and renewal."

The Categorization

Before we classify values into certain categories or groups, let us try to enlist them. A few values are: truth, beauty, goodness, sincerity, obedience, respect, honesty, worship, devotion, service, satyam, shivam, sundram, purity, simplicity, acceptance of one's fault or mistake, universal love, brotherhood, broadmindedness, service to others and secularism. There can endless number of values if we consider it from various angles. It is rather difficult to put them in specific classifications. Surely many type of classifications will be required for presenting all of them.

Walter's Classification: Walter G. Everett in his book 'Moral Values' classifies human values in the following eight groups:

Economic Values: These are indicated by market price and they include all purchasable things. Economic values are instrumental in the sense that they are used as means to obtain other values. Some writers do not believe that these are values in the strict sense but only in a secondary or derivative sense.

Bodily Values: These values relate to the health efficiency and beauty of the physical life.

Recreation Values: These refer to the values of play and leisure enriching the life.

Values of Association: These may be called the social values as they include numerous forms of human association-from friendship and family life to worldwide relationships.

Character Values: Here we may include the whole range of desirable, personal and social virtues including justice, benevolence, self-control and truthfulness.

Aesthetic Values: Beauty of nature and works of art are the aesthetic values.

Intellectual Values: Values concerning knowledge and quest for an attainment of truth can be included in this group.

Religious Values: Religious values include worship, devotion etc.

Parker's Classification According to Interest: Parker has given another classification of values according to interest. The different groups suggested by him are as under:

(i) Biological values
(ii) Economic values
(iii) Affecting values
(iv) Social values
(v) Intellectual values
(vi) Aesthetic values
(vii) Moral values
(viii) Religious values

Classification in Terms of Ultimate Realities: Plato advocated another classification in terms of ultimate realities. These are:

(i) Goodness
(ii) Beauty
(iii) Truth

These values of life have been enunciated by Indian thinkers as Satyam, Shivam and Sundaram.

ORIGIN OF VALUES

Values are there within the individuals and they develop in them as are the situations all around and the circumstances they are placed in. A good person in the teeth of bad environment may become outlawed and shun his goodness, truth, honesty and sincerity.

Various sources of values are:

Religion: Different religions propagate different values. Analyzed and properly understood, almost all religions lay emphasis on the same values.

Hindu religion advocates self-realization or MOKSHA. Everyone ultimately tries to merge his ownself with universal God.

Christianity, Islam, Sikhism emphasis a particular way of life based on the doctrines and principles of respective religions.

In the recent past, the new discipline 'Study of Comparative Religions' has come up in different centres of higher learning. In Punjabi University, Patiala, the Department of Comparative religions is housed in Guru Gobind Singh Bhawan. The very structure of the building shows different religions in human society and ultimately all merging into one. The basic philosophy behind all religions is that God is one and the same whatever may be His garb in different religions. Young scholars from India are seen going to foreign countries specially U.S.A. for their doctoral work in this new discipline. Surely this discipline will affect considerably in propagating right values among the youth.

All the religions of the world recommend the following common values of life:

(i) Simplicity
(ii) Pursuit of truth
(iii) Dignity of labour
(iv) Tolerance
(v) Broadmindedness
(vi) Welfare of mankind
(vii) Attainment of bliss-Moksha
(viii) Holy life
(ix) Purity and simple living

Philosophy: Philosophy of life is another important source of values. Philosophy involves deep and critical thinking and thus it is able to have its own list of different values. Values of life change with the change of time and change of philosophy. For example idealism is in favour of values of life, such as truth, goodness, and beauty.

Literature: Literature is also an important source of values. Literature and social life are closely interlinked. Values of social life are reflected in different forms of literature, such as essays, stories, poems, prose writings etc. The study of literature affects the mind of the learner. The study of good literature has far reaching effects on the youth.

Social Customs: Social customs, social functions, cultural heritage, social beliefs, social practices advocate different types of values. Since the society goes on changing with the passage of time, the same way the values also go on changing.

Science: Apparently science seems to be against religious beliefs and thus there seems to be end of all good values. Actually it is not so. Science is rather an important social institution and is source of values. Through science, we are able to develop knowledge through observation, experimentation and rational thinking. Science provides us with a new set of values which have their own utility and usefulness.

According to Barber, the values more favourable for science are the following:

(a) Rationality.

(b) Utilitarianism.

(c) Universalism.

(d) Individualism.

It is true that science helps us to think scientifically and act rationally.

According to Russell, "The effects of science are various and of very different kinds. There are direct intellectual effects, the dispelling of many traditional beliefs and the adoption of others."

DETERIORATION OF VALUES

Different types of values make the individual grow and develop rightly. The values are the assets of an individual. In the absence of moral, social, cultural, and economic values, man has no worth, and is considered insignificant. The society whose individuals have lost values may be called a poor and backward society. Indian society has been a very good example of high traditions and conventions replete with all type of values. If we compare the present situation with that of the past, it is all depressive, and sorrowful. Over the years, there have been all types of deterioration. Too much erosion of values is seen all around.

The erosion of values is everywhere and at all levels leading to the spread of greed, self-aggrandizement, gross-injustice, abuse of human rights, perversion of power, callousness, insensitivity, depravity of taste and behaviour, pettiness, waste and plunder and man's wallowing for the low and dark dimensions of his consciousness.

S.N. Ghosh says in his paper 'Key to Value Orientation', "The more we pursue this fragmented science in the name of development or removal of poverty, the more we would proceed towards mass impoverishment and elitist parasitism, when more and more people are thrown in the vortex and have to compete for survival, all values, piety, compassion, spirit of sacrifice, truthfulness, independence, courage, fellow feeling, love etc. come under a blight from which only the very exceptional persons can escape." Dr. T. Ramji observes, "Man is the monarch of the external world of emotions and passions to a large extent. There is a crisis of character in our age, owing to deterioration of values in social, economic, political and religious spheres of life." He further says, "In the midst of material prosperity, there is a sense of frustration and gloom. In the midst of abundance, we find poverty in a large section of society."

Dr. Sampuran Singh has analyzed the present position of Indian society and the erosion of social values. In his book 'The Holistic Education' in the foreword of his book Vimla Thakur remarked, "Thoughts, ideologies, codes of conduct and sets of values, psychological pattern of behaviour have failed in transforming man. Man with the help of thought organization has created a marvellous scientific and technological world, but human being, as an individual is unhappy and frustrated, not at peace with himself, not at harmony with the different layers of his being."

Why there has been erosion of values in social groups is a question which needs contemplation, and pondering over by one and all. Surely those who are responsible for it should reconsider everything and review everything with the motive of setting everything right. The educationist should also exert and think of ways and means for improving the deteriorated social set up of life. The research workers should also work in this area of crisis and help in bringing about improvements.

Why Erosion of Values?: The erosion of values has started from the top and it has gone down through different channels causing havoc all around. Perhaps the only possibility is that a revolutionary type of change would be able to set things right. Erosion of values is discernible in the following institutions in the country:

Political Institutions: The political groups of the country ruling or the sitting has set many worst examples by showing erosion of values before the public. All types of quarrels among the different political groups, first verbal and then of physical type, are being noticed by the public. With the advancement of Science and Technology, the use of T.V. has now revealed the workings going on in different meetings to one and all in the public. One important person of the Govt. abusing the other or throwing a chair upon public others or beating them is seen by within the country or abroad. Persons of higher or lower ranks, and especially the youth and the budding children are adversely affected by this type of activities. The political groups have thus led to the erosion of values among masses.

Erosion in political standards and values are of the following type:

(i) The political leaders exploit the masses to achieve their narrow and selfish ends.

(ii) The so-called political people lack code of conduct and they indulge more and more in political corruption.

(iii) In the light of constitutional provisions and guarantees given there in, far less is actually provided.

(iv) The leaders keep their vested interest in the fore front and national interests are ignored.

(v) There is lack of true leadership. Many high-ups in the political circles don't deserve the rank but they continue holding it shamelessly.

(vi) Police atrocities and brutalities are committed on the advice of politicians.

(vii) Scandals, militancy, lawlessness, indiscipline are on the increase in the society. Often politics is involved.

Educational Institutions: The educational scene in its true sense can be seen in the universities (so called centres of higher learning), the colleges and the schools. Politics one way or the other has entered in the sacred profession of teaching. Elections of teachers and students are held there for which all types of political pressures are used. Quarrels, physical fighting, disrespect to the chair and to the high-ups can be seen. Then teachers going on strike, the students going on strike and sometimes both teachers and students going on strike together—all this is deteriorating the social values day by day. The educational institutions are meant for betterment of the individual and the society but they are now helping in creating an unwanted type of social environment. Every now and then, the Heads of the institutions are seen quarrelling with the staff or the students. Corruption on the part of the authorities is spreading and making the younger groups imitate it. Some examples are given below:

(i) Selfishness on the part of teaching and administrative community is seen.

(ii) Cooperation, fellow feelings, brotherhood, social service, etc. are disappearing in the institutions.

(iii) All types of corruption, malpractices from the top to bottom are on the increase.

(iv) Self-discipline, hard-working, honesty, sincerity are disappearing.

(v) Disobedience is spreading all around.

(vi) Everyone is becoming more and more materialistic and money minded-all at the cost of values.

Scene at Home: The scene at home has also become similar to the ones being seen in politics and centres of education. Quarrel between the parents, quarrel of youngers with the elders, quarrel between different members of the family and same age group are now multiplying. Almost every home stands disintegrated as far as love, affection and respect are concerned, which is similar and parallel to the sight in educational institutions and Parliament House of the country. The situation at home and in family is reflected as:

(i) Self-centredness and selfishness are spreading.

(ii) Respect for others, obedience to elders are fast decreasing.

Neighbourhood Sight: The streets joining different homes present their own added gloom and deterioration in this direction. There is jealousy and hatred of one with the other. Mutual give and take relationship, the we-feeling etc. are disappearing. Help from one neighbour to the next can hardly be seen in times of difficulty. Respect of elderly persons living in the neighbourhood is also fast disappearing. This is evident from the following:

(i) Spirit of cooperation, fellow feelings are vanishing.

(ii) Individualized style of living and self-centredness are increasing.

Sight at Informal Social Gatherings: There are informal types of social gatherings in the bazars, on the railway stations, in the trains, in the buses, etc. The elderly persons are seen standing whereas the youngsters continue sitting occupying seats in the moving bus or the train. Gone are the days when people out of respect offered the seat to the ladies and surely to the aged and elderly persons. Now even on making special request nobody vacates the seats for the ailing person even. Respect for others, sympathy, kindness, etc. are now fast disappearing. The present trend is:

(i) Social sensitiveness is disappearing from the minds of the people.

(ii) The feelings of oneness, common brotherhood are matters of the past. None seems to be caring for others.

(iii) Respect for others, sympathy and kindness for those in difficulty are missing.

Religious Institutions: Religious institutions have also gone down in moral standards to a great extent. Politics has entered into these organizations and there are sights showing erosion of values. Sympathy for a poor person is no longer the consideration there. Give and take relationship has become the basis in matters of service rendered by the religious organizations. The present situation might have been caused due to ill-will and unwanted type of behaviour shown by the public or the so-called devotees.

Setting Things Right: Erosion of values in the social circles need be checked vehemently by one and all concerned. It is the duty of one and all to shoulder their responsibility with full sincerity and help in setting things right. Before we think of ways and means to check, the further erosion of values let us think of the sources of values.

DEMAND OF THE TIME

The social environment all around is deteriorating day by day. There is erosion of social, economic, political and cultural values. No doubt, there has been great advancement in the field of Science and Technology, but it has changed the attitude of the people considerably. People now have more or less materialistic attitude. It has led to different types of conflicts, such as old beliefs and new beliefs, old values of life and new values of life. Now only value oriented education can deliver the goods rightly and help to change things for betterment.

Views Related to Value Oriented Education

Indian Education Commission: In this context, Indian Education Commission (1964-66) puts forth the views: "The weakening of social and moral values in the younger generation is creating many serious social and ethical conflicts in western societies and there is already a desire among some great western thinkers to balance the knowledge and skills which science and technology bring with the values and insights associated with ethics and religion at its best. In the situation that is developing, it is equally important for us to give a proper value orientation.

About value oriented education, Challenge of Education: a Policy Perspective mentions, "One of the major crises facing education in India is that of value orientation. It has been usually argued that the main focus during the last three decades has been on quantitative expansion and consequently adequate attention could not be paid to maintaining standards and quality of education. The output of the educational system is not only of poor quality but degradation of the moral values has also been noticed."

National Policy on Education (1986): Following points are mentioned in the National Policy of Education-1986:

> "The growing concern over the erosion of essential values and an increasing cynicism in society has brought to focus the need for readjustments in the curriculum for the cultivation of social and moral values".

In our culturally plural society, education should foster universal and eternal values, oriented towards the unity and integration of our people. Such value education should help eliminate obscurantism, religious fanaticism, violence, superstition and fatalism.

Apart from this combative role, value education as a profound positive content is based on our heritage, national goals, universal perceptions. It should lay primary emphasis on this aspect.

Views of Educationists and Thinkers: Regarding value oriented education, different educationists and thinkers of India have put forth their views as under:

> Mahatma Gandhi wanted education should be for the hand, head and heart. Education for the heart was the spiritual training for him. According to him, the aim of education is self-realization the summum bonum of life and education.

Rabindranath Tagore said, "The greatest use of education is not merely to collect facts, but to know man and to make oneself known to man."

Aurobindo gave a higher and clearer dimension to education of values. He recognized the dormant spirituality in every individual. His scheme of education for spiritual values was two-faced. He believed that our education should provide the opportunity for teaching of higher values. At the lower level all should be educated in higher values. In the second phase only those who can pursue the spiritual values should be given spiritual education at higher levels.

Swami Dayanand laid emphasis on the role and responsibility of parents in the scheme of value education. According to him it is the duty of parents to give instructions in value to their children which draws injunctions from the tradition of ancient Indian education.

Swami Vivekanand defines education as "Education is a manifestation of divine perfection already existing in man." He further says, "We want education by which character is formed, strength of mind is increased, the intellect expanded and by which one can stand on one's feet."

Dr. Radha Krishnan says, "Education is not limited to the imparting of information or training in skills. It has to give the educated a proper sense of values."

The Characteristics of Man: A few characteristics of a man with values are listed below:

(a) A man with values looks fine. All tend to appreciate him as well as his activity.

(b) 'A man of words' finds appreciation all around. Whatever one says, sticks to it firmly.

(c) Respects the elders—considers them to be his guide, depends upon them and remains a person of their faith and confidence.

(d) Tolerance and patience are fully with him. He tolerates others and does not lose patience for a while.

(e) A true national worker for the betterment of society, community and the nation.

(f) Ever ready to help others, considers the service of others as his prime duty.

(g) Sympathetic attitude—he never scoffs or laughs at others in times of difficulty, rather he shares the troubles with a sympathetic outlook.

(h) Works diligently, never shirks work.

Values of life are, therefore, ornaments which shine like stars in the personality of the individual who possesses those values. It is therefore, very important that values be inculcated.

Inculcation of Values

Approaches: There are different approaches for inculcating values. They are briefly discussed here below:

Direct and Indirect Approach: Direct approach means teaching values directly to others. Here efforts are made cautiously to teach different values to others. The approach may work for sometime but many a time, it has its disadvantages. There may be reaction of the learners and sometimes they may give opposite opinions. That can prove rather more dangerous.

Indirect approach of teaching values is more convenient, effective and lasting. Here, teaching is done indirectly. The learner reads books and is able to catch up values of life here and there. In day to day life situations, he learns values incidently.

Formal and Informal Approach: When the learners are taught about difficult values by using formal ways, it may not leave much effect. Here, materials from books are taught with a motive of teaching certain values. Television is shown by using formal situations in order to inculcate different values. On the other hand, in informal approach the learner or the receiver of values is unaware of values. He reads some material from the books and is able to pick up values of life incidently. This type of learning is of greater value and lasts longer.

Curricular and Co-curricular Approach: According to curricular approach, separate syllabus is framed which aims at teaching values to the learners. The syllabus is prescribed and teaching is done to finish this syllabus. In the text-books, the values maybe integrated in different chapters. Thus, the students have curricular programme which helps them to learn different values.

In co-curricular programme, different activities such as singing, poem recitation, drama, debate, declamation contest, essay writing competition, etc. are organized with a motive of inculcating different values of life in the students. There can be social service activities, physical exercises, games and sports. Different activities will help in the inculcation of variety of values in students.

Ways and Means for the Inculcation of Values in Schools: The school authorities can organize various activities and functions for the purpose of inculcation of values in the students. The head of the institution and the teaching staff can plan and organize a number of programmes for this purpose. A few such programmes are briefly explained here:

(a) The text-books prescribed for the students should contain stories with certain moral lessons. Teachers interested in writing text-books for the children can help in making the text-books of this type. Even supplementary readers or books for the children may be written by some teachers in collaboration with others and help in the achievement of this goal.

(b) Prizes may be given to the deserving students for showing honesty, bravery, gallantry, truth, etc. The award of prizes be given to the students in social gathering or functions.

(c) Declamation contest maybe organized in the institution on themes related to values of life. The contest may be intra-school and inter-school. Participation in the contest by way of speakers and also by way of audience will have a good deal of impact.

(d) National Service Scheme (N.S.S.) need to be popularized and its programme of activities be organized vigorously. The students interested in social service at the railway station, at the general bus stand, in the social festivals, in the hospitals, in the villages, in the slum areas be able to do a lot. In this way they will imbibe values of life permanently.

(e) A few projects for value education may be started in educational institutions under the guidance of some teachers. The students may start their own canteen on no-profit no-loss basis. Different groups may control it turn by turn and make its functioning successful. Some students may start a cooperative store where books and stationery on wholesale rate may be purchased and sold to all the students studying in that school. The basis of the cooperative store should be no-profit no-loss. It will make the students hardworker and they will also understand tips of business and the margin of profit-loss, etc.

In the same way, students' cooperative banks, students' cooperative post office, etc. may be set up in the institution under the guidance of some teachers. All these practices will inculcate good values of life among the students. These students will come out as successful and worthy social beings.

Educational Institutions should shoulder the responsibility and strive in every possible way for the inculcation of values in students. The beginning years in the school are more conducive for it. The teachers will be able to achieve the aims while devoting less tune and by paying far less attention as compared to the situation which would be otherwise.

(f) Extension lectures based on morality or value oriented education may be arranged in the institution. Eminent persons specialized in this field may be invited. Listening to the lectures, discussions, etc. will help the students to have clarification with regard to values.

(g) The head of the institution and the teaching personnel should be the living examples of values. The institution in itself should be made a centre for moral instructions. It should propagate higher values of life.

(h) Book exhibitions on literature related to values be organized in the institution by extendable invitations to noted publishers/booksellers of this area of knowledge. The exhibitions should be thrown open to the students and the community. It will have its effects on one and all.

(i) Educational TV can work wonders in this field. Some good teachers can bring out materials related to values in the form of TV serials. Showing such films to the students and the community be made a regular feature of the school.

(j) Art and painting exhibitions on themes like moral, social, cultural values, etc. be organized in the institutions. Paintings of distinguished artists depicting values be displayed. Such exhibitions will have their effects on the growing personalities of children. Some children might develop then-interest in this area of knowledge. On the spot, Art and Painting competitions may be organized on themes related to different types of values. Students of different age groups may be invited from institutions of the region or the state as may be considered proper. Prizes may be given for excellent performances in different age groups. It will highlight the themes of values among the children and through them to the families and the community.

(k) Some journal on the theme of values in life may be brought out by an institution. It can be done by some voluntary organization also. Suitable articles can be invited for publication. The journal may be monthly or quarterly as is possible and its circulation should be popularized. It should be suitably priced so that it is within the reach of majority.

(l) Skit, drama, competition, etc. may be organized in the institution. Assistance may be sought from the District Public Relations Officers. The themes should have values in life-social, moral, cultural, political, educational, etc. The different institutions should be encouraged to participate in the competition enthusiastically.

(m) Value oriented education should be made compulsory in all the schools. One teacher may be entrusted with the duty of assessing the whole with teaching of the school in terms of value education. Strenuous efforts should be made to achieve the desired aims with the cooperation of the staff and students.

(n) Morning assembly should be made compulsory in all the educational institutions. It can be of half an hour duration. Apart from morning prayer, good thoughts may be read out by some students and staff members. Religious and national songs may be sung and poems may be recited.

(o) House examinations may be arranged in Value Education. All students may be asked to qualify it at junior levels say in standard V, standard VIII and also at standard XII. It should also be at degree level which may be organized by the university or by the college itself. No student should be considered to have passed the examination without having passed in Value Education or Moral Education or the so called Religious Education.

Views of Different Commissions on Education for Values: The importance of Value Education has been recognized by different Education Commissions and Committees appointed by the Government. Their views are as under:

(a) The Hartong Committee (1929) felt that religious instructions can be given in common schools outside the school hours.

(b) The Central Advisory Board of Education felt in 1946 that religious and moral instruction was important and that it should be left to community to which the pupils belong.

(c) The Secondary Education Commission Report in 1953 favoured that religious and moral instruction should be given in school, and outside school hours on voluntary basis.

(d) The Sriparkasha Committee on Religious and Moral Instruction had recommended that Religious and Moral Education should be imparted in all educational institutions.

(e) The Education Commission of 1964-66 has also strongly recommended for the direct and indirect teaching of social, moral and spiritual values to our children. The Commission has recommended that the, University Department of Comparative Religion should produce suitable literature for teaching of universal social, moral, religious and spiritual values.

Value-crisis in India has to be checked by one and all concerned with it directly or indirectly. Then and then only we can hope to see the bright future of the countrymen and see India as prosperous nation. There is need of re-consideration, re-planning, restructuring and re-execution of educational programmes. Let us also follow the views expressed by different Commissions on education for the development of values and act wisely and rightly.

Human Rights Education

Human Rights have ushered in a new era. Fukuyama's conceit (I mean it in both senses) that the triumph of Western liberalism has stopped the clock of change—has put an end to history—is already waning. We may reflect that human rights themselves have played a sacrificial role in this process, for the demise of the regimes of Eastern Europe was accelerated by a megaphone rhetoric of human rights from States, including our own, with an embarrassing capacity for overlooking human rights abuses among their own allies and clients and even within their own frontiers. The message between the lines has been that human rights are a commodity like any other, capable of being traded for political or economic advantage, and the rhetoric little more than the conduct of politics by other means.

Politicization of Human Rights

This is not, however, a complaint about the politicization of human rights. They are by nature political, for they seek to condition how States treat individuals. The reason why it is we who feel able to lecture others about them is that human rights are historically and ideologically the property of the liberal democracies of the West. In their received and accepted form, whether one takes the European Convention or the Universal Declaration as the example, they enshrine values which are universal neither in time nor in place. They are in essence the enlightenment's values of possessive individualism, derived from the historic paradigm, which has shaped our world, of the conscious human actor whose natural enemy is the State—a necessary evil—and in whose maximum personal liberty lies the maximum benefit for society.

To accept, as we can and should, that this view is rooted in time and place is not to consign it to the bin of relativism, for the same has been and will continue to be true of all historic proclamations of self-evident and universal truths. (The two most self-evident truths of life on this planet are after all that the earth is flat and that the sun goes round it.) The truth that all men are created equal was far from self-evident to the slaves owned by some of the men who proclaimed it at the dawn of American republicanism.

That free speech or family life is today a fundamental individual right is by no means self-evident in a good number of the contemporary world's States, where history and conditions have made it apparent that they are primarily the State's business; and it is entirely conceivable that the States of Western Europe may during the coming century recast their thinking about family life and the right of the incurably or expensively ill to life itself as social and economic pressures be are down on ethics and theology. Who will then be right: our grandchildren or us?

It is perfectly possible to recognize the localization of ideas in time and place and to assert that they are none the worse for it; indeed, that ideas which pretend to universality are historical delusions. To do so, however, carries two corollaries. One is that as times change our premises and assumptions about the content of fundamental rights will change.

Secondly, what is made of currently accepted rights in each country and each generation by its courts and adjudicators is itself a function of time and place. (Law spends its life stretched on the rack between certainty and adaptability, sometimes groaning audibly but mostly maintaining the stoical appearance of steady uniformity which public confidence demands.) But lest the mask become the face, it is important that new generations of lawyers should become actively curious about why the certainties of the law themselves change constantly.

How and why is it that the same American Constitution in 1896 legitimated racial segregation in public services and then in 1954 forbade it? How does it come about that not dissimilar abortion laws have in recent years been struck down by Canada's Supreme Court as too restrictive and by Germany's Constitutional Court as too permissive? On our own patch, how did it come to be self-evident to the Court of Appeal in 1925 that it was perfectly all right for an education authority to sack married women teachers on the ground that their duties lay at home or, in 1948, that it was perfectly all right for Wednesbury Corporation to use its cinema licensing powers to stop young people going to the pictures on Sunday?

Not one of these decisions, each of them affecting what we would recognize now as fundamental human rights, is intelligible today except by situating the reasoning of the deciding court in its peculiar time and place; and the same will, I hope, be true of the decisions handed down by this judicial generation—for it would be only in an ossified and retrograde society that the laws of one generation were good enough for the next.

Precedent, far from becoming redundant, takes on an organic role in this scheme of things—not perhaps in the grand Tennysonian image of freedom slowly broadening down in a kind of Fabian long march to happiness, but a centuries-long culture of reasoning and principle which ebbs and flows, so that, for example, the charge of contempt of court made on behalf of a Zairian asylum-seeker against the holder of one of the three great offices of State, the Home Secretary, could found upon Sir Edward Coke's assertion of the sovereignty of the courts in the face of the Crown's prerogatives and upon Wilkes's recovery of punitive damages from an earlier Home Secretary, Lord Halifax, for the unlawful issue of a general warrant. A former jobbing electrician who became a distinguished teacher of law once told me that in both jobs he had found the most useful part of his equipment to be a well-filled box of junk; and while I would not put the great cases I have been referring to in that class, an eclectic mind is not a bad asset in a modern lawyer.

The ministerial contempt case illustrates, too, the way in which modern public law has carried forward a culture of judicial assertiveness to compensate for, and in places repair, dysfunctions in the democratic process. It is a remarkable fact that a judiciary which has taken a public battering in recent years over miscarriages of criminal justice has in the same period earned large public approbation for its willingness to prevent and correct abuses of governmental power.

When the history of modern judicial review is written, it will recount how the coming of the adult franchise through the two great nineteenth century Reform Acts was matched by the introduction of the Northgate Trevelyan civil service. This replaced ministers' placement with an intellectual and administrative elite from the same schools, universities and clubs as the judges themselves, and encouraged the judiciary to retreat from its prickly Victorian invigoration of the executive into a passivity. This passivity by the 1950s, had allowed executive and local government an unprecedented measure of unchallenged power, to the extent that even the administrative tribunals set up to adjudicate between citizen and State were treated as instruments of departmental policy.

It will also, I hope, observe how the subsequent reassertion of judicial oversight of government which has been the achievement of the 1970s and 1980s in this country has been replicated all over the common law world as judiciaries have moved to fill lacunae of legitimacy in the functioning of democratic polities—a process of which the Pergau Dam decision can stand as a sharp recent illustration. The historian's conclusion may well be that the last three decades of the twentieth century have seen a judicial refashioning, with popular support sufficient to mute political opposition to it, of our organic constitution. If so, its consequence is that we have today both in this country and in those with which it shares aspects of its political and judicial culture a new and still emerging constitutional paradigm.

This is no longer of Dicey's supreme parliament to whose will the rule of law must finally bend, but of a bipolar sovereignty of the Crown in Parliament and the Crown in its courts, to each of which the Crown's ministers are answerable—politically to Parliament, legally to the courts. That the government of the day has no separate sovereignty in this paradigm is both axiomatic and a reminder of the sharpest of all the lessons of eastern Europe: that it is when State is collapsed into party that democracy flounders.

Primacy of Democracy

To assume a jurisdiction of this kind is of course to assume, without having argued it, the primacy of democracy. It is therefore worth remembering how temporary and vulnerable the desirable sense of democracy is. A term of abuse synonymous with mob rule in Burke's vocabulary, its contemporary feel-good usage finds its origin in America, where from its first known modern use in the Rhode Island Constitution of 1641 it became a vehicle of challenge to the colonial power in the hands of Hamilton and his contemporaries and in due course a vehicle of challenge in this country in the hands of the Chartists and their successors to the rotten boroughs and aristocratic oligarchies which electoral reform was eventually to sweep away.

But although the power of the world has become such that there is barely a regime anywhere in the world which has not sought during the twentieth century to characterize itself as democratic, there is nothing which determines that the notion of democracy as the higher-order law beneath which constitutions must operate is there for all time. If anything, history should lead us to expect the converse; but apart from watching phlegmatically as the great oxymoron of the nineteenth century, the nation States, fissiparate and super States now arm the world's poor nations to kill each other, we cannot peer very far into that darkness.

For these and other reasons one sees trouble with the concept of a higher-order of law as the basis of human rights adjudication. To postulate such a law is to attract all the theological problems which attend any argument from a first cause and which can ultimately only be answered by an act of faith. (It may be in the end that a society's consensus about its basic values is an act of faith, but my own preference is to reason, as Hobbes or Bentham might have done, that it is society itself which is given and which poses certain overriding needs for its own existence.) While shared perceptions of what those needs are change as societies change, there are moral and practical continuities—of which the democratic principle is one—which can be powerfully represented as fundamental values, at least within the temporal and social horizons of each society.

This relatively modest foundation for the legitimacy of human rights has perhaps the virtue that, without reducing all discourse to incoherent subjectivity, it recognizes that a single 'right' outcome to every issue is attainable, if at all, only locally and temporarily, and that just as the only universal truth is that there are no universal truths, true objectivity may well consist in recognizing the reality of history and of change. When the future Chief Justice Hughes of the US said eighty years ago, "The Constitution is what the judges say it is", he was speaking of all rights instruments at all times, and to a realist concerned with human rights he was offering not despair but hope.

This will be thought perverse by many whose views I respect and who point to what happens when the judges are put in the driving seat in order to show the that way constitutional madness lies. They point, among many other examples, to the record of the Privy Council as a constitutional court composed chiefly of English judges, veering between indefensible interference with democratic decisions (for example with the legislation by which Canada was trying to replicate Roosevelt's New Deal, and which the Privy Council actually wrecked because Canada could deploy no equivalent of Roosevelt's threat to pack the Supreme Court), and indefensible abstention in the face of illiberal and oppressive conduct by Commonwealth regimes.

They point too, to the outcomes of a series of cases from Northern Ireland decided in the House of Lords and in the European Commission and Court of Human Rights, in which principle seems to have taken second place to expediency and the lesson of Liverside v. Anderson to have been forgotten. These critics are opposed, however, by a respected school of rights discourse which holds that once fundamental human rights are articulated and set down, to attack them for their outcomes is to substitute venality for principle and to drag rights adjudication in the political mud.

For reasons elaborated, there should be little sympathy with this critique: it not only makes historical assumptions about the primacy and universality of currently accepted principles of political and social conduct, but assumes the neutrality of adjudication and at worst ascribes rogue decisions to rogue judges. It is equally plain, nevertheless, as the end of the century approaches that the argument for a bill of rights for the United Kingdom is being won by its proponents, and that the off-the-shelf solution of incorporation of the European Convention heads the list of possible measures if only on the practical ground that adherence to a set of standards enforceable on the State by an international tribunal but not by its own citizens in its own courts makes no sense at all.

Moreover, the House of Lords has now recognized that our constitution knows such a thing as a fundamental law—the European Communities Act 1972—capable of overriding subsequent primary legislation if the courts find the two to be in conflict; so self-evident in fact was the doctrine that the House in Factortame (No. 2) found it unnecessary to articulate it before giving it effect.

As to the shape of a UK bill of rights I shall have a little more to say; but my present argument is that our agenda for the twenty-first century is not necessarily confined to a choice between a rights instrument interpreted for better or for worse by a judiciary with a long record of illiberal adjudication, and rejection of any rights instrument in favour of parliamentary government. Certainly, the better government becomes, the less scope there will be before judicial review of it: it is not mere piety to say that the aim of the nominated judges is to work themselves out of a job.

But for the foreseeable future we have a problem, shared in large part with other developed democracies: how to ensure that as a docility we are governed within a law which has internalized the notion of fundamental human rights. If posing it this way means adopting the rule of law, like democracy, as a higher-order principle, we likewise have the social consensus, which alone—and without the need of a leap of faith—can accord it that primacy.

And if in our own society the rule of law is to mean much, it must at least mean that it is the obligation of the courts to articulate and uphold the ground rules of ethical social existence which we dignify as fundamental human rights, temporary and local though they are in the grand scheme of things.

The largely unexplored avenue to this end, and the one I want to explore, is what I will perversely call the principle of outcomes. In common with the critics of a bill of rights I believe that in a democracy people have every right to scrutinize and appraise not merely the integrity of the judicial process but what it actually delivers. It is one thing, however difficult, to explain to the public that a directed acquittal because of an improperly extracted confession seeks to preserve the integrity of legal process as a greater good than the conviction of a possibly guilty individual without due process; it is another to try to justify, by reference to the legal principles which undoubtedly explain them, the kinds of award made in major libel actions. There is nothing wrong with the argument that if this is the due result there is something wrong with the principles or the processes that have produced it.

Refusing to accept the objectionable outcome alongside the welcome one is not simply allowing predilection to triumph over principle: it is to recognize that outcome—the result we want—is symbiotic with principle, because it is only for their concrete effect that we reconsider principles worth having and fighting over. If I thought there were any self-evident truths I would rank this high among them.

Take the right to life, qualified as it ordinarily is in favour of limited inroads made into it by law. No rights instrument I know of tells you whether capital punishment is compatible with this fundamental right, but nobody suggests that for this reason the right is not worth articulating or that courts cannot adjudicate on it. It is simply that argument about the content of the right cannot be conducted in purely overrun principally legal terms, and the answers given by constitutional courts are inevitably and rightly a function of that large debate.

Democratic Society

The new transitional Constitution of South Africa, a country which till recently led the world in the rate of judicial executions, accords the right to life and permits derogation to any extent which is reasonable and justifiable in an open and democratic society, but not so as to negate the essential content of the right in question. The first case in the list of the new Constitutional Court has been a challenge to the constitutionality of the death penalty.

Its judgement, whichever way it goes, will resolve an issue which politicians had consciously decided was better left to the courts, even if (as one suspects) the prohibition on derogations which negate the essential content of the right makes the outcome fairly certain.

The Canadian Charter of Rights and Freedoms puts it very differently: "Everyone has the right to life... and the right not to be deprived thereof except in accordance with the principles of fundamental justice", but the words are capable of giving rise to much the same debate. In tomorrow's world the role which courts have had to accept as society's arbiter and conscience is a role capable of embracing issues of this kind without forfeiting the epithet judicial.

It is not a new role; it was the English courts which, however reluctantly, grasped the nettle that legislators would not touch and declared slavery—at least on these shores—illegal; although it is a fine irony that the famous phrase of Lord Stowell in the case of the Slave Grace in 1827, that the air of England was too pure for a slave to breathe, appears to have originated in a sixteenth-century decision of the Court of Star Chamber, which had used the same metaphor in depriving an Englishman of his imported slave. But to say that the courts are likely to continue to discharge this role, whether under the name of public policy or of human right adjudication, tells us little about how and by what standards they will do it.

Until recently it was to Canada that we could most usefully look from this country for a prognostication of how a common law judiciary might be expected to interpret and apply a modern rights instrument. These messages have been mixed: it has become apparent that the big battalions are getting an unfair share of Canadian rights adjudications; but there have been many decisions to cheer up liberal thinkers. But it is in Australia that the real problem has recently been highlighted: its High Court has reached into the bowels of the country's now elderly Constitution and extracted certain modern human rights—a process that outcome watchers might applaud; but it has proceeded in one case to apply them to an effect which, seen from this side of the globe, looks so partial as to justify every fear the outcome watchers have expressed.

In the first of two cases decided on the same day in 1992, a statute which criminalized criticism, justified or not, of members of the Industrial Relations Commission was struck down as creating a fetter on free speech out of all proportion to the permissible objective. In the second, the court struck down a statutory provision which, in order to stop the loading of the dice in elections in favour of candidates or parties with wealthy supporters who bought television advertising time and used it to promote them, provided for free airtime for all parties and allowed full and free journalistic coverage, but banned other broadcast political advertising in the run-up to elections.

The reasoning in the second case went like this: the Australian Constitution of 1900 contains no bill of rights and gives the courts no express power to review primary legislation; but it is predicated on the primacy of representative government, which in turn depends on the full and free communication of ideas; so that any legislation which obstructs the fullest desired flow of opinion in the electoral process is unconstitutional. In Australia too the Constitution appears to be what the judges say it is, and these two decisions and their more recent successors have serious implications.

First, they illustrate vividly the trend in the free-market democracies for the courts, with a great measure of popular support, to keep government within the law by—if necessary—strong and innovative measures. In the UK we are already some way down the road of legislative review, and legislation may well carry us the rest of the way by the end of the century. Whether it does so by entrenchment, giving a power to strike down legislation on human rights grounds as well as European Union ones, or by infiltration along the lines of the New Zealand Bill of Rights Act 1990, may not matter very much—at least if we can expect in the latter event to emulate the approach to outcomes adopted by Sir Robin Cooke in a recent leading case. He said: "It is necessary to be alert in New Zealand to the danger that both the courts and parliament at times may, or at least be asked to give, lip service to human rights in high-sounding language, but little or no real service in terms of actual decision." And he went on to hold that there was now a cause of action for breach of the Bill of Rights Act, basing himself—to be fair—on a 1979 decision of the Privy Council.

Secondly, however, the cases illustrate the fickleness of outcomes. Speaking for myself as a citizen I applaud the first and deplore the second. The first cuts down an indefensible protection of public figures from civilized criticism. But the second adopts, it seems to me, a very particular and partisan view of what free speech is: because it demands a free flow of ideas, the court holds that to accord a hearing to ideas in proportion to the wealth of those who hold them is not only a democratic course but the only democratic course; and in doing so it assumes a symmetry which simply does not exist between freedom of speech and freedom of information.

In Britain where we have lived all our lives with Representation of the People Acts predicated (despite judicial inroads) on a financially limited and level playing field for all contenders, and with a complete prohibition on political advertising on television, the fallacy is more readily seen. In the United States, by contrast, the Australian decision is prefigured by a long history of legislative attempts to stop wealth buying seats, frustrated every time by a Supreme Court with both eyes fixed mesmerically on the First Amendment, and with results that are well known in terms of the wealth needed to run for office.

The Australian decision certainly makes it harder to defend the fitness of the courts to undertake constitutional adjudication on human rights issues, for the High Court of Australia has taken to be self-evident and universal views which many would regard as partial and highly contentious in a democracy.

What then is to be done? The answer, whether we like it or not, is in large part being determined for us. The courts of these and other countries—India prominent among them—are by now engaged on a broad highway of constitutional adjudication along which issues of fundamental rights relentlessly present themselves.

In this country, as I have outlined, the modern growth of public law and the internationalization of our jurisprudence have moved adjudication towards a new catholicity of subject-matter and a greater preparedness to intervene to right wrongs in the polity. The only choice in this situation—and it is a choice which the judiciary can make for itself but which Parliament can no longer realistically make for 'it is to retreat from rights adjudication into the long sleep of Wednesbury and before, or to develop the role with which we are now becoming familiar and to continue to move in the direction of a rights culture compatible with constitutional adjudication in a democracy.

With all its pitfalls, the latter looks to be the only worthwhile choice. There is no means of standing still, but neither is there any virtue in proceeding down the path of constitutional and human rights adjudication without taking very careful stock indeed of where it might lead us. This is why it is to outcomes as much as to principles that we need to look for the future, recognizing that even then the future will one day be the past and its decision be seen, like ours, to be creatures of a dialectic of time, place and principle. It is also why there is nothing unprincipled in arguing from outcomes.

The first and most important lesson that experience is teaching us is that human rights can be treated as commodities and, like commodities, appropriated by those who have the means to do so. I began by mentioning this on the international plane, but it is equally true domestically, and the free speech issue provides perhaps the sharpest illustration of how and why. The splendour of American First Amendment jurisprudence sets a standard, which nobody can ignore: the marketplace of ideas, the heresy that grows into orthodoxy. It is between the glories of the First Amendment and the horrors of a Ministry of Truth that the region of debate lies, for all societies place a restraint at some point on who can say what.

Time and again in recent years it has been the free speech issue which has come banging at the court's door, asking it to open up, in the name of fundamental human rights— in this country from the Sunday Times thalidomide case to the Sinn Fein broadcasting ban, in Australia in the television broadcasting case and a number which have followed it. I do not for a moment contest the right of any of them to do so, nor the vast importance of the Miltonic freedom, and I might privately applaud what each plaintiff or applicant was setting out to achieve. But if I ask myself: why of all the human rights issues there are, should it be the issue of free speech which is constantly at the head of the queue for rights adjudication? The answer is very clear: it is because for the mass media free speech is a valuable commodity and litigation a worthwhile investment in it.

This in itself in no way negates the importance of the issue, for there is no law against doing well in the process of doing good; but it throws up a series of further issues which either a future rights instrument or the courts are going to have to address. For example, freedom to speak includes freedom to keep silent. In relation to the State, this is one thing—though not a thing beyond the reach of our law if we are prepared to take freedom of information seriously.

For a transitional corporation on which hundreds of millions of people depend for their information about the world, it is another: the power to suppress information, of which we should firmly deny the State control, is a power possessed by the media corporations. Does human rights theory then have anything to say about a transitional media corporation which, in order to secure satellite TV rights for China, agrees not to transmit BBC broadcasts because they have a standard of objectivity which the Chinese government dislikes? Is it perhaps a corollary of the right to speak freely that others have a right to listen freely, and not merely to hear what those who control the media think they should hear? If so, who is to articulate it and on whose behalf?

Are human rights there for corporations or for people? Are they a form of property or a constraint on power? If freedom to speak is a right, does it carry correlative obligations towards those who wish to hear? Above all, by what possible test of democracy or of equality before the law is it possible to pose a State, which maintains a high standard of public service broadcasting, as the unique natural enemy of individual liberty, and a media corporation possessing far greater communication resources than any State, as a disempowered candidate for freedom from State interference with its right of free expression?

And where in this grand contest does the intended human beneficiary of the dialogue sit? However the problem is posed, it is as impossible to discuss principles divorced from outcomes as it is outcomes divorced from principles: if the reception of news and information at large is a principle which matters, the operative matrix in which the principle is to be cast cannot matter less.

If then, without abandoning principle, we are to escape the cold wind of history, which blows, sooner or later on higher-order laws and self-evident truths, it is to our present epoch's consensus about society's ground rules that we have to turn. To admit this is to admit, as perhaps we should, that different societies will agree on different ground rules, and to accept accordingly that we have both a right to review and recast our standards and an obligation to make the case for the adoption of them by others rather than continue to assert loftily that ours, being self-evident, are the only acceptable ones. It certainly denies us any moral right to preach to others what we do not practise ourselves.

One of the keynotes of our epoch was struck by the Civil War radical John Warn who, writing in 1649, looked for 'a spirit of understanding big with freedom and having a single respect to people's rights' (a phrase 150 years ahead of its time). Wan contended that justice was anterior to law and postulated as the prime function of law 'the protection of the poor against the might'.

One of the principles we have derived from the upheavals of the seventeenth and eighteenth centuries is the primacy of democracy, but it is a principle which carries with it a baggage of inchoate assumptions—free speech according to means is only one of them—which are capable of subverting the principle itself. Both in enacting our own rights instruments for the future and in applying them by adjudication it is important to understand that such principles are not self-implementing and that in their application they can readily be hijacked by those who already possess the greatest power in society.

It is only by being rigorous, as Warr was, about a second such ground rule or principle, substantive equality before the law, that it becomes feasible to set about fireproofing the juridical elements of life in a democracy and to be serious about preventing the appropriation of legal rights and democratic processes for private or partial ends. There is a potential tension, in other words, between the principle of democratic government and the principle of equality before the law. If human rights theory has an urgent job in the coming years it is to turn this tension from its present destructive motion towards a creative balance between the individual whom democracy offers to empower and the sources and the repositories of power, both within and outside the apparatus of State, which a democracy has both to licence and to control.

This is why a rights instrument for the new century needs to address in its terms the imbalances and appropriations of power which threaten the values—possibly even the meaning:—of democracy; and it is equally why a judiciary charged with upholding the rule of law in a democracy has in making its adjudications to address the same questions. To take a modest example, in the US an enacted right of reply has been struck down as an unconstitutional interference with freedom of expression—conceiving the freedom, therefore, as a form of property—and an informal right of reply is resisted here for the same reason. In an attempt to meet this problem, an ANC draft of South Africa's transitional constitution proposed to provide: There shall be freedom of thought, speech, expression and opinion, including a free press, which shall respect the right to reply.

The last clause of the formulation was omitted from the final document, but the issue remains a real one and the Constitutional court may one day be asked to decide, since the legislature has declined to do so, what responsibilities are bound up with this and other human rights.

Judicial Culture

If then we are to anticipate a continuing debate about outcomes, these too can and should be debated in terms of principle, focused now by experience on the more complicated subtext, which every rights instrument silently carries. To say that the courts are not fit to absorb and respond acceptably to such a debate is to assume both too much and too little; too much because our judicial culture has historically pretended to be insulated from public debate and so has always had to disguise its social and ethical judgements as value-free adjudications; and too little because our capacity for open and intelligent response to the wider issues of human rights is as a consequence largely unexplored: it is a language in which we are not entirely illiterate but are certainly dyslexic, and in which with remedial help we can probably do a great deal better.

The tale told in Canada that a Supreme Court judge, debating an early Charter case (Canada, Charter of Rights and Freedoms) and told by his clerk that Dworkin has written something on the point, said 'Who's Dworkin?', while apocryphal, can stand as a parable of the expansion of a common law universe under the impulse of rights adjudication—for many of today's Charter decisions have a degree of legal literacy and an intellectual catholicity which our courts have so far been able (I am thinking principally of the Tony Bland case) to touch only briefly.

I hope that in constitutional adjudication, which is what our public law cases are, we shall be moving in the not too distant future toward the reception of Amicus and Brandeis briefs—the kind that were desperately lacking in the Gillick case. To do so will help us to escape the pincers which at the moment are closing on us: the pressures, which cannot be wholly resisted, towards omnicompetent adjudication, and the want of any corresponding expansion in the data and culture with and within which we carry it out. There are no guarantees that better educated the courts will get everything right, but to be sent as history is sending us on a voyage without modern navigational aids and supplies is to experience the worst of both worlds, the old and the new. My argument is that we should assemble the equipment and go on.

Fundamental Rights

If, as is almost inevitable, this voyage is going increasingly to take us into the deep water of fundamental rights, this is a culture which English lawyers are going to have to acquire and absorb. To rest, as our courts sometimes do, on the laurels of having been the first to articulate a number of the freedoms the world now takes for granted is not really enough, not least because the content of these rights has at present to be subordinated giving the courts a currently watertight defence for illiberal decisions.

But where, in John Mortimer's metaphor, we have so far survived by 'clinging to the wreckage', rights adjudication under a fundamental law of some description is going to mean that we have to learn to swim. This much is uncontentious. What may be more contentious is the proposition that the waters in which we shall be swimming are shark-infested and that our human rights armoury at present gives us little protection against the predators.

The notion that the prime function of human rights and indeed the rule of law is to protect the weak against the strong is not mere sentimentality. It is the child of an era of history in which equality of treatment and opportunity has become perceived—as it is not perceived in societies based on status—as an unqualified good, and of a significant recognition that you do not achieve equality by proclaiming it but only by levelling up from the inherited or systemic inequalities which make some social actors too weak to make use of their rights and others strong enough to stifle their aspirations.

The deconstruction of the State as provider as well as entrepreneur is now a worldwide phenomenon; but because power in every society on this planet is and perhaps always will be unequally distributed, every society today has a problem not just with Leviathan, against whom contemporary rights instruments continue to be directed, but with Jaws. It is going to be the task of those who write and those who implement the human rights instruments of the next generation to build on the jurisprudence of substantive race and gender equality which has been one of the real achievements of this generation, so as to distinguish between the strong and the weak as claimants of fundamental rights and to avoid what one writer has characterized as a culture in which self-respect and human dignity depend upon being in a position to make strident, querulous and adversarial claims.

I have not embarked on the vexed questions of group rights as against individual rights or of social and economic rights as fundamental human rights. As to the first, it seems to me that the dichotomy of individual and group involves at least in part a false antithesis, for as individuals we are defined by our relationships with others, and which social cadre is to be the context of an individual's rights is itself a function of the rights debate; so that the invite women comes by political choice to have rights as a Canadian citizen which deny the relationships of an aboriginal culture recognized but not entrenched by the Charter of Rights and Freedoms.

Nor have I entered the debate about whether the right to shelter or to work can or should rank as a human right, for these are in my view questions to be answered by social consensus from time to time, not by definition a *priori* and certainly not by derivation from some higher law.

Simply observe that the right not to suffer racial or sexual discrimination, which we now take as axiomatic, was entirely foreign—except perhaps as an aspiration—to the thinking of our grandparents' generation; that rights to education or to justice could only have been treated as self-evident in their time—which is our time—by societies that could afford to provide them; that the right to an unpolluted environment which the Indian High Court has in recent years extracted from the constitutional right to life depends less on what a society can afford than on what it cannot afford; and that it is not easy to see how in any humane society a right to shelter and food deserves any less regard than the right to life.

MULTICULTURAL EDUCATION

As compared to civil, political, economic and social rights, cultural rights are often dealt with a sense of neglect. Under developed is the term that was chosen as the title of the seminar organized in 1991 at Fribourg University,' and was then broadly accepted. It suggests that, in comparison with other categories of human rights— civil, political, economic and social-cultural rights are the least developed as far as their scope, legal content and enforceability are concerned.

Indeed, they need further elucidation, classification and strengthening. However, the term 'development' suggests the process of the creation of new rights. This point of view may be challenged as the existing list of cultural rights is relatively exhaustive. Therefore the problem is linked rather to the fact that these rights are neglected, underestimated, missing or forgotten, and that they are treated as 'poor relatives' of other human rights.

This neglect can be seen in the fact that although, in accordance with the International Covenant on Economic, Social and Cultural Rights, cultural rights are usually enumerated together with economic and social rights, they receive much less attention and quite often are completely forgotten. As observed by Eide, although the expression 'economic, social and cultural' is widely used, in most cases concern appears to be limited to economic and social rights. This can be observed not only in the doctrine but in state practice.

Every year the Commission on Human Rights discusses the question of the realization in all countries of the economic, social and cultural rights contained in the Universal Declaration of Human Rights and in the International Covenant on Economic, Social and Cultural Rights. An analysis of statements during the debate on this item once again shows that, though cultural rights are mentioned together with economic and social rights, in fact attention is limited to economic and social rights, with cultural rights not being debated. This neglect can also be found in reports presented by the States Parties to the International Covenant on Economic, Social and Cultural Rights on its implementation. The attention paid to cultural rights formulated in Article 15 is far from satisfactory.

What are the reasons for the reserve demonstrated by the doctrine and state practice in relation to cultural rights? They are manifold. Cultural rights are scattered throughout a great number of instruments, both universal and regional, adopted by the United Nations, by the specialized agencies and by the regional organizations. This, in the absence of any codifying treaty or declaration, opens the way for various classifications and groupings. In some cases cultural rights are presented as an aggregate—as one right, the right to culture. Such a presentation indeed raizes doubts about the clear or precise content of cultural rights.

Among important sources of reservation concerning cultural rights, one should mention fears and suspicions of states that the recognition of the right to different cultural identities, the right of identification with vulnerable groups, in particular minorities and indigenous peoples, may encourage the tendency towards secession and may endanger national unity. For this very reason, the introduction of cultural rights in the Charter of the United Nations was blocked during the San Francisco Conference. By the same token, the cultural rights of persons belonging to minorities are not mentioned by the Universal Declaration of Human Rights. They were only recognized by Article 27 of the International Covenant on Civil and Political Rights in 1966.

During the last decade of the twentieth century, cultural rights have received increasing attention from international governmental and non-governmental organizations, as well as from human rights specialists. Among the manifold reasons for which they have become a subject of international debates and discussions, there is no doubt an acknowledgment of the fact that the cultural factor can be found among the most important sources of internal conflicts. Violations of cultural rights of various groups, rejection of the right to be different, to have different cultural identities, have become very dangerous pathologies which fuel aggressive ethnonationalism, xenophobia, racism and anti-semitism.

Therefore culture and respect for cultural rights have also been recognized as an essential element in the prevention and resolution of conflicts. This has resulted in increased attention being paid to the elaboration and respecting of the cultural rights of persons belonging to minorities, indigenous people and other vulnerable groups.

At the end of the twentieth century there is also a full recognition of the importance of culture not only for development in its economic dimension, but also for 'human development, understood by the World Summit for Social Development (Copenhagen, 1995) as the social and cultural fulfilment of the individual. Without the implementation of cultural rights—the right to education, the right to participate in cultural life—and without the freedom of artistic, scientific and intellectual activities and pursuits, human development is impossible. The observance of cultural rights, in particular the right to cultural identification, is seen now as a constitutive element of the respect for human dignity.

Reflection on the interrelation between culture and development was initiated by a series of initiatives undertaken by the United Nations system. The General Assembly, by its resolution 41/187, proclaimed the World Decade for Cultural Development (1988-97) and asked UNESCO to play the role of lead agency. Among four of the Decade's objectives, three—affirming and enriching cultural identities, broadening participation in culture and promoting international cultural cooperation—are directly linked to the implementation of cultural rights.

In 1992, the Director-General of UNESCO, in accordance with the request formulated by the General Conference and supported by the General Assembly,' established the World Commission on Culture and Development chaired by Javier Perez de Cuellar. The Commission's mandate obliged it to prepare a World Report on Culture and Development and proposals both for urgent and long-term action to meet cultural needs in the context of development'. The World Commission met six times and set in motion a dynamic of international cooperation through the preparation of regional reports, expert contributions, specially commissioned papers and studies, as well as thematic workshops. During the fourth meeting, the World Commission discussed cultural rights and the right to development. The report of the World Commission on Culture and Development, under the title 'Our Creative Diversity', was published in 1995. Among its ten recommendations for international cooperation, Action 7 is entitled 'Protecting cultural rights as human rights'.

In line with Chapter 9 of the report of the World Commission, 'Rethinking cultural policies', UNESCO organized in Stockholm, from 30 March to 2 April 1998, an Intergovernmental Conference on Cultural Policies for Development. The main objective of the conference was the elaboration of strategies and a plan of action for such policies, as well as to review UNESCO's own preparatory contribution in this. Cultural rights were presented in the preparatory paper for the conference, in a section of its background document, and was referred to in the Action Plan on Cultural Policies for Development adopted by the conference which states, 'Access to and participation in cultural life being a fundamental right of individuals in all communities, governments have a duty to create conditions for the full exercise of this right.

In the 1990s, cultural rights of persons belonging to minorities became an important part of the general discussion and international regulations concerning these groups. In 1992, the General Assembly adopted the Declaration on the Rights of Persons Belonging to National or Ethnic, Religions and Linguistic Minorities, which contains a number of provisions dealing with the cultural rights of these persons.

The question of how to improve the protection of the cultural rights of minorities was introduced into UNESCO's programmes in 1992. Studies endorsing the implementation of cultural rights for Europe, Africa, Asia and Latin America were prepared. In 1994, the Executive Board put on its agenda a special item, the protection and promotion of the cultural rights of persons belonging to minorities and indigenous people within UNESCO's field of competence.

As the problem of minorities became especially acute in Europe, various initiatives aimed at the preparation of normative instruments were undertaken by European organizations. In October 1993, the summit of heads of state and government of the Council of Europe called for the preparation of a protocol complementing the European Convention on Human Rights in the cultural field with provisions guaranteeing individual rights, in particular for persons belonging to national minorities.

In 1994, the Framework Convention for the Protection of National Minorities was drawn up and opened for signature. The Convention enumerates the cultural rights of persons belonging to minorities and invests the state with the duty to protect them. A few years earlier the Organization on Security and Cooperation in Europe, during its 1990 Copenhagen meeting, adopted the Concluding Document which presented an exhaustive list of the cultural rights of persons belonging to minorities.

Apart from actions aimed at the protection of the rights of minorities and indigenous people, international governmental and non-governmental organizations as well as the academic community have undertaken in recent years a number of efforts aimed at the better understanding, consolidation and recognition of cultural rights. UNESCO, in its Medium Term Programme 1996-2001 states: 'The definition and content of cultural rights must be clarified and measures must be identified which could improve their effective implementation. The recognition of academic freedom is another important aspect of the promotion of cultural rights.'

In line with this aim, together with the Council of Europe and the University of Fribourg, Switzerland, UNESCO organized a number of meetings and prepared publications concerning cultural rights.

To sum up this rather selective presentation of the developments concerning cultural rights in the 1990s, one can say that they raised awareness concerning the importance of cultural rights. Though these rights still remain a neglected category of human rights, perhaps by the end of the century they could at least be considered less 'forgotten'.

Definition of Culture

Although the notion 'culture' is essential for the formulation, understanding and scope of 'cultural rights', it is impossible to find, among dozens if not hundreds of definitions used, one which is universally accepted. Different formulations and meanings of this term are proposed in different contexts. Thus, as suggested by Stavenhagen, culture may be identified with the accumulated material heritage of humankind or may be regarded rather as the process of artistic and scientific creation; or it may be understood as the sum total of the material and spiritual activities and products of a given social group which distinguishes it from other similar groups.

During a meeting on 'Cultural rights as human rights' held at UNESCO Headquarters in July 1968, experts for the first time discussed a definition of culture in the context of cultural rights. The working paper prepared by the secretariat referred to 'mass culture', 'popular culture', 'traditional culture' and 'world culture'. The word 'culture' has been used both in a very wide and in a restricted sense. In the widest sense, it really means the very essence of man, including the sum total of human activities; culture is precisely that which makes man different from nature. Boutros-Ghali noted that there are three separate meanings of culture: culture as a way of life, cultures of universal significance and certain forms of culture that are peculiar to certain communities. Thapar referred to international, national and sub-national culture. The experts agreed in the final conclusions:

> Culture is a human experience which is difficult to define, but we recognize it as the totality of ways by which men create designs for living. It is a process of communication between men; it is the essence of being human. Culture is everything which enables man to be operative and active in his world, and to use all forms of expression more and more freely to establish communication among men.

As stated by the report of the World Commission on Culture and Development: 'A great deal of confusion arises in both academic and political discourse when "culture" in the humanistic sense is not distinguished from "culture" in its anthropological sense, notably culture as the total and distinctive way of life of a people or society. In the context of development, the Commission adopted a broader understanding of culture.

It is worth noting that, during the general discussion conducted during the seventh session of the Committee on Economic, Social and Culture Rights (1992), on the right to take part in cultural life as recognized in Article 15 of the International Covenant on Economic, Social and Cultural Rights, it was also stated: 'that culture meant a way of life... Culture mirrored and shaped the economic, social and political life of a community.

Analysis of various UNESCO instruments allows us to discover a tendency towards the acceptance of a broader understanding of 'culture'. Thus the Declaration of the Principles of International Cultural Cooperation of 4 November 1966 states, in Article III: 'International cultural cooperation shall cover all aspects of intellectual and creative activities relating to education, science and culture.' As far as the aims of international cultural cooperation are concerned, Article IV stresses that it should: 'enable everyone to have access to knowledge, to enjoy the arts and literature of all peoples, to share in advances made in science in all parts of the world and in the resulting benefits and to contribute to the enrichment of cultural life'.

The Recommendation on participation by the people at large in Cultural Life and Their Contribution to it of 26 November 1976 explains, in its preamble:

> Culture is not merely an accumulation of works and knowledge which an elite produces... is not limited to access to works of art and the humanities, but is at one and the same time the acquisition of knowledge, the demand for a way of life and the need to communicate.

Similarly, the Final Report of the 1982 World Conference on Cultural Policies states that, without attempting to lay down a scientific or over-rigid definition of culture, delegates were in agreement in understanding the term 'culture', not in the restricted sense of the fine arts, literature and philosophy, but as distinctive and specific features and ways of thinking and organizing people's lives. The report states:

> Culture therefore covered artistic creation together with the interpretation, execution and dissemination of works of at,

physical culture, sports and games and open-air activities, as well as the ways in which a society and its members expressed their feeling for beauty and harmony and their vision of the world, as much as their modes of scientific and technological creation and control of their natural environment.

The broad anthropological definition of culture was accepted by the Council of Europe. The Arc-et-Senans Declaration (1972) on the Future of Cultural Development explains: 'Culture, as experienced by the majority of the population today, means much more than traditional arts and the humanities. Nowadays, culture embraces the education system, the mass media, the cultural industries.'

The Declaration on Culture Objectives (Berlin, 1984) states: 'Considering the determining role of culture, as a whole of values which gives to human beings their reason to be and to act [...] the main aim of all societies is to enable everyone to achieve personal fulfilment.'

As with the term 'culture' itself, which has broader or narrower interpretations and meanings, cultural rights may also be presented in a twofold manner. The broader understanding of cultural rights means that they also embrace the right to education, the right to participate in scientific progress and the right to information.

This approach is based on the assumption that the above-mentioned rights are so closely linked with other cultural rights that, in some cases, a separation is almost impossible. Indeed, creative activity can sometimes hardly be divided into scientific or artistic, as in many cases new forms and methods of artistic expression are determined by scientific and technological progress.

The essence of the protection of moral and material interests is identical and independent of the fact that they result from either scientific or literary production. Similarly, one may say that, without the right to information, without the right to seek, receive and impart information and ideas through any media, neither cultural nor scientific and educational cooperation is possible.

Law for the Whole Word: The concept of cultural rights was born as part of a new approach to human rights, their 'socialization', which was articulated after the Second World War. During the discussion preceding the adoption of the United Nations Charter, several Latin American states proposed the inclusion of cultural rights. Though the notion of cultural rights was not in the end introduced into the Charter, nevertheless the very fact that human rights were included within the competence of the Economic and Social Council is sometimes interpreted as evidence that the Charter departed from the narrowly interpreted conception of human rights.

On 10 December 1948, the General Assembly adopted the Universal Declaration of Human Rights which, in Article 27, states:

1. Everyone has the right freely to participate in the cultural life of the community, to enjoy the arts and to share in scientific advancement and its benefits.
2. Everyone has the right to the protection of the moral and material interests resulting from any scientific, literary or artistic production of which he is the author.

The Declaration also provides, in Article 22, that everyone is entitled to the realization, through national effort and international cooperation, of the economic, social and cultural rights indispensable for his dignity and the free development of his personality. The right to education is formulated by Article 26.

A step forward in the development of the concept of cultural rights was made in the International Covenant on Economic, Social and Cultural Rights which, in Article 15, provides:

1. The States Parties to the present Covenant recognize the right of everyone:
   (a) to take part in cultural life;
   (b) to enjoy the benefits of scientific progress and its applications;
   (c) to benefit from the protection of the moral and material interests resulting from any scientific, literary or artistic production of which he is the author.
2. The steps to be taken by the States Parties to the present Covenant to achieve the full realization of this right shall include those necessary for the conservation, the development and the diffusion of science and culture.

3. The States Parties to the present Covenant undertake to respect the freedom indispensable for scientific research and creative activity.
4. The States Parties to the present Covenant recognize the benefits to be derived from the encouragement and development of international contacts and cooperation in the scientific and cultural fields.

The text of paragraph 1 is slightly different from Article 27 of the Universal Declaration of Human Rights, as it does not include the phrase that identified the cultural life as that 'of the community'. This change was made because, in some cases, the 'cultural life of the community, in the singular, may be interpreted restrictively to exclude the right of minorities or other groups to participate in their own independent cultural life.

As far as paragraph 2 is concerned, there was, in the Commission on Human Rights and in the Third Committee, considerable debate about whether or not certain goals of scientific and cultural development should be set out. It was proposed that states should undertake to ensure the development of science and culture in the interest of progress and democracy and to ensure peace and cooperation among nations. These proposals were rejected as it was felt that a statement of aims might provide states with a pretext for abusive control of science and culture.

During the debate relating to paragraph 3, certain states found the term 'indispensable' which described freedom as too restrictive. A section of the Third Committee decided to retain the word which the right of the state to impose upon the exercise of that freedom limitations required in the interests of national security, public order and morality.

Although presented in terms of a single right, Article 15 in fact recognizes four different rights. Paragraph 4, which speaks about international cooperation, is worded, by the inclusion of the phrase, recognize the benefits to be derived from', in such a way that it is difficult to speak about binding obligations.

Among the United Nations human rights instruments which, apart from the International Bill of Rights, confirm provisions concerning cultural rights, too deserve special attention. The Convention on the

Elimination of All Forms of Discrimination against Women (1979) which, in Article 13, paragraph c, formulates states' obligation to ensure for women, on the basis of equality of men and women, 'the right to participate in recreational activities, sports and all aspects of cultural rights'. The same right is *mutatis mutandis* guaranteed for the child by Article 31 of the Convention on the Rights of the Child. Articles 28 and 29 also provide the child's right to education, whereas Article 30 speaks about the cultural rights of the child who belongs to a minority or an indigenous group.

Norms at Work

The American Declaration of the Rights and Duties of Man of 1948 is the first inter-state instrument presenting a catalogue of cultural rights. Article XIII provides:

> Every person has the right to take part in the cultural life of the community, to enjoy the arts and to participate in the benefits that result from intellectual progress, especially scientific discoveries. He likewise has the right to the protection of his moral and material interests as regards his inventions or any literary scientific or artistic works of which he is the author.

Important provisions concerning cultural rights are also enshrined in the Protocol of San Salvador.

The African Charter on Human and Peoples Rights of 1981 formulates both the right of every individual to freely take part in the cultural life of his community (Article 17) and the duty of individuals to preserve and strengthen positive African cultural values in their relations with the other members of the society, in the spirit of tolerance, dialogue and consultation and, in general to contribute to the promotion of the moral well-being of society. The Charter also speaks about collective rights, the rights of all peoples to their cultural development with due regard to their freedom and identity and in the equal enjoyment of the common heritage of mankind.

The European Convention of Human Rights (1950) does not specifically protect cultural rights, though its Article 20 mentions the right to information and Article 2 of the Protocol speaks about the right to education.

Among instruments adopted by the Council of Europe which are relevant to cultural rights one can mention the European Social Charter (1961), the Convention on the Protection of the Cultural Heritage (1985), the Convention on the Protection of the Archaeological Heritage (1992), the European Sports Charter (1992), the European Charter for Regional or Minority Languages (1992) and the Framework Convention for the Protection of National Minorities (1994).

Significance of UNESCO

An impressive number of standard-setting instruments concerning cultural rights have been adopted by UNESCO, which, by its Constitution, is obliged to give fresh impetus to the spread of culture, to maintain, increase and diffuse knowledge and to recommend to the nations concerned the necessary international conventions. Furthering this mission, UNESCO has elaborated nearly 30 standard-setting instruments: conventions, declarations and recommendations dealing with various aspects of cultural rights.

The first convention for the protection of cultural rights was prepared by UNESCO under the influence of the Universal Declaration of Human Rights. To guarantee the right of authors to the protection of their moral and material interests, in 1952 UNESCO convened the Intergovernmental Copyright Conference, which adopted the Universal Copyright Convention, revised in 1971.

Other important conventions include the Convention against Discrimination in Education (1960), the Convention on the Means of Prohibiting and Preventing the Illicit Import, Export and Transfer of Ownership of Cultural Property (1970) and the Convention concerning the Protection of the World Cultural and Natural Heritage (1972).

Of nearly 20 declarations and recommendations dealing with various cultural rights, the three best known are the Declaration on the Principles of International Cultural Cooperation (1966), the Recommendation on Participation by the People at Large in Cultural Life and Their Contribution to it (1976) and the Recommendation concerning the Status of the Artist (1980). Conventions, declarations and recommendations adopted by UNESCO protect and develop the rights to education, to cultural identity, to information, to participation in cultural life, to creativity, to benefits from scientific progress, to the protection of material and moral interests of authors, and to international cultural cooperation.

An original contribution of UNESCO to the development of the concept of cultural rights is the proclamation and elaboration in a series of normative instruments of the right to the protection of and access to the cultural heritage.

Are cultural rights recognized and listed by fundamental laws? Does the analysis of constitutions allow us to formulate a positive answer? In general, one may say that there are three ways in which cultural rights are mentioned. They may be recognized as a specific category of human rights when constitutions, for example, presenting the fundamental rights of citizens contain a chapter or a part on economic, social and cultural rights. Such a chapter may be found in the constitutions of Croatia (1990), Macedonia (1991), Poland (1997), Slovakia (1992) and Surinam (1987), among others. The Indian Constitution (1949), in the part dealing with fundamental rights, has one specific article (29) on cultural rights.

Some constitutions recognize cultural rights indirectly when they have the stipulation confirming the binding character of international human rights instruments. The constitution of the Czech Republic (1992) provides, in Article 10, 'The ratified and promulgated international treaties on human rights and fundamental freedoms [...] shall be applicable as directly binding regulations, having priority before the law.'

Similarly, the Constitution of Romania (1991) states, in Article 20, 'Constitutional provisions concerning the citizen's rights and liberties shall be interpreted and enforced in conformity with the Universal Declaration of Human Rights, with the Covenants and other treaties Romania is a party to.' These formulations may be interpreted as the recognition of cultural rights which are listed in the International Bill of Rights and other human rights instruments binding these countries.

The majority of constitutions do not utilize the term 'cultural rights' but enumerate concrete rights belonging to this category. In fact, it is almost impossible to find a constitution which does not list at least one cultural right. Among these, the most frequently quoted is the right to education. Many constitutions—for example, Portugal (1976, amended in 1982), the Republic of Korea (1980), Egypt (1980) and Bulgaria (1991)—formulate the right to freedom of artistic, scientific and intellectual activity and creativity and confirm the protection of the moral and material interests of authors.

Several constitutions Panama (1972), Spain (1978), Peru (1993)—recognize the right of the citizen to access to or participation in culture or cultural life. The right of access to information is mentioned, *inter alia*, by the constitutions of Estonia (1988) and Romania (1991).

The right to cultural identity, and linguistic and educational rights are relatively broadly presented in the constitutions of countries in which there are indigenous people and minorities. The cultural rights of indigenous peoples (communities) are formulated in the constitutions of Latin American countries: Argentina, Bolivia, Brazil, Colombia, Ecuador, Guatemala, Honduras, Panama, Paraguay, Peru, Mexico and Nicaragua. The cultural rights of persons belonging to minorities are presented in the constitutions of several Central and Eastern European countries: Bulgaria, Estonia, Hungary; Lithuania, Moldova, Romania, Slovakia and Slovenia. These constitutions recognize the right of members of minorities to their cultural (ethnic, national) identity and the right to participate in decision making concerning their cultural affairs.

An analysis of constitutional provisions allows us to conclude that cultural rights are recognized by national constitutions, though none of them contains an exhaustive list of these rights. One may also observe that a longer list of cultural rights may be found in constitutions which were adopted relatively recently, in the 1990s.

Despite the fact that international human rights instruments analyzed earlier in this chapter formulate concrete cultural rights, their general enumeration or a full list is far from being agreed upon. For this very reason, the World Commission proposed the establishment of an inventory of cultural rights. As none of the human rights instruments gives in full an enumeration of cultural rights, a call for the preparation of a comprehensive, codifying instrument was formulated by UNESCO. Thus, the Programme and Budget for 1994-95 mentioned the need to draft a standard-setting instrument on cultural rights. The continuation of international reflection aimed at the better definition and understanding of cultural rights was also foreseen by the Programme and Budget for 1998-99.

What are the causes or sources of misunderstanding and differences concerning the presentation of a comprehensive list of cultural rights? There are many. First, there is, or rather was, a tendency to replace the whole category of cultural rights with 'the right to culture'. Although the International Bill of Rights does not use this term, it was referred to by specialists and appeared in documentation, programmes and publications of the United Nations and UNESCO.

This right was mentioned frequently during the seminar on cultural rights organized by UNESCO in 1968 and during conferences on cultural policies held in the 1970s. Still, in the publication United Nations Action in the Field of Human Rights (1992), the paragraph dealing with cultural rights is entitled 'The right to culture'. Fortunately, in the 1990s, the references to this right are less frequent. Probably, 'the right to culture' appeared in human rights vocabulary by misinterpretation. Article 27 of the International Covenant on Civil and Political Rights speaks about the right of persons belonging to minorities to enjoy their own culture.

The term 'their own culture' should be interpreted as the right to cultural identity for persons belonging to minorities and not as the general right of everybody to culture. In a situation where there is no accepted definition of culture and where at the same time there is an agreement to understand culture in a very broad anthropological sense, the right to culture is too general to have any precise legal meaning. Therefore it may only be understood as the right to a cultural identity, to a cultural heritage.

Differences among various proposed lists of cultural rights are often linked with the tendency to incorporate and to present as cultural rights numerous human rights with cultural dimensions. Thus Article 1 of the Declaration on the Right to Development (1986) provides that every human person is entitled to participate in, contribute to and enjoy economic, social, cultural and political development. There is no need to formulate a separate right to cultural development. This may mean that the holistic, comprehensive right to development will be divided into four independent rights. Many freedoms, such as the freedom of thought, conscience and religion, the freedom of opinion and expression, the freedom of peaceful assembly and association, are indisputable for the implementation of cultural rights. They are intimately linked with the right to cultural identity or the right to creativity, but there is no need to add them to the list of cultural rights.

This tendency to incorporate human rights with cultural dimensions may be observed in the preliminary list of cultural rights established by Leander. This impressive inventory based on a detailed analysis of existing legal instruments, contains 50 rights grouped under 11 titles: the rights to physical and cultural survival; the rights to association and identification with the cultural community; the rights to and respect for cultural identity; the rights to physical and intangible heritages; the rights to religious belief and practice; the rights to freedom of opinion, expression and information; the rights to choice of education and training; the rights to participation in the elaboration of cultural policies; the rights to participation in cultural life and rights to create; the rights to choice of endogenous development; and the rights to people's own physical and cultural environment.

Catalogues of cultural rights may serve various purposes. They may be elaborated for use either as a basis for codification or for progressive development. They may present binding standards or suggestions and proposals. In some cases, confusion concerning cultural rights is caused by putting on the same level conventions, declarations and recommendations adopted by intergovernmental organizations, and drafts or resolutions and proposals formulated by non-governmental organizations or experts. For example, the list of cultural rights proposed by the Secretariat of the Council of Europe was based on texts of conventions and recommendations of the Committee of Ministers; resolutions of the Parliamentary Assembly, resolutions of the Congress of Local and Regional Authorities of Europe; resolutions or recommendations of European Conferences of Specialized Ministers; and of charters and declarations adopted by seminars or conferences. Obviously the legal character of these texts varies substantially.

Work to prepare a draft declaration on cultural rights in order to present it to the UNESCO General Conference for evaluation and adoption was conducted over several years by the so-called 'Fribourg Group'. In 1998, the draft prepared by the group was published. It enumerates six rights: to cultural identity and heritage; to identification with the cultural community, to participation in cultural life; to education and training; to information; and to participate in cultural policies and cooperation. The draft declaration, which also contains definitions of 'culture', 'cultural identity' and 'cultural community', presents fundamental principles and speaks about responsibilities for its implementation. No doubt this is a contribution to efforts aimed at the recognition of cultural rights as an integral and important part of human rights. However, the need to elaborate a short text has led to a very 'aggregated', combined presentation of some cultural rights.

Analysis of international human rights instruments allows us to propose the following list of cultural rights.

Importance of Cultural Identity: This right, indirectly formulated by Article 27 of the International Covenant on Economic, Social and Cultural Rights stipulating that persons belonging to minorities have the right to enjoy their own culture, may be seen as an articulation of the right provided by Article 1 of UNESCO's Declaration on Race and Racial Prejudice (1978): 'All individuals and groups have the right to be different, to consider themselves as different and to be regarded as such.'

During the World Conference on Cultural Policies (Mexico City, 1982), delegates emphasized people's growing awareness of their cultural identity, of the pluralism stemming from it, of their right to be different and of the respect of one culture for another, including that of minorities. They observed that the affirmation of cultural identity had become a permanent requirement, both for individuals and for groups and nations.

In the Recommendation on Cultural Identity, the Conference called upon member states (1) to respect and work to preserve the cultural identity of all countries, regions and peoples and oppose any discrimination with regard to the cultural identity of other countries, regions and peoples, and (2) to promote the development of cultural identity through all appropriate means.

At present, the right to cultural identity is recognized by human rights instruments and constitutions, in particular those concerning the rights of minorities adopted in recent years. Article 29 of the International Convention on the Rights of the Child provides that the education of the child shall be directed to: The development of respect for the child's parents, his or her own cultural identity, language and values'.

The right to respect for cultural identity means that everyone, alone or in a community with others, may freely choose his or her cultural identity in its various aspects such as language, religion, heritage and traditions; that everyone may have one or several cultural identities and may freely decide whether or not to identity with one or more cultural communities. Nobody can be subjected against his or her will to forced assimilation.

Role of Culture in Life

This right is mentioned by nearly all universal and regional human rights instruments dealing with cultural rights, though its legal content is open to broader or narrower interpretations. It has two aspects, passive and active. Both of them are mentioned by the Recommendation on Participation by the People at Large in Cultural Life of 26 November 1976, which explains:

> By access to culture is meant the concrete opportunities available to everyone, in particular through the creation of the appropriate socioeconomic conditions, for freely obtaining information, training, knowledge and understanding and for enjoying cultural values and cultural property.

The Recommendation also adds an active dimension of participation which embraces:

> The concrete opportunities guaranteed for all—groups and individuals—to express themselves freely, to communicate, act and engage in creative activities with a view to the full development of their personalities, a harmonious life and cultural progress of society.

The Recommendation deals with measures to be undertaken by member states to democratize the means and instruments of cultural activity. Participation in cultural life presupposes involvement of the different social partners in decision making related to cultural policy as well as in the conduct and evaluation of these activities. The broadening of access to and participation in cultural life has to be seen as one of the main objectives of cultural policies.

Education and the Constitution: During the general discussion by the Committee on Economic, "Social and Cultural Rights on the right to education (1998)," an agreement was reached that four elements define its core content:

1. no one shall be denied a right to education;
2. everyone is entitled to basic (primary) education in one form or another, this includes basic education for adults. Primary education must be compulsory and free. No one may withhold a child from primary education. A state has an obligation to protect this right from encroachment by third persons;
3. there is a free choice of education, without interference by the state or a third person;
4. the minorities have the right to be taught in the language of their choice, in institutions outside the official system of public education.

International instruments also establish state duty concerning human rights education." Education should constitute the free and full development of cultural identity/identities in respect of cultural diversity plurality and tolerance. In accordance with its mandate, UNESCO has adopted a number of normative documents, conventions and recommendations ensuring the enjoyment of the right to education for everyone. The best known among these is the Convention Against Discrimination in Education, which was adopted on 14 December 1960 by the General Conference and which entered into force in 1962.

The right to education is intimately linked to the right to teach. In 1966, an intergovernmental conference convened by UNESCO, with the participation of the International Labour Organization, adopted the Recommendation Concerning the Status of Teachers. In its preamble it underlines that the right to education is a fundamental human right and recognizes the essential role of teachers in educational advancement and the importance of their contribution to the development of man and modern society.

UNESCO's activities for the implementation of the right to education are by no means limited to the preparation of normative documents. The organization also undertakes operational programmes assuring access to education of refugees, migrants, minorities, indigenous people, women and the handicapped. The fight against illiteracy is an absolute priority among the organization's current activities, since collective development proceeds from the education given to each individual human being. At present, the right to education has been placed on the agenda of the Commission on Human Rights. K. Tomagevski has been nominated as the special rapporteur on this right and has presented a preliminary report.

Importance of Creativity

The right to creativity is formulated by human rights instruments and constitutions in the context of freedom from limitation and external interventions. The Recommendation Concerning the Status of the Artist of 27 October 1980 calls upon member states to encourage all measures tending to strengthen respect for artistic creation. It emphasized that governments should help to create and sustain not only a climate encouraging freedom of artistic expression but also the material conditions facilitating the release of creative talents. It stipulates: 'Since freedom of expression and communication is the essential perquisite for all artistic activities, Member States should see that artists are unequivocally accorded the protection provided for in this respect by international and national legislation concerning human rights.

A number of normative instruments adopted by UNESCO are of direct relevance in promoting the right of everyone to benefit from the protection of interests resulting from intellectual property. Most important amongst them is the Universal Copyright Convention of 1952, as revised in 1971. Both conventions require that each contracting state protect the rights of authors and other copyright holders. Article I, identical in both conventions, stipulates:

> Each Contracting State undertakes to provide for the adequate and effective protection of the rights of authors and other copyright proprietors in literary, scientific and artistic works, including writings, musical, dramatic and cinematographic works, and paintings, engravings and sculpture.

UNESCO has also sponsored the International Convention for the Protection of Performers and Producers of Phonograms and Broadcasting Organizations, adopted in Rome in 1961, and the Convention for the Protection of Producers of Phonographs Against Unauthorized Duplication of Their Monograms, adopted in Geneva in 1971.

New information and communication technology requires protection against electronic piracy and the violation of the interests of copyright holders. New intellectual property rights like those concerning databases also need regulation.

Benefits of Information

In accordance with the formulation of this right in the United Nations standard-setting instruments, everyone is entitled to seek and receive information, and to participate in its production and dissemination, as well as to obtain the correction of false or distorted information. Freedom of information is rightly regarded as one of the pre-requisites for the exercise of human rights and constitutes a very potent confidence-building measure.

Accordingly, Article 1, paragraph 2(a) of the UNESCO Constitution stipulates that the organization will: 'collaborate in the work of advancing the mutual knowledge and understanding of peoples, through all means of mass communication and to that end recommend such international agreements as maybe necessary to promote the free flow of ideas by word and image'. In implementing the right to information, UNESCO strives to eliminate various barriers to the free movement of books, publications and other printed materials. Four agreements have been prepared for this purpose.

The end of ideological rivalry between East and West allowed the organization to adopt a clear-cut strategy concerning freedom of information and free flow of ideas. The organization took an unequivocal position on this subject, foreseeing the encouragement of the free flow of information and promotion of its wider and better balanced dissemination, without any obstacle to the freedom of expression. The Major Programme on Communication, Information and Informatics is inspired by the principle of freedom of expression and its corollary:

freedom for all to choose their information. This is reflected in action aimed at promoting press freedom, pluralism and media independence, and at supporting efforts in member states to set up independent, pluralist media. The ultimate aim of this strategy is to provide practical responses to the challenges arising from the process of democratization going on in many countries and the demands of sustainable development.

Growth and Advancement of Science: This right is recognized, though in a general form, by the International Bill of Rights and regional instruments. Few of the standard-setting documents adopted by UNESCO are relevant to the promotion of this right. The Recommendation on the Status of Scientific Researchers adopted in 1974 underlines that each member state should use scientific and technological knowledge for the enhancement of the cultural and natural well-being of its citizens and to further the ideals and objectives of the United Nations.

Over the last decade, UNESCO has done work on the human and cultural implications of scientific and technological progress and, at a conference in Brasilia in 1985, participants urged the use of science and technology for peaceful ends, and rejected 'any application that places the survival of humanity in jeopardy'. Despite the limited number of standard-setting instruments dealing with the right to benefit from scientific progress, it is reflected in UNESCO's programmes.

In its activities concerning bio-ethics, UNESCO has attached special attention to the human genome. On 10 November 1997, the General Conference adopted by consensus a Universal Declaration on the Human Genome and Human Rights, the result of four years of deliberations and work of the UNESCO International Bio-ethics Committee.

Treasures of Culture

This right embraces the enjoyment and protection against destruction and illegal appropriation of cultural heritage both national and international (global). The largest group of UNESCO instruments dealing with cultural rights are those devoted to the protection of cultural property in time both of peace and of war. In 1954, UNESCO convened in The Hague an Intergovernmental Conference which adopted the Convention for the Protection of Cultural Property in the Event of Armed Conflict. The Convention contains provisions for the safeguarding of movable or immovable property of great importance to the cultural heritage of peoples, irrespective of its origin or ownership, and makes respect for such property obligatory. The safeguarding of such property implies that the state within the territories of which it is situated will take all necessary protective measures in time of peace. Respect for protected property is an obligation both on the territorial state and on its enemies in time of armed conflict.

The Convention on the Means of Prohibiting and Preventing the Illicit Import, Export and Transfer of Ownership of Cultural Property of 14 November 1970 defines cultural property qualifying for protection not only on historical, archaeological or artistic grounds but also in the interest of science.

The Convention concerning the Protection of the World Cultural and Natural Heritage adopted by the General Conference on 16 November 1972 defines international protection of the world cultural and natural heritage as: 'The establishment of a system of international cooperation and assistance designed to support States Parties to the Convention in their efforts to conserve and identify that heritage.' The items protected by the Convention are those of outstanding universal value from the point of view of history, art, science or aesthetics.

The Convention lays down two basic principles: that each state party recognizes the duty of ensuring the conservation of elements of the world heritage situated on its territory, and that it is the duty of the international community as a whole to cooperate in ensuring the conservation of the heritage which is of a universal character. The World Heritage Committee designates the items which, being regarded as forming a part of the world heritage, fall under protective measures provided for by the Convention.

Global Assistance and Culture: As foreseen by Article 15 of the International Covenant on Economic, Social and Cultural Rights, the States Parties recognize the benefits accruing from the encouragement and development of international contacts and cooperation. The right to international as well as internal cultural cooperation is provided, expressis verbis, by normative instruments concerning the rights of minorities.

The Declaration of the Principles of International Cultural Cooperation adopted by UNESCO on 4 November 1966 states, in its Article I, that every people has the right and duty to develop its culture. It explains in Article VI that cultural cooperation is a right and duty for all peoples and all nations, which should share with one another their knowledge and skills.

The aims of international cultural cooperation, bilateral or multilateral, regional or universal, are, *inter alia*, to spread knowledge, to stimulate talent, to enrich cultures, to develop peaceful relations and friendship among the peoples, and to raise the level of the spiritual and material life of man in all parts of the world.

WOMEN EDUCATION

Education is the most important instrument for human resource development. Education of women, therefore occupies top Priority amongst various measures taken to `improve the status of women in India. In recent years, the focus of planning has shifted from equipping women for their traditional roles of house-wives and mothers to recognizing their worth as producers, making a major contribution to family and national income.

Efforts have been made over the past three decades of planned development to enrol more girls in schools and encourage them to stay in schools, to contribute their education as long as possible, and to provide non-formal educational opportunities for women. The fulfilment of the Constitutional directives in respect of providing free and compulsory education up to the age of 14 years has been included as one of the components of the 'Minimum Needs Programme' and given overriding priority.

Education in India is constrained by the socio-economic conditions of the people, their attitudes, values and culture. During the pre-British era, education was linked to the socio-religious, institutions, reinforcing the patriarchal social structure. During the British period, education became a tool of colonial power, enabling a small minority to have access to education, and all the benefits it entailed. The social reformers of the nineteenth century raised the demand for women's transformation but to make them more capable of fulfilling their traditional roles. Since

Independence, the policy makers have argued for universal education and for making education as a tool for bringing about social equality.

In spite of concerted efforts to improve the enrolment of girls and provide adult education for women, their educational status is still far from satisfactory. Female enrolment in educational institutions is low as compared with males and dropout rates are higher. There are also regional and inter-group disparities.

The factors which do not permit the closing of the existing gap between the education of men and women are many. While undertaking a review of the educational system at the time of formulation of the National Policy on Education 1986, if was noted that the system is caught in a state of ambivalence, aiming at creating an equal society, while at the same time not disturbing the class, caste and gender relationships. Issues in women's education are, therefore, not issues only of educational sector, but they extend to issues of environment, employment production processes. Indeed, the entire gamut of social and, economic policy has a bearing on women's education. The need for educating girls is not considered worthwhile. In urban areas, by and large, there is a greater acceptance of its need than in rural areas. Some other factors responsible for low enrolment are:

(i) The requirement for older girls to stay at home to take care of siblings when mothers are away at work;

(ii) Need for girls to work in order to help in augmenting the family income;

(iii) Early marriage of girls;

(iv) Social customs that hinder female mobility after puberty;

(v) Lack of relevance of school curriculum; and

(vi) Lack of facilities in the form of school buildings, hostels and women teachers, etc.

Programmes and Planning

Women's education has assumed special significance in the context of the country's planned development.' This is because women constitute nearly half the nation's population representing a valuable human resource and play an important role in the development of the community and the national economy. Education enables women to acquire basic skills and abilities, and fosters a value system which is conducive to raising their status in society. Recognizing this fact, great emphasis has been laid on women's education in the five-year plans.

The First Five-Year Plan advocated the need for adopting special measures for solving the problems of women's education. It held that women "must have the same opportunities as men for taking all kinds of work and this presupposes that they get equal facilities so that their entry into the professions and public services is in no way prejudiced". It further added that "at the secondary and even at the university stage it should have a vocational or occupational basis, as far as possible, so that those who complete such stages may be in a position, if necessary, to immediately take up some vocation or other".

Accordingly the educational facilities for girls continued to expand in the subsequent plans. The major schemes undertaken encompassed elementary education, secondary education, university education, postgraduate education and research, technical education, scholarships, social/adult education and physical education. The Second Plan continued the emphasis on overall, expansion of educational facilities. The Report of the National C committee on Women's Education (1959) made a strong impact on the Third Five-Year Plan. It launched important schemes like condensed school courses for adult women, Bal Sevika training and child care programmes. Subsequent plans supported these measures and also continued incentives such as free text-books and scholarships for girls. This trend continued in the Fourth and Fifth Five-Year Plans.

Although there was a large-scale expansion of facilities for education up to the Fourth Plan, vast disparities existed in the relative utilization of available facilities by boys and girls at various stages of education. Hence, the major thrust in the Fifth Plan was to offer equality of opportunities as part of the overall plan of ensuring social justice and improving the quality of education imparted.

To promote enrolment and retention in schools in backward areas and among underprivileged sections of the population, in addition to the incentives like free distribution of text-books, mid-day meals, etc., girls were to be given uniform and attendance scholarships. In spite of these schemes, it was noticed that insufficient numbers of women teachers resulted in low enrolment of girls. To remove this bottleneck, scholarships were given to local girls to complete their education and training leading to a teaching career. Besides, condensed and correspondence courses were organized for the less educated women. Emphasis as also laid on the need for orientation of the curriculum to meet the special needs of girls.

A landmark in the Sixth Plan was the inclusion of women's education as one of the major programmes under Women and Development which was an outcome of the publication of the report of the Committee on the Status of Women in India. The programmes for universalization of elementary education were specially directed towards higher enrolment and retention of girls in schools.

It was envisaged to promote Balwadi-cum-creches attached to the schools to enable girls responsible for sibling care at home to attend schools. Women teachers, where necessary, were to be appointed in rural areas to encourage girls education. Science teaching in girl schools and colleges had to be strengthened to achieve greater participation of women in science and technology. Streamlining the admission policies to promote greater enrolment of women in engineering, electronics, agriculture, veterinary fishery and forestry courses was stressed. For boosting the education of women belonging to backward classes, the number of girls' hostels were to be increased. Instead of adding more separate women's polytechnics, which were developed as multipurpose institutions for imparting training in arts, crafts, etc. coeducational institutions were encouraged as far as possible. The adult education programme too received a fillip.

The Seventh Plan envisages restructuring of the educational programmes and modification of school curricula to eliminate gender bias. Enrolment of girls in elementary, secondary and higher education courses, formal as well as non-formal, has been accorded high priority. At the elementary stage, education has been made free for girls. Sustained efforts are to be made through various schemes and measures to reach 100 per cent coverage in elementary education.

Financial assistance schemes to voluntary agencies to run early childhood education (preschool centres) as adjuncts of primary/middle schools are to be expanded, particularly to help evolve innovative models suited to specific learner groups or areas. Efforts are to be made to enrol and retain girls in schools, especially in rural areas, and also to enrol children belonging to Scheduled Castes, Scheduled Tribes and other weaker sections. Teacher training programmes are to receive continued priority with a view to increase the availability of trained women teachers, and thereby to enhance girls' enrolment and retention in schools. Incentives by way of distribution of uniforms, free text-books and attendance scholarships to needy girls are to be continued.

Non-formal elementary education is to be expanded to benefit girls in the age group of 6-14 years. Talented girls are to be encouraged to pursue higher education. It is also proposed to expand the 'Open Learning System', including correspondence courses for them. In order to promote technical and vocational education for girls, more women's polytechnics are to be set up and programmes for vocationalization of education are to be expanded.

To expedite education among the girls of the Scheduled Castes and Scheduled Tribes, additional facilities will continue to be provided under the "Development of Backward Classes" sector. Girls above the matriculation stage will get higher scholarships/stipends than male students. Financial assistance is envisaged for construction of hostel buildings for girls at the district level and for purchase of equipment, furniture utensils, books and periodicals in these hostels.

Under the National Sports Policy, participation of women and girls in sports and games is to be encouraged. Stress is to be laid on the identification of sports talent among women, and provision made for sports scholarships, coaching and nourishment support for promising girls with a view to improve the standards of their performance in competitive games. Besides, the schemes for encouraging traditional folk, tribal and hill arts and cultural activities are to be expanded and strengthened.

Assessment of Situation

Notwithstanding the planned objectives and endeavours, actual progress in upgrading the educational status of women has been slow. The literacy level among women has risen from 7.9 per cent in 1951 to 24.3 per cent in 1981 (excluding Assam). Among males, the corresponding rise was from 24.9 to 46.3 per cent. Thus the gap in percentage literacy points between male and female literacy increased from 17 in 1951 to 22 in 1981. In absolute terms too, the number of illiterate women has increased during the period, from 158.7 million to 241.7 million (excluding Assam). Women comprised 57 per cent of the illiterate population in 1981, and girls formed 70 per cent of non-enrolled children in the school age group.

There are disturbing regional variations in the levels of literacy in the country. The literacy rate for women varies from 65.7 per cent in Kerala, as per 1981 census, to 11.4 per cent for Rajasthan. The gap between male and female literacy, rates in percentage points is only 9.5 in Kerala, but 24.9 in Rajasthan. States like Madhya Pradesh, Uttar Pradesh and Bihar are also lagging behind in girls education. Certain ecological constraints like difficult terrain, variety of dialects as in Arunachal Pradesh, migratory habits due to unfavourable weather as in parts of Jammu & Kashmir, etc. have also been instrumental in perpetuating low levels of literacy in such areas for the population as a whole and particularly for women.

Primary Education

High Priority has been accorded to elementary education in the National Development Plans to fulfil the requirements under Article 45 of the Constitution for universal, free and compulsory elementary education for children up to the age of 14 years.

By the end of the Sixth Plan, it was apparent that in order to achieve universal elementary education, an additional enrolment of 255.3 lakhs is required of which the girls constitute 140.7 lakhs, *i.e.*, a little more than 55 per cent. Besides, there is a sharp fall in the number enrolled at the middle level, *viz.*, from nearly 332 lakhs to 91 lakhs indicating a large dropout rate, wastage and stagnation. The enrolment ratio falls from 76.7 to 36.3. The retention of girls in schools from classes I to VIII, therefore is a task requiring urgent attention.

Among Scheduled Tribes particularly, the enrolment of girls is far below that of boys. At the primary stage, the enrolment of Scheduled Tribes boys is almost double the enrolment of girls, and the difference increases at higher stage. Girls belonging to Scheduled Castes communities are also lagging behind boys.

The ratio of Scheduled Castes boys to girls in the elementary classes is 2:1. In the VI to VIII classes, 61.9 per cent of girls in the general Population are enrolled, whereas among Scheduled Castes this proportion is only 20.9 per cent. The reasons for Scheduled Castes and Scheduled tribes girls lagging behind boys. The ratio of Scheduled Castes boys to girls in the elementary classes is 2:1. In the VI to VIII classes, 61.9 per cent of girls in the general population are enrolled, whereas among Scheduled Castes this proportion is only 29.9 per cent.

The reasons for Scheduled and Scheduled tribes girls lagging behind the boys are mainly rooted in socio-economic conditions and environmental constraints such as inaccessibility of schools in tribal areas. Irrelevance of formal education curriculum to the immediate environment is also responsible for low initial enrolment and subsequent dropout rates. Among the urban and rural poor, the compulsion on girls to assist in household chores including care of younger siblings, and on children of both sexes to work for their own survival and contribute economically to the household income, forces them to remain outside the education system.

According to the Fourth Educational Survey (1978), in the plains 95 per cent of the rural population have access to a primary school within one kilometre of their habitation (having a population of 360 persons or more). Middle schools are available to 78.8 per cent of rural people within three kilometres from their habitation. But commuting to distant schools does pose a problem for girls.

There are very few separate schools for girls. The parents, particularly in rural areas, are reluctant to send their daughters to co-educational schools. Moreover, in most schools, the teachers are male. Despite considerable emphasis in the plans, the proportion of women teachers continues to be low Provision for accommodation for women workers including teachers is far from satisfactory.

A large number of primary and middle schools, in rural areas especially, lack facilities such as a proper building, adequate number of teaching rooms, drinking water and toilets for girls. More than 85 per cent primary and 70 per cent middle schools in rural areas do not have these facilities, according to the Fourth All India Educational Survey (1978). Hostel facilities for girls continue to be meagre.

Secondary Education

There is a progressive rise in the rate of enrolment in secondary education of girls during the various Plan periods as seen below:

> The enrolment ratio of girls in the age group 15-18 years for secondary classes is 14.3 per cent as against 29.3 per cent for boys. Secondary education continues to be more or less confined to urban areas, and is affordable and accessible largely to the higher castes and the upper and middle economic strata. Although a large number of secondary schools have come up in rural areas, their enrolment particularly, in respect of girls is low. The main constraints in improving secondary and higher level education among girls have been a lack of availability of trained lady teachers, dearth of separate institutions for girls and lack of hostel facilities.

The 10+2+3 system of education has been introduced with the aim of establishing a uniform pattern of education all over the country in terms of its structure, curriculum and mobility across the States. This system has laid a common foundation for higher education without differentiation between boys and girls. Both girls and boys under the new system Will learn the rudiments of science and mathematics, social sciences and humanities up to matriculation and thus gain a holistic base education which will equip them to play an active and meaningful role in the employment market.

University Education

In the higher educational courses, girls constitute 24 to 50 per cent of the students enrolled depending upon the type of courses. The most popular course with girls has been teachers training where they already constitute nearly fifty per cent of those enrolled. The number of girls in science courses had risen to 41 per 100 boys in 1984-85. In engineering and technology courses, however, the enrolment of girls is only 6 for 100 boys. This Proportion has to be enhanced through suitable incentives in the form of scholarships and other facilities for girls studying for these courses.

Girls enrolled for higher education, particularly those in science and technical courses, are mainly from the higher economic strata.

There is a need to introduce positive measure to improve the enrolment to girls in higher education courses in rural areas and, among backward groups like SCs and STs.

Non-formal Education

The concept of adult education has found support in several Plan Programmes. However, until the Sixth Plan, no special emphasis was given to women's education. In the Sixth Five-Year Plan, adult education was included as a part of the Minimum Needs Programme and the goal of reaching 100 per cent literacy by 1990 was set under the New Twenty-Point Programme. Adult education centres exclusively for women were set up, which provided education in subjects like health, nutrition and family planning. An effort was made to build up an awareness about these sub among women through discussions, talks and distribution of relevant literature.

Under the Adult Education Programme, apart from increasing adult literacy, the content of education was to be modified to incorporate new value systems regarding the role of women in the family, and community. The Seventh Plan also envisages, among other schemes, the preparation of district level plans with local community participation, both for activating, and implementing the literacy programme, and the creation of special mechanisms to monitor the progress of implementation at the State level.

The Integrated Rural Development Programme (IRDP), National Rural Employment Programme (NREP), Training of Rural Youth in Self-employment (TRYSEM), and other such programmes, are also to have a component of functional literacy for women beneficiaries. The programme of Functional Literacy for Adult Women (a component of the ICDS programme) was unfortunately abandoned, though the concept of utilizing Anganwari workers, who belonged to the villages and were in contact with young mothers, could have been an effective mechanism for imparting non-formal education. The scheme has since been revised to focus on issues of immediate relevance to women but has yet to be introduced.

The scheme of 'condensed courses of education and vocational training' for adult women was started in 1958 under the aegis of the

Central Social Welfare Board, and was suitably expanded over the years to vocational training in areas with high employment potential. Measures are to be taken to enhance the competence of the teaching staff /training institutions involved in this programme.

The various programmes, however, have not yet been able to make any significant impact on literacy levels of the Indian population, particularly on women. According to a World Bank Report in 2000 A.D., there will be 500 million illiterates in India, constituting 54 per cent of the world's population of illiterates. As per the Seventh Plan, the total number of adult illiterates is about 900 lakhs of whom 580 lakhs are women. Although it is encouraging to note that the proportion of women in the adult education centres has gone above 50 per cent (52.34 per cent in 1984-85), women still constitute about 5.7 per cent of the illiterate population. Among these, literacy levels of SC mad ST women are still worse. Even those treated as literates, have very low levels of literacy, scant opportunities for continuing education and use of literacy skills. Therefore they often relapse into illiteracy.

Initiatives for Women

The National Policy on Education (NPE)-1986 is a landmark in the approach to women's education. It has attempted for the first time to address itself to the basic issues of women's equality. In the section titled "Education for Women's Equality", the policy states:

> Education will be used as an agent of basic change in the status of women. In order to neutralize the accumulated distortions of the past, there will be a well-conceived edge in favour of women. The National Education System will play a positive, interventionist role in the empowerment of women. It will foster the development of new values through redesigned curricula, text-books, training and orientation of teachers, decision makers and administrators.

It gives overriding priority to the removal of women's inhibiting their access to and retention in elementary education. Emphasis has been laid on women's participation in vocational, technical and professional education at different levels as also to promote women's participation in non-traditional occupations and existing and emergent technologies.

The Programme of Action for Implementation of NPE (POA) spells out the meaning of women's empowerment:

Women become empowered through collective reflection and decision making. The parameters of empowerment are:

(a) Building a positive self-image and self-confidence.

(b) Developing ability to think critically.

(c) Building up group cohesion and fostering decision making and action.

(d) Ensuring equal participation in the process of bringing About social change.

(e) Encouraging group action in order to bring about change in the society.

(f) Providing the wherewithal for economic independence.

The programme entails the following:

(i) A phased time bound programme of elementary education for girls, particularly up to primary stage by 1990 and up to the elementary stage by 1995.

(ii) A phased time bound programme of adult education for women in the age group 15-35 by 1995.

(iii) Increased women's access to vocational, technical, professional education and existing and emergent technologies; and

(iv) Review and reorganization of educational activities to ensure that they make a substantial contribution towards women's equality, and creation of appropriate cells/units therefore.

A number of measures have been suggested to achieve the state's objectives of the National Policy on Education. The Action Plan enunciates that every educational institution should take up by 1995 active programmes for the development of women. All teachers and non-formal education/adult education instructors should be trained as agents of women's development. Special programmes should be developed by research institutions to promote general awareness and positive self-image amongst women through programmes like discussions, street plays, wall papers, puppet shows, etc. Preference in recruitment of teachers up to school level should be for women.

National Literacy Mission (NLM) which aims at eradication of illiteracy in 15-35 age group by 1995 concretizes what is envisaged in NPE as regards literacy and adult education. The Mission document emphasizes the importance of imbibing the values of national integration, conservation of environment, women's equality, observance of small family norm, etc., and goes on to say that "the focus of NLM would be on rural areas, particularly women and persons belonging to the Scheduled Castes and Scheduled Tribes."

For universalization of elementary and adult education, the present programme of non-formal centres for girls needs to be extended to all educationally backward pockets of the country. Increased assistance should be given to voluntary organizations to run non-formal education centres for girls. In rural areas, special support services should be provided to relieve the girls from sibling care and other household work like fetching water, fuel, etc. Skill development linked to employment opportunities in the villages is required to be given priority so that there is an incentive on the part of the parents to educate girls.

It is necessary to develop adult education programmes for women linked with upgradation of their skills and income generating activities. Skill development for girls should be a continuous process of learning and should be supported by programmes administered by others such as Polytechnics, Industrial Training Institutes (ITIs), Women's Centres in Agricultural and Home Science Colleges, etc. Centres should be set up in a phased manner vocational training, provide opportunities for retention skills and application of this learning for improving their living conditions.

Their are 104 ITIs functioning exclusively for women and 97 wings in general ITIs reserved for women would need to be revamped during 1988-90 in terms of diversification of trades and courses, keeping in view the job potential and facilities for vocational counselling, imparting information about credit, banking, entrepreneurial development and women's access to technical education, etc.

Women's studies programmes would also have four dimensions, *viz.*, teaching, research, training and extension. Women's issues would be incorporated in courses under various disciplines. Research would be encouraged on identified areas/ subjects. Seminars/workshops would be organized on the need for women's studies, and for dissemination of information and interaction. Educational institutions would be encouraged to take up programmes like adult education, awareness building, legal literacy, information and training support for socio-economic programmes of women's development, instructional programmes through media, etc., which directly benefit the community and bring about the empowerment of women.

All the foregoing endeavours will be planned, coordinated, and evaluated continuously both at the national and state levels. The Women's Cell in the National Council for Educational Research and Training would be revived and strengthened. National, Institute of Educational Planning and Administration and Directorate of, Adult Education would have cells to plan and administer women's training programmes. The Women's cell in the University Grants Commission would, be strengthened to monitor the implementation of various programmes at the higher education level. It is proposed that women cells should be set up in all the States.

The Context

The programmes for women's education will have to be implemented as a priority so that women attain a comparable level of education by 2020 AD. The strategy to be adopted for raising literacy levels and education among women has to keep, in view the vast cultural, geographical and ecological variations as also the problems relating to poverty and ignorance.

The cultural and geographical variations call for decentralization of educational planning. Within the national perspective planning, implementation and monitoring of educational programmes has to be done at district and block levels, keeping in view the socioeconomic and geographic parameters of the area. The vocational and occupational components have to be designed in accordance with the availability of resources and job opportunities in the regions. Voluntary organizations and women's groups active in the area should be involved in the task.

In view of the social and cultural handicaps that have operated against women's education and taking account of the multiple roles that women are required to play, the need for adopting set of objectives specific to women's education is imperative. The objectives to be achieved by 2000 AD in regard to women's education are:

(i) Elimination of illiteracy, universalization of elementary education and minimization of the dropout and stagnation rate in the age group 6-14 years, to negligible proportions.

(ii) Ensuring opportunities to all women for access to appropriate level, nature and quality of education and also the wherewithal for success comparable with men.

(iii) Substantial vocationalization and diversification of secondary education so as to provide a wide scope for employment and economic independence of women.

(iv) Making education an effective means for women's equality by (a) Addressing ourselves to the constraints that prevent from participating in the educational process; (b) Eliminating the existing sexist bias in the system; (c) Making necessary intervention in the content and scope of education to inculcate positive and egalitarian and (d) Ensuring that teachers perceive this as one essential role.

(v) Providing non-formal and part-time courses to women to them to acquire knowledge and skills for their social, cultural and economic advancement.

(vi) Impetus to enrol in various professional degree courses so as to increase their number in medicine, teaching, engineering fields substantially.

(vii) Creating a new system of accountability, particularly of the basic educational services, to the local community, inter alia, by active involvement of women.

In brief, it is reiterated that the goals and strategies spelt out in the National Policy on Education, POA and the National Literacy Mission will ensure a much larger access for women to education.

High priority has to be accorded to creating awareness, through the various communication media, of the need for women's education and their active participation in economic and political development of the nation.

The curricula for school as well as university education have to be reviewed and revised so as to remove sex bias, inculcate among the masses a recognition of equality between men and women, and make women aware of their own potentials as well as provide them necessary opportunities to develop their capabilities in every field. Greater accessibility of educational facilities to girls is to be achieved by reducing the distance of schools from village habitations, and expanding non-formal elementary education, adult education, and the open school system.

Appointment of lady teachers in schools would help draw more girls to schools and instil confidence among their parents. Towards this end, provision of quarters for lady teachers would be essential. Efforts should be directed at training local women as teachers. Provision of creche facilities and Balwadis near the elementary and secondary schools for girls would enable the girls to attend schools and ensure care of younger siblings. Incentives like midday meals, better rates of scholarships, freeships, etc., would go a long way in preventing dropout.

Above all, better health facilities, smaller families, and relief from drudgery through improved technology for household chores, are essential prerequisites for better enrolment of girls at school and higher educational institutions. Inputs from other sectors are, therefore, important. Greater coordination of health, employment, welfare and education interventions will have an effect on the status of women and girls.

According to Educational Statistics for 1984-85 published by the Ministry of Human Resource Development, the enrolment of girls at primary level, which covers the age group 6-11 years, is 331.9 lakhs. Surveys and field research have pointed out that there is 25 per cent inflation in the enrolment figures, and 22 per cent enrolment is outside the age group. Thus the effective enrolment gets reduced by about 47 per cent. Accordingly, the coverage for 1984-85 for the 6-11 years age group may be estimated as 176 lakhs. The population projected for the age group is 422.7 lakhs. This means that only 40.7 per cent of the girls in the age group 6-11 are enrolled in schools. On a similar basis, the enrolment of 11-14 years age group gets reduced to 48.1 lakhs (from 90.7 lakhs) which is only 19.2 per cent of the population of 249.9 lakhs estimated for the age group. The population projections for the girls in the age group 6-11 years and 11-14 years for 1989-90 are 462 lakhs and 2,67 lakhs respectively. In order to have full coverage, the additional enrolment required would be 286 lakhs for 6-11 age group and 219 lakhs for 11-14 years age group, the total being nearly 5 crore. The task appears to be stupendous. Along with enrolment, there is the problem of very high dropout rates. Stemming from highly inflated enrolment rates and subsequent dropouts in the 6-11 years age group, enrolment of 11-14 years age group girls, even at primary level, may not be possible even by 1995.

In view of the social and cultural handicaps that have operated against women's education, the need for adopting a set of objectives specific to women's education is imperative. These would need to encompass the elimination of illiteracy and measures for retention of girls in schools, substantial vocationalization and diversification to enhance economic opportunities for women, improvement in the quality of education in terms of the values it promotes and inculcates, and finally the provision of access to professional courses for women. Such measures would be necessary as also efforts to remove the inherent prejudices working against women's education.

1. Awareness needs to be generated among the masses regarding the necessity of educating girls so as to prepare them to effectively contribute to the socio-economic development of the country, to strengthen their role in society and to realize their own capacities. The media and various forms of communication have to be geared to this end.
2. A fruitful rapport has to be established between the community at large and the teachers and other education personnel. As per the Programme of Action under National Policy on Education-1986, every educational institution should actively participate in bringing about such awareness.
3. Involvement of local leaders, voluntary agencies and women's groups is also necessary. Mahila Mandals need to be revitalized and reoriented to provide an effective forum for the purpose. One measure to achieve this could be to assign the responsibility to Mahila Mandals for ensuring that all children in a community attend school. An incentive scheme should be introduced to motivate panchayats to ensure 100 per cent enrolment of girls in their villages.

4. Early childhood care and education introduces children into the school system gradually and smoothly. When children get used to attending schools, it ensures in some measure retention of children, including girls, at elementary stages also. Hence there is needed to have a comprehensive and effective programme of early childhood care and education linked to an integrated package of learning for women. The most comprehensive example of this is the Integrated Child Development Services Programme which needs to be universalized.
5. For improving enrolment and minimizing dropouts and wastage in case of girl students, it would be helpful if learning is made more attractive by providing adequate teaching materials in schools.
6. The number of teachers should also be increased so that the interaction between the teacher and the taught, which is so essential for good education also increases. This would help in the retention of girls in schools and would be more effective if teachers from the area are employed. In single teacher schools, the teacher must be a woman. In Orissa all jobs of primary teachers have been reserved for women.
7. School curricula should be imaginatively developed to stimulate creativity 'largely through play rather than overburdening children' with formal or rote learning. Regional language should normally be the medium of instruction.
8. School timings should be flexible and fixed to suit local conditions and the needs of the working girls and must be available within the walking distance of the child. A substantial increase is required in the number of schools for girls.
9. In addition to incentives like free text-books, free supply of uniforms, award of attendance scholarships and mid-day meals, facilities such as proper school building, safe drinking water, and toilet, etc., need to be provided to encourage school enrolment and retention of girls especially girls from educationally deprived social groups and from hilly, tribal, desert and remote areas and urban slums.
10. Local talent must be developed in order to meet the need for recruiting women teachers at the primary and elementary levels

especially in rural and tribal areas. In this endeavour national agencies like CAPART and CSWB, voluntary agencies, Mahila Mandals and local self-government agencies can make a significant contribution. They can also play a useful watchdog function to ensure that educational and other programmes are run efficiently and effectively.

11. There should be a reservation of 50 per cent posts for women teachers in elementary schools. Women teachers working in the rural areas should be provided suitable accommodation.
12. Multi-entry system for girls who cannot attend schools continuously should be adopted.
13. Wherever necessary, schools meant exclusively for girls may be set up. The recommended distance of 3 kilometres for locating a middle school is a handicap for many girls. To ensure participation of girls in middle schools, it is necessary to provide hostel facilities.
14. The Savitribai Phule Foster Parent Scheme of Maharashtra could be adopted in other States/Union Territories to help poorer families to at least complete primary school. Under the scheme, well to do persons and organizations are persuaded to adopt one or more out of school girls and contribute in cash or kind or both @ Rs. 25 per month for her education. The money can be spent on uniforms, stationery or anything else, needed by the girls or also partly used to alleviate the economic distress of the parents. The Zila Parishad, Block Education Officer and headmasters play a pivotal role in implementing the scheme, which is purely voluntary and if district level officers are appointed for coordination of programmes for women, they could also actively take it up.
15. Condensed courses of education at elementary and middle school levels for girls must be started in all the rural areas and for weaker sections of the urban community.
16. Many girls in the 11-14 years age group would first have to be brought into the primary stage through non-formal education. By devising alternative education approaches non-formal schooling and through like intelligent use of technology, the pace of middle school education can be accelerated. If retention up to 73 per cent is achieved up to class V, universal elementary education may be possible in some parts of the country by 2000 AD. Other

backward areas would have to be given much more attention in, professional as well as financial terms to enable them even to universalize primary education for girls by 1995. The National Literacy Mission will need to address these issues on a priority basis.

17. Special efforts are necessary for bringing tribal children particularly, girls into the school system. Tribal dialects, extreme poverty, problems of commuting, rigidity of formal education and its irrelevance to the tribal culture and the tribal's distrust of the ways of the mainstream society, must be borne in mind in formulating strategies.
18. The educational forecasts, may look more achievable if the system is opened up for flexible non-formal education which 'the below average states' should be persuaded to adopt in a large measure. The existing educational infrastructure particularly, in tribal and rural areas should be made effective and responsible.
19. Non-formal education is an alternative to the formal system which has the potentiality of becoming the major programme of education for girls who cannot attend school during normal school hours due to various reasons. The Central Government is already implementing a centrally sponsored scheme under which grants to the extent of 90 per cent are provided towards maintenance of non-formal education centres exclusively for girls in nine educationally backward states. This programme should be strengthened further and extended to other states where education of girls is lagging behind. It should at least cover all the pockets of low enrolments of girls and areas of high dropout rate. Besides literacy, it must also provide relevant information on skill development and inculcation of positive self-image among girls.
20. Secondary education for girls should entail:

(i) A ten-year course in general education learning and diversified higher secondary education which may be either terminal or lead to further professional preparation; and (ii) Diversified courses after Grade VIII in technical subjects, *viz.*, agricultural technology, health services, food production activities such as dairy and poultry and non-traditional areas need to be untroubled. A legal literacy component is also recommended at this stage.

21. Diversified courses leading to occupational preparation should be of parallel duration to the general secondary courses. In addition, there should be a variety of short and long term, whole time, part-time and apprentice courses. The trend of thinking is now to place emphasis on the last. Keeping in view the rapid modernization and advancement in technology for agriculture, there is an urgent need for skilled artisanship, for promoting productive activities on the one hand, and a variety of learning programmes for adjustment of the rural society to socio-economic change on the other. Efforts should be made to ensure that girls have every opportunity to enter into apprenticeship in areas that are non-conventional, and incentives be provided for the same. Further, at least 30 per cent seats should be reserved for girls in apprenticeship training courses on a non-transferable basis.

22. General and vocational training courses should be combined so that prospects of a career immediately on completion of schooling may attract girls from weaker sections. While designing the vocational courses, available occupational opportunities as well as the need to overcome market stereotypes should be kept in view.

23. Since secondary education has remained almost beyond the reach of weaker sections, liberal incentives and other facilities to release the girls from household chores appear to be essential. It would also help to locate the institutions in the areas of their habitation.

24. Multiple entry system should be introduced in the secondary classes. Part-time education facilities should also be made available.

25. Condensed courses should be organized in cooperation with local vocational training institutions to cover all rural areas and areas inhabited by weaker sections in urban areas. Such courses may be organized for small groups of girls, and combined with job training. Efforts should be made to cover atleast 215 lakhs women in the age group 15-30 years under the condensed courses programme wherever possible the condensed courses of

the CSWB should be expanded and strengthened. New programmes that are to be initiated must avoid duplication in the areas where the CSWB's programmes exist.

26. Correspondence courses and self-study programmes can be especially useful for girls desirous of continuing education but are unable to do so because of circumstances. Apart from imparting elementary education and knowledge about farming techniques, the curriculum for non-student girls should include courses of training in occupational skills. Similar programmes should also be designed for girls in the urban areas.
27. The open school system should be expanded extending the facility to all the girls in rural and backward areas.
28. Science education for girls has been neglected so far. Secondary schools for girls must be helped to build good science programmes over the Eighth Five-Year Plan. Special scholarships for girls opting for science courses need to be instituted at the secondary and higher education levels.
29. Special scholarship may also be offered to rural women, who opt for teachers' training, especially those who complete the condensed courses at the secondary stage.
30. There is a need to open more colleges and polytechnics for girls, especially in rural areas.
31. Incentives like scholarships, freeships, etc., should be provided to enable girls from rural areas to pursue higher education for girls belonging to weaker sections. In addition to freeships and scholarships hostels should also be provided to meet their requirements for food and lodging.
32. Girls should be encouraged to enter professional courses. Reservation of seats for girls in such courses may be considered to level out the existing bias in access to certain professional streams.
33. Vocational counselling and guidance service be organized exclusively in a more meaningful way to help girls in colleges and universities opt for suitable courses relevant to their talents and interests, and free of traditional bias.

34. Vocational and technical education for women, both formal and non-formal, should be a major feature of the programmes of rural universities. The women's wings of the universities could undertake large-scale extension programmes in order to activate girls and women in the surrounding areas to take advantage of educational and occupational facilities of various types, particularly those leading to meaningful employment, essential for reducing women's marginalization.
35. In order to increase the representation of rural girls in higher education courses, 30 per cent seats, may be reserved for girls to begin with.
36. All agencies, involved with preparation of curricula prescription of text-books and organization of educational processes will have to evince awareness towards women's issues. University/College Departments of Women's Studies, appropriate voluntary agencies, women's groups, etc., should be involved in giving a new perspective to the various issues of content and processes of education. Women's universities and women's centres in colleges need to take an active role in women's development and in influencing the attitudes of Future generations.
37. Facilities for part-time self-study and correspondence courses should be provided on a large-scale to enable girls who are not in a position to join higher educational institutions on a regular basis, to continue their studies.
38. In addition to courses leading to degree/diploma, short courses in specific subjects through summer school sessions, and ad hoc programmes like seminars, workshops, etc., should be organized for working women with a view to upgrading their knowledge and skills, not necessarily leading to degrees.
39. Integrated learning programmes for women are recommended which will not only lay emphasis on literacy but on empowering women through awareness building on social issues, bringing about attitudinal change, promoting skill training for employment, providing information on healthcare, nutrition and hygiene as well as on legal rights. Such programmes are beginning and must continue to be designed and structured so as to be relevant for

the vast majority of rural women. The revised scheme linked to ICDS known as the 'Women's Integrated Learning for Life', should be introduced as an integral part of the non-formal education system.

40. Entrepreneurship development programmes should be organized separately for education of women in the age group 18-30 years, with a minimum of matriculation level of education. The objective of such training should be to:

    (i) Make them aware of the various opportunities for self-employment; (ii) Motivate them to take up self-employment; (iii) Impart needed skills and training; (iv)Promote motivation for achievement among them; and (v) Create access to resources such as capital, credit, etc.

41. A large number of girls cannot participate in whole day education programmes. Provision of non-formal and part-time programmes, with flexible school hours and sensitivity to the agricultural cycle are, of particular importance. In addition to the primary and upper primary stages, distance learning opportunities need to be provided at secondary and higher secondary levels.

42. Adult education will have to be composed of three interrelated stands aimed at:

    (i) Continuous flow of new information especially to rural and tribal areas, particularly to inculcate positive attitudes towards women;

    (ii) Continuous training of the people in the use of modern tools and methods of production; and

    (iii) Acquisition of permanent reading and computation skills.

    Following from the above, three types of programmes may be offered to the learner:

    (a) Information and literacy.

    (b) Information and training in new technology and literacy.

    (c) Information and training in new technology with or without literacy. Continuous information flows relating to human affairs, gender relations and the use of science and technology for betterment of life would be the common factor in all the three programmes.

43. The growing availability of communication media should be directed towards keeping up information flows and portraying positive images of women in non-conventional roles. Audio-visual materials, combined with non-formal training arrangements, could impart to various population groups the kind of instruction they need in the use of new technologies. Involvement of mass media in motivating women to attend literacy classes is most essential.

44. Rapid strides in the development of technologies and tools for the reduction in women's drudgery and easy access to work places, water and fuel supply, child care, health services and population control can contribute significantly to the success of learning programmes for women. Women's literacy programmes would succeed better if they centre around women's concerns and also provide opportunities of recreation and sharing of experiences.

45. District plans should be prepared keeping in view literacy requirements of the learners and identifying agencies which can take up such programmes in districts.

46. All women working in industries or employed elsewhere should be made literate by the employers by allotting time from the working hours for their education. Place of teaching, teachers and teaching material should be arranged by them. Necessary legislation to this effect may be enacted.

47. At least 50 per cent seats in pre-service courses in all teachers training institutions should be reserved for women. Spatial planning to ensure that women from rural areas are selected as teachers is essential.

48. Provision of composite teacher training courses for women who have had insufficient education to improve their educational qualifications along with their training, should be made.

49. The existing Integrated Rural Development Programme, National Rural Employment Programme, Development of Women and Children in Rural Areas, Training of Youth in Self-Employment Programme, Integrated Child Development Programme, etc.,

should have a component of literacy for their women beneficiaries. Training should be provided to the functionaries of various development departments by Directorate of Education in the States.

50. The State Resources Centres should produce suitable learning material for women on a priority basis. Literature for neoliterates should be suitably devised by experts, keeping in view the needs of different groups of learners.

51. Decentralization is the key to the successful application of the strategies outlined above in this decentralized approach, the village cluster or the block level is seen as most appropriate for the delivery of programmes. It is, therefore, necessary that the block is allocated a flexible budget so as to make funds available to village clusters/ villages for innovative educational activities and for equalization of educational opportunity.

52. An overall coordination of health, welfare and educational inputs would be most desirable. This would entail (a) Convergent policies in these sectors; (b) Coordination of delivery mechanisms; and (c) Pooling of allocations.

53. The strategies spelt out in the National Policy of Education, 1986, the Programme of Action for its implementation and the National Literacy Mission and the successful achievement of the goals, imposed in these documents, would be important for improvement in the status of women.

Denial of Education

As centuries rolled on, Aryan culture was firmly entrenched in this land. Indian women were trapped more and more in the web of myth and lost their sense of self and will. The goddesses were robbed of their glory even though they were still seated on a high pedestal. Men's obsession was to pull them down to earth by having the women sing their praises and do their will. Only when the women pleased them and satisfied their ego-needs, did they call them the goddesses of the household (Girhya Lakshmi).

The moment women defied male idiosyncrasies, they were called devils. Men took upon themselves the responsibilities of protecting and feeding the women who were consequently destitute and completely dependent. The women were not allowed to move outside the household without male company since it was taken for granted that they were incapable of defending themselves. Women became frail and weak creatures and believed that if any man other than their husbands touched them or cast a lustful glance towards them they were defiled and dishonoured.

Hence, their only path to an honourable existence was to give the men unflinching loyalty, submit to their care and deny their own self and will.

Perhaps in no other culture does such a duality exist where women have been mythically placed upon a high pinnacle while at the same time pulled down to dust in reality. In no other civilization the women's status in the social milieu has been raised so high and simultaneously, so brutally lowered as in the Indian culture.

In other cultures women are usually labelled as either saint or sinner, while in India she is both. Years of being enmeshed in the many strands of this web have deeply affected the position of the Indian women.

Women of the early Aryan civilization were highly respected. This society, however, as patriarchal, therefore, the birth of a girl was generally an unwelcome event. As early as in 2000 BC charms and rituals ensured the birth of a son in preference to that of a daughter. These charms are reported in the ancient Atharva Veda. Even though a son was desired and preferred, the birth of a daughter was a source of great pleasure to the family. Alteker points out that some scholars of this period were of the opinion that a gifted and well-mannered daughter might be a source of pleasure to the family. No restrictions were placed on girls in performing religious rites. The marriage of a daughter was not a difficult problem since she was free to choose her husband.

The marriage of girls used to take place at the age of 16 or 17 years. The women were not restricted and were allowed freedom of movement within the society, even-in the company of their lovers. The wife occupied the honoured place in the family as the mistress of her household. Marriages were mostly monogamous. Widow remarriage was usually permitted within the family. Parents desired their daughters to marry the husbands of their choice. During the early Vedic period, the prayer of an anxious father used to be "May Saviter lead and bring to thee the husband whom thy heart desires". Pinkham notes: It is important for us to note that a wife was on a level of equality at the hearth which was the altar of sacrifice.

Around 1500 BC, the education of the daughters confined to the family. Religious and secular training was given only to girls from rich and cultured families. Men performed functions in the religious sacrificial rites, which had previously been the wife's domain. Girls were married at about the age of sixteen years, and divorce and widow remarriage were, still permitted.

Gradually circumstances changed. As ancestor worship gained popularity, sons alone were permitted to perform religious rites. Women became "valued only as the vehicles for bearing sons, and when they were unfit or unwilling to perform this function, they were considered useless". The value of the sons increased further, and they began to be regarded as investments for the future. Without a son, no man or woman could hope to go to heaven. The position of the daughter was greatly undermined. Still the women were not debarred from the study of the Vedas and there existed very few taboos regarding the rearing of girls.

During the Epic period in India, the birth of daughter became an exceedingly negative event because of the prevalence of marriage customs, which subordinated the position of women. Still, a daughter was regarded as a prized possession, and family took a keen interest in her rearing. In Mahabbarata, Draupadi is described as the common property of the five brothers. She was put at stake in a gambling bout.

Sita, the ideal woman character of Ramayana, was put to fire ordeal to prove her chastity. She was denounced by Lord Rama to prove himself as an deal king. Draupadi did not accept her subordinate position and fought in an open assembly when Duryodhana the winner of the bout, sought to derobe her. Sita, on the other hand, took her humiliations with fortitude and goodwill toward her husband. However, by this time the right of the husband over his wife or a man over a woman has generally accepted by the society irrespective of whether women acknowledge it willingly or not.

This willing acceptance, even today, is considered as the ideal of womanhood. Sita is worshipped in most of the devout homes for her absolute obedience to her husband. Everywhere in India her example is exalted to be followed by all women. Sita had great strength of character and virtue. She pursued what she considered to be right. Her love for the husband was limitless. Her character was of utmost purity and chastity.

If we for the sake of argument forget for the time being the divinity of Rama and Sita there arises a doubt in our minds that such a character might have been drawn to satisfy the male ego by the male poets. It might be possible that Sita's character was enfolded in the myth of male supremacy and female subordination so that the women's sole aspiration in life became the loyalty and the service to her husband who was put at the level of God to her. This emphasis on chastity and service to the husband may lead to the conclusion that the women of this period were put on pedestal as goddesses only if they lived the ideal and the virtuous life according to the most rigid standards set by a male dominated society.

The witch type of the nature of women is demonstrated in the Ramayana through the story about Kaikeyi and Manthra. Kaikeyi tried through deceit to obtain the throne for her son. Manthra prompted her to do so. Hence both are branded as great culprits at the opposite end of the spectrum from Sita.

An aspect worth noticing in the character portrayal of Mahabharata heroines is the strong willed women. They are depicted as "resolute, full of fire, passionate in comparison with the often slackened, spineless men". Perhaps the Indians of this period were not in full control of their women and were frustrated enough to seek means of controlling them. One such means was to put an exceedingly high value on loyalty and chastity. Meyer points out that in Indian literature no ideal of a man is found; however, idealistic character portrayals of women are outstanding, especially in the Epic period". We may not entirely agree with this view as the portrayal of characters of Shri Rama, Shri Krishna and other heroes of Epic period cannot be ignored and yet there seems to be truth in this observation that women of this period were certainly of strong will.

During the post-Vedic period the age of marriage of girls was nine or ten years. Since the marriage was performed at such a young age, the choice then was not that of the girl but of the parents or other elders. A woman was debarred from revoking her marriage but the husband was free to throw his wife out of his household if she was not submissive. Widow marriage became unacceptable and was banned by 500 AD. The dictum that "the wife ought to revere her husband as a god even if he was vicious and void of any merit was accepted as applying to all women". The Law of Manu became the accepted way of life. It stated that the father should protect his daughter while she was young, her husband when she was married, and her son when her husband was no longer there. This law contributed to woman's inferior status in society and denied her all decision making rights.

Kautilya was in favour of marrying girls at a tender age. He advocated the marriage of girls when menses appear. He advocated the punishment of parents who did not marry their daughters at proper time. According to Jha: "Probably Kautilya advocates early marriage with a view to maintaining the chastity of girls, preventing 'women' from joining nunneries, check love marriages, utilizing the fertile period of girls for bringing forth offspring, and increasing the population at a time when frightful wars of conquest reduced Hindu population by one-half".

Kautilya propagates the subjection of women in married life. The wife must remain under the control of her husband. As the girls were to be married at an early age their education was totally neglected. Kautilya considered that a wife must be fully devoted to her husband and blindly follow him. The woman's freedom of speech was totally curbed and since her individuality was denied she was kept ignorant.

At this time, Buddhism developed in India as a revolt against Brahmanism, a too formal ritualistic religion prevalent about six centuries before the birth of Christ, Buddhism soon spread throughout India and dominated the nation until about 800 AD. Buddhists still maintained women in an inferior position through an emphasis on celibacy for men who made women appear unclean or as objects simply for men's pleasure.

Women were admitted to the Buddhist order as a gradual change occurred. According to Altekar, "this change was the beginning of a movement, which led to new attitudes about female education among ladies in commercial and aristocratic familes". Several ladies from Buddhist families led lives of celibacy with the aim of understanding and following the eternal truths of religion and philosophy.

Some women like Sanghamitra went to foreign countries to propagate Buddhism. Also, many women of the Jaina faith devoted their time to learning and became famous scholars. However, these were early exceptions. For the majority of women, no educational gains were made between 300 AD and 800 AD because of either Buddhism or Jainism.

The celibate Jaina monks considered women as the temptresses that perpetuated the misery that was life. This attitude certainly did not deter in general the Jainas from marriage or begetting of children. Women were given place of honour in the household. However, the monkish tales about celibacy did contribute to ambivalence among the Jaina men in their behaviour pattern with their women. Jaina men enjoyed their women in spite of the religious discourses about their evils.

The road back to educational equality was slow and difficult. By 500 AD the religious influence had obligated all education for women. The model women were exposed to remodelled. Women were exposed to such literature, which highlighted dependence and punishment for breaking the norms of conduct imposed on them by indifferent priests. A blind faith developed among the women through a process of awe and forced reverence. The Puranic literature cites examples where the husband was carried on his wife's shoulders to the house of a prostitute. The wife's willingness to put her husband's needs above hers' proved that she was a sati.

This literature which seems to have been developed by male Hindu priests completely subjugated the will of women. It emphasized husband worship along with the notion that a woman's salvation was possible only by doing that which her husband desired. An abundance of stories about Pativarta Nari or the husband worshipping woman influenced women to perform every kind of unnatural act for the sake of their husbands. Women started taking pleasure in their morbid existence. Eventually they became even greater fanatics than men in opposing their freedom. Perhaps they were so removed from the idea of an independent existence that even the thought of such responsibility frightened them. It may be said that it is human nature that one wants to stay with the familiar even if it is destructive because the unknown is scary.

Muslims considered marriage as a contract. In certain respects the Muslim law gave woman a higher position in the society than the medieval Hindu law. However, the purdah or veil as well as the women's ignorance of the law diminished this small difference. The Muslim men believed that their women would remain safe only if they were not exposed to temptation. Thus the women were denied the right to make choices.

The Muslims like Hindus believed that the women's only path to salvation lay in the service to their menfolk. Divorce was shunned and many myths were woven about the dutiful wife who was prepared to sacrifice her all for her husband. Muslim had put all types of restrictions on the movement of their women outside their households and by and large they were restricted from having any contact with men who did not belong to their immediate family. Chastity was valued and the husband considered it his conjugal duty to keep his wife away from temptation.

According to the Holy Quran women were respected because they bore children. Progeny was very important to the Muslims as defenders in warfare against unbelievers. Hence among Muslims there also developed ambivalent feelings towards their women. Women were respected for being mothers but at the same time they were restricted from having any freedom of action. They were completely subjugated by the dominant males. Due to a number of environmental factors affecting the Indian Muslims the feelings of respect were overcome by the need or restriction. Most of the legal rights of the women were virtually subjected to the male will.

The early Muslim period was one of great instabilities. Local feuds and conversions were dominating the social life. The fanaticism and religious intolerance closed the doors to rationality. The women were the worst sufferers of the irrationality of the ignorant priests and religious fanatics. Their spirit of inquiry was crushed, as they were not allowed any interaction with learned or open minded persons. The women were left with no option but to submit to their submissive role and suffer indignities and cruelties in silence. Dubey describes the personality and the character of the women that emerged during this period: They had no status in society; none in their own estimation. They were more like puppets, which move when someone pulls the strings than individual human beings with minds of their own.

At this time the patriarchal type of family in its perfectly developed state was generally in existence. The senior male in the family was the undisputed head. Hindu women could not claim any patronage since the law of succession did not give them independent right of inheritance. The inheritor of the property was made responsible for looking after the widow of the deceased. However, in spite of their low social status, women were still the ideal of conjugal devotion, and the family was the most intimate and enduring social relationship. Dubey considered that "the Hindu family was an ideal family, the Hindu parents .... Mothers were not equalled by any people on the earth in tenderness towards their progeny and attachment to the family ties".

This attachment to their families was not an exercise of free will for the women. They only knew to be dutiful wives and loving mothers. No other options were open to them. In most cases, motherhood was the only solace for them in their subordinate existence. As mothers, they elicited respect, and through their sons, they ruthlessly made attempts to dominate their daughter-in-laws and other poor and dependent relatives. The condition of the women in the Indian society continued to remain low. The disruption of the Mughal Empire in the eighteenth-century and the consequent confusion throughout the country added to the women's miseries. At the beginning of British rule, the marriage age was lowered to three or four years. Since hygienic conditions were poor and disease and famine were common, a large number of girls became widows in their early childhood. These child widows were ill treated and considered a curse to their families.

The use of the veil became popular, particularly among the Muslims. The higher-class women were kept away from the males by means of purdah even a glimpse of a woman's fully clothed and veiled body by a stranger was not tolerated. While travelling, dark clothes also covered the vehicle, and when the women entered it and left it, the male servants or the carriers had to be removed from their presence.

The observance of purdah was not only to safeguard the honour and chastity of women, it also kept them for special pleasure of the men. Certainly, the veil produced a special type of feminine beauty, which was pale and passionate with mystic eyes, and the mind of a child. Such women seemed to appeal to the morbid taste of the pleasure lovers. When a woman is unlimited and has free social interaction with the opposite sex, her sexual impulses are toned down. Perhaps those who put their women in purdah do so to obtain more sexual pleasure out of them.

During the period of Muslim rule, quite a number of upper caste Indian widows burned themselves on the funeral pyres of their husbands. This was known as the sati system. The Sanskrit word sati means "true wife" or "good woman." Thus a woman was considered true to her husband when she burned her body with him after his death. Akbar, the Mughal emperor, made efforts to stop this practice about 1600 AD. He, however, was unsuccessful. When the British became the rulers, they found this practice so firmly entrenched that they also had no luck in disrupting it. The magnitude of the tradition is further understood by noting that in the year 1803, 275 women were burned at their husbands' funeral pyres within 30 mile radius of Calcutta. Within six months of the year 1804 in the same area, the number was 115.

The British passed an Act in 1829 to stop the burning of widows. However, the practice continued in rural parts of India as late as 1905 when a few people participated in a sati ceremony in Bihar and were condemned to prison. The Hindu priesthood strongly resisted the British India law. They argued that Vedas, their holy text, sanctioned the practice, therefore, alien rulers could not suppress this practice. When the religious texts were examined, it was found that the Hindu priests had falsified them to support this rite.

The prevalence of the sati system and the opposition of its abolition by the orthodox priests show the extent to which a society can degenerate in the name of religious law. It also shows the strong influence of myth which the men and women came to believe. The honour of a family became so strongly linked with the widow burning that the kinsmen of a widow could cruelly push her into the fire. Unfortunately, the abolition of sati system did not end the miseries of the Hindu widows. Their burning was stopped, but they were still treated worst than the pet animals of the household.

They were not allowed to remarry and had to pass their lives depending on the charity of their kinsmen and serving them like domestic servants. The plight of the young widows was extremely bad. They were not only tortured but also many times sexually exploited by the unscrupulous males in the family or the neighbourhood.

Unfortunately sati system is still not completely wiped out. In September 1987, a young widow of 18 years Roop Kanwar was burnt at the funeral pyre of her deceased husband, a bare seven months after her wedding. The burning took place before a large gathering of people. The illiterate village folk endorsed the sati pratha and the rural women developed worshipful attitude toward the burnt widow. She became a deity. The myth woven centuries ago around the virtuous wives and self-destroying satis as goddesses seemed to persist in the minds of the people. It is worth noticing that all those women and men who supported and organized the burning of Roop Kanwar were not totally illiterate. They were some that were educated.

Yet the type of education which they had received did not result in opening the vistas of their minds. This has in fact opened the question of quality of education, which these persons had received. In the case of these persons education which they had received had completely failed in developing in them a positive attitude towards modernity and a will to fight against orthodoxy perpetuated by a corrupt and ill formed priestly class.

The institution of prostitution continued to flourish as a respectable way of life and the dancing girls were patronized by the nobles and landowners of their villages or towns. Chakraborty writes that in 1853, the Chief Magistrate of Calcutta reported that his town with its 416,000 people supported 12,419 such women. Of these upwards of 10,000 were Hindus including several daughters of the Kulin Brahmins.

Existing along with the customary form of prostitution, which was quite common in large part of the country there was another form of prostitution that of Devdasi cult or temple prostitution. In early times, the practice of offering virgins to the deity was common. Some examples can also be found in the temple precincts of Sumerian culture in Mesopotamia. In India, the Dravidians who may have borrowed it from Egypt or Mesopotamia probably introduced this custom.

In the Rig Veda there is a clear reference to the dancing girl. Usha, the goddess of dowri, is compared to a dancing girl wearing embroidered garments and baring her bosom. In the Atharva Veda there is also a reference to the existence of women called Gandharva grihtas (possessed or owned by Gandharvas). They do not marry and exist for the pleasure of gods and men.

The cult of Devadasi originated in the early civilization and became prevalent in South India between the sixth and the thirteenth centuries AD. During the reigns of Pallavas and Cholas all big temples recruited girls for temple prostitution. The temple dancers were married to the temple deity at a young age. They were taught music, dancing and the classical literature. After seven years of practice, the rite of worship of anklets (gajjai puja) took place. This was the first wearing of the anklets for the dancer. It has been traditional for families to offer their daughters as Devadasis or servants of the gods. In spite of the Devadasi Protection Act of 1934, some families still continue with this tradition in Maharashtra and Karnataka. In most other parts of India, this practice has been abolished.

The courtesan in India has filled a need for the men, which the wives were unable to meet. It seemed normal to a wealthy male that wives are kept for progeny and prostitutes for pleasure both sexually and aesthetically. The high-class courtesans throughout most of India's history were the most learned women in the country. Santosh Chatterjee in one of his articles has observed that "Be she of heaven or this earth, the courtesan in India had dual purposes in her life. She was in one way an object of lust for men, in another way she was the repository of all the delightful acts of music, dancing and personal decoration'.

The cult of Devadasis supported the envelopment of women in the web of myth regarding self-sacrifice and negation of will for men's pleasure. Women lost their individuality partly due to the contrivance of men and partly due to their need for the advantages they gained by being submissive.

Many factors contributed to women's dependent state. Numerous pregnancies during their most active years left her unfit and unable for engaging themselves in any type of employment except in the case of very poor or destitute women. Men accepted the responsibility of looking after the material needs of the women but in return for this they demanded from them unflinching loyalty and devotion.

They denied them any opportunity to develop them physically or mentally or to develop their own will power. Thus women became weak and inferior to men as human beings. This degeneration of the women in India was at its peak by the end of the eighteenth century. By the beginning of the nineteenth century the entrapment of the women in the mythical web was so complete that in almost all the spoken languages of India women were, described as evil, an appendage of men, and always open to temptation.

And so such sayings were quoted:

"To educate a women is like placing a knife in the hands of a monkey".

"Where there are women, there is trouble".

"Woman is a poisonous creeper, avoid her company; her love destroys faith, caste, wealth and money".

"He who is guilty of sin easily begets daughters".

WOMEN EMPOWERMENT

In last decades, along with the growth of population, there has been a shift in the population from rural to urban areas. The increasing urbanization has led to problems like crime and juvenile delinquency, alcoholism and drug abuse, housing shortage, over-crowding and slums, unemployment and poverty, pollution and noise, and communication and traffic control among others.

But if cities are places of tensions and strain, they are also the centres of civilization and culture. They are active, innovative, and alive. They provide opportunities to achieve one's aspirations. If the future of our country is linked with the development of rural areas, it is equally linked with the growth of cities and metropolitan areas. But before analyzing these problems, let us understand the basic concepts.

SHIFT TOWARDS CITIES

Urban: What is an 'urban area' or a city or a town? This term is used in two senses—demographically and sociologically. In the former sense, emphasis is given to the size of population, density of population and nature of work of the majority of the adult males; while in the latter sense, the focus is on heterogeneity, impersonality, interdependence, and the quality of life. The German sociologist, Tonnies (1957) differentiated between rural and urban communities in terms of social relationships and values. The rural gemeinschaft community is one in which social bonds are based on close personal ties of kinship and friendship, and the emphasis is on tradition, consensus and informality, while the urban gesellschaft society is one in which impersonal and secondary relationships predominate and the interaction of people is formal, contractual and dependent on the special function or service they perform.

The emphasis on gesellschaft society is on utilitarian goals and competitive nature of social relationships. Other sociologists like Max Weber (1961:381) and George Simmel (1950) have stressed on dense living conditions, rapidity of change and impersonal interaction in urban settings. Louis Wirth (1938:8) has said that for sociological purposes a city may be defined as 'a relatively large, dense and permanent settlement of socially heterogeneous individuals'. Scholars like Ruth Glass (1956) have defined city in terms of factors like: size of population, density of population, main economic system, type of administration, and some social characteristics.

In India, the census definition of 'town' remained more or less the same for the period 1901-51; but in 1961, a new definition was adopted. Up to 1951, 'town' included (1) collection of houses permanently inhabited by not less than 5,000 persons, (2) every municipality/corporation/notified area of whatever size, and (3) all civil lines not included within the municipal units.

Thus, the primary focus in the definition of town was more on the administrative set-up rather than the size of the population. In 1961, certain tests were applied for defining a place as 'town'. These were: (a) a minimum population of 5,000, (b) a density of not less than 1,000 persons per square mile, (c) three-fourths of its working population should be engaged in non-agricultural activities, and (d) the place should have a few characteristics and civic amenities like transport and communication, banks, schools, markets, recreation centres, hospitals, electricity, and newspapers, etc. As a result of this change in the definition, 812 areas (with 44 lakhs people) declared as towns in the 1951 census were not so considered in the 1961 census. The 1961 basis was adopted in the 1971, 1981 and 1991 censuses too for defining towns. Now demographically, areas with population between 5,000 and 20,000 are considered as small towns, those with population between 20,000 and 50,000 are considered as large towns, those with population between 50,000 and one lakh are considered as big cities, those with more than 10 lakhs people are considered as metropolitan areas, and those with more than 50 lakhs people are called mega cities.

Sociologists do not attach much importance to the size of population in the definition of city because the minimum population standards vary greatly. For example, in the Netherlands a minimum population of 20,000 is required for a place to be designated as urban; in France, Austria and West Germany, it is 2,000; in Japan it is 3,000; in the USA it is 3.500; and so on. As such, they give more importance to characteristics other than the population size. Theodorson (1969:451) has defined 'urban community' as "a community with a high population density, a predominance of non-agricultural occupations, a high degree of specialization resulting in a complex division of labour, and a formalized system of local government.

It is also characterized by a prevalence of impersonal secondary relations and dependence on formal social controls." According to Robert Redfield (American Journal of Sociology, January 1942), 'urban society' is characterized by a large heterogeneous population, close contact with other societies (through trade, communication, etc.), a complex division of labour, a prevalence of secular over sacred concerns, and the desire to organize behaviour rationally toward given goals, as opposed to following traditional standards and norms.

Urbanization: Urbanization is the movement of population from rural to urban areas and the resulting increasing proportion of a population that resides in urban rather than rural places. Thompson Warren (Encyclopaedia of Social Sciences) has defined it as "the movement of people from communities concerned chiefly or solely with agriculture to other communities, generally larger whose activities are primarily centred in government, trade, manufacture, or allied interests".

According to Anderson (1953:11), urbanization is not a one-way process but it is a two-way process. It involves not only movement from villages to cities and change from agricultural occupation to business, trade, service and profession, but it also involves change in the migrants' attitudes, beliefs, values and behaviour patterns. He has given five characteristics of urbanization: money economy, civil administration, cultural changes, written records and innovations.

Urbanism: Urbanism is a way of life. It reflects an organization of society in terms of a complex division of labour, high levels of technology, high mobility, interdependence of its members in fulfilling economic functions and impersonality in social relations (Theodorson, 1969: 453).

The Characteristics: Louis Wirth (1938:49) has given four characteristics of urbanism:

Transiency: an urban inhabitant's relations with others last only for a short time; he tends to forget his old acquaintances and develop relations with new people. Since he is not much attached to his neighbours, members of the social groups, he does not mind leaving their places.

Superficiality: an urban person has the limited number of persons with whom he interacts and his relations with them are impersonal and formal. People meet each other in highly segmental roles. They are dependent on more people for the satisfaction of their life needs.

Anonymity: urbanites do not know each other intimately. Personal mutual acquaintanship between the inhabitants which ordinarily is found in a neighbourhood is lacking.

Individualism: people give more importance to their own vested interests.

Ruth Glass (1956:32) has given the following characteristics of urbanism: mobility, anonymity, individualism, impersonal relations, social differentiation, transience, and organic type of solidarity. Anderson (1953:2) has listed three characteristics of urbanism: adjustability, mobility, and diffusion. Marshal Clinard (1957) has talked of rapid social change, conflict between norms and values, increasing mobility of population, emphasis on material things and decline in intimate interpersonal communication as important characteristics of urbanism. K. Dewis (1953) has highlighted eight characteristics of the urban social system: social heterogeneity (people of different religions, languages, castes, and classes live in urban areas.

There is also specialization in occupation), secondary association, social mobility, individualism, spatial segregation, social tolerance, secondary control and voluntary associations. Lious Wirth (1938:124) has given five characteristics of urbanism: heterogeneity of population, specialization of function, anonymity, impersonality and standardization of life and behaviour. Though these characteristics present an exaggerated picture of the urban man and his life, an analysis there of is necessary.

Heterogeneity of Population: The large population in cities can be largely attributed to migration from different areas which leads to people of different backgrounds and beliefs living together. This mixture of people affects the working of informal controls—mores and institutions—and reliance on formally designed mechanisms for regulating the behaviour of individuals and groups increases.

People no longer share the common sentiments, and being exposed to new ideas imported from other cultures through contacts with migrants, they challenge the out-moded beliefs and practices and adopt such new attitudes and lifestyles which help them in improving their economic status and coping with problems of adjustment. The influence of family and neighbourhood decreases and people come into conflict on the question of tightness of behaviour.

Specialization of Function and Behaviour: The heterogeneity and the large size of population of a city favour the development of specialization. Since the city has many facets of life and an individual can participate only in some of them, he becomes choosy and takes interest only in a few fields. Specialization in function encourages a diversity of life patterns. Doctors, engineers, businessmen, lawyers, bureaucrats, factory workers, teachers, clerks, policemen, for example, have different life patterns, different interests, and also different philosophy of life. Each specialist group makes its own contribution to the community and thus a division of labour is created.

The cloth merchant say, sells only cloth, and depends on many other specialists to manufacture, process and distribute cloth so that it reaches his shop. Such a division of labour permits an individual to benefit from a broader range of services than his own knowledge and capabilities provide. Each inhabitant in the city becomes dependent on specialists such as physicians, masons, mechanics, shopkeepers, tailors, washermen, and so on. He need not learn the techniques of each profession.

Specialization provides to an individual diverse opportunities to act, to express himself and to develop his potentialities. However, the contacts become secondary and formal and the sense of living a common life and having common concerns is destroyed. The relationship between two persons remains for a short duration till they gratify each other's purpose.

In a social order characterized by a heterogeneous population and diversity in behaviour patterns, there is a greater likelihood of confusion among several alternatives for proper behaviour in a given situation. For example, a student finds other student using unfair means and getting first division. He then thinks, should he do the same thing? One person finds another person giving Rs. 10,000 and getting a job of a police sub-inspector. He becomes confused whether he should report the case and get the bribe-taker arrested, or should he develop an attitude of indifference? These moral, social, and legal dilemmas are overwhelming in the city life.

Anonymity and Impersonality: High population density in the city erodes a sense of personal identity leading to loneliness and a loss of a sense of belonging. Hundreds of people watch a movie in a picture-house, enjoy and laugh together but when the film ends, the common emotions disintegrate into anonymity and impersonality. On the other hand, this very anonymity is the crux of personal freedom. The lack of interest in others releases the individual from heavy pressures towards conformity. In many cases, his responsibility to others ends with payment. Even when he becomes a member of a voluntary group like a club for instance, his participation could be minimum. He does not have to win the acceptance of other members or to engage in the accommodative process of fitting himself into the frame of their expectations. He may observe others but he may not necessarily be carried away by their stimuli.

One advantage of anonymity is that individuals are not judged according to their parents' lower class status but are evaluated on the basis of their appearance and behaviour in casual contacts. The anonymity and impersonality of urban life gives an individual, who aspires for a higher status, a greater opportunity to take advantage of symbols of higher status, like wearing attractive clothing, improving his mode of speech and manner so as to gain the acceptance and to impress persons of high positions, maintaining contacts with them and ultimately achieving the goals he seeks through these contacts.

Standardization of Behaviour: The urban life necessitates an individual to standardize his behaviour which ultimately helps him and others (with whom he interacts) to understand each other and make interaction simpler. For example, a shopkeeper finds the same questions being asked by a succession of customers. The customers are then seen as types—the person who haggles over price, the fellow who goes for quality, the man who is merely looking without any intention of buying, and so on. The experienced shopkeeper quickly judges the type of customer he is dealing with and uses the sales strategy he regards as most effective for a particular type of customer.

This helps both the shopkeeper and the customer to handle the sales transaction in a simple and quick fashion. Such standardized expectations and behaviour are part of urban life. Markets, clubs, restaurants, buses, newspapers, TV, radio, and schools/colleges present a largely standardized picture. A person who is unable to fit into such a life finds himself out of step, and is faced with the problem of adjustment. The large size of the city population lends particular force to the standardization of behaviour. This does not mean that the divergence of individual orientations is not possible.

Sorokin and Zimmerman (1962:56-57) have identified the following characteristics of the urban social system:

Non-agricultural Occupation: While agriculture is the main basis of the rural economy, trade, industry and commerce are the chief supports of the urban economy. It is this difference in occupation that ensures that rural people work in natural environments. Urban people on the other hand work mostly in artificial and unnatural environment in which the heat, cold and humidity are controlled by innovative skills. According to James Williams (1958), working in unnatural environment affects people's attitudes and behaviour patterns. It is, thus, because of the occupational differences that in urban areas we find liberals as well as conservatives, moderns as well as traditionalists, and unsociables as well as sociables.

Size of Population: Urban communities are much bigger in size than rural communities. The availability of job opportunities on one hand, and the materialistic as well as educational, medical and recreational facilities on the other hand attract people to cities.

Density of Population: In villages, people have to live near their fields to supervise the agricultural pursuits but in urban areas, people's residence depends on the location of their offices, market, children's school/college and so forth. This leads to a high density of population in areas which abound in these facilities.

In India, the average density of population per square mile in metropolitan cities varies between 3,000 and 5,000 persons. This high density has its own benefits as well as disadvantages. The advantages are that social contacts multiply, all necessary facilities are easily approachable and selection of friends becomes easier. The disadvantages are that inhabitants have very formal and impersonal relations with each other and their mental stresses increase.

Environment: Bernard (1971) has talked of four types of environment: material (climate), biological (animals and plants), social, physiosocial (machines, gadgets, instruments) and psychosocial (customs, traditions, institutions, etc.) and composite (economic, political and educational systems). The urban environment is more polluted. Besides, because of being surrounded by educational institutions and hence being more educated, an urban dweller is more rational, secular, and competitive.

Social Differentiation: In urban areas, people are differentiated on the basis of occupations, religion, class, living standards and social beliefs. Yet, they are dependent on each other and act as a functioning whole.

Social Mobility: Urban areas provide opportunities for change in social status because of which, as compared to villages, there is more upward mobility in cities. The mobility may be horizontal or vertical. Besides social mobility, we also find geographical mobility in urban areas.

Social Interaction: Relations among urban inhabitants are secondary and impersonal. People are more concerned with the status and skills of other persons than with their beliefs and ideologies. Control is also so formal that many a time it creates deviant behaviour.

Social Solidarity: In comparison to mechanical solidarity in rural areas, there exists organic solidarity in urban areas. In such a solidarity, though each person has his own individuality and personality, he depends more on others for their specialized roles.

The above description of the characteristics of urbanism as a way of life gives a feeling as if personal relations, primary groups and social intimacy do not exist in the cities. If consciously developed organizations serve the interests of the individuals, the primary groups also admit members through birth. Primary-group members are tied together by a fusion of concerns for one another. Their relations are more emotional and intensive. Within the group, a member performs variety of functions unlike specified functions in secondary groups.

For example, in a family, a mother serves as a cook, a nurse, a moral instructor and a manager of tensions for the children and the family members. Although the social change has weakened the bonds of family, neighbourhood and peer groups yet the old kind of functioning of these groups has not completely stopped nor' have the primary relations vanished. Performing obligatory roles in the family, maintaining social participation within the neighbourhood, sharing common interests of castes and, acting as a source of support to one's kin and friends continue to be important and significant features of urban life. A number of studies in India (like those by Kapadia, Sachchidanand, R.K. Mukerjee and M.S. Gore) have shown that rural people who migrate to cities continue to maintain links with their families and kin in the village. In cities too, they not only share their problems with persons belonging to the same and adjoining villages but also with members of their caste. This makes their adaptation to city life easier.

The Growth: While cities have existed since ancient times, until recently they represented only a relatively small proportion of the population. The lives of the great majority of the people were predominantly shaped by the rural community or village. The massive growth of cities and metropolitan areas, and the shift of a significant proportion of the population to urban areas has been a characteristic feature of past six decades or so. Urbanization was an offshoot of the industrial revolution which created a demand for a large number of workers at centralized locations.

The growth of cities depends not only on birth and death rates and migration but also on political, religious historical and economic factors. Political centres can be the capital of states (Bhopal, Jaipur, Bombay, Calcutta, etc.) or the areas of political activities (Delhi), or the training centres for the military (Kharagvasla), or centres for defence production (Jodhpur); economic centres are areas which predominate in trade or commerce (Ahmedabad, Surat); industrial towns are places with factories (Bhilai, Singrauli, Kota, Ludhiana); the religious cities are those where people go on pilgrimage (Hardwar, Varanasi, Allahabad); and educational centres have educational institutions (Pilani).

In India, the urban population in 1971 was 109.11 million, in 1981 it was 160.1 million, and in 1991 it was 217.18 million. It is expected to increase to 291 million by March 2001 (The Hindustan Times, January 19, 1997). While in 1921 the urban population was only 11.3 per cent of the total population of the country; in 1951 it increased to 17.6 per cent, in 1971 to 20.2 per cent, in 1981 to 23.8 per cent and in 1991 to 25.7 per cent (Census of India, 1991, Series 1, 2). Again, in the 1911-21 decade, the urban population increased by 8.3 per cent, in 1921-31 it increased by 19.1 per cent, in 1931-41 by 32 per cent, in 1941-51 by 41.4 per cent, in 1951-61 by 37 per cent, in 1961-71 by 38.2 per cent, in 1971-81 by 35.4 per cent, and in 1981-91 by 40.4 per cent. Thus, during the four and a half decades between 1941 and 1985, the growth rate of urban population was between 3.4 and 3.8 per cent every year. During 1985-90, the average annual growth rate for urban areas was 2.95 per cent as compared to 1.65 per cent for rural areas for the same period. The growth rate for urban areas will increase during the next two decades whereas the growth rate for rural areas will decrease. As per the UN projections, urban areas in India will be marked by a growth rate of 3.03 per cent during 2015-2020, while rural areas will have a reduced growth rate of 0.34 per cent during the corresponding period. Also as per UN projections, 45.2 per cent people (about 630 million) will live in urban areas in India by 2025 AD. This is close to the total population of India in 1981 which was 684 million (The Hindustan Times, November 29, 1995).

The share of agricultural employment in the total employment of main workers reduced from 72 per cent in 1961 to 64 per cent in 1991 (Census of India). By the year 2001, anything between 18 to 20 crore people would be added to the rural population and of this addition, at least 10 crore of them will come to urban areas in search of jobs.. Further, while in 1931, the total number of cities with more than one lakh population was 32, it increased to 107 in 1961, 216 in 1981 and 317 in 1991 (excluding Jammu and Kashmir). The number of bigger cities with more than ten lakhs population increased from two in 1941 to nine in 1971,12 in 1981, and 23 in 1991 (Census of India, 1991, Series 1, Paper 2:251). Such growth affects the social, economic and political life of the people.

Of the total number of 4,689 urban settlements (in 1991) in India, Uttar Pradesh has the largest number of towns (704), followed by Tamil Nadu (434), Madhya Pradesh (327) and Maharashtra (307). According to the 1991 census, 65.2 per cent population was living in cities with more than one lakh population, 10.9 per cent in cities with population between 50,000 and one lakh, 13.2 per cent in cities with population between 20,000 and 50,000, 7.8 per cent in cities with population between 10,000 and 20,000, and 2.6 per cent in towns with population between 10,000 and 5,000 (Census of India, 1991, Series 1, Paper 2). Four major cities of India with more than 50 lakhs population, according to 1991 figures are: Calcutta (109 lakhs), Mumbai (126 lakhs), Delhi (93 lakhs), and Chennai (54 lakhs) (The Hindustan Times, May 30,1991).

Role of Society

The social effects of urbanization may be analyzed in relationship to family, caste, social status of women, and village life.

Urbanization and Family: Urbanization affects not only the family structure but also intra and inter-family relations, as well as the functions the family performs. Several empirical studies of urban families conducted by scholars like I.P. Desai, Kapadia, and Aileen Ross, have pointed out that urban joint family is being gradually replaced by nuclear family, the size of the family is shrinking, and kinship relationship is confined to two or three generations only.

In his study of 423 families made in 1955-57 in Mahuva town in Gujarat, I.P. Desai (1964) found that 5 per cent families were nuclear (residentially as well as functionally), 74 per cent were residentially nuclear but functionally and/or substantially (in property) joint, and 21 per cent were joint in residence and functioning as well as in property. Of the 95 per cent joint families (joint in functioning and/ or property, and/or residence), the degree of functionality was low in 27 per cent cases (that is, they were joint only in functioning), high in 17 per cent cases (that is, they were joint in functioning and property), higher in 30 per cent cases (that is, they were joint in functioning, property and residence but were two generation families), and highest in 21 per cent cases (that is, they were joint in residence, functioning and property and were three-generation families). This shows that though the structure of urban family is clanging, the spirit of individualism is not growing in the families.

Kapadia (1959) in his study of 1,162 families in rural and urban (Wavsari) areas in Gujarat in 1955 found that while in rural areas, for every two nuclear families there were three joint families; in urban areas, nuclear families were 10 per cent more than joint families. Ross (1961) in her study of 157 Hindu families belonging to middle and upper classes in Bangalore in 1957 found that (1) about three-fifth (or 60 per cent) of the families are nuclear and two-fifths (or 40 per cent) are joint; (2) of the joint families, 70 per cent are small joint (couple+unmarried children+married sons without children, or two or more married brothers with children) and 30 per cent are large joint families (parents of unmarried children unmarried children+married sons with children); (3) the trend today is towards a break with the traditional joint family form into the nuclear family unit; (4) small joint family is now the most typical form of family life in urban India; (5) there is a cycle of family types; (6) a growing number of people now spend at least part of their lives in single units; and (7) relations with one's distant kin are breaking or weakening.

R.K. Mukherjee (1973) also, on the basis of his study of 4,120 families in West Bengal in 1960-61, has said that replacement of joint family by nuclear family units is a fait accompli.

Though intra-family and inter-family relations are changing, it does not mean that youngsters no longer respect their elders, or children completely ignore their obligations to their parents and siblings, or wives challenge the authority of their husbands. The important change is that the 'husband-dominant' family is being replaced by 'equalitarian' family where wife is given a share in decision-making processes.

The parents also no longer impose their authority on the children nor do the children blindly obey the commands of their parents. The attitude of youngsters is motivated by respect rather than fear. I.P. Desai maintains that "in spite of strains between the younger and older generations,, the attachment of the children to their families is seldom weakened". M.S. Gore (1968) writes: "even in joint family, the eldest male consults his children and this consultation is not formal". Ross (1961), however, thinks that "the feelings of family obligation and emotional attachment to family members will almost certainly weaken and the authority of the patriarch break down. When this happens, there will be little left for identity within the larger kinship group", Our own feeling is that family in urban India (and for that matter in the whole country) will never disintegrate but it will remain a strong unit.

Urbanization and Caste: Caste identity tends to diminish with urbanization, education and the development of an orientation towards individual achievement and modern status symbols. Urbanites participate in networks which include persons of several castes. According to Rajni Kothari, the structure of particularistic loyalties has been overlaid by a more sophisticated system of social and political participation with crosscutting allegiances. Andre Beteille (1966:209-10) has pointed out that among the westernized elite, class ties are much more important than caste ties.

The educated members of some castes with modern occupations sometimes organize as a pressure group. As such, a caste association competes as a corporate body with other pressure groups for political and economic resources. This type of organization represents a new kind of solidarity. These competing units function more as social classes than as caste structures.

Yet other change we find today is the fusion of sub-castes and fusion of castes. Kolenda (1984:150-51) has identified three kinds of fusion: (i) on the job and in newer neighbourhoods in the city, persons of different sub-castes and of different castes meet. They are usually of approximately equal rank. Neighbourhood or office group solidarity develops. This has been found common in the government colonies in big cities; (ii) inter-subcaste marriages take place, promoting a fusion of subcastes. This is because many a time it is difficult to find a sufficiently educated groom for an educated daughter within his own sub-caste, but one may find it in neighbouring sub-caste; and (iii) democratic politics fosters the fusion of sub-castes and of adjacent castes. One example is the Dravida Munnetra Kazagam (DMK) and the Anna Dravida Munnetra Kazagam (ADMK) parties of Tamil Nadu composed of the members of higher non-Brahmin castes.

Urban dwellers do not conform to caste norms strictly. There is a change in commensal relations, marital relations, social relations, as well as in occupational relations. A study of caste system in Bihar revealed that urbanization does did affect all characteristics of the caste system uniformly. On the basis of the study of 200 persons belonging to five different castes (Brahmins, Rajputs, Dhobis, Ahirs and Chamars), it was found that all respondents had married in their own castes, though 20 per cent of the respondents living in cities (against 5 per cent in rural areas) were in favour of inter-caste marriages. As regards occupation, not a single respondent in the city was engaged in his traditional caste occupation, though 81 per cent respondents in rural areas were still engaged in their traditional occupations. Likewise, caste solidarity was not as strong in urban areas as in the rural areas. Caste panchayats were very weak in cities. G.S. Ghurye (1952), K.M. Kapadia (1959), A.P. Barnabas, Yogendra Singh, R.K. Mukerjee, M.N. Srinivas, Yogesh Atal and S.C. Dube have also referred to the impact of urbanization on caste.

Status of Women: The status of women in urban areas is higher than that of rural women. Urban women are comparatively educated and liberal. Against 25.1 per cent literate women in rural areas, there are 54 per cent literate women in urban areas according to the census of 1991. Some of them are working too. As such, they are not only aware of their economic, social and political rights but they even use these rights to save themselves from being humiliated and exploited. The average age of girls at marriage in cities is also higher than the corresponding age in villages.

However, in the labour market, women are still in a disadvantaged situation. The labour market discriminates against women and is opposed to equality of opportunity—understood in a comprehensive sense to include equality of employment, training and promotional opportunities. In this sense, change is not possible in the sex segregated labour market whose structures ensure that the career patterns of women will normally be marked by discontinuity, unlike the normal male career patterns which assume continuity.

Because of the constraints of the sex segregated labour market, women tend to cluster in a limited range of occupations, which have low status and are poorly paid. Women normally prefer teaching, nursing, social work, secretarial and clerical jobs—all of which have low status and low remuneration. Even those women who have surmounted the hurdle to professional education are disadvantaged as they find it difficult to reconcile to the competing demands of a professional career and home.

It is difficult for women to remain single or to combine marriage with career. Apart from the general expectation that all wives must be housewives, it has been noted that women are called upon to sacrifice their career when the need arises, thereby subordinating their own career to that of their husbands. This often creates frustration among women, leading to psychotic illness in a few cases. Rural women, however, do not have to face such problems.

It has been further found that in the cities of India, the high level education among girls is significantly associated with the smaller family size. Though education of women has raised the age of marriage and lowered the birth rate, it has not brought about any radical change in the traditional pattern of arranged marriages with dowry.

Margaret Cormack (1961:109) found in her study of 500 university students that girls were ready to go to college and mix with boys but they wanted their parents to arrange their marriage. Women want new opportunities but demand old securities as well. They enjoy their newly found freedom but at the same time wish to carry on with old values.

Divorce and remarriage are the new phenomena we find among urban women. Today women take more initiative to break their marriages legally if they find adjustment after marriage impossible. Surprizingly, a large number of divorces are sought by women on the grounds of incompatibility and mental torture.

Politically also, urban women are more active today. The number of women contesting elections has increased at every level. They hold important political positions and also possess independent political ideologies. It may, thus, be concluded that while rural women continue to be dependent on men both economically and socially, urban women are comparatively independent and enjoy greater freedom.

Urbanization and Village Life: During the past half a century, urban development in our country has led to the centrifugal movement of village people to the urban areas that were located within fairly easy access of public utilities. Many migrated to cities because of the availability of jobs there. Those who continue to live in villages also enjoy many of the conveniences of city life, although they are miles removed from the urban centres.

The excellent highways, automobiles, radio, television and newspapers keep the villagers in contact with the city culture and civilization. The combination of rural residence and urban employment, and urban residence and rural contact has resulted not only in certain modifications of social patterns but also in adjustments to a new way of life.

The villagers are now more aware of the city lifestyle and they have been influenced by it in such a way that they no longer lay undue emphasis on caste, creed... They have become more liberal in their approach. They no longer live in isolation. Many cultivators have accepted the new farm practices. Not only have their values and aspirations changed but there is a change in their behaviour too. The *jajmani* system is weakening and inter-caste and interclass relations are changing. There is a change even in institutions of marriage, family and caste panchayats. Instead of depending on traditional methods of treating the diseases, they now use modern allopathic medicine. Similarly in elections, they give importance not as much to the social status of the candidate as to his individual potentialities and his political background.

But this in no way mean that traditions have ceased to be important in villages. Individualism as not been able to replace familism, nor has secularism been able to replace the bond with the sacred.

The Problems: Urban problems are endless. Drug addiction, pollution, crime, juvenile delinquency, begging, alcoholism, corruption, and unemployment are a few of them. Let us analyze the incidence and prevalence of seven crucial problems that are not covered in other chapters of this book. These are: (i) housing and slums, (ii) crowding and depersonalization, (iii) water supply and drainage, (iv) transportation and traffic, (v) power shortage, (vi) sanitation and (vii) pollution.

Housing and Slums: Housing people in the city 'house-lessness' is a serious problem. Government, industrialists, capitalists, entrepreneurs, developers, contractors, and landlords have been unable to keep pace with the housing needs of the poor and the middle class people. According to the 1988 UNI report (The Hindustan Times, 9 May, 1988), between one-fourth and half of the urban population in India's largest cities lives in makeshift shelters and slums.

At least 15 per cent of the nation's families are deprived of houses, more than 60 per cent of the houses have inadequate lighting and air facilities, and 80 per cent of the rural and 30 per cent of the urban population lives in mud-houses. Millions of people are required to pay excessive rent, that is, one which is beyond their means. In our profit-oriented economy, private developers and colonizers find little profit in building houses in cities for the poor and the lower middle-class people, and they consider it gainful to concentrate instead in meeting the housing needs of the rich and the upper-middle class.

The result has been higher rents and a scramble for the few available houses. Almost half of the population are either ill-housed or pay more than 20 per cent of their income on rent. In some states, the Housing Boards and the City Development Authorities have tried to remedy the city housing problem with active financial support from the Life Insurance Corporation, HUDCO and such other agencies.

They even charge the total housing cost in monthly instalments on an interest varying between 9 per cent and 11 per cent. But engineers and contractors profit a lot from these government efforts. They use poor-quality material in construction and finish the houses contravening the laid down specifications. The buyer soon finds that the roof leaks, the plaster peels off, there are cracks in the walls, and the electric fittings break down. Such ventures bring bad name to housing boards and even of a few honest bureaucrats associated with such housing schemes. No wonder, housing in the cities even today continues to be a gigantic problem next only to food and clothing.

The estimated shortage of houses at the beginning of the Eighth Plan was about 30 million units, out of which about 8 million were required for the urban areas. By 1997, the shortage was expected to grow to 12 million units in urban areas. In Delhi alone, which has seen a population increase from 6.2 to 9.3 million between 1981 and 1991, there is an addition of 60,000 people each year who need to be provided with new housing. Almost 70 per cent of Delhi's population, according to an UNI report, lives in sub-standard conditions.

With the country's slum population of 1991 standing at nearly 40 million, slum dwellers form 44 per cent of the population in Delhi, 45 per cent in Mumbai, 42 per cent in Calcutta, and 39 per cent in Chennai. The situation is no better in the eight other metropolizes of Bangalore, Hyderabad, Ahmedabad, Kanpur, Pune, Nagpur, Lucknow and Jaipur. The slum population, governmental efforts notwithstanding, is expected to show a sizable increase by 2000 aggravating to the housing problem and the squalor conditions. The living conditions in slum areas are characterized by over-crowding, poor environmental conditions, scarcity of health and family welfare services and total absence of minimum level of residential accommodation. As a result, conditions of people living in slums is far more pathetic than in rural areas.

Let us take a look at the slum-dwellers of Bangalore, for an example. According to a survey conducted here in 1992, this Garden City has 464 slums with a total slum population of 8.51 lakhs. Only 10 per cent of the slum population here has the facilities for sewage disposal. About 55 per cent of the slum habitats live below the poverty line with a monthly income of less than Rs. 1,000.

The average age of marriage is 18.3 years, as compared to 20.3 years for urban areas of Karnataka as a whole. The urban areas of Karnataka have an infant mortality rate of 42 per thousand but the slum dwellers of Bangalore have infant mortality rate of 77.8. Similarly, crude birth rate is 32.5 against 23.1 for urban Karnataka as a whole. Nine out often pregnant women are in the age group of 15-29.

The concept of spacing births has not gained acceptance. Only 40 per cent children between the ages of one and two are fully immunized. The incidence of diseases is high among children. On an average a slum household spends 5 per cent of its income on medicines, private doctors fees and transportation for treatment.

The reasons for not going to government municipal hospitals are distance, long waiting time and rude behaviour of staff (The Hindustan Times, November 29, 1995). This is the scenario obtaining in the slums of Bangalore, despite the fact that the Government has provided a network of 92 dispensaries, 16 hospitals, 3 pediatric centres, 37 Urban Family Welfare Centres, 31 maternity homes, two maternity hospitals, and 200 Anganwadis. We only need to strain our imagination to visualize the plight of slum-dwellers in other cities. The order of development in squatter settlements is people, land (sites), shelter and services. People first select a site which meets their social and economic needs, build shelters and then wait for the services to move in over a period of time.

Although the settlements fulfil the needs of people, they violate city planning regulations. It is, therefore, believed that the current order of development ought to be land (site), people, shelter and services. Now the government, apart from encouraging the poor for going in for low cost non-formal housing technologies, has formulated several plans and given many concessions to promote more and better housing. This includes contribution of Rs. 100 crore to the National Housing Bank, setting up a separate Social Security Fund with a corpus of Rs. 100 crore, and creating a National Scheduled Caste and Scheduled Tribes Finance and Development Corporation.

Crowding and Depersonalization: Crowding (density of population) and people's apathy to other persons' problems (including their neighbours' problems) is another problem growing out of city life. Some homes are so overcrowded that five to six persons live in one room. Some city neighbourhoods are extremely overcrowded. Overcrowding has very deleterious effects. It encourages deviant behaviour, spreads diseases, and creates conditions for mental illness, alcoholism, and riots. One effect of dense urban living is people's apathy and indifference. City dwellers do not want to 'get involved' in other people's affairs. Some people do take interest in accidents and in cases of molestations, assaults and even murders but others choose to be mere onlookers.

Water Supply and Drainage: We have reached a stage where no city has round the clock water supply. Intermittent supply results in a vacuum being created in empty water lines which often suck in pollutants through leaking joints. Cities like Chennai, Hyderabad, Rajkot, Ajmer, and Udaipur get water from the municipality for less than an hour a day. Many small towns have no main water supply at all and are dependent on tube wells. Even a relatively planned and serviced city like Delhi has now to reach as far as 180 km to the Ramganga for augmentation of water supply.

Bangalore pumps water from far away with a lift of about 700 metres. Most towns and cities which normally get good rain every year, have been undergoing the agony of acute water shortage in the last eight-nine years. What seems to be sadly lacking is a national water policy which would assess the total water resources and then allocate water. This is in spite of the State Chief Ministers' meeting at Delhi in September 1987 which approved the National Water Policy which aimed at giving priority to drinking water requirements.

When we look on the other side of the water supply, that is, drainage, we find the situation equally bad. One of the less known facts about India is that there is not a single city which is fully sewered. Not even Chandigarh can claim this distinction because the unauthorized constructions in and around it lie outside the purview of the main system. Because of the non-existence of a drainage system, large pools of stagnant water can be seen in every city even in summer months. Just as we need a national water policy, we also need a national and regional drainage policy.

Transportation and Traffic: The transportation and traffic picture in all Indian cities is unhappy. A majority of people use buses and tempos, while a few use rail as transit system. The increasing number of scooters, motorcycles, mopeds and cars make the traffic problem worse. For example, in Mumbai, automobiles have trebled (from 3.1 lakhs to 8.73 lakhs) and in Delhi increased by four times (from 5.92 lakhs to 23.7 lakhs) between 1986 and 1996 (The Hindustan Times,

November 29, 1996). They pollute the air with smoke. In Mumbai alone, the daily pollutants let out into the air is about 3,000 tons, of which 52 per cent come from automobiles, 2 per cent from domestic fuels, and the remaining 46 per cent from industries.

The number of buses plying in metropolitan cities like Delhi, Mumbai, Chennai and Calcutta is not adequate and commuters have to spend about one to two hours to get into a bus, which means leaving the house two hours in advance in the morning to reach their place of work and reaching home two hours late in the evening.

The main reason for being in this mess is that the low income of the commuters forces them to live in areas with cheap accommodation which necessitates extensive travel. Further, since our citizens cannot afford to pay high fares for the use of a public transport system, the fares have to be kept very low which results in all city bus services sustaining such annual losses as hamper their expansion or maintenance a fleet adequate to meet city needs.

Power Shortage: Closely linked with transportation is the question of power shortage. The use of electrical gadgets has increased very much in cities, and on the other hand, the establishment of new industries and the expansion of the old industries has also increased dependence on electricity. Most states are not in a position to generate the power that they need with the result that they remain dependent on the neighbouring states. Conflict over supplying of power between two states often creates severe power crisis for people in the city.

Sanitation: Municipalities and municipal corporations in Indian cities are so riddled with corruption and inefficiency that they have time for all things but the interest in sanitation of the city, particularly in removing garbage, cleaning drains, and unclogging sewers. The sweepers rarely and reluntantly perform their assigned duties and every few months threaten to go on strike on the issue of wages, etc. The garbage disposal fleets operate to a third or half of their capacity. If removing garbage work is assigned to private contractors, they always complain of non-payment of money and stop working on slight pretexts. There is, thus, total lack of motivation to tackle the basic sanitation needs of the cities.

The spread of unauthorized slums in congested urban areas and lack of civic sense among the settlers in these slums further adds to the growing mound of filth and diseases. Even the major cities of our country reflect the sanitation crisis. Of about 3,000 to 5,000 tonnes of garbage generated in one day in a metropolitan city, hardly 50 to 60 per cent is cleared. Out of 1,500-2,000 million litres of sewage generated in a day, hardly 1,000 to 1,500 litres a day is collected.

This is when the total budget of municipal corporations of cities like Delhi, Calcutta, Mumbai and Chennai varies between Rs. 1,000 and Rs. 1,500 crore per annum (India Today, October 31, 1994:63-66). Municipal machinery works only in the VIP areas, totally neglecting the seweage, water or garbage collection in other colonies. According to UMCEF, lakhs of urban children die or suffer from diarrhoea, diphtheria, tetanus, and measles, etc. because of poor sanitary conditions and water contamination. Many cities report a good number of malaria and filaria cases every year.

More than half our battle against these diseases can be won if our municipal officials sincerely devote time to cope with sanitation problem and if our people become more responsible to the need for cleanliness.

The outbreak of the plague in some cities in our country in 1994 has created some awareness among the officials and the general public but covering the whole city by seweage, arranging the disposal of garbage, cleaning drains and community toilets, etc. are such big problems that clean environment, community hygiene and city sanitation still remain and are likely to remain serious problems in decades to come.

Various forms of racketeering in municipal work exit in our cities. For instance: (a) since payment for garbage removal is made on the basis of trips and not the weight of the garbage pickup vehicles, a large number of trips are shown on records and money is split between the contractor and the municipal employees; (b) a large number of vehicles used for garbage-collecting operations are actually used for outside work; (c) debris is diverted and sold to private parties for filling up building sites while payment for debris disposal is also taken from the municipality; and (d) drivers of trucks and dumpers sell diesel meant for sanitation trucks.

Obviously, the basic problem is excessive urbanization and the resultant slumming of the cities. But because our politicians use migrants as vote-banks, they remain unconcerned with taking necessary civic action. Lack of understanding at the planning level, lack of coordination between the concerned agencies, mismanagement of municipalities, and lack of necessary funds to be provided by the state governments will always remain barriers in putting sanitation maintenance cycle in proper shape. If cities continue to treat sanitation and sewage as low-priority areas, over coning health crisis in urban areas will be an insurmountable task in years to come. As a long-term remedy, what is needed is using new techniques of refuse collection, new technology for the disposal of garbage, and a fundamental change in the municipal infrastructure, and land use planning.

Pollution: Our cities and towns are major polluters of the environment. Several cities discharge 40 per cent to 60 per cent of their entire sewage and industrial effluents untreated into the nearby rivers. The smallest town contributes its share of garbage and excreta to the nearest waterway through its open drains. Urban industry pollutes the atmosphere with smoke and toxic gases from its chimneys. Areas recording higher levels of air pollution abound with many ailments which particularly affect children below five years and people above fifty years of age. The high synergistic effect of sulphur dioxide, nitrogen dioxide, etc. causes these diseases. The ambient air quality in Delhi gives it the dubious distinction of being the fourth most polluted city in the world.

The issue of environmental pollution in urban areas is considered so significant that even the Supreme Court ordered in July 1995 for the strict enforcement of environmental laws leading to closure or relocation of about 146 hazardous industries in Delhi by November-December 1996. The orders led to even agitations among the affected workers in pecember 1996, but the Apex Court stuck to its decision of not locating industries within the National Capital Region (NCR) but shifting them by where in the neighbouring states. The vehicular emissions in Delhi account for 64 per cent of Delhi's air pollutant load, power plants are responsible for 16 per cent and industries account for 12 per cent. The closure of industries in Delhi was however stayed until June 1997.

Similar significant role was played by the Supreme Court in yet another judgment on environment protection in Andhra Pradesh in October 1996. The judgment banned shrimp (small marine fish) culture within 500 metres of the high tide line along the 6,000 km coastline and dismantling of all structures within the restricted zone by March 1997. The country earns more than Rs. 600 crore in foreign exchange through export of shrimp from Andhra Pradesh and Tamil Nadu alone. According to an estimate by the Central Pollution Control Board, the effluent generation from acquaculture farms in the east coast alone was about 2.37 million cubic metres (The Hindustan Times, January 6, 1997).

The poison we put in the environment comes right back to us through our air, water and food, slowly seeping into our bodies and showing up as cancer, immune disorders or as hormonal system disorders. No wonder, the doctors claim that the worsening environmental condition in India has increased the chances of catching cancer dramatically in the four metros—Delhi, Mumbai, Bangalore and Chennai—the chances of having cancer are as high as 7 to 11 per cent during a life time. A conservative estimate of cancer patients in India by the year 2001 stands at eight lakhs. Of course, the poor suffer more than the rich from environmental degradation.

The Causes: Following McVeigh and Shostak (1978:198-205), who have linked urban problems in the United States to four factors, we can identify following five major causes of problems of urban life in India: (i) migration in and out of the city, (ii) industrial growth, (iii) apathy of the government, (iv) defective town planning, and (v) vested interest forces.

Migration: As already indicated, people migrate to towns/cities because of the relatively better employment opportunities available there. In India, the migration has four patterns: rural to rural, rural to urban, urban to urban and urban to rural. Though rural to rural migration is by far the most prevalent form of movement but rural to urban and urban to urban migration is equally crucial. The 1971 census figures pointed out that in 71.3 per cent cases, migration was from rural to rural, in 15 per cent cases, it was from rural to urban, in 8.8 per cent of cases it was from urban to urban, and in 4.9 per cent cases, it was from urban to rural (Bose, 1979:560). The figures must be approximately the same today (in 1997). The analysis of intradistrict migration (short-distance migration), interdistrict or intrastate migration (medium distance migration) and inter-state migration (long distance migration) shows that about 68 per cent migrations are short distance, 21 per cent are medium distance and 11 per cent are long distance migrations (Bose, 1979:187).

The entrance of the rural poor into the city depletes sources of revenue. On the other hand, the rich people today prefer to live in sub-urban areas. This movement of the rich causes financial loss to the city. This migration to the city and away from the city aggravates problems.

Industrial Growth: While the urban population growth rate is 4 per cent in India, the industrial growth rate is about 6 per cent per annum. The Eighth Five Year Plan postulated an industrial growth rate of 8 per cent per annum. This growth was expected to take care of the additional job requirements in the cities. The tertiary sector also provides refuge to the migrants, though their earnings remain at low level.

Apathy of the Government: The administrative mismanagement of our cities is also responsible for the mess in which city-dwellers find themselves. Municipal governments have not kept pace with city growth, either spatially or in terms of management infrastructure. There is neither the will nor the capacity to plan for the future. There is also no skill and capability to manage what exists. Until we improve the capacity of our cities to govern themselves, we cannot emerge from the urban mess. On the other hand, the state governments also put many restrictions on local governments in raising necessary funds for dealing with particular urban problems.

Defective Town Planning: A more alarming factor in the general deterioration in the standard of civic services is the growing sense of helplessness of our planners and administrators. From the Planning Commission downwards, there seems to be a fatalistic acceptance of the uncontrolled growth in our metropolitan cities. In fact, a member of the National Commission on Urbanization had expressed a feeling that very little is being done in our country to plan the growth of the cities in a proper way.

Vested-interest Forces: The last cause of urban problems is the vested interest forces that work Against people but enhance private commercial interests and profits. The city residents are usually powerless to affect decisions that the elite take to further their own interests. power and profit. When these powerful elite can make more money. they adopt plans and programmes no matter how many people are hurt in the process.

The Solutions: Some measures have to be adopted if we want to remedy urban problems. The measures suggested are as follows:

Rapid Progress

One important solution to our urban problems is the systematic development of the fast growing urban centres and planning an investment programme which, over the next 20 years or so, could give rise to a large number of well distributed, viable urban centres throughout the country. So far we have been focusing attention on programmes for providing wage employment in rural areas through IRDP, NREP and JRY to hold people back in the villages. While there is ample justification for providing rural employment, this by itself is not enough. It is not possible to provide gainful employment in the agricultural sector beyond a certain point. For this purpose, we have to emphasize on programmes which can permit multifunctional activities to sustain people in cities.

Planning Procedure

Urban planning is almost city-centred. We have always been talking of town and city planning but never of the planned development of the whole region so that population is logically dispersed and activities are properly distributed. City planning is an ad-hoc solution but regional planning could be a more lasting one. For example, instead of providing houses to slum-dwellers in cities through city development authorities if through regional planning migrants could be diverted to other areas which may provide attractive employment, the pace of growth of existing cities could be checked. It is time that at least beginning from the Ninth Five Year Plan (1997), the Government of India helped the states in setting up regional planning organizations and evolving meaningful regional settlement plans.

Encouraging Industries to Move to Backward Areas: Land pricing policy which gives land in large chunks at throwaway prices has to be replanned to encourage industries to move to backward areas/districts. This will also take care of linear development of metropolitan and big cities. A policy of the state taking over potential high value land in and around large cities with a view to exploiting its full cost at a later date also needs serious consideration.

Municipalities to Find Own Financial Resources: People do not mind paying taxes to the municipality if their money is properly utilized to maintain roads, provide sewage system, reduce water shortage and provide electricity. It is a well known fact that cities suffer from crippling resource constraints. If deterrent punishment is given to the corrupt municipality officials, there is no reason why the municipal corporations should find it difficult in collecting money from the residents of the city. A city must bear the cost of its own development. High financial support from state government is becoming difficult. By revising property, water and electricity taxes, money can be collected and more money per head per annum can be made available for providing necessary amenities. When any new industry or business is located in a city or on its periphery, it could be moderately taxed so that additional money becomes available to the local body.

Encouraging Private Transport: Why should city transport be a public monopoly? When the transport is handled by state employees, it has been noticed that they tend to have extremely rudely and callously. Backing of the trade union encourages them to go on strikes frequently. It is necessary then that private transportation be encouraged. Privately operated mini bus and tempo services will charge a little more fare but commuters would not mind paying this in view of the better services.

Amendment of Rent Control Acts: Laws which inhibit the construction of new houses or giving of houses on rent must be amended. Which landlord would like to spend Rs. 3 or 4 lakhs or so on a two-three room tenement and give it on rent for Rs. 500-700 a month or so for the next 10 to 20 years without having the authority to increase the rent or get it vacated on appropriate grounds. Maharashtra has taken a lead in amending the Rent Control

Act which has made thousands of houses available for rent. A similar step in other states would be welcome.

Adopting Pragmatic Housing Policy: In May 1988, the central government presented the National Housing Policy (NHP) to the parliament which aimed at abolishing 'homelessness' by the turn of the century and upgrading the quality of accommodation to a fixed minimum standard. Such policy sounds too ambitious and Utopian.

It is a dream impossible to accomplish in a span of remaining four years by which time the twentieth century will have become past. The government policy and planning has to be more down to earth. This is not to say that the concept of NHP is irrational. The NHP strategy is broadbased. It seeks to provide easy access to finance as well as land and materials for building houses at reasonable rates. It also seeks to encourage manufacturers to use new type of building materials. Moreover, it seeks to review the entire gamut of laws relating to land tenure, land acquisition and ceiling to apartment ownership, municipal regulations and rental laws. But these are all thorny issues.

The NHP is oriented towards rich developers, landlords and contractors. The NHP has to discourage luxury housing and promote cooperative and group housing societies. It has to develop special schemes for the poor and low-income people. It has also to favour providing incentives to employers to build houses for the employees. It has to increase its authorized capital of Rs. 100 crore which cannot go anywhere near to meeting the financial needs. Unless, a more pragmatic NHP is adopted, it will be impossible to achieve the set goals.

Collective Responsibility

One proposal by innovative planners and some radicals envision a structural decentralization of local self government itself. This could entail the creation of 'neighbourhood-action groups', to be called 'community centres' consisting of representatives of residents and municipality officials. These centres will identify and act upon neighbourhood needs. For example, many new colonies have come to be established in many cities in which as many as 10,000 to 50,000 people reside. Thus, these colonies are small towns by themselves.

Some taxes like house tax, road tax, light tax, etc., could be passed on directly to these community-centres instead of giving them to municipalities.

The centres would direct the affairs of the neighbourhood without reference to the city municipal corporation and use the collected money in maintaining roads, lights and so forth. The argument for this kind of decentralized structure within the city is that the same system that allows lakhs of people a substantial control over their civic destiny denies them an effective role in shaping the institutions that shape their lives. Community centres will allow them to create their own exclusive environment.

To conclude, it may be pointed out that the effects of urbanization and urbanism and the problems of cities can never be solved until urban planning is modified and radical measures are taken. These should not be based on the profit motive which would benefit a few vested interests. The use of land, technology, and taxes should be for the benefit of the people and not for the benefit of a few powerful interest groups. City-dwellers have to become politically active and organize themselves and agitate to change the existing economic and social systems in the cities.

Women Emancipation

Liberty for Women

According to experts, the status of women—social and political—can be defined as the degree of equality and freedom enjoyed by women in the shaping and sharing of power and in the value given by society to this role of women. The Indian Constitution guarantees political equality through the institution of adult franchise and Article 15 which prohibits discrimination inter alia on grounds of sex.

It should be kept in mind that this recognition of political equality of women was a radical departure not only from the socio-cultural norms prevailing in traditional India but also in the context of the political evolution of even most advanced countries at that date. With the exception of the socialist countries, no other State in the world had accepted women's equality as a matter of course. The United States and the United Kingdom granted franchise to women only after World War I, after decades of struggle by their women.

Most other countries, Eastern or Western, conceded it only after World War II. Japan granted franchise to women in 1946, China in 1949. The exceptions were Thailand and the Philippines which granted a limited franchise, similar to the Indian case, in 1932 and 1933 respectively. Amongst the West European countries, France granted franchise to women in 1945, Switzerland in 1971. However, in case of India, the two major forces which acted as a catalyst in the achievement of political equality of women were the national movement and the leadership of Gandhi, who declared himself to be "uncompromizing in the matter of women's rights."

According to Gandhi in Young India, 17.10.1929: Women must have votes and an equal legal status. But the problem does not end there. It only commences at the point where women begin to affect the political deliberations of the nation. The nineteenth century reform movement and the spread of education among the women had definitely initiated the process of improving the status of women.

However, this process was essentially limited to improving the position of women within the traditional family structure. Predominant social attitudes, particularly among the upper and middle-classes, continued to regard domestic life as women's sole occupation. Nevertheless there was a minority of women who voluntarily participated in both social welfare and revolutionary movements. They were active in the cause of women's education, welfare of the weaker sections in society and relief to distressed persons during emergencies like floods, droughts, famines, etc.

A still smaller group became involved in the revolutionary movement, actively participating as couriers, distributing literature, looking after various institutions and risking police repression, imprisonment, and even capital punishment. In both these cases, the women received a certain degree of support from their families in such activities, either overt or covert. Most of them came from the affluent or middle-class families in urban areas.

Collective Sense

The social attitude to this first awakening was one of reserved acceptance, extending sometimes to admiration and pride in the heroism displayed by some of these women. But it by no means amounted to accepting this as a norm for women's role and behaviour in society. The nineteenth century reformers professed concern for the low status of women, but their efforts were concentrated towards improving women's position within the family, for the purpose of strengthening the family as the basic unit of social organization.

Raising the status of women was seen only as granting her the right to property, remarriage after widowhood, abolition of child marriage and the right to education. A characteristic of this movement was its elitist approach. Most of the demands were relevant only for a limited section of women, *i.e.*, the upper and middle-classes. They did not represent the problem affecting the majority of women. The social change envisaged was a limited one of transformation within the system, rather than that of the system. The turn of the nineteenth century witnessed some results of the dissemination of education to women, though restricted, and the impact of the ideas of the reformers in the variations taking place in the status of women.

This was manifested in the emergence of women's organizations, when women entered public life in even larger numbers than before. This period saw the birth of organizations such as The Women's Indian Association (this was later merged in the All India Women's Conference), the National Council for Women and The All India Women's Conference. It also opened a new chapter in the women's movement for equality.

A demand for women's franchise was started in 1917 when a deputation of Indian women led by Sarojini Naidu, presented to the British Parliament a demand for the enfranchisement of women on the basis of equality with men. The constitutional reforms of 1919 left the matter to the discretion of the elected legislatures in the provinces and finally the Reforms Act of 1921 enfranchised a very small fraction of the Indian population including women.

This right to vote, however, was subject to certain reservations: women could vote only if they had qualifications of wifehood, property and education. These qualifications, apart from making the women's right dependent on her marital status, in fact restricted it to an infinitesimal minority of women. The gap between the radical nature of the demand and actual achievement was a characteristic of the period till Independence.

It represented not only the reluctance of the foreign rulers to accept the democratic aspirations of the people, but also their own political view regarding the restricted role of women in Indian society. They could not believe that Indian society would ever regard women as equal partners of men. Nor could they expect women to act independently of the men, as a separate political force.

Therefore, women did not feature in the framework of representation of classes, communities, and interests, which was offered by the colonial authorities as the solution of the Indian question. A transformation of the attitude to women was precipitated by the Gandhian view regarding women's role in the social revolution and reconstruction: Woman is the companion of man gifted with equal mental capacities. She has the right to participate in the minutest details of the activities of man, and she has the same right of freedom and liberty as he... By sheer force of a vicious custom, even the most ignorant and worthless men have been enjoying a superiority over women which they do not deserve and ought not to have. (Gandhi, *Young India*, 26.2.1918). Since resistance in satyagraha is offered through self-suffering. It is a weapon pre-eminently open to women.... She can become the leader in satyagraha which does not require the learning that books give but does require the stout heart that comes from suffering and faith. Gandhi, *Young India*, 24.2.1940.

As a result, responding to his call, women of different communities and all walks of life came out to join the struggle—as political campaigners, joining protest marches and demonstrations, as constructive workers, participating in and often taking charge of the village reconstruction programmes, as workers in the cause of social and economic justice working for the removal of untouchability and other forms of social oppression. The highly educated and the not so well educated joined hands to spread literacy and develop self-reliance among the people.

Women who had spent their lives behind purdah came out to fight orthodoxy, superstition and communal separatism. Social legitimation for such activity was not forthcoming at first but the women joined the men to fight in the movement. Events proved that without the cooperation of women the freedom struggle would not have been so successful. Under Mahatma Gandhi's direction the civil disobedience movement and the salt satyagraha saw women in the forefront. The breaking of the forest laws, boycott of foreign cloth and liquor shops resulted in women suffering police repression, incarceration in prisons and other indignities. Scores of women were in the vanguard of the movement.

According to Nehru in Discovery of India: Our women came to the forefront and took charge of the struggle. Women had always been there of course but now there was an avalanche of them which took not only the British Government but their own menfolk by surprize. There were these women, women of the upper or middle cases, living sheltered lives in their homes, peasant women, working class women, right women—pouring out in their tens of thousands in defiance of government orders and police *lathis*. It was not only the shouring of courage and daring but what was even more surprizing was the organizational power they showed.

Naturally, such united participation had a direct impact on the attitudes of women also. A meeting of representative women's organizations in 1930 drafted a memorandum demanding immediate acceptance of adult franchise without sex discrimination. It was turned down by the Government, but in 1931 the Karachi Session of the Indian National Congress took the historic decision, committing itself to political equality of women, regardless of their status and qualifications. The Government of India Act of 1935 increased the number of enfranchised Indians, the proportional suffrage rights of women and relaxed some of the previous qualifications.

Freedom and Studies

All women over 21 could vote provided they fulfilled the conditions of property and education. Independence brought the promise of actual liberation and equality. The Constitution pledged the nation to obtaining a just society, based on the principles of equality and dignity of the individual, and proclaimed the right to political and legal equality as fundamental rights of all Indians.

The guarantee against discrimination in employment and offices under the State opened the avenues to offices of power and dignity. It has been argued that political equality is meaningless in a country where the mass of the population suffers from poverty, continuous threat of starvation, illiteracy, lack of health, and inequality of class, status and power. It is more so in the case of women who suffer from another dimension of inequality, namely the weight of traditional attitudes that regard them as physically, intellectually and socially inferior to men.

It is, however, clear from Mahatma Gandhi's statement that the equal and political rights of women were only to be a starting point to enable the society to transform itself by ending all exploitation, a process in which women would be the prime movers. Looked at from this angle, political rights and status appear as only instrumental for achieving general equality of status and opportunities and social, economic and political justice.

It, therefore, becomes important to examine the efficiency of this instrument in the practical operation of the political process. We have used the following indicators for this examination:

The urge from within the people to participate in the political process is a basic requirement for a democracy. The role of women in this field can be measured by the turnout of women voters and number of women candidates in each election. Since attitudes play a major role in determining political behaviour, the level of awareness, commitment and involvement of women participating in politics, particularly their autonomy and independence in political action and behaviour, are important measures of their political status. If political rights are only an instrument to achieve other goals. then this is the crucial measure of women's political status. Yet this is the most difficult to measure.

Quantitative data is of little use because they may not indicate the actual reality in the political process. We have tried to measure this by looking at the women's view of their own roles and efficacy in the political process, and society's attitude to these new roles of women. This is indicated by the success of women candidates at various, elections, the efficiency of women's pressure groups, the nature of the leadership and women elites in parties and Government, and the effectiveness of campaigns for women's mobilization particularly on issues that directly concern them.

During our examination we have tried to separate certain myths from the actual state of affairs, by indicating the gaps that exist between popular notions and opinions and empirical realities, between what the law provides and the policy demands on the one hand and what society actually permits on the other. The evidence for our examination has been collected by various means, from published research on Indian political behaviour, some first-hand studies sponsored by the Committee, comments of political workers and parties, and the views of the large number of women belonging to different socio-economic categories, whom the Committee met who, during the tours, came across the committee.

Democratically participation in politics has to be viewed at the levels of acquisition and exercise of power and rights of a citizen. The study of general elections at these two levels offers certain quantitative measures of participation of citizens both as voters and as candidates. Unfortunately the statistics for the first two general elections do not throw light on the number of women candidates or voters. Our comparison, therefore, has to be limited to the last three general elections, *viz.*, those of 1996, 1998 and 1999. The percentage turnout of men and women voters in the last three general elections to the Lok Sabha and the overall picture of women participation indicate that the difference between percentage turnout of men and women voters has been decreasing.

Between 1996 and 1998 the percentage of women who exercised their franchise increased nearly by 11 per cent but in 1991 it decreased by 7.1 per cent. This decrease is, however, nearly equal to the fall in the total voting percentage in that year. Since the difference between men and women voters does not show any substantial increase, it may be inferred that there was no significant change in the trend, which is visible when we compare the figures of 1996 and 1999.

During the nine year period, while the total voters' turnout increased by only 0.90 per cent increase in the percentage of women voters was 2.25 per cent. A comparison of the turn out in different States shows that the States of Orissa, Bihar, Madhya Pradesh, Himachal Pradesh, Rajasthan and Uttar Pradesh registered a low turnout of total voters. The turnout of women voters in these States was still lower, resulting in a high difference between men and women. Assam and Jammu & Kashmir also come under this category.

These States are generally known for the educational and social backwardness of their women. All the demographic indicators, *viz.*, sex ratio, literacy rate, life expectancy, etc., point to a low status of women in these States. This is reflected in the low participation. It has generally been found that there is a close relationship between literacy and political awareness. The States and Union Territories which have registered the maximum mobilization of women voters generally have a high female literacy rate. It should, however, be noted that it is impossible to establish a similar correlation between education or economic development and exercise of franchise by women.

One great difficulty about the Indian political scene is that it is impossible to generalize about the interrelationship between any factor and political behaviour. Patterns of political behaviour from different regions show different relationships, influenced as they are by interrelated factors like the social status of women, their economic position, the cultural norms and the overall regional outlook towards women's participation in the wider society. The state-wise number of contestants has been generally in accordance with the total number of seats allocated to the States. The maximum number was in UP, except in 1971, when Bihar (then), the next biggest State in terms of Lok Sabha seats, took the lead by one candidate. The record of Madhya Pradesh is also high except in 1971, when it dropped.

This indicates that there is no correlation between the general level of women's participation, (which is consistently low in UP, and Bihar), and the selection of women candidates, which is mostly done by the parties. Punjab, where women's participation rate has outstripped that of men in the urban areas, has fewer number of candidates. Kerala and Maharashtra show increase in the number of candidates over the years, and West Bengal a sudden one in 1971, but the most visible trend is the stagnation or even decline in the number in most States. Karnataka, though not backward in any sense, did not put up a single woman candidate in three of the general elections, and only one in the other two. Similarly, Jammu & Kashmir, Nagaland and most of the Union Territories never put a single woman candidate. Women in Manipur, Andhra Pradesh, Tamil Nadu, Karnataka and Orissa were particularly vocal in criticizing the political parties for sponsoring so few women. In their view the small number of candidates represented not the aspiration of women, but the indifference of political parties in nominating them.

Elements at Work

The determining factors of the number of women candidates from different regions are obviously not related to the level of poll participation, literacy or economic and social position of women in a region. On the other hand, the States where women's position is relatively low have a record of higher number of candidates. On the whole, we have to note that the number of women seeking elections either for the Lok Sabha or for the State Assemblies, has been in no way comparable to their proportion in the population. Apart from the election figures, our discussion with different groups of women in all the States points towards certain general conclusions. At the level of participation, women have improved their response to the political rights conferred by the Constitution.

Keeping other things equal, overall development such as literacy, increased mass communication, etc., may help to draw a larger number of women into the political mainstream. The present participation of women in the political process, however, presents sharp contrasts. The overall statistics indicate that women, participation though improving, is still so small as to be discouraging, specially when compared with that of men. Though there has been a substantial number of new women entrants.

Factors at Work

During our tours we were informed by many women that there has been a large number of dropouts from active participation. When these are from families with long political traditions, they indicate a certain process of disillusionment. This is also corroborated by some of the State studies mentioned earlier. Muslims and tribal women show a lower level of participation both as voters and candidates, though there are exceptions to this.

A survey on Muslim women indicates that a large number of the women interviewed had voted in the previous election. The surveyor also met tribal women in Tripura, Meghalaya and Baster (MP), who, though not formally educated, have a keen interest in politics and participate regularly in voting. Women of Scheduled Castes and other intermediary groups reveal a higher participation rate. In West Bengal, women from these groups were more aware and participated relatively more than the tribal women. Studies in Gujarat and Maharashtra have also corroborated this fact.

We met a number of women from these communities in villages in different states, whose determination to participate in elections was quite obvious. In terms of voting participation, the rural-urban difference seems to be narrowing down, though the belief in the lower participation of rural women continues to be widespread.

During the general elections of 1972, the Committee had appointed some observers. The results of their investigation, as well as those of their studies show that urbanization *per se* does not have much influence on women's participation. On the other hand, the argument that domestic duties prevent them from participation is more commonly voiced by women in urban areas, and those belonging to the middle classes, in particular.

During our tour to many villages we came across women who have been exercising their franchise, and were fully conscious of the power that this right gave them. A group of Scheduled Caste women whom we met in a village in Madhya Pradesh had not only voted in the last elections but were very much conscious of the power conferred on them by the franchise. They were emphatic that they would hereafter vote only for such candidates who will continue to take interest in their welfare even after the election.

In a village in UP, Scheduled Caste and Muslim women were very vocal, not only about their franchise, but also about the secrecy of the ballot. There is a general consensus that the political parties have neglected their task of politically educating and mobilizing women adequately. They have also tended to ignore the claims of women in nominating candidates for elections.

This criticism was voiced even by successful women legislators. Majority of the women candidates come from relatively well-to-do families, with a sprinkling of members of old princely houses. Only one party has occasionally backed women candidates from Scheduled Castes or Tribes and Muslims. Majority of the women candidates are educated, though their levels vary.

About 70 per cent to 80 per cent of the women Members of Parliament are, however, relatively better educated. In terms of political socialization or background, the smaller group among the candidates come from families with fairly long traditions of political participation.

They are, therefore, highly articulate, have a sharp perspective of politics, and have continued in the struggle for power through several successive elections. The larger group consists of new entrants. Some of them had no previous political experience but entered the political arena through elections, for the first time.

One of the most effective deterrents to women's active participation as candidates is the increasing expense of elections. Women were emphatic that families were still not prepared to finance the elections of their women from family funds, though they would do so for the men. Since most women have no economic resources of their own, their aspirations could only be fulfilled if they were fully backed by a political party. Because of this factor, the majority of women candidates today are those who have some independent means under their thumb.

Some other factors which deter many women from active participation in politics are the threats of violence and character assassinations which have increased recently. This was mentioned to us by many legislators and political workers. Some of them have a long record of political activism, but still hesitate to face candidature at elections. It must be kept in mind that these three indices used to assess political roles are largely heuristic devices, which usually overlap in describing the empirical situation.

Attitudes have a bearing on participation and impact, while attitudes in turn depend to a great extent on impact and levels of participation. Relative differences in the political attitudes of men and women have been studied by various scholars and form a feature of most of our political literature since Independence. Certain broad trends can be discerned, the most important of which are mentioned below.

The point which emerges in the very beginning of our analysis is that there is no single homogeneous pattern. Levels of political awareness vary from region to region, from class to class and from community to community, and are conditioned greatly by the political culture of the area, the approach of the political parties to the women and the quality of local leadership.

Therefore, it is generally held that political awareness varies with the levels of modernization in a given area, with concomitant factors such as literacy rates, education and exposure to urbanization and mass media. This correlation however seems more apparent than real, as proved by studies in different regions.

It has already been indicated that the distinction in the influence of literacy and education on awareness and participation exists there. While the former is generally found to be an important determinant for both awareness and participation, education does not command a similar influence.

Urban and Rural Variables

While a correlation can be established between education and awareness, this does not always extend to participation. We have also noted that similarly, urbanization alone cannot be identified with high political awareness or participation. In terms of urban rural variables, there is no significant difference in political awareness. On an average, working women including professionals, indicate a higher degree of awareness, but this is not necessarily reflected in their participation.

There is a uniform finding from different regions regarding the complaint of urban middle-class women that they find their family responsibilities a handicap to political participation. There is no positive relationship between higher socioe-conomic status and the degree of awareness. We may cite a few illustrations from Prof Sirsikar's study:

In Gujarat, the high income group women are less aware and participate less in the political process; in Maharashtra, the higher the socio-economic status, other factors being equal, lesser is the proportion of women who participate. This is further borne out by the apathy of professionals with high socio-economic status. By and large, politics constitutes a peripheral interest for women from this strata, though a significant number of women legislators come from an affluent background. Most studies on political behaviour have so far held that women are considerably influenced by their husbands and family wishes in political matters.

During the course of our tours, however, we received ample evidence that this pattern is beginning to change and many women now exercise considerable autonomy in using their right of franchise. They emphasize their ability to do so because of the secrecy of the ballot. Many women told us that though their husbands still try to influence their judgement "they can't find out whom we have really voted for." In rural areas the influence of village elders plays an important role in determining political choice which also influence the women's behaviour.

However, it would not be correct to describe this as a universal rule. In spite of such changes, it is still evident that there is a difference in the level of political information and perception regarding implications of the right of franchise, etc., between men and women, both quantitatively and qualitatively. Most scholars have attributed this to the lack of interest shown by political parties, in improving the political knowledge of women. Some have also levelled this charge against the women's organizations and pressure groups.

A study of urban voters in Rajasthan provides an illustration 44.5 per cent of the women did not have any clear cut idea about their criterion for voting: 19.5 per cent considered the personality of the candidates, 22.3 per cent caste and family as a factor, while only 8.3 per cent and 5.5 per cent considered the party and the issues respectively.

In a way, all the State profiles indicate one common trend that women are concerned with problems that affect their day-to-day lives. The issues are price-rise, non-availability of essential commodities, hoarding and black marketing, adulteration, unemployment and poverty. On several occasions during the last few years, women have organized protests against these problems. There are indications of growing trends of disillusionment with the political process among women. This may be partly attributed to their reactions against the prevalence of corruption and inefficiency in political circles but a great deal of such attitudes is on account of their feelings of ineffectiveness in solving problems which affect their lives.

According to a study conducted in West Bengal, about 25 per cent of the respondents stated that having votes has not helped women and even men. About 8 per cent stated that they would not vote on principle since it did not help in any way. Another study done in Rajasthan in 1971 showed that 42 per cent of the women interviewed including housewives and working women, supported revolution for social progress as opposed to the 'ritual' of elections.

The majority of respondents in this study felt that the problems of the country needing solution in order of priority were as follows: (1) employment and poverty; (2) rising prices; (3) corruption; and (4) law and order. The freedom movement and the period immediately succeeding independence brought the involvement and commitment of women in the political process. However, the institutionalization of this process resulted in difference in perception of goals and methods of achievement.

The absence of a movement in the period after Independence explains the low involvement of women in the political process. Such involvement is however always visible during national emergencies. It was repeatedly brought to our notice that the unity between political, economic and social issues that characterized the freedom movement was one of the causes for women's high degree of participation. The divorce between social problems that affect women directly, and the political process, has been one of the major causes of women's lower political engagement.

Altough the percentage of political participation and the number of women contestants have shown a gradual increase, their record of success at elections, however, presents a very different picture. The number and percentage of successful women candidates for the Lok Sabha had been declining steadily from 33 (50.6 per cent) in 1962 to 21 (25.9 per cent) in 1971. The variations in the number of contestants and those elected are uneasily accountable. The sharp decline in successful candidates in 1971 had been attributed to the sudden increase in the number of independent women candidates which increased from 10 in 1967 to 31 in 1971, only one of whom was elected, thus bringing the percentage of successful contestants down to 25.9 per cent. The trend continued in later elections, till 1999.

This however, does not explain why the parties' nominations should have been so few. A state-wise comparison of successful women candidates for the Lok Sabha shows that the number of successful candidates has been greater in UP, Bihar, Madhya Pradesh and Andhra Pradesh where the number of contestants has also been greater. Orissa, Haryana, Goa, Daman and Diu and Manipur are the only areas where women contested but were never returned. Percentage-wise Karnataka was the most successful. It set up only one candidate in 1962 and 1971 and elected the same. Bihar, UP, Madhya Pradesh, Tamil Nadu and West Bengal were the only States which sent women to the Lok Sabha in every election.

In terms of the overall performance, however, Andhra Pradesh and Assam may also be considered satisfactory. Analyzing the first general elections Smt. Laxmi N. Menon had inferred that the number of women candidates was in inverse proportion to the percentage of literacy among them. This hypothesis is confirmed when tested against the figures of subsequent elections in Madhya Pradesh, Bihar and UP. But Orissa, Jammu & Kashmir and Rajasthan do not substantiate this hypothesis. On the other hand, Kerala, West Bengal, Maharashtra and Tamil Nadu do not support the reverse of this view, *i.e.*, the number of women contestants does not decline relatively with a higher literacy rate.

We may infer, therefore, that literacy is not one of the facts that determine the number of women contestants or their success. The backing of the party which sponsors them, the personality of the contestants, including their family background, and the campaign strategy adopted, play a much more important role in determining the success or failure of women candidates. Women representatives in the State Legislatures also present a varied pattern.

New Approach

The most significant trend, however, is either a decline or stagnation in the percentage of successful contestants. In the First General Elections (1952), Gujarat elected four out of five women candidates to the Gujarat Assembly. In 1962 the number increased to 15 out of 24 but it dropped to 8 out of 17 in 1967 and 8 out of 21 in 1972. In the case of Karnataka, except for 1957 and 1962 the ratio of female to male representatives has been extremely low, the number of successful candidates dropping to 7 in 1967 and increasing marginally to 11 in 1972. In Maharashtra the number of successful candidates improved from 5 in 1952 to 14 in 1957 but has been declining ever since.

The Rajasthan Assembly, which had 24 women between 1957 and 1962 contained only 6 in 1967-68. The West Bengal Assembly had

14 women in 1962, but had only 6 in the next assembly. The election manifestos of the parties indicate that practically all of them agree that women constitute a backward section of the society to whom special privileges should be granted to bring them on a par with men.

The parties also agree that the existing gap between men and women should be reduced to the minimum possible. The India National Congress is pledged to implement the principles of the Constitution. The recent manifestos of the party have emphasized development of education and employment opportunities for women. The Congress has consistently maintained its position as the party sponsoring the largest number of women candidates both at Parliamentary and State Assembly elections.

The number of women contestants sponsored by the Congress, however, has remained much below its stipulated target of 15 per cent of the total candidates. This percentage was initially decided by the party in 1957 and has been repeatedly reiterated since then but to no effect. The Congress Mahila Front had been active in mobilizing women in support of the party. In recent years it has been voicing the demand of women workers within the party.

In some States it is becoming very critical of the neglect of women's demands by the official leadership. There is a general feeling among women political workers that they do not have enough opportunities to develop or demonstrate their organizing ability. Exclusion from the decision making bodies within the party is responsible for considerable resentment among women political workers. The Communist Party of India believes that in the capitalist system complete equality of women is impossible. Only a socialist system can liberate women fully by ending all types of exploitation.

Women have a role to play in bringing about the social revolution which cannot be achieved if they remain in a backward condition. According to its election manifesto the party stands for equality of women in every sphere of national life. The party demands equal pay for equal work, removal of all restrictions on employment of married women, extension of maternity benefits to all employed women and enforcement of the social laws that have been enacted to improve their status.

The party appreciates the need for adequate financial allocation and extra facilities for women's education. It promises to achieve removal of all disabilities to secure women's equality with men in inheritance of property, marriage and divorce laws, entrance to education institutions, professions and services. The greatest cause of women's inability to enjoy these rights was their economic dependence and poverty. Attempts to implement the equal pay for equal work principle by industrial tribunals have invariably ended in retrenchment of women workers.

Poverty also prevented them from enjoying the protection of the social laws enacted to improve their status. The answer to this handicap lay in fuller participation of women in the process of social production which should not be limited to small scale and cottage industries only. They suggested specific protection against retrenchment of women and drew the attention of the Committee to a trade union demand for 20 per cent reservation of jobs for women in industry.

In their opinion, this could be insisted upon in selected industries like textiles where the number of women workers has been declining. Free legal aid, particularly for women in adverse economic circumstances should also be provided to enable them to utilize the rights provided under the social laws. Regarding education, while the party supported co-education as the ultimate object, they noted the possible necessity of secondary schools for women.

Hostel accommodation and generous provision of stipends was also essential to improve women's education. The party believes that genuine equality between the sexes is impossible in a capitalist order, and can only be realized in the process of a socialist transformation of society. The party declares itself as opposed to any kind of discrimination against women. It is critical of the poor progress in the field of women's welfare since Independence and demands greater facilities for women's education, removal of social disabilities, equal rights in matters of marriage, admission to professions and other services and equal pay for equal work.

This party also holds that the nation cannot progress if its women remain in their present condition of illiteracy, limited opportunities for development and as victims of obscurantist customs and prejudices.

In a recent conference, the representatives of the party emphasized the need for economic independence of women without which there could not be real equality between men and women in any sphere of life-social, political, legal or even family life. In the absence of economic independence, women were as good as private property of men.

In this context, they felt that the growing problem of rural unemployment was posing an increasing threat to the security and status of women in the rural areas. With the increase in landlessness and the decay of village industries, new avenues for employment of the vast masses of rural women were imperative. In the absence of land, basic economic security and literacy, rural women have been unable to enjoy their constitutional and legal rights to an even greater extent than their counterparts in the urban areas. This extreme poverty was also the real cause for the low enrolment of rights in schools in these areas.

Their suggestions to the Committee included the following: (i) Mass employment and mass education including education of women about their emancipation. (ii)Free education of girls at all levels. (iii) Inclusion of principle of equal pay for equal work in the fundamental rights and removal of existing disabilities in the law of inheritance, marriage and divorce and admissions to profession and service. (iv) Equal shares of land and job facilities for peasant women and maternity benefits, and common kitchens for all working women. (v) Implementation of constitutional and legal rights and propaganda against orthodoxy and conservative attitudes towards women.

The objective of the party is advancement of women and is keen to take special steps to remove social and educational disabilities, to enable them to discharge their responsibilities to the family, society and nation, without any fundamental change in the traditionally established principles of social organization. The party promises to enlarge and make more substantial the property rights of women, granting them absolute rights as members of their husband's family. Some time ago, in a workshop, the representatives of the party emphasized the need to increase the consciousness and political participation of women without which the Constitutional guarantees would remain unimplemented.

Their suggestion included the spread of civic and political education to foster a sense of national pride and political awareness to students, housewives and working women also who needed to be taught their civic and political rights and duties. It was their view that legislation could not improve the status of women, when society including women themselves continued to foster a sense of male superiority at all stages. In spite of outstanding performance of some women in politics, science, etc., most women are conservative, backward and wholly dependent on men.

Governmental and non-governmental efforts must combine to develop not 'independence' but 'individuality' of women so that they can cooperate in family, social and national life. Illiteracy and unemployment were the causes of their low position. They were highly critical of the present trend in advertising and films which used the female figures in very bad taste. They felt that there should be some restriction or control on the mass media as these trends were leading to immorality and degeneration, particularly amongst the youth of the country.

The problem of security, particularly for working women was becoming more acute, and it was necessary to provide more hostels for working women. Regarding social laws, they said that women who protest against polygamy receive no protection and hence were afraid to do so in public. In cases of divorce, courts should examine the reasons for a woman seeking a divorce and not go by the 'matrimonial wrong' theory.

Their suggestions included: (i) free education for girls up to the end of secondary stage, (ii) night schools for working women, (iii)vocational training in village school, (iv) compulsory home science classes in every school, (v) expansion of condensed course, and (vi)development of mobile libraries.

Similarly, to promote employment they suggested: (i) reservation of some jobs for women in different spheres (ii) legislation on equal pay for equal work, (iii) relaxation of conditions for employment of women, particularly rural areas.

While only a very few women were able to reach the highest level of power and authority, those who did so were recognized for their administrative prowess and capacity to manage their affairs. Since 1952 there have been a number of women ministers in the Union Government—some of them were Deputy Ministers, while some became Ministers of State, a few attained Cabinet rank and one was Prime Minister. There is one Deputy Chairperson of Rajya Sabha and several in the panel of Chairmen of both houses of Parliament.

Besides this, many others have been members of various standing and ad hoc committees. About 26 of the women parliamentarians had previous experience of holding political offices in the States, either in the pre-independence ministries formed in 1937 or in the post-Independence period. At the State level several women have held the office of Governor, Chief Minister, Speaker and Deputy Speaker since Independence. Though only few have held cabinet rank, women have held office in most of the States.

Compared to their overall number in the legislatures, the number holding offices was not low. One of the common characteristics of the women leaders in the political process during the period immediately after Independence was their experience of participation in the freedom movement. The women members of the Constituent Assembly which also functioned as the Central Legislative Council in the first 5 years after Independence were mostly veterans of the freedom struggle.

Most of them had worked in the movement for women's welfare and development. They were the spokesmen of the women's cause in the Legislative Body and played an important role in mobilizing public opinion in support of the social legislations that changed the legal status of women within the first few years after Independence. Some of them also played their part in shaping the policies and programmes of women's development that were taken up by the Government of India. While most of the women leaders who had attained a national stature during the freedom struggle were to be found in the circles of the Central Government or legislatures, in the States a new generation of women entered the political process. The accounts from the States emphasize that experience of social work, specially among women, while it is still considered a qualification for candidates seeking representation in local bodies, has ceased to be an important qualification for women representatives in the legislatures.

As pointed out by some of the political workers interviewed by the Committee, political conflicts these days, particularly at the State level seldom reflect social differences. The issues are primarily economic which are used by various political parties to seek power in the State Government structure. The women who have been involved in this process mostly come from the economic and political elite of the States and their entry into the political process, particularly representation, depends more on their support within the party rather than on the electorate.

Their electorate campaigns are held by party workers among whom women form a minority. Only some women candidates have attained their position through active political and organizational work among the masses. Women candidates and legislators have rightly seen their roles as representatives of the people. Both in Parliament and in State legislatures they have been more concerned with problems of a general nature relating to issues of national and State importance. In the earlier years, while women participated in such general discussions, on questions relating to women, their championship of women's causes cut across party lines and evoked concerted articulation.

In recent years, however, women legislators have not shown such concern or interest in problems that affect women specifically. During a recent debate in the Rajya Sabha on a private resolution on equal pay for equal work for women, not even one-third of the women members attended the discussion and only a few spoke. This lack of interest has led to criticism by women outside the circle of active politicians that the women political elite today are not much concerned with the problems affecting large masses of Indian women.

Thus, an analysis of debates and discussions in the legislative bodies indicate the very meagre attention given by these institutions to women's problems. It would appear that the political elite of the country, of both sexes, had come to believe that the problem of women had practically been solved with the measures—legal and administrative—adopted in the first few years after Independence. The very articulate debates on women's problems that took place in the earlier period, in which women members invariably played a major role has not been repeated in the later years. The reason for this lack of concern among the political elite to the problems of women is the absence of an active women's movement.

While the number of political organizations seeking to mobilize women is now much higher than in the earlier period, their identification with different political parties prevents most of them from arousing women's consciousness for the solution of problems which are specific to women. It has already been pointed out the significant gap between the degree of politicization and participation of women and its reflection in the representation of women in the legislative bodies. States which have a larger group of women representatives both in the State Assemblies and in Parliament are also States where the level of politicization among the masses of women is low.

States where political mobilization of women seems to have developed more have very few women members in the legislature. It would appear, therefore, that the institutionalization of political activities has resulted in a failure on the part of women to exert adequate pressure on political institutions for solution of the problems that affect their lives. A number of women who have entered the power structure have reached it mainly through certain ascriptive channels.

This, coupled with their small numbers in the legislatures as well as decision-making bodies within the parties explains their inhibition and failure why they are unable to voice the problems pertaing to women folk in India.

Environmental Education

Ecology is an interdisciplinary branch of biology which deals with the study of distribution structure, various aspects of life of organisms and their interaction with the environment.

The French Zoologist, Isodore Geoffrey St. Hilaire proposed the term ethology for "the study of the relations of the organisms within the family and society in the aggregate and in the community." St. George Jackson Mivart coined the term hexicology, which he defined as "devoted to study of the relations which exist between the organisms and their environment as regard the nature of the locality the frequent, the temperatures and the amount of light which suit them, and their relations to other organisms as enemies, rivals or accidental and evolutionary benefactors."

The Definition

The term ecology (Oekologie) was first used by Reiter in 1885 followed by Ernst Haeckel in 1886. It was coined by combining two Greek words oikos (meaning 'house' or 'dwelling place') and logos (meaning the study of) to denote such relationships between the organisms and their environment. Thus, literally, ecology is the study of organisms 'at home'. Mishra has defined ecology as the study of interaction of form, function and factors. Krebs described ecology as "the scientific study of interactions that determine the distribution and abundance of organisms."

Ecology differs from other branches of biology firstly it comprehends physical environment alongwith organisms and secondly it deals with level of biological organization. The various levels of biological organization are called biological spectrum.

Level of Organization	***Basic Division of Biology***
Organic molecules	
Subcellular organelles	
Cells	Cell Biology
Tissues	History
Organs	
Organ Systems Organisms	Anatomy, Physiology
Biochemistry	
Population	
Communities	Ecosystems
Ecology	

However, the recent development in study of ecology has been the recognition of the fact that the biotic (living) and abiotic (non-living) components of the nature are not only inter-related but both these components function in an orderly manner as a definite system, thus presently it is considered to be the structure and function of ecosystems.

Ecology is a synthetic branch of science which obtains source materials from several other disciplines like climatology, geography, geology, limnology, mathematics, physics, chemistry, microbiology besides other branches of biology. It is because ecology is to deal with the study of interactions of living beings among themselves as well as their physical environment.

The physical environment consists of soil, water, air and energy. It provides both habitation and raw materials for the synthesis of organic food. Several other life processes are dependent upon the physical environment, *viz.*, germination of seeds, pollination, respiration, hibernation etc. like components of living world, the various constituents of physical environment are inter-related. Some of their interactions are useful to living organisms *e.g.*, ozone, nitrogen and carbon dioxide filter ultraviolet rays from incoming solar radiations while infra red rays are absorbed by the water vapours present in the atmosphere.

Each level of organization has properties peculiar to it that are not identifiable at the levels below. But studies at higher levels must take account of the lower levels. Ecology has three levels of organization such as population, communities and ecosystems. However, a strict demarcation between lower and ecological levels cannot be made since the latter also involve the study of effects on the constituents of lower levels of organization.

Population: A population is a group of individual organisms of the same species (in breeding individuals) in a given area. It is also called local population. A local population adapted to its particular environment is called ecotype. A species may have several ecotypes. The different ecotypes have different genetic set-ups within the broad frameworks of the gene pool of the species. They are capable of interbreeding. Where two ecotypes meet, a continuous change from one type to another occurs due to interbreeding. It is called ecotine.

Community: A community is a group of population of different species in a given area. It may include all the population in that area—all plants, all animals and microorganisms or may be defined more narrowly as a particular group such as the fern community, or the seed-eating biocommunity of that area. The different population do not remain secluded but show interactions and inter-dependence.

Vegetation: A vegetation is a group of plants growing under the same climate over a wide range.

Ecosystem: An ecosystem is a segment of nature consisting of a community of living organisms and the physical environment, both interacting with each other and exchanging materials between them. Ecosystem ecology emphasizes the movements of energy and nutrients among the biotic and abiotic components of the ecosystems. Because the ecosystem is the highest level of biological organization, all ecological concepts can be set within its framework. The biotic components of any ecosystem are linked as foodchains. Food chains are interlinked to form complex food webs. Food webs are the basic units of ecosystem ecology. Thus ecology begins with population and culminates in ecosystem.

Biosphere: The different ecosystems of the world are not independent rather exchange material among themselves. The biologically inhabited part of the earth consisting of all the ecosystems of the world is called biosphere.

The Structure

Like other sciences ecology too has its own principles and basic concepts. Earlier, stress was laid down on describing structural components and their relationships but later on emphasis was laid on the functional aspects of various components. There is also a trend to study historical or evolutionary causes of ecological phenomena.

Basic Requirements

1. The different types of organisms living in a particular environment are not only independent and mutually reactive but affecting each other in various ways. Animal population, Flora and vegetation are interdependent through the environment and are mutually reactive.
2. Environment, which is actually a complex of several interrelated and dynamic (variable) factors some of which become critical at critical stages of the life cycle of the species. It, therefore, works as a sieve selecting organisms that can flourish in it.
3. The species put each effort to maintain its uniformity in structure, function, reproduction, growth and development by preservation of its genetic pool. However species have sufficient plasticity to modify themselves according to changing environment by virtue of somatic plasticity (ecads) or by recognition of their genes during sexual reproduction (ecotypes).
4. It is not only the environment which influences the life of organisms, but organisms too modify their environment to make it more congenial for their growth, development, reproduction and dispersal. The modified environment may become less suitable for the community already living in it. The dynamic environment and organisms make ways for the development of different kinds of organisms through a process known as succession. The process continues till the development of a community which is now more or less stable and is now able to keep itself adjusted in equilibrium with the environment. This final stage of community is called a climax.

5. According to Clements and Shelford (1939), under similar climatic conditions, there may develop more than one communities, some reaching to climax stage, others under different stages of succession. This complex of many communities growing in a particular area, sharing a common climate is called a biome.

Influencing Elements

1. The basic structural and functional units of nature are ecosystems. An ecosystem is a segment of nature consists of community of living organisms and physical environment both interacting and exchanging materials between them.
2. Discrete biological unit consists of a number of population each occupying a specific functional position with respect to other organisms with which it interacts. It is called ecological niche.
3. The degree of success of a particular population in an area is determined by the parameters of both abiotic factors as well as interaction with other types of population. These interactions among organisms can be positive, negative or even neutral.
4. Also, there are involved energetics of ecosystem, as energy is the driving force of this system. The flow of energy in the ecosystem is unidirectional or non-cyclic. The radiant energy is trapped by the autotrophic organisms (producers) and is transferred as organic molecules to the heterotrophic organisms (consumers) and decomposers. Energy is lost during its transfer from one trophic level to the next. Organisms use the energy in respiration.
5. A number of inorganic nutrients are taken up by living organisms for their metabolism and body building and are called biogenetic nurtrients. These chemical components keep on moving between biotic and abiotic components of an ecosystem in defined cycles called biogeochemical cycles.
6. Human beings have exploited the ecosphere to an extent that only economically important plants are allowed to grow in an ecosystem. This caused a reduction in species diversity and natural interaction amongst organisms and physical environment.
7. Under natural conditions, different population undergo succession. Ecosystem undergo an orderly process of change with time,

passing from a less complex to a more complex state. This process involves not only changes in species but also changes in physical environment of a community. The terminal or stabilised state is known as climax.

The Progress

1. Present day organisms are the product of evolution of the past organisms.
2. By knowing the evolutionary aspects of each ecological phenomena, we can predict the future shape of events under different sets of conditions.

Factors of Atmosphere

Plant ecology is divided into four branches—autecology, synecology, system ecology and applied ecology. A perusal of the developmental history of ecology reveals that ecological studies made from time to time are based upon three principles aspects—taxonomic affinities, habitat and level of organization.

Autecology: This is also known as ecology of individuals where we study individual species or population in relation to its environment from the time of seed germination up to setting of fruits and seeds *i.e.*, seedling growth, vegetative growth and reproductive growth. An applied branch of autecology is agronomy which studies the various aspects of crop plants.

Synecology: Under natural conditions, however, organisms-plants, animals, microbes, etc., live together as natural group affecting each other's life in several ways. Thus, more complex situations exist where the unit of study, instead of single organisms are groups of organisms known as community. Synecology deals with the study of plant communities, including the composition, organization and development in relation to environment. It is divided into several branches according to the aspect under study:

Habitat Specialization (Habitat Ecology): Organisms are influenced and modified by the habitat in which they live. Therefore, they can be studied in a group according to the habitat, *e.g.*, freshwater ecology, marine ecology, grassland ecology, forest ecology, desert ecology, etc.

Community Type (Community Ecology): In ecology no organism can be studied in seclusion because of the inter-dependence and interaction amongst various members of a community. Therefore, community is studied as a single entity, *e.g.*, forest ecology, grass land ecology.

Taxonomic Group: In early days of ecology, botanist and zoologists engaged themselves separately in the study of ecology of plants and animals respectively. This leads to the development of such sub-divisions as (i) Plant ecology, and (ii) Animal ecology. In each sub-division there are further specializeds like ecology of pines, insect ecology, avian ecology, bacterial ecology and ecology of mosquitoes etc. However, modern ecologists feel that the principles in the study of plants and animals are not only much similar, but these two great groups of organisms are inseparably inter-related with each other. Therefore, modern ecology studies inter-relations and inter-dependence of all organisms.

Levels of Organization: Depending upon the level of organization, synecology can be divided into many types:

(i) Population Ecology. The study of growth, structure and regulation of population of organisms.

(ii) Community Ecology. Study of inter-dependence and interaction amongst various members of community.

(iii) Ecosystem Ecology. It deals with interactions of living and non-living parts of nature besides the flow of energy, biochemical cycling, trophic levels etc.

(iv) Biome Ecology. Study of different communities living in a particular climate or area.

(v) Genecology. It is the study of ecology in relation to genetics.

There are some specialized branches of Ecology.

(i) Geographic Ecology. The study of geographical distribution of plants and animals.

(ii) Radiation Ecology. The study of effects of radiation on environment and organisms.

(iii) Sociology. The study of ecology and ethology of mankind.

(iv) Ethology. The interpretation of animal behaviour under natural surroundings.

(v) Space Ecology. The effect of space on the growth, development, reproduction and behaviour of organisms and cycling of resources so as to sustain life for long periods in the space.

System Ecology: It deals the analysis and understanding of the structure and function of ecosystem. It employs mathematical models.

Applied Ecology: The study of the human needs and the applications of ecological concepts, *e.g.*, agriculture, forestry, land use etc.

There are basic fundamental principles which govern the various aspects of organisms and components of environment. The following are the fundamental principles of ecology:

(i) All living organisms and physical environment are mutually reactive. The organisms interact among themselves and affect each other and physical environment.

(ii) The physical and biological processes follow the principles of uniformitarianism which states the same physical and biological processes, as the environment is influenced by human activity.

(iii) Natural hazards affect adversely the biological communities in general and in particular. When biological processes are associated with physical events, yet severe hazards are created.

(iv) Sustained life on earth is a characteristic of ecosystem, not of individual organisms or population.

(v) Environmental principles of holistic nature of natural environment which largely affect the biological communities in a biospheric ecosystem.

(vi) Ecosystem is a fundamental unit of ecological study because it comprises both biotic and abiotic components.

(vii) Ecosystem functions through the input of energy mainly solar radiation which is trapped by green plants and is used to prepare food through the process of photosynthesis. The solar radiation is the main driving force of the ecosystem.

(viii) The ecosystem productivity depends on:

(a) The availability of the amount of solar radiations to the primary producers.

(b) The efficiency of plants to convert solar energy into chemical energy.

(ix) Ecosystem instability results when an ecosystem becomes unable to adjust with environmental changes.

(x) Man being an active agent of environmental change, modifies the ecosystem through the exploitation of natural resources.

THE GADGETS

Ecology is an interdisciplinary approach for studying environment. It is considered both science and art. It concerns both the aspects doing and understanding. An ecologist has to work with living system and various environmental components. In ecology various types of tools and techniques are used. It employ scientific and non-scientific methods, tools and techniques. An ecologist has to begin with observations of living organisms and environmental components. The observations are quantified and statistical techniques are used to analyse the relationships and interdependence. The observation tool and correlation techniques an commonly used by ecologists the qualitative and quantitative method: and tools are employed in ecology.

Qualitative Methods	*Quantitative Methods*
(i) Observations	(i) Observation
(ii) Historical	(ii) Experimental
(iii) Longitudinal	(iii) Cross-sectional
(iv) Descriptive	(iv) Project method
(v) Sampling Technique	(v) Sampling technique

The qualitative is the subjective approach while qualitative is objective and scientific approach.

THE ENVIRONMENT

The term "Environment" which etymologically means surroundings, is considered as a composite term for the conditions in which organisms live and thus consists of air, water, food and sunlight which are the basic needs for all living beings and plant life, to carry on their life functions. The environment also includes other non-living things, temperature, wind, electricity etc. In other words, environment consists of both biotic and abiotic substances. Environment creates favourable conditions for the existence and development of living organisms. Environment can be defined in number of ways:

(1) "Environment is the sum of all social, economical, biological, physical or chemical factors which constitute the surroundings of man, who is both creator and moulder of his environment."

(2) "Environment refers to the sum total of conditions which surround man at a given point in space and time."

(3) "Environment is the representative of physical components of the earth where in man is the important factor influencing his environment."

"Environment" is assuming great importance in our dairy life. Though environment is a very broad term but in common parlance it is the 'limited surround' that affects the functioning of the world in which we live, thus in our daily life, what we are really concerned about is the "Biosphere". The part of the biosphere which can be affected by the present day technology, is called the Technosphere' and in the part of 'Ecosystem' that is badly affected.

It is very difficult to maintain ecological balance until and unless poverty elimination programmes are persued effectively. Our then Prime Minister in his speech on 6th July 1987 in the meeting of the World Commission on Environment and Development emphasized that there should be global commitment for mass poverty elimination. If we are able to improve the quality of life of the poor, we will be able to protect and regenerate the environment.

After the scientific and industrial revolution in the recent past, there has been immense impact of man on his environment. Man has failed to realize that any new factor upsets the balance of the ecosystem as a whole. All the devastating effects of man's effect to control nature have occurred because he has upset the balance relationship of the organisms that make up the environment. Huge industrial installations every year, introduction of faster mode of transport and sprouting up of large crowded cities (Urbanization) are the main outcomes of the modern civilization. These and a large number of many others are contributing to what is called environmental pollution. Increasing industrialization is also causing much danger to man's life because it is also responsible for defouling or polluting of environment by man.

Mankind will perish if the protection of the environment does not become an integral part of all the development programmes because we cannot cheat the "Mother Nature".

Reliable on plant foods rather than animal foods is ecologically more viable and sustainable because of the tremendous loss of energy in the food chain of ecosystem. The conservation of natural resources especially forests and wild life got attention in both developed and developing countries. Late Sanjay Gandhi gave much attention to the preservation of trees find cultivating more of them.

The Government of India, along with other Governments participated in a United Nations sponsored conference on the human environment in June 1972 at Stockholm (Sweden). The conference concluded that the decline in environmental quality is due to increasing pollution, loss of vegetable cover and biological diversity and excessive concentration of harmful chemical in the environment.

In May, 1986 Government of India passed the Environment Protection Bill which afterward became an act. The act gave a wide meaning to the environment and concluded that the environment included water, air land and the living creatures such as plants, animals and human beings. To implement Environment Protection Act throughout India our Government launched National Environmental Awareness Campaign, organized All India Essay Competitions on environment for the school children, National Seminars on various aspects of the environment, established Environmental Education Centres (Ahmedabad).

The subject of environment got immense national priority. Its protection and promotion was made one of the twenty programmes of the Prime Minister. How the plant life and healthy environment affect our mental health is not even cleared to the well informed people. There is an equal need for protection to oil and petroleum by minimizing its wastage.

It was categorically emphasized in an exhibition on "Our Environment and Our Future" held at International Trade Fair, New Delhi in 1989. We alongwith other developing countries, have to find alternative path to an alternative good. A goal which ultimately is the true goal of development—an environmentally sound and sustainable development. Time has reached when we are facing challenge to our intellect and wisdom for saving the humanity from extinction. I arises from our activities constricting the environment and depleting the biosphere, especially so in the name of development. We have to plan our actions ecologically for the sustenance of the environment and development. Perhaps the greatest challenge facing the present generation is need to balance apparently conflicting responsibilities of caring for the exploitation, preservation and conservation of environment around them.

Mishra (1991) presented an excellent account of planning for environmental management. The four basic requirements of environmental management recognized by him are, (i) impact of human activities on the environment (ii) value system, (iii) Plan and design for sustainable development, and (iv) environmental education.

The conservation of natural resources especially forests and wild life, mineral, metals and oil got attention of the Govt. in both developed and developing countries. The problem is however, grave in over populated, poor and educationally backward society in which India is placed. Population, poverty and environment are interrelated. India has often been described a rich land with poor people. The nexus between poverty and environmental degradation can hardly be over-emphasized. The low level literacy, economic backwardness and over population are some of the important aspects of Third World States Culture.

A nation can be called super power largely due to its natural resources. All the branches of science should be involved in promoting the rational use of natural resources environmental protection, its improvement and welfare of human society.

The organisms live on different surroundings of the earth which include biotic (living) and abiotic components which form the environment. The individual pass through various stages in the life cycle *i.e.* from birth to death. They have capabilities to continue their race from generation to generation. With the death of old individual new one start their cycle of life.

For the existence of all living organisms on the earth, they need the system which sustains life. The important system is the environment which covers all living and non-living systems. So it is necessary for every layman and literate person to know the meaning of the environment.

The Structure

Environment can be conveniently divided into two categories

(1) Natural Environment

(2) Man-made Environment

Natural Environment: It means the environment that comes into existence without interference of man. The natural environment system operates through self-regulating mechanism called homeostatic environment mechanism *i.e.* any change in the natural ecosystem brought about by natural process is counter balanced by changes in other component of the environment. Many components together coordinate to form a natural environment which helps in sustenance of life. The environment consists of mainly two components:

A. Abiotic or Non-living components

B. Biotic or Living Components.

Abiotic Components: They are those components which are not living but can support other living organisms. These are the basic components of Environment and when these components become unbalanced they will prove fatal for the living organisms. These are of three kinds:

1. Inorganic Substances. These include elements like Nitrogen, Calcium, phosphorous, water and gases like carbon dioxide and oxygen. These substances are required for the synthesis of organic substances and are called inorganic nutrients or biogenetic substances.
2. Organic Substances. They are substances dispersed from dead bodies of organisms or are derived from their excretions. Organic substances together called organic detritus. It produces humus

which is essential for maintaining proper soil aeration, hydration and fertility. Humus contains nucleic acids, amino acids, proteins, lipids, carbohydrates etc. These are again sent back to the environment after decomposition by decomposers.

3. Physical Factors. They include climatic, edaphic and topographic factors *e.g.* light, temperature, humidity, wind, rain, soil, topography and background etc.
   - (i) Light. It provides solar energy for photosynthesis. Maximum light energy is available at equator. It decreases towards poles. In a tree more energy is available to upper leaves than the lower leaves. Their rate of photosynthesis is accordingly higher.
   - (ii) Temperature. On the basis of temperature range, there are four life zones—tropical (hot throughout the year), subtropical (hot during summer and cool during winter), temperate (pleasant summer and cold winter with occasional snowy and arctic or alpine (Snowy throughout except for brief summer).
   - (iii) Rainfall. Amount and priodicity of rainfall determine type of vegetation.
   - (iv) Humidity. Transpiration is inversely related to humidity. Humid areas have abundant dense plant growth with numerous animals and epiphytes.
   - (v) Wind. It controls weather, transpiration, pollination and dissemination of propagules.
   - (vi) Soil. Its texture, pH and fertility determine the type of vegetation and animal community depends on it.

In addition to these, other abiotic components are:

(a) Lithosphere. Outer most layer of the earth

(b) Hydrosphere. Part of the earth having water resources

(c) Atmosphere. It is a cover around the earth having a number of gases

Biotic Components: The living organisms form the biotic component of the environment. Every living organism in the Biosphere depends upon one another and these living organisms which exist in

Biosphere forming the biotic community of the environment are as follows:

(a) Producers or Autotrophs. They are autotrophic plants which synthesize organic compounds from inorganic raw materials in the presence of energy usually derived from the sun. Organic compounds serve two purposes—body building and liberation of energy during the process of respiration. All other organisms depend upon the producers for getting their food and energy contained in it.

(b) Consumers or Heterotrophs. They are also called phagotrophs. Consumers are animals which ingest other organisms or their particulate organic matter. They are of two main categories—herbivores and carnivores. The herbivores or primary consumers directly feed on plant matter, *e.g.*, rabbits, deer, cattle, goats, horses etc.

Carnivores feed on the flesh of other animals. Secondary consumers or primary carnivores eat the herbivores *e.g.*, frog, molluse, small birds etc. The secondary consumers, in turn are eaten by tertiary consumers and so on. The carnivores which are not further prayed upon are called top carnivores, *e.g.*, Lion.

Since organic matter is resynthesized by consumers, they are also called secondary producers.

(c) Decomposers. They include bacteria, actinomycetes and fungi. They decompose the complex compounds in the dead organic matter of plants and animals and again recycle the elements into the environment.

Man-made Environment: Man is the most powerful environmental agent, spearheaded by modern technologies capable of modifying the environment according to his needs to a great extent without taking into account to his needs to a great extent without taking into account its consequences. Increase in the scientific technologies which are the product of human brain is now deteriorating the environment. Urbanization, industrialization and commercialization all have lead to more critical conditions. The condition of villages in worse as there is no proper sewerage and sanitation system. Increase production leads to spoilage of the environment and alter the composition of natural products.

The development of any country depends on its geographical and environmental conditions. From the ancient time man is continuously exploiting and struggling with nature. Degradation of environment started with the development in the early man's life in the form of many inventions and discoveries. These resulted in the development of new tools and implements. He also made developments in other fields such as industry, nuclear and other technological developments which are causing degradation of environment.

Development: From the early time man is putting efforts for development such as agriculture, urbanization, industrialization, commercialization etc. All these developments have put stress on the environment because these required large spaces which forests have to be cut without taking into account its consequences. Advancement in agriculture lead to use of more chemical fertilizers, pesticides, weedicides, insecticides without taking into consideration their ill effects. The urbanization stresses on basic necessities like food, shelter clothing which directly influenced the forests. Industrialization posed a serious threat to biotic and abiotic components of the environment. As more and more industries are being set up those are polluting the environment with their emission and discharge effluents.

Population Stress: As population is increasing day by day their basic demands are at the increase. The ecological balance of the earth is disturbing because the natural resources are limited to meet their demands. This increase in population causing destruction of the environment. Therefore, it is necessary to save our environment by sustainable development. The increase in population should be at a rate that the resources should be exploited in a way that they not depleted.

Present Scenario: As we have already depleted lot of our natural resources it is the need of the day we should have a control on the unlimited use of our resources so that we could improve our environment. For this proper planning and management of resources as well as the environmental impact assessment should be done before establishing any developmental activity. Every person of the country should be aware of the consequences of changed environmental conditions. Non-governmental organizations also play important role in educating people and controlling environment. So it is important to safeguard our environment which in turn safeguards the living beings.

Role of Environment

The term ecosystem was introduced by A.G. Tansley in 1935. Before him, Mobins had used the term biocoenosis while Forbes coined the term Microcosm for the community of the organisms. Sukachev employed the term biogeocoenosis as synonym of ecosystem.

> "Ecosystem is a segment of nature consisting of community of living beings and the physical environment, both interacting and exchanging material between them."

According to Evans "the ecosystem involves the circulation, transformation and accumulation of energy and matter through the medium of living organisms and their activities.

According to Fitzpatrick a group of organisms interacting among themselves and with environment is known as ecosystem.

An ecosystem may be small like a drop of pond water (micro ecosystem) or may be as large as ocean. Each ecosystem has a distinct community with a distinct environment. Therefore, different ecosystems are identified by their bionics *e.g.*, freshwater ecosystem, marine ecosystem, desert ecosystem, grassland ecosystem, tropical ecosystem. However, these ecosystems are not isolated. All the ecosystems of the world are inter-related and exchange materials amongst themselves. Therefore, some workers consider the whole earth as ecosystem and call it biosphere or ecosphere.

The Importance

1. Ecosystem study gives information about the amount of available solar energy in an area.
2. It gives data about the availability of mineral elements, their utilization and recycling.
3. Inter relationships between various types of organisms as well as between organisms and abiotic environment can be known.
4. Productivity of producers and consumers is known.

5. The maximum number of producers and consumers of various categories which can be supported in the ecosystem is known.

PRACTICAL FACTORS

(i) The ecosystem is a unit of organisms connected to one another and to their environment within given space and time limit.

(ii) Any system composed of physical, chemical and biological processes within a space and time unit.

(iii) It is composed of three basic components-biotic (biome), abiotic (habitat) and energy components.

(iv) It occupies certain well defined area on the earth-space and time unit.

(v) Ecosystem of any given space-time-unit represents the sum of all living organisms and physical environment.

(vi) It is an open system which is characterized by continuous input and output of matter and energy.

(vii) There are complex sets of interactions between biotic and abiotic components including energy components on the one hand and among the organism on the other hand.

(viii) It is powered by energy of various sorts but the solar energy is the most significant and tends to be relatively stable equilibrium. It has the natural resource system.

(ix) It is well organized and structured system. The study of ecosystem development is helpful in the environmental planning from ecological point of view.

VARIOUS TYPES

Ecosystem can be natural or artificial, large or small, permanent or temporary, complete or incomplete.

Natural Ecosystem: It is an ecosystem developed under natural conditions without any major interference by man and based upon the particular kind of habitat, these are further divided into two sub categories.

(a) Terrestrial ecosystem, *e.g.*, forest, desert, grassland etc.

(b) Aquatic ecosystem, *e.g.* freshwater lake, pond, river, sea.

Artificial Ecosystem (man-engineered): It is an ecosystem which is created and maintained by human beings, *e.g.*, garden, orchard, crop jand, aquarium, dam, village, town, city, piggery, poultry etc. Agro ecosystem is the single largest man-made ecosystem which has large number of variations.

Macro Ecosystem: A large ecosystem such as ocean, forest etc.

Micro Ecosystem: A small specific part of a large ecosystem with its own specialization *e.g.*, sub-alpine ecosystem, valley ecosystem.

Temporary Ecosystem: An ecosystem which persists for only a short duration like rain water pond.

Permanent Ecosystem: Which persists throughout *e.g.*, forest or a lake.

Incomplete Ecosystem: Which lacks one or the other component *e.g.* cave, sea bottom, city (all lack producers), rain water pond with bloom of toxic algae (lack consumers).

The Structure

An ecosystem consists of two types of components—biotic and abiotic. Biotic components are living beings, the abiotic components are non-living that includes inorganic substances, organic substances and physical factors.

The living organisms present in an ecosystem form the biotic components. They are classified into three categories—producers, consumers and reducer or decomposer.

Producers: They are autotrophic plants which synthesize organic food from inorganic raw materials using the energy of sun (exception—chemosynthetic bacteria). On land producers are usually large rooted green plants while in deep water ecosystems they are rootless algar floating or submerged in water. Autotrophs are sometimes called primary producers.

Consumers: They are mainly animals. They are unable to synthesize their food so depend upon other organisms or particulate organic matter (food) produced by producers. They are known as heterotrophs. They are of two main categories, herbivores and carnivores. The herbivores called primary consumers depend upon green plants for their food.

Insects (aphides, bugs, ants), rodents and ruminants are the common herbivores in terrestrial habitats and small crustaceans and molluscs in aquatic habitats. Goat, Cow, deer, rabit etc., are the common animals which are primary consumers. The herbivores are used as food by primary carnivores (secondary consumers) (*e.g.*, grasshopper, frog) which in turn are used as food by secondary carnivores (tertiary consumers) (*e.g.* snake that eats frog or birds which eat fish). In addition there may be top carnivores which are not further preyed upon (*e.g.*, Falcon, Lion etc.)

Decomposers: (Osmotrophs = Saprotrophs = (Sapros = to decompose) (also called micro-consumers). They include fungi and bacteria which attack the dead bodies of producers and consumers and break down the complex compounds of dead protoplasm, absorb some of the decomposition products and release inorganic nutrients to the environment for reuse by the producers.

Thus there is a cyclic exchange of materials between living community and the abiotic environment of an ecosystem.

The non-living factors prevailing in an ecosystem form the abiotic components. These are further divided into following three parts:

(i) *Climatic:* Includes light, temperature, wind, water etc.

(ii) *Inorganic Substances:* Nitrogen, calcium, sulphur, phosphorus etc.

(iii) *Organic Compounds:* Protein, carbohydrates and lipids which are linked between abiotic and biotic components.

The various steps through which food energy passes into an ecosystem are called trophic levels. All green plants or producers belong to first trophic or T_1-level. All the herbivores or primary consumers derive their energy from the producers belong to second trophic or T_2-level, where as all the primary carnivores or secondary consumers belong to third trophic level or T_3 and the secondary carnivores or tertiary consumers belong to fourth trophic level or T_4. Quartenary consumers (Top carnivores) generally belong to T_5 trophic level. Decomposers form the last or detritus trophic level (T_6).

Food Supply

A food chain is a series of population through which food energy moves in an ecosystem. A food chain is simple if it has only one trophic level besides the decomposers. A complex food chain has both producers and consumer trophic level. The idea of food chain was introduced by C. Elton. This idea describes the linear series of species, generally involving plants (autotrophs), herbivores and one or two successive sets of predators (a predator chain) or alternatively, the series of parasites and hyperparasites exploiting a host (a parasitic chain), saprophytic chains exploiting dead tissues are now known to be very important.

It is a network of food chains which become interconnected at various trophic levels so as to form at number of feeding connections amongst different organisms of a biotic community. An organism can operate at more than one trophic level and obtains its requirement of food from different sources. Similarly an organism may be eaten by a number of different-organisms. Therefore, in nature linear and independent food chains are very rare. Instead several food chains are linked together. A food web opens several alternate pathways for the flow of food energy. It also allows an organism to obtain its food from two or more types of organisms of the lower trophic level.

Thus a field mouse may be eaten by a wild cat, a snake or an owl. Similarly wild cats eat a number of herbivores like squirrel, birds, mice etc. A wolf or jackal can eat both rabbit and deer. The food web helps in maintaining the stability of the ecosystem by keeping the different species under check and maintain a state of equilibrium called homoeostasis.

Importance of Energy

Biological activity needs utilization of energy. Solar energy is transformed from radiant to the chemical form in photosynthesis and from chemical to mechanical and heat form in cellular activities. Entrance of energy, its retention within the ecosystem and dissipation into space are governed by laws of thermo dynamics.

(1) Energy can not be destroyed or created but is simply converted from one form to the other.

(2) Processes involving energy transformation will not occur spontaneously unless there is degradation of energy from non random to a random form.

In an ecosystem all energy is provided by the sun of the sunlight energy only 1 per cent is stored by plants in photosynthesis. This small amount of energy is sufficient to maintain all life on the surface of the globe. All of the energy stored by the autotrophs in the form of the food is available to the herbivores as food. Herbivores are primary consumers but they can store only 10 per cent of this energy in their biomass and remaining 90 per cent is used by them in life activities.

In the same way herbivores are eaten by carnivores *e.g.* lion eats a deer. Thus only 10 per cent of energy of lower trophic level can be captured by the organisms of next higher trophic level. This is known as Ten per cent law.

An ecological pyramid is graphic representation of a parameter like number, biomass or energy in a food chain at successive trophic levels with producers at the base, top carnivores at the top and other consumers forming intermediate tiers. The ecological pyramids are of the following types.

In this type of pyramid the number of individual organisms at each trophic level is shown. The pyramid may be upright or inverted. In grassland and crop ecosystems the pyramid may be upright where the producers are maximum in number and primary, secondary and tertiary consumers constitute the successive tiers, last tier makes the apex.

In a tree ecosystem the pyramid is inverted *i.e.*, one single tree which is primary producer has got large number of birds on it (Primary consumers) which have large number of insects outside their body (Secondary consumers).

The total fresh or dry weight of all living organisms in a certain unit area is called biomass. The amount of new biomass produced in a single growing season is called yield. The pyramid of biomass may be upright (terrestrial ecosystem) or inverted (aquatic ecosystem). In terrestrial ecosystem (Forest) the biomass of primary producers is maximum and biomass of top carnivores is minimum. In aquatic ecosystem the biomass of consumers is more than that of primary producers.

The type of pyramid shows energy accumulation pattern at different trophic levels. Such a pyramid of all ecosystem is upright. Primary producers are characterized by maximum value and at each successive tiers of consumers the energy value per square metre per year is decreased by approximately 1/10. Thus there is noted a gradual decrease in the energy content at successive trophic level from producers to consumers.

In nature ecological grouping of plants and animals extends over large areas. Two major types of ecosystems are recognized in nature. These are:

1. Aquatic ecosystem: Further divided into
   (a) Fresh water ecosystem
   (b) Marine ecosystem
2. Terrestrial ecosystem. The major terrestrial ecosystem of the world are of four types
   (a) deserts
   (b) grasslands
   (c) tundra
   (d) forests

Water Supply

It has a structure having the abiotic and biotic components. Location, size, depth and substrates of a pond influence the biology of pond ecosystem. A pond ecosystem is a self-sufficient, self-regulating system.

Abiotic Components: Temperature, light, pH of water and several basic inorganic and organic substances like H_2O, Co_2,O_2, N_2, PO_4, Ca, S and carbohydrates, proteins, lipids etc., make the abiotic components.

Biotic Components

Producers: This category includes green plants which may be submerged, free-floating or amphibious *e.g.*, Hydrilla, Ceratophyllum, Utricularia, Vallisnaria, Jussiaea, Wolffia, Lemna, Eichornia, Azoll, Salvinia, Trapa: They are minute floating and suspended algal phytoplanktons like Ulothrix, Spirogyra, Oedogonium, Chlamydomonas, Volvox, Pandorina, Eudorina, Anabaena.

Consumers: These include

(i) Primary Consumers: Herbivores

(a) Zooplanktons: Some protozoans - Dileptus, Coleps, Euglena etc. rotifiers, Lecane, Asplanchana etc., Crustaceans, Cyclops, Stenocrypis etc., feeding upon phytoplanktons.

(b) Benthos: Larvae of insects, beetles, fishes, mites, molluscs, crustaceans. Their biomass is determined.

(ii) Secondary consumers: Insects, water beetles, frogs, fishes etc. feeding upon primary consumers are included under this group.

(iii) Tertiary Consumers: Big fishes eating small fishes belong to this group.

(c) Decomposers: Several bacteria, fungi and actinomycetes represent this group *e.g.*, Aspergillus, Saprolegnia, Fusarium, Rhizopus.

System of Ecology

Forest Ecosystem is considered as an example here. Forests are natural plant communities with dominance of phanerogams. In India forests occupy approx. 1/10 of the land area. Forests can be divided into the 4 broad categories.

1. Tropical (wet evergreen, semi evergreen, moist deciduous and dry deciduous)
2. Sub-tropical
3. Temperate
4. Alpine

Abiotic Components: This includes inorganic and organic substances present in the atmosphere and soil. The climate (temperature, light, rain fall etc.) and soil (minerals) vary from forest to forest. In addition to minerals the occurrence of litter is the characteristic feature of majority of forests.

Through litter decomposition approx. 90 per cent energy trapped in the ecosystem by autotrophs dissipates into space as heat energy. The litter fall increases with decreasing latitudes.

Biotic Components

(a) Producers: They are mainly represented by trees but shrubs and ground flora are also found. Depending upon the kinds of the forests the flora varies.

(b) Consumers:

(i) Primary Consumers are small animals feeding on tree leaves include ants, beetles, flies, bugs, spiders, leaf hoppers etc. neelgai, deer, elephants, moles, squirrels and fruit bats are large animals which feed upon shoots and/or fruits.

(ii) Secondary consumers are different kind of birds snakes, lizards, feeding on primary consumers.

(iii) Tertiary Consumers are tigers and lions are top carnivores.

(c) Decomposers: Streptomyces (Bacteria) and Fungi (Aspergillus. Alternaria, Fusarium) are helpful in decomposing the litter.

Effect of Secularism

Secularism in education refers to an attitude of mind that omits religion from curriculum of 'public schools' in contrast to the religious institutions like 'madarsas' and 'maqtabs' which revolve their educative process around their religious tenets. Of late, efforts are being made to bring these institutions in the mainstream and add scientific and technological aspects to their curriculum.

Nevertheless, omission of religions from the curriculum encouraged the rise of a strongly "secular temper of mind" which gets along with the educative process without any "religious observances" wherein children are well adjusted to meet the principal "scientific and social demands of the everyday world about them". The secularist is concerned with the world here and now, and lays emphasis on continued adjustment in obedience to natural laws by means of a scientific method.

He has no religion except a secular outlook which demands a non-religious approach to religion and morals "which rest on the self-sufficiency of man's own natural powers to direct his own destiny" (Brubacher). It, however, does not mean that the school dispenses with the spiritual values. Secularism in education provides equal access to spiritual values by all irrespective of caste, creed, religion, gender and cultural origin.

These spiritual values are not wedded to any religion or sect, and are based on "secular views". Democracy and secularism, generally, go together, and consider "man to be captain of his social destiny". However, in the Indian context, the word secular was added in the Constitution in 1977 (42nd amendment) and has been a cause of great confusion, mistrust and apprehension, especially amongst the minorities as the political parties give it their own twist and significance.

The Perception

Derived from Latin Sacculum meaning this presemage, the word secularism was first used by George Jacob Holydake in the nineteenth century. He accorded it a social and ethical value status. As such, secularism acquired a social and ethical connotation and referred to a system which considered all men equal in opportunity, participation and belief in spite of one's caste, creed, religion and belief. Secularism, therefore, became the hallmark of liberal and tolerant social and moral practices.

Important Dimensions

Secularism has the following essential features:

1. Primary emphasis on the material and cultural upliftment of individual and society.
2. Respect and reverence for truth irrespective of source for better social and moral character of society.
3. Concerns for this age or world and its improvement.
4. An independent, unbiased and positive attitude of life which does not root itself in any single divine faith and commandment.
5. Liberal, permissive, progressive and tolerant social and moral order.
6. As against the view of Bradlaugh, secularism and religion are not necessarily hostile. As a matter of fact, secularism is a state of harmonious coexistence of various religions, so much so that it becomes a religion by itself.
7. Secularism is equality of all religions in a state.
8. Secularism is absence of a state religion.

Secularism in Practice

Secularism is an essential characteristic of any democratic educational system and goes well with the accepted norms of educational theory and practice to an extent that education would, perhaps not be democratic if it was not secular. As such, the dynamics of educational change in the modern society covers the entire domain of educational objectives, content and procedures.

These may also be called the variables of education/teaching, and have the following ramifications:

Teacher	*Content*	*Pupil*
1. Development	1. Universal	1. Interest
2. Knowledge	2. Flexible	2. Ability
3. Tasks	3. Secular	3. Aspirations
4. Instructional Interventions	4. Global	4. All-round development
5. Ideology	5. Diversified	5. Knowledge, Attitude and Skills
6. Attitude	6. Play oriented	6. Variability of individual differences.
7. Status	7. Vocational	
	8. Graded	
	9. Updated and relevant	
	10. Distance Education	

Dynamics of Educational Change: It may reasonably be assumed that the entire educative process in a democratic setup revolves around secularism and in cultivating secular attitudes and values. We shall presently discuss the role of various components of education in this regard.

Secular Experience

Aims: Aims are values in expressed form. As such, the educational aims of a democratic educative process must cherish and aspire for secularism in education. The Secondary Education Commission 1952-53 recommended the following aims of education having a direct bearing on secularism.

"Education system must make contribution to the development of habits, attitudes and qualities of character which will enable its citizens to bear worthily the responsibilities of democratic citizenship and to counteract all those fissiparous tendencies which hinder the emergence of broad national and secular outlook."

Development of Democratic Citizenship: India is a secular, socialist, democratic republic, and as such education should produce dynamic, resourceful and enterprizing citizens. It should help one develop the intellectual and emotional ability and control to sift the right from the wrong in a dispassionate and scientific manner.

Training in the Art of Living Efficiency: For the wholesome development of the child, and for the benefit of society, education should develop in him a spirit of accommodation based on discipline, cooperation and tolerance. It should foster such socially desirable aims, acceptable attitudes that make the child to be a responsible and efficient member of the society.

The Kothari Commission 1966 recommended the following measures to consolidate democracy by means of social, national and moral values which inversely consolidate secular education:

Develop Social and National Unity: For national reconstruction, national unity is an essential need. In the absence of national unity, self-centred individuals try to achieve their own motives without caring for the interests of the nation. This makes the nation weak and backward. Thus, national unity is greatly essential for national reconstruction. But the feeling of national unity can be developed through education only. Hence, the aim of education should be to develop social and national unity.

Consolidate Democracy: Education is necessary for the success of democracy. Hence, to consolidate democracy is another aim of education. To achieve this aim, education should be so organized as to provide more and more effective experiences to children to inculcate in them the qualities of democratic living. Then only, national consciousness will stimulate national outlook, sense of national character and responsibility.

Comments: Whatever be the effect of the educational process regulated by the aims prescribed by society, there is a "unanimity of opinion on the point" that children at the time of leaving the school are in an incomplete state of development". This deficiency is to be filled up in later life by religion and social and moral integration, and consolidation of faculties and inclinations. Secularism is one way of doing it where integration takes place without subscribing to any religious sect and faith. Secularism, therefore, is vital for peaceful coexistence, growth and prosperity, and is, in fact, attitudinal and progressive.

Educational values help imbibe secular values, and educational aims provide appropriate direction and keep the educative process on track by exercising vigilant control and rectification, leading it to Sarvadharmambhave wherein every religious tenet and creed enjoys equal opportunity and status. National Educational Policy 1986 and India Vision 2002-2020 are the cardinal points toward total secular education as a matter of state policy irrespective of the occasional crying foul of saffronization and appeasement.

Curriculum: The first question in curriculum construction is whether it should be shaped by the social culture and the demands of the society, or according to the needs of an individual. In spite of the profound respect for the individual in a democratic setup, preference is given to the social order in curriculum construction. Secular curriculum should be universal, flexible, global, play-oriented, graded and relevant, and should address to the society rather than an individual, community or sect. It should be culture-oriented, and as best of the culture is contained in tradition, let curriculum be tradition-oriented, permitting little permissiveness and aberrations, which will soon disappear into the body-structure.

The content of the curriculum and its presentation goes a long way in developing secularism in a society. A long history and a long line of tradition may have certain aberrations at some point, but it does not mean that these should be blown out of proportion to ignite racial and religious feelings, or to fan the fires of passion, hatred, suspicion and ill will.

In contrast to it, even if there are such historical incidents of acrimony and cruelty, these should either be ignored, glossed over or toned down. As it is, one such omission would not change the course of history and tradition of a people. Tolerance is the key word. The curriculum should be so designed that it develops better understanding of each other's views with compassion and respect. Secular education should have secular curriculum presenting the learning experiences in different forms at different stages of learning and comprehension to absorb it. Inclusion of science subjects broadens one's outlook and perception, and, therefore, helps develop secular attitude.

The current misconception about saffronization of education and tankering with the curriculum is based either on misrepresentation or misconception. Social studies, especially, History is the favourite target of this onslaught, at times rousing passions beyond reason and control. In fact, how much of History has been distorted, if distorted at all, in the recent times by those who aim at diluting presentation of some unpleasant incidents in the course of our history.

The author remembers the manner in which History was taught during the pre-Independence era raking up hatred resulting in the partition of the country. Does teaching of history aim at dividing people to the extent it did in the Indian subcontinent? We are talking about History because it is a hotbed of controversy and mistrust. The same is true of other social subjects though not related as directly and intimately with tradition.

Teacher Tasks and Behaviour: Teacher has specific tasks and behaviour in a democratic set-up: his knowledge, development and preparation; use of strategies or other instructional interventions; manipulation of environment; ideology and attitudes should be such that they help create a democratic and secular impression on the pupils. The teacher must tell what is relevant at an appropriate level, and skip the rest for the time the pupils are matured enough to understand things on their own and in their own perspective.

The teacher should be professionally honest, capable, impartial, discrete, progressive and enlightened without being unduly charged with any specific faith, creed or tenet, showing equal respect to all religions in a conscientious and fair manner. He is the promoter and upholder of creating a social climate in the society that helps generate secular values and traditions in the country. Such is the teacher who would infuse secular attitudes and knowledge amongst his students for a better, prosperous and glorious tomorrow where everyone lives in amity, harmony and peace.

Pupils and Secularism: In the ultimate analysis it is the pupil on whom all secular manipulations and interventions are working; it is the pupil who has got to be secular in his approach and outlook. The other components and variables simply help him reach there by providing necessary and amicable facilities and environment. Today's pupils are tomorrow's citizens and would be at the helm of the things in various spheres of life in their own right.

Whatever they imbibe today would manifest itself in their social, moral, political, literary and religious views and actions. Secular attitudes are those socially desirable attitudes that help one understand and tolerate others' point of view, accept it with respect and compassion in the interest of general well being, welfare, progress and prosperity. Pupils should, therefore, be provided opportunities to develop secular bent of mind, attitude and culture. This will be the signal contribution of education toward secularism in society.

Main Characteristics

Briefly speaking secular education has the following characteristics:

1. Moral outlook.
2. Development of wider vision.
3. Pluralistic outlook.
4. Democratic values.
5. Cultural development.
6. Synthesis of spiritual and material values.
7. Humanitarianism.
    1. Traditional bias and narrow outlook.
    2. Too much emphasis on theoretical learning and absence of a solid value system.

3. Lack of knowledge of secular social and moral outlook, and a general apathy to celebration of each other's festivals to inculcate a spirit of secular understanding and living.
4. Neglect of mixed group interaction and lack of mutual faith and trust.
5. Cross purpose of various constitutional provisions which created more confusion and mistrust about the need and meaning of the word secular (1977/42nd amendment) in the Constitution which already had adequate projective devices by means of Articles 25 to 28, as well as 29 and 30, which were enough to dispel any misgivings by some sections of the society.

BIBLIOGRAPHY

Aggarwal, J.C. : *Development and Planning of Modern Education with Special Reference to India*, Vikas Publishing House, New Delhi, 1982.

———— : *National Policy on Education*, Arya Book Depot, New Delhi, 1979.

Aparna Basu : *The Growth of Education and Political Development in India 1898-1920*, Oxford University Press, Delhi, 1970.

Barrie, H. : *The Theory and Practice of Vocational Guidance*, Pergamon Press, London, 1968.

Bekar, A. : *The Union and the States in Education : A Study in Educational Finance and Planning*, Shabd Sanchar, New Delhi, 1976.

Bertrand, R. : *On Education*, Unwin Books, London, 1971.

Bhatia, S.C.: *Education and Socio-Cultural Disadvantage*, Xerxes Publications, Delhi, 1982.

Bhatnagar, A. : *A Study of Some Rural Communities in Punjab*, The Minarva Associates, Calcutta, 1972.

Biswas, D. : *Educational Pattern in India*, MacMillan Pvt. Ltd., Delhi, 1966.

Buch, M.B. : *A Survey of Research in Education, Centre of Advanced Study in Education*, M.S. University of Baroda, Baroda, 1974.

———— : *Second Survey of Research in Education 1972-1978,* Society for Educational Research and Development, Baroda, 1979.

Cattell, B.B. : *Abilities: Their Structure, Growth and Action*, Houghton Mifflin Co., Boston, 1971.

Chauhan, B.R. : *Scheduled Castes and Education*, Anu Publications, Meerut, 1975.

Chauhan, S.S. : *Principles and Techniques of Guidance*, Vikas Publishing House, New Delhi, 1982.

Chourasia, G. : *Challenges and Innovations in Education*, Sterling Publishers, New Delhi, 1977.

Cole, S. Brem Beck : *Education and National Concern*, Holt, Rinehart and Winston, New York, 1966.

Crow, A. : *Education and Socio-Cultural in India*, Xerxes Publications, Delhi, 1982.

Denis, L. : *Education and Social Justice*, Sage Publications, London, 1977.

Desai, A.R. : *Rural Sociology in India*, Popular Prakashan, Bombay, 1978.

Don, Adams : *Education and Modernisation in Asia*, Addison Wesley Publishing Company, London, 1970.

Ehsanul Haq : *Education and Political Culture in India*, Sterling Publishers, New Delhi, 1981.

Erickson, C.E. : *A Basic Text for Guidance Workers*, Englewood Cliffs, Prentice Hall, 1955.

Freeman, F.S. : *Theory and Practice of Psychological Testing*, Oxford and IBH Publishing Company, New Delhi, 1965.

Freire, P. : *Education : The Practice of Freedom*, Writers and Readers Publishing Cooperative, London, 1976.

Ganguly, S.N. : *Tradition, Modernity and Development: A Study in Contemporary Indian Society*, MacMillan Company of India, Delhi, 1977.

Garret, A. : *Interviewing: Its Principles and Methods*, Family Service Association of America, New York, 1942.

Gaur, J.S. : *Occupational Literature : An Annotated Bibliography*, NCERT, New Delhi, 1978.

Ghiselli, E.E. : *Personnel and Industrial Psychology*, McGraw Hill Book Co., New York, 1965.

Ghosh, S.C. : *Educational Strategies in Developing Countries*, Sterling Publishers, New Delhi, 1976.

Goel, S.C. : *Education and Economic Growth in India*, MacMillan Company of India Ltd., Delhi, 1975.

Gore, M.S. : *Papers in the Sociology of Education in India*, NCERT, New Delhi, 1967.

Guilford, J.P. : *Fundamental Statistics in Psychology and Education*, McGraw Hill, New York, 1965.

Halping, W. : *Administrative Theory in Education*, MacMillan Company, New York, 1967.

Hamrin, S.A. : *Initiating and Administering Guidance Services*, Bloomington, McKnight and McKnight Publishing Company, London, 1959.

Haragopal, G. : *Administrative Leadership and Rural Development in India*, Light & Life Publishers, New Delhi, 1980.

Henry, W. : *Behaviour Changes Through Guidance*, McGraw Hill, New York, 1964.

Hoppock, R. : *Occupational Information—Where to Get It and How to Use It in Counselling and Teaching*, McGraw Hill Book Co. Inc., New York, 1957.

James, A.R. : *Vocation, Education and Guidance: A System for the Seventies*, Charles E. Marril Publishing Co., Columbus, 1970.

Jeffries, C. : *Illiteracy : A World Problem*, Pall Mall Press, London, 1967.

John W. : *Education and the Development of Nations*, McGraw Hill Book Co., New York, 1975.

Joshi, R.N. : *Education—Elsewhere and Here*, Bharatiya Vidya Bhavan, Bombay, 1979.

Kamat, A.R. : *The Educational Situation and other Essays on Education*, People's Publishing House, New Delhi, 1973.

Kidd, J.R. : *Education for Perspective*, Indian Education Association, New Delhi, 1969.

Kishore Gandhi : *Issues and Choices in Higher Education: A Sociological Analysis*, B.R. Publishing Corporation, Delhi, 1977.

Kripal, P. : *A Decade of Education in India*, Indian Book Company, Delhi, 1968.

Krumboliz, J.D. : *Counselling Methods*, Holt Rinehart and Winston, New York, 1976.

Lester, D. : *An Introduction to Guidance Principles and Practices*, Eurasia Publishing House, New Delhi, 1962.

Louis, Malassis : *Education and Development in India*, Croom Helm, New York, 1976.

Miller, Carroll H. : *Foundations of Guidance*, Harper and Brothers, New York, 1981.

Mukherjee, R.K. : *The Social Structure of Values*, S. Chand & Company, New Delhi, 1994.

Mukherji, S.N. : *Administration of Education in India*, Acharya Book Depot, Baroda, 1982.

Naik, J.P. : *Educational Planning in India*, Allied Publishers, Bombay, 1965.

——————— : *Elementary Education in India : A Promise to Keep*, Allied Publishers, Bombay, 1975.

——————— : *Some Perspectives on Non-Fomal Education*, Allied Publishers, New Delhi, 1977.

——————— : *The Single Teacher School : Studies in Education and Psychology*, Government of India, Delhi. 1973.

Nair, P.R. : *Primary Education, Population Growth and Socio-Economic Change*, Allied Publishers, New Delhi, 1981.

Narayan, G. : *A Study of Some Rural Communities in India*, Anu Publications, Lucknow, 1985.

Niblett, W.R. : *Essential Education.* University of London, London, *1955*.

Nural Hasan, S. : *Challenges in Education. Culture and Social Welfare*, Allied Publishers, Bombay, 1977.

Ohlsen, M.M. : *Group Counselling*, Holt Rinchart and Winston, New York, 1977.

Oldhan, J.N. : *Village Education in India : The Report of Commission of Enquiry*. Oxford University Press, London, 1972.

Pandey, S.N. : *Education and Social Changes in Bihar (1900-1921) : A Survey of Social History of Bihar from Curzon to Non-Cooperation Movement*, Motilal Banerasidas, Delhi, 1976.

Premi, M.K. : *Educational Planning in India : Implications of Population Trends*, Sterling Publishers, New Delhi, 1972.

Rajagopal, M.V. : *Kothari Commission on School Education: A Recapitulation and Review*, Telugu Vidyardhi Prachuranalu, Machilipatnam, 1967.

Ram Reddy, G. : *Patterns of Panchayati Raj in India*, MacMillan Company of India, Madras, 1977.

Rao, V.K.R.V. : *Education and Human Resource Development*, Allied Publishers, Bombay, 1966.

Roeber, E.C. : *Organisation and Administration of Guidance Services*, McGraw Hill, New York, 1955.

Rudolph, R. : *Education and Politics in India Studies in Organisation, Society and Policy*, Harvard University Press, Cambridge, 1972.

Russell, B. : *Education and the Social Order*, Unwin, London, 1977.

Ruth, S. : *Counselling Techniques in College and Secondary School*, Haarper and Brothers, New York, 1937.

Safaya, R. : *Innovations and Latest Trends in Education*, The Associated Publishers, Ambala Cantt., 1976.

Saini, S.K. : *Development of Education in India : Socio-Economic and Political Perspective*, Cosmo Publications, New Delhi, 1980.

Saran, G. : *Education and Social Change : A Study of Some Rural Communities in Punjab*, The Minarva Associates, Calcutta, 1972.

Saraswat, R.K. : *Personnel and Industrial Psychology*, McGraw Hill Book Co., New York, 1975.

Saxena, S. : *Education Planning in India : A Study in Approach and Methodology*, Sterling Publishers, New Delhi, 1974.

Sayalu, A. : *Scheduled Caste Elite : A Study of Scheduled Caste Elite in Andhra Pradesh*, Booklinks Corporation, Hyderabad, 1978.

Sharma, G.S. : *Educational and Cultural Development of the Minorities—A Study in Social Effects of the Judicial Trends in India*, ICSSR, New Delhi, 1973.

Shipman, M.D. : *Education and Modernisation*, Faber and Faber, London, 1971.

Shrimali, K.L. : *A Search for Values in Indian Education*, Vikas Publishers, Delhi, 1974.

Shukla, P.D. : *Towards the New Pattern of Education in India*, Sterling Publishers, New Delhi, 1976.

Singh, T.R. : *Scheduled Castes and Education*, Mohan Publications, Allahabad, 1987.

Singhal, R.P. : *The New Educational Pattern in India*, Vikas Publishing House, Delhi, 1916.

Singla, M.M. : *The Constitution of India—Studies in Perspective*, The World Press, Calcutta, 1975.

Smith, G.E. : *Education and Politics in India Studies in Organisation, Society and Policy*, McGraw Hill, New York, 1955.

Station, F. : *Dynamics of Adjustment*, MacMillan Co., New York, 1953.

Stephen, J. : *Administration of Public Education*, Harper and Brothers, New York, 1962.

Thoreasen, C.E. : *The Rural World : Education and Development*, Croom Helm, London, 1976.

Tiwari, D.D. : *Thoughts on Education,* Chugh Publications, New York, 1972.

Vaughan, T.D. : *Educational and Vocational Guidance Today*, Routledge and Kegan Paul, London, 1968.

Wren, C. : *The Counsellor in a Changing World, Washington*, American Personnel and Guidance Association, New York, 1962.

BIN TRAVERLER FORM

Cut By: Klagleidy #3 **Qty** 25 **Date** 09.15.26

Scanned By: ______ **Qty** ______ **Date** ______

Scanned Batch ID's

______ ______ ______

Notes / Exceptions

______